Palgrave Studies in Minority Languages and Communities

Worldwide migration and unprecedented economic, political and social integration present serious challenges to the nature and position of language minorities. Some communities receive protective legislation and active support from states through policies that promote and sustain cultural and linguistic diversity; others succumb to global homogenisation and assimilation. At the same time, discourses on diversity and emancipation have produced greater demands for the management of difference.

This series publishes new research based on single or comparative case studies on minority languages worldwide. We focus on their use, status and prospects, and on linguistic pluralism in areas with immigrant or traditional minority communities or with shifting borders. Each volume is written in an accessible style for researchers and students in linguistics, education, politics and anthropology, and for practitioners interested in language minorities and diversity. We welcome submissions in either monograph or Pivot format.

More information about this series at
https://link.springer.com/bookseries/14611

Michael Hornsby · Wilson McLeod
Editors

Transmitting Minority Languages

Complementary Reversing Language Shift Strategies

palgrave
macmillan

Editors
Michael Hornsby
Faculty of English
Adam Mickiewicz University
Poznań, Poland

Wilson McLeod
Celtic and Scottish Studies
University of Edinburgh
Edinburgh, UK

Palgrave Studies in Minority Languages and Communities
ISBN 978-3-030-87909-9 ISBN 978-3-030-87910-5 (eBook)
https://doi.org/10.1007/978-3-030-87910-5

Cover illustration: Morse Images/Getty Images

This Palgrave Macmillan imprint is published by the registered company Springer Nature Switzerland AG
The registered company address is: Gewerbestrasse 11, 6330 Cham, Switzerland

Contents

List of Figures

Wider Community Stance and Irish-Speaking Families in the Gaeltacht

Creating Language Shift: Factors Behind the Language Choices of Māori Speakers

'We Had to Make a Choice': The Contentious Debate Over Language Replacement in Transnational Adoptive Families

List of Tables

Wider Community Stance and Irish-Speaking Families in the Gaeltacht

Creating Language Shift: Factors Behind the Language Choices of Māori Speakers

Transmission of Breton Among Immersion-School Students: The Impact of Home Language

Introduction

Michael Hornsby

Most studies on language maintenance emphasise the importance of community, or where the language has ceased to be a community-based language, of close-knit social networks in maintaining or revitalising a minority or heritage language in the face of socially dominant languages and cultures (García 2003). In his highly influential work entitled *Reversing Language Shift* ('RLS'), Fishman (1991) is adamant that the whole process hinges on successful intergenerational language transmission in the home and community. In other words, if intergenerational transmission of a minority language (Stage 6 in his so-called Graded Intergenerational Disruption Scale) does not meet with success, the subsequent stages of the model will also achieve limited—if

M. Hornsby (✉)
Faculty of English, Adam Mickiewicz University, Poznań, Poland
e-mail: mhornsby@wa.amu.edu.pl

M. Hornsby and W. McLeod (eds.), *Transmitting Minority Languages*, Palgrave Studies in Minority Languages and Communities,
https://doi.org/10.1007/978-3-030-87910-5_1

any—success, resulting in the continuation of the language's precarious position. Fishman writes (p. 95):

> The home-family-neighborhood-community complex is the normal 'whole' of childhood life and of intergenerational mother tongue transmission. Accordingly, it must remain at the center of RLS-efforts, no matter what are the stages that necessarily come thereafter.

It should be noted, however, that how transmission of the language plays out in practice can vary considerably: some communities exhibit more language solidarity than others, and most authors agree that attitudes and ideologies which speakers associate with their languages (and with those who speak them) will be a determining factor in the survival of a language (Woolard 1998; Schieffelin et al. 1998; Wölck 2004; Lasagabaster and Huguet 2007). Pervasive attitudes in the minority/heritage language environment, such as the value placed on bi- or multilingualism by the individual, the family, the school and society at large (García 2009), and the acceptability of the public use of a minority language in the presence of monolingual majority speakers (Wölck 2004) are also factors which may encourage or discourage the maintenance of a given language in a particular environment. We also need to factor in the real or perceived usefulness of a particular language (Grin and Vaillancourt 1997; Henley and Jones 2005) as well as more intimate perceptions, such as regarding language as a core cultural value (Woolard and Schieffelin 1994) in individual families' decisions concerning the language to be used in the home. The centrality of the family to the achievement of wider language revitalisation goals is also echoed in Spolsky's (2012) characterisation of the family as the 'critical domain' in language policy. However, as Spolsky rightly points out (p. 3), typically language policy has focused on the higher echelons of social organisation, such as the national government. In response, researchers have begun to make explicit connections between language practices at the micro-level of family language policy as it is typically conceptualised in terms of human organisation at the regional, state and supranational level.

Not unsurprisingly, research has shown that environments in which caregivers make a conscious decision to use the minority language with their children in the first place; sustain high and varied minority language input with their children; and use management strategies which mandate responses in the minority language are more likely to lead to intergenerational language transmission than those that do not (e.g. Lanza 1997; Ó hIfearnáin 2013; Altman et al. 2014; Curdt-Christiansen 2016; de Houwer and Bornstein 2016). However, on the other hand, the decision to transmit a particular language in a minority setting may not always be so clear-cut, and caregivers may find themselves having to maintain a fine balance in making various decisions—for instance, not using a strict management style once the child has established a preference for the majority language, since this might disrupt family relationships, as well as negatively affect the child's relationship with the minority or heritage language in question (Kopeliovich 2013; Smith-Christmas 2016).

In the case of minority and heritage languages, until relatively recently, the prevailing pattern has been one of transmission in a home/communal setting by 'native' speakers of the language in communities in which the language is widely spoken, as has been described by Hindley (1990), Fishman (1991) and Krauss (1992), inter alios. This mode of transmission has typically been identified, and indeed valorised, as the most important source of language reproduction. As the intergenerational transmission of many minority languages begins to break down, however, minority language and diaspora communities are resorting to other modes of transmission, out of necessity, to complement traditional mechanisms and secure language maintenance. As a recent study on intergenerational transmission by Kircher (2019) notes, 'L1, proficiency, and attitudes on the solidarity dimension predicted a large proportion of the variance [in transmission] – but not all of it, indicating that other variables were at play' (p. 14). This volume thus brings together a number of studies of these alternative modes of transmission and considers these 'other variables' in a variety of sociolinguistic contexts, examining the complex and diverse practical, ideological and personal challenges that arise.

By far the most prominent alternative mechanism to facilitate language maintenance is immersion schooling, a topic which has given rise to extensive research (e.g. Ó Duibhir 2018: 26–56). The present volume focuses not on the role of formal schooling per se, but on the wider range of 'non-traditional' mechanisms and strategies that parents of different kinds have adopted to facilitate their children's acquisition of minority or heritage languages. These may involve distinct categories of parents (e.g. those who have acquired or who are acquiring the minority language in adulthood) or structured programmes of different kinds (e.g. language nests with a key role for older fluent speakers), or more personal, domestic strategies involving forms of language management in the home. It is vital to note, though, that there has been little critical analysis on what 'successful' intergenerational transmission looks like and how it should (or can) be measured, whether through the family or through the schools. As Schwartz and Vershik (2013: 1) point out, gauging 'success' tends to be influenced by an output-driven outlook, such as using 'balanced bilingualism' as a benchmark. Research on minority and heritage languages has thus been largely guided by the implicit understanding that successful intergenerational transmission should produce age-appropriate carbon-copy speakers modelled on earlier generations of the minority/heritage language community. Ó hIfearnáin (2015: 50) critiques this expectation, in which each generation is expected to faithfully reproduce the speech of the generation that went before, 'with any change being framed as degeneration, [and] variation is defined as variance from the imagined pure local norm of older speakers'.

More broadly, Spolsky has discussed the terms to describe what we think is happening in situations of language endangerment and shift, especially in efforts to reverse these trends, finds them 'sloppily presented' (2008: 152). He is more comfortable with the term *revitalisation* to signify where intergenerational transmission is restored and/or *revernacularisation* (where a written language is restored to daily life, such as happened with Hebrew), as opposed to language *revival*, which he finds too vague. Of particular note here is his adoption of the term language *regeneration* (after Hohepa 2000: 153), which has not been used extensively in the literature since, but which describes the school-based teaching of a dying language, and which it is useful to bear in mind in relation to a number of case studies within this volume. Indeed, overall the chapters here implicate all of the processes mentioned above and echo Spolsky's observation that, even though we tend to identify the situations described here as examples of language maintenance and/or revitalisation, they each 'suggest different processes, different goals (apart from assertion of identity and mobilization of ethnic movement around a language), and different levels of achievement' (Spolsky 2008: 153).

Thus, the different case studies presented in this volume do indeed present a wide range of situations and a wide range of understandings of what it means to maintain or restore (intergenerational) transmission. A number of chapters discuss, or touch on, what is commonly understood as 'traditional' intergenerational transmission, from a minority or heritage language perspective: maternal and/or paternal L1 input producing the next generation of L1 speakers. The chapter by Smith-Christmas and Ruiséal ("Conceptualising Successful Intergenerational Language Transmission in Terms of saibhreas: Family Language Support in the Corca Dhuibhne Gaeltacht"), for example, considers language revitalisation in terms of the Family Language Policy model and argues for a concrete and holistic strategy to conceptualise and realise 'successful' intergenerational language transmission. Taking the linguistic situation in the Corca Dhuibhne Gaeltacht (Co. Kerry, Ireland) as their case study, they discuss the *saibhreas* ('richness') model and its three constituent components—competent language use; local language use; and embodied language use—and show how this approach provides a tangible means by which to understand how caregivers frame their visions of 'success' and how they go about bringing this success into being. In particular, they argue that their notion of 'embodied language use', which encourages the child to want to speak the minority language as a 'way of being' rather than viewing language as an artefact, is applicable to other minority language contexts.

A similar intergenerational focus can be found in the chapter by Ó hIfearnáin ("Wider Community Stance and Irish-Speaking Families in the Gaeltacht"), in somewhat similar but much weaker sociolinguistic circumstances than those described in the Smith-Christm as and Ruiséal chapter. The case of the transmission of Irish in less favourable conditions, such as in the so-called 'weaker' Gaeltacht (Irish-speaking) areas, is examined by Ó hIfearnáin here, where he discusses the situation of the Muscraí Gaeltacht in south-west Ireland. He critiques aspects of the prevailing discourse of the imminent and terminal decline of Irish as a community language by showing how the wider community in a 'weak' Gaeltacht area provides some of the support mechanisms that allow it to sustain a small but consistent number of Irish-speaking families in its midst. If the language ideologies and practices of a core set of parents and families, and their social networks, are key for maintaining Irish, as Ó hIfearnáin shows, so too are those of the peripheral linguistic community in the area.

Still with an intergenerational focus, but quite different again in the circumstances described, Macleod's chapter ("Family Language Policy in the Face of a Shrinking Community Language: Gaelic on the Isle of Lewis") reports on families who have endeavoured to re-establish Scottish Gaelic in their families and repairing the broken intergenerational link. They have managed this with very little support in terms of targeted interventionist activity or support, apart from school assistance. Macleod shows how they had to take matters into their own hands and recruit the assistance of grandparents and other family members in their own family language policy. The research shows that even when individuals have failed to become fully active speakers themselves, their agency on behalf of their children in creating networks of practice can still be successful. By involving grandparents, the extended family and the local community in general, the chapter shows how taking an active role in supporting a Gaelic language choice can go a long way towards repairing interrupted intergenerational transmission.

Other chapters also focus on intergenerational transmission, but add a migration dimension into the mix. Karpava, Ringblom and Zabrodskaja (chapter "Comparing Family Language Policy in Cyprus Estonia and Sweden: Efforts and Choices Among Russian-Speaking Families") examine the transmission of Russian as a heritage language in transnational situations, comparing and contrasting how Russian-speaking parents go about doing this in Cyprus, Estonia and Sweden. They find that, even though parents act as Russian language teachers, buy Russian books and organise Russian language extra-curricular activities, this might not be sufficient without the conscious and consistent use of the heritage language by the Russian-speaking parents in order to transmit Russian to their children. The influence of the wider society in these three situations is strikingly different: Greek Cypriots are generally very positive towards Russian, in Estonia, sometimes negative and even downright hostile attitudes towards Russian have been noted, while Sweden falls somewhere in between.

In the case of transnational adoption, language transmission of both the origin language and the adoptive language is complicated as adopted children struggle from the beginning between two linguistic identities and trying to adapt to the language policy of the family. Fiorentino's chapter ("'We Had to Make a Choice': The Contentious Debate Over Language Replacement in Transnational Adoptive Families") documents the process of language replacement in one example of transnational adoption, showing how a difficult position arises when a child has two different linguistic 'entities' and suggests ways to build an inclusive, multicultural identity in such situations.

The above chapters engage with a fairly conservative understanding of what it means to transmit a language intergenerationally. However, we can note that '[i]n contrast to how it is often conceptualised in sociolinguistic and language policy literature, intergenerational transmission is not binary, but a much more dynamic, muddled, and nuanced process, and one in need of further investigation' (King et al. 2008: 918). Chantreau and Moal's chapter ("The Transmission of Breton in the Family: The Effect of Family Rupture and Recomposition") thus shifts the discussion somewhat, studying how families in a minority language setting, in this case Breton, can (like families anywhere) experience disruption and drastic changes in circumstances when parents/caregivers decide to separate. They note that often previously established family language policies tend not to come to the fore when renegotiating how the family unit will operate in the future. Newcomers into a recomposed family set-up can also drastically alter previous linguistic practices, whether they be stepchildren or a new step-parent. As the authors note, it is not possible to identify a homogenous influence of family separation or recomposition on the family transmission of Breton, since each case is particular.

Although language transmission is typically understood within the framework of a single family, the sources of relevant input may in fact be much wider. The chapter by Kasares, Ortega and Amorrortu

("Basque Intergenerational Transmission from a Language Socialisation Perspective") aims to unpick this complexity by showing that transmission does not happen only in the family and at school, but all domains of social life in the minority language, including leisure and sports activities, and cultural products and events. The holistic nature of language socialisation acknowledges that the whole community is involved in the process and makes visible those agents that have a true impact on language transmission, but who are often invisible. Acknowledging this diversity of agencies can also help develop community-based strategies, as well as language planning objectives. In a similar way, Nandi, Manterola, Reyna-Muniain and Kasares (chapter "Effective Family Language Policies and Intergenerational Transmission of Minority Languages: Parental Language Governance in Indigenous and Diasporic Contexts") investigate how activist parents from autochthonous as well as diasporic contexts have to negotiate conflicts between the realities of social pressure, political imposition and public education demands on the one hand, and the desire for cultural loyalty and intergenerational language transmission on the other. This involves a certain level of flexibility in the choices made between Castilian and Galician or Basque and involve continuous negotiations, variations and mutations on a daily basis between various actors and stakeholders. The chapter shows how these actions take place over multiple levels, ranging from the government level to the family level, involving parental control over children, and the case studies in the chapter illustrate how the parents manage and coordinate all these various demands.

Other chapters pick up the challenge to explore the notion of language transmission (whether intergenerationally or by other means) more broadly. A number of chapters look at routes of transmission for minority languages which are not necessarily intergenerationally based. The chapter ("Native and Non-native Speakers' School Language Practices and Transmission in Upper Lusatia") by Dołowy-Rybińska, for example, shows how the acquisition of Upper Sorbian in Upper Lusatia by students in the Sorbian language education system does not, just in itself, confer membership of the language community, but this process does become easier in the case of Catholics because the linguistic appropriation of the whole 'Catholic space' is accepted by the Sorbian community and even non-Sorbs are at least expected to understand the language in this setting. Thus, cultural and religious participation allows group members to belong in ways that mere linguistic competency does not. Transmission of Upper Sorbian through the schools needs to be accompanied by other factors if a new speaker of the language is to be accepted by the community, something which few actually manage to do.

With alternative ways of language transmission becoming more usual in a number of minority language communities, the critique sometimes arises that this is cause for concern, so far as 'authentic' language is concerned. Kennard's chapter ("Transmission of Breton Among Immersion-School Students: The Impact of Home Language") tackles the oft-repeated discourse that immersion students in Brittany do not speak 'correct' Breton, or at least a type of Breton that would be recognisable to their grandparents' generation and thus 'authentic'. Kennard challenges this, and her study finds that even when immersion students do use Breton at home often with their parents, while being beneficial, not having this input does not necessarily mean that teenaged speakers will lag behind their peers in certain areas of native-like production, even though a somewhat patchy acquisition of Breton morphophonology among some speakers is detectable. Drawing on other studies of adolescent speakers of minority languages, Kennard suggests that the impact of home background on language acquisition is minimal and surmises that the effect of immersion students' linguistic background on their morphological and morphophonological output is more stable than on their phonological production.

In the case of Guernésiais (in the Channel Isle of Guernsey), Sallabank (chapter "Peer-to-Peer Endangered Language Transmission Among Adults") argues that the successful maintenance of this highly endangered language lies in its peer-to-peer transmission amongst adults, which can then lead on to the development of proficient new speakers. Given that almost all fluent speakers of Guernsiais are now elderly, the author considers how this may, in fact, be a much more effective strategy in this particular language setting than the more usual emphasis on intergenerational transmission within the family or through the schools. Sallabank concludes that adult-to-adult peer language transmission is not only vital as a language management strategy, it is also a valid aim in its own right.

Of course, many situations of language revitalisation do seek to restore intergenerational transmission. Olsen-Reeder, in "Creating Language Shift: Factors Behind the Language Choices of Māori Speakers", considers whether, after 40 years of Māori language revitalisation, it is too early to talk of a successful reinstatement of intergenerational transmission of the language since, he proposes, that can only be measured effectively by examining the linguistic practices of the fourth generation, which has yet to appear in this particular context. He therefore turns his attention to intragenerational transmission and the importance of children hearing and observing their parents or grandparents talking Māori to each other. If the practice of Māori-speaking becomes perceived as something only children do actively, they may cease speaking Māori and perpetuate a cycle of adult-to-child communication, but not adult-to-adult communication. And, if this cycle becomes habitual, intergenerational transmission is probably not going to be possible. He concludes that there is a pressing need to make a more concerted effort to convince adult Māori speakers to communicate in the language amongst themselves, if revitalisation is to be deemed successful.

These case studies do show that the intergenerational transmission of minority and heritage languages, in the settings showcased here at least, does continue to happen. The chapters in this volume by Smith-Christmas and Ruiséal, as well as the chapters by Macleod and by Karpava, Ringblom and Zabrodskaja, are testament to this. Those parents who do choose to engage in such transmission are working to buck an increasing trend which pressurises minority and heritage language speakers to disengage from the transmission process. The examples given here show what can be done in the cases of maintaining or restoring the intergenerational links of language transmission, which were the norm for most present-day linguistic minorities only one or two generations ago. However, despite Fishman's reservations against improving the 'ethnolinguistic wellness' (Fishman 1991: xii) of regional, ethnic and religious languages against a premature dependence on schools, especially schools controlled by speakers of the dominant societal language, we have to recognise the fact that minority and heritage language transmission is becoming heavily reliant on educational institutions. We also need to take note that these efforts are not always deemed 'successful' or sufficient, and further research is needed in order to unpick how the outcomes (or, at the very least, the perceptions of the outcomes) of immersion or bilingual education can be improved. Edwards and Newcombe (2005) discussed this issue fairly early on, and the title of their article, 'When School is not Enough' accurately sums up the perception that in order for minority and heritage language transmission through the schools to be considered successful, children need additional input. This volume gives some examples of how this additional input is working out in practice, particularly in the Basque Country (chapter "Basque Intergenerational Transmission from a Language Socialisation Perspective") and in Aotearoa/ New Zealand (chapter "Creating Language Shift: Factors Behind the Language Choices of Māori Speakers").

The volume also aims to push the boundaries of what we commonly understand by 'transmission' and to this end the inclusion of chapters which deal with the importance of the participation of the minority community in language and cultural transmission (Dołowy-Rybińska) or of peer input (Sallabank) are important in our understanding of how language acquisition is happening at the present time among minority and diasporic communities. Overall, then, this volume aims to add to the conversation on the importance of maintaining and ensuring the survival of minority and heritage languages in the twenty-first century and beyond. As Valdés (2017: 74) has noted, '[i]t is increasingly clear […] that the continued use of non-dominant societal languages in various modes (e. g., language survivance, distributed language use) still continues to matter to individuals and communities'. The editors and authors of chapters in this volume believe their present contributions will help to highlight the importance of language to minority and heritage communities to a wider audience.

References

Altman, C., Z. Burstein Feldman, D. Yitzhaki, S. Armon Lotem, and J. Walters. 2014. Family Language Policies, Reported Language Use and Proficiency in Russian-Hebrew Bilingual Children in Israel. *Journal of Multilingual and Multicultural Development* 35 (3): 216–234.

Curdt-Christiansen, X.L. 2016. Conflicting Language Ideologies and Contradictory Language Practices in Singaporean Multilingual Families. *Journal of Multilingual and Multicultural Development* 37 (7): 694–709.

de Houwer, A., and M.H. Bornstein. 2016. Bilingual Mothers' Language Choice in Child-Directed Speech: Continuity and Change. *Journal of Multilingual and Multicultural Development* 37 (7): 680–693.

Edwards, V., and L. Pritchard Newcombe. 2005. When School Is Not Enough: New Initiatives in Intergenerational Language Transmission in Wales. *International Journal of Bilingual Education and Bilingualism* 8 (4): 298–312.

Fishman, J.A. 1991. *Reversing Language Shift: Theoretical and Empirical Foundations of Assistance to Threatened Languages*. Clevedon: Multilingual Matters.

García, M. 2003. Recent Research on Language Maintenance. *Annual Review of Applied Linguistics* 23: 22–43.

García, O. 2009. *Bilingual Education in the 21st Century*. Chichester: Wiley-Blackwell.

Grin, F., and F. Vaillancourt. 1997. The Economics of Multilingualism: Overview and Analytical Framework. *Annual Review of Applied Linguistics* 17: 43–65.

Henley, A., and R. Jones. 2005. Earnings and Linguistic Proficiency in a Bilingual Economy. *The Manchester School* 73 (3): 300–320.

Hindley, R. 1990. *The Death of the Irish Language: A Qualified Obituary*. London and New York: Routledge.

Hohepa, P.W. 2000. Towards 2030 AD (2) Māori Language Regeneration Strategies, Government, People. *He Pūkenga Kōrero: A Journal of Māori Studies* 5 (2): 10–15.

King, K.A., L. Fogle, and A. Logan-Terry. 2008. Family Language Policy. *Language and Linguistics Compass* 2 (5): 907–922.

Kircher, R. 2019. Intergenerational Language Transmission in Quebec: Patterns and Predictors in the Light of Provincial Language Planning. *International*

Journal of Bilingual Education and Bilingualism. https://doi.org/10.1080/13670050.2019.1691499.

Krauss, M. 1992. The World's Languages in Crisis. *Language* 68 (1): 4–10.

Kopeliovich, S. 2013. Happylingual: A Family Project for Enhancing and Balancing Multilingual Development. In *Successful Family Language Policy*, ed. M. Schwartz and A. Verschik, 249–276. Dordrecht: Springer.

Lanza, E. 1997. *Language Mixing in Infant Bilingualism: A Sociolinguistic Perspective*. Oxford: Oxford University Press.

Lasagabaster, D., and A. Huguet, eds. 2007. *Multilingualism in European Bilingual Contexts. Language Use and Attitudes*. Clevedon: Multilingual Matters.

Ó Duibhir, P. 2018. *Immersion Education: Lessons from a Minority Language Context*. Clevedon: Multilingual Matters.

Ó hIfearnáin, T. 2013. Family Language Policy, First Language Irish Speaker Attitudes and Community-Based Response to Language Shift. *Journal of Multilingual and Multicultural Development* 34 (4): 348–365.

Ó hIfearnáin, T. 2015. Sociolinguistic Vitality of Manx After Extreme Language Shift: Authenticity Without Traditional Native Speakers. *International Journal of the Sociology of Language* 231: 45–62.

Schieffelin, B.B., K.A. Woolard, and P.V. Kroskrity. 1998. *Language Ideologies: Practice and Theory*. New York: Oxford University Press.

Schwartz, M., and A. Vershik, eds. 2013. *Successful Family Language Policy*. Dordrecht: Springer.

Smith-Christmas, C. 2016. *Family Language Policy: Maintaining an Endangered Language in the Home*. Basingstoke: Palgrave Macmillan.

Spolsky, B. 2008. Riding the tiger. In *Can Schools Save Indigenous Languages: Policy and Practice in Four Continents*, ed. N.H. Hornberger, 152–160. New York, NY: Palgrave Macmillan.

Spolsky, B. 2012. Family Language Policy – The Critical Domain. *Journal of Multilingual and Multicultural Development* 33 (1): 3–11.

Valdés, G. 2017. From Language Maintenance and Intergenerational Transmission to Language *Survivance*: Will 'Heritage Language' Education Help or Hinder? *International Journal of the Sociology of Language* 243: 67–95.

Wölck, W. 2004. Universals of Language Maintenance, Shift and Change. *Collegium Anthropologicum* 28: 5–12.

Woolard, K. 1998. Introduction: Language Ideology as a Field of Inquiry. In *Language Ideologies: Practice and Theory*, ed. B.B. Schieffelin, K.A. Woolard, and P.V. Kroskrity, 3–47. Oxford: Oxford University Press.
Woolard, K.A., and B.B. Schieffelin. 1994. Language Ideology. *Annual Review of Anthropology* 23: 55–82.

Intergenerational Transmission

Conceptualising Successful Intergenerational Language Transmission in Terms of *saibhreas*: Family Language Support in the Corca Dhuibhne Gaeltacht

Cassie Smith-Christmas and Orlaith Ruiséal

Introduction

In his seminal work *Reversing Language Shift* ('RLS'), Fishman (1991) is adamant that this titular process hinges on successful intergenerational language transmission in the home and community. The centrality of the family to the achievement of wider language revitalisation goals is also echoed in Spolsky's (2012) characterisation of the family as the 'critical' domain in language policy. However, as Spolsky rightly points out (p. 3), typically language policy has focused on the higher echelons of social organisation, such as national governments. It has been mostly through

C. Smith-Christmas (✉)
National University of Ireland, Galway, Ireland
e-mail: Cassandra.Smith-Christmas@nuigalway.ie

O. Ruiséal
Oidhreacht Chorca Dhuibhne, Ballyferriter, Ireland

M. Hornsby and W. McLeod (eds.), *Transmitting Minority Languages*, Palgrave Studies in Minority Languages and Communities,
https://doi.org/10.1007/978-3-030-87910-5_2

the emergent field known as 'Family Language Policy' ('FLP'; Luykx 2003; King et al. 2008) that researchers have made explicit connections between language practices at the micro-level of the family and language policy as it is typically conceptualised in terms of the regional, state and supranational level. Especially in the early years of its trajectory, FLP's emphasis lay in identifying the factors that lead to successful intergenerational transmission. These factors can be distilled into three main types: ideological factors, input factors and output management factors (cf. Spolsky's 2004 model of language policy, which has been very influential on FLP research). Perhaps not surprisingly, research has shown that FLPs in which caregivers make a conscious decision to use the minority language in the first place; sustain high and varied minority language input with their children; and implement management strategies which mandate responses in the minority language are most likely to result in successful intergenerational transmission (e.g. Lanza 1997; de Houwer 2007; Ó hIfearnáin 2013; Altman et al. 2014; Curdt-Christiansen 2016). However, given the complex and multilayered nature of the relationship between language, family and society, there are various nuances to this general premise, and caregivers often find themselves having to navigate a fine balance in making various decisions—for instance, not using a strict management style once the child has established a preference for the majority language, as this might jeopardise family relationships and cause the child's relationship with the minority language to deteriorate (Kopeliovich 2013; Smith-Christmas 2016; Higgins 2019).

Despite FLP's early focus on the factors which lead to successful intergenerational language transmission, however, there has been little critical analysis on what 'successful' intergenerational transmission looks like and how it should (or can) be measured. As Schwartz and Verschik (2013: 1) point out in their interrogation of 'success' in FLP, gauging success tends to be guided by an output-driven outlook, and as Smith-Christmas et al. (2019) discuss, FLP research has been largely guided by the implicit understanding that successful intergenerational transmission equates to the child's language use as an age-appropriate carbon copy of their caregivers' language use. This point resonates with Ó hIfearnáin's (2019) critique of the term 'language maintenance' (which is often used interchangeably with intergenerational language transmission) in implying stasis rather than taking into account the dynamic, negotiated nature of language use.

Our aim in this chapter is to provide a means to conceptualise success in intergenerational transmission in a way that privileges the dynamic and emotional aspects of language use. To do this, we will propose a model, which we refer to as the *saibhreas* model, as a means to understand how caregivers envisage successful intergenerational transmission and how they go about bringing this success to fruition. *Saibhreas* translates to 'richness' in Irish, the language under scope in this chapter, and we will illustrate how *saibhreas* is comprised of three intersecting components: competent language use, local language use and embodied language use. This model was conceived through work with *Tús Maith*, the complementary family language support programme in the Corca Dhuibhne Gaeltacht in south-west Ireland. After introducing the background to the research, the chapter will go on to discuss the three constituent components of *saibhreas* and illustrate the various balances that caregivers must strike in terms of formulating and achieving their goals, especially in terms of issues related to purism and authenticity. The chapter will conclude by discussing how although the *saibhreas* model was developed in the context of autochthonous minority language revitalisation efforts, it can also be a lens for examining intergenerational language transmission in other contexts.

Research Context

This research is situated in the Corca Dhuibhne Gaeltacht, which is in the west of County Kerry. The term 'Gaeltacht' refers to an area that is officially designated by the state as 'Irish-speaking', and which entails certain legal and administrative provisions to ensure this designation, such as Irish being the medium of education for Gaeltacht schools (see Ó hIfearnáin, this volume). This particular research forms part of a case study of Oidhreacht Chorca Dhuibhne (OChD), the area's Irish language development centre, which was one of the six ethnographic case studies comprising the Smithsonian Institution's Sustaining Minoritized Languages in Europe (SMiLE) initiative. Although the case studies were designed and implemented to investigate a range of research questions, our case study centred on the intersection of the family and community, which built on both authors' experience with FLP in a research and professional capacity, as well as their previous collaboration on the Irish Research Council-funded project 'The Challenges of Minority Language Maintenance: Family Language Policy in Scotland and Ireland' (GOIPD/2016/644). In particular, the SMiLE project 'The Intersection of Language and Community in Corca Dhuibhne' centres on *Tús Maith*, the family support programme, of which second author Orlaith Ruiséal is director. The fieldwork for the SMiLE project was carried out between June 2018 and May 2019 and involved participant observation by both Cassie Smith-Christmas and Orlaith Ruiséal in a number of different activities (all of which were coordinated and facilitated by Orlaith Ruiséal in her duties as director), ranging from weekly activities, such as a parent-toddler group and a drama group, to seasonal activities such as the children's visit with Santa.

The participant observation also included a continuing professional development (CPD) day for practitioners working with child-centred language initiatives in the Corca Dhuibhne Gaeltacht as well as the other Gaeltacht areas within the province of Munster. The composition of the group included practitioners who worked as part of the *Cúntóirí Teanga* (language assistant programme) in local schools (all of which are Irish immersion schools by virtue of their location within Gaeltacht areas); *naíonra* (Irish immersion pre-school) leaders and co-leaders; and practitioners as part of *Cuairteoirí Baile* (home visitor) programme. The day consisted of a morning workshop designed to help practitioners identify common 'trouble spots' in children's speech and to effectively deal with these trouble spots. The workshop was led by one of the OChD staff members who has wide experience working with different types of Irish speakers and who has also worked in Irish language publishing. During the second part of the CPD day, practitioners learned rhymes and games to teach to children. Several practitioners took turns leading this part of the day, one of whom was a language assistant at one of the primary schools in Corca Dhuibhne. Following the CPD Day, first author Cassie

Smith-Christmas interviewed this language assistant and observed two of her school sessions as well as interviewed one of the home language visitors and participated in one of the home visits. Prior to the CPD day, Cassie had also interviewed the head teacher of the observation school, the *naíonra* leader and the workshop facilitator.

Throughout the entirety of the interviews for the project (42 in total, approximately 20 hours of recordings), the concept of *saibhreas teanga* 'richness of language' emerged as a key point of import for interviewees, for both those whose language revitalisation efforts specifically involved children (e.g. practitioners and caregivers) and those speakers involved in other facets of language revitalisation (e.g. adult language learning and support). Discursively, *saibhreas* was constructed as the goal for various strands of language revitalisation: if children and/or adult language learners had *saibhreas*, then 'success' had been achieved. Similarly, speakers who had *saibhreas* were held up as extremely positive examples in the community. In many ways, at face value, *saibhreas* may look like being a 'native' or 'authentic' speaker, or similar to the construction of *blas* as in Will's (2012: 37) exploration of Scottish Gaelic:

> *blas* may be described as a set of linguistic and paralinguistic elements, including dialectal and register variants, prosody, and the use of idiomatic expressions, which combine to bestow an almost palpable aesthetic quality to one's speech.

While initially *saibhreas* appeared to have a similarly 'ephemeral' nature, it did not appear to have the same exclusionary function often associated with 'authenticity' (see Woolard 2018). This premise was especially evident in the CPD day, which functioned as what Hornberger (2015) refers to as a 'rich point' in the data and allowed Smith-Christmas to concretise the elements of *saibhreas* into three distinct, yet overlapping, components, as summarised in the diagram (Fig. 1).

As seen from the model, language use is *saibhir* 'rich' if it is competent, local and embodied. The following section will give more background on *Tús Maith* and then go into a detailed discussion of what we mean by each intersecting component of the model, centring on how caregivers and practitioners discursively construct each component. We will also

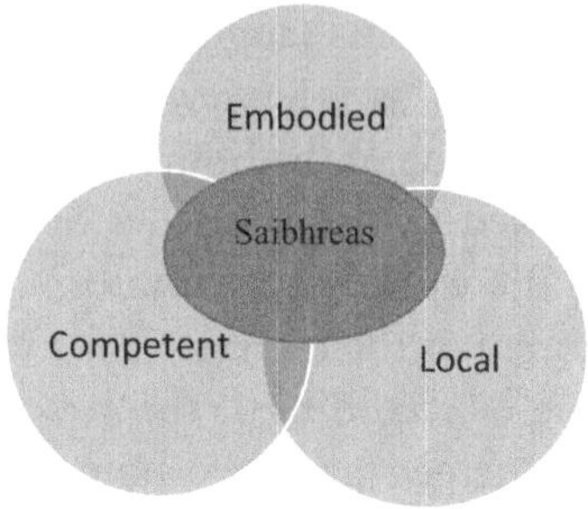

Fig. 1 *Saibhreas* model

look at the specific ways they foster each component in their teaching and practice and especially how they strike a balance between their goals for *saibhreas* and the purist-borderline-exclusionary aspects that these components can engender.

Background: *Tús Maith* and Intergenerational Transmission in the Corca Dhuibhne Gaeltacht

The most recent (2016) census shows that of a population of 6,948 people, 1,928 (28.7%) use Irish daily outside of the education system in the Corca Dhuibhne Gaeltacht. This number and corresponding proportion is taken to be a proxy for the number of speakers for whom Irish functions to some degree as their home and community language. The proportion of daily speakers who use the language outside the education system, however, is much lower in An Daingean, the main town on the peninsula, and the areas to the east of An Daingean (17%), but much higher to core areas west of An Daingean (54.3%), with the remaining areas at 29.1% (Plean Teanga LPT Ciarraí Thiar 2018: 19–21). In terms of gauging the rate of intergenerational transmission in this area, perhaps the most useful benchmark is a survey, conducted the same year as the most recent census, of the language background children entering *naíonraí*. For many of the children, this would have been their first main site of language socialisation outside of the home: the survey reports that of the 88 children in the Corca Dhuibhne Gaeltacht entering local *naíonraí*, 20% of them could be classed as *cainteoirí dúchais* 'native speakers'; 6% could be classed as having *Gaeilge mhaith* 'good Irish'; 41% as having *ar bheagán Gaeilge* 'some Irish'; and 17% with *tuiscint ar an nGaeilge* 'understanding of Irish'. 16% of the children were classified as *gan tuiscint ar an nGaeilge*, meaning that they did not understand any Irish at all (Plean Teanga LPT Chiarraí Thiar 2018: 26). On the whole, these numbers suggest that intergenerational transmission in Corca Dhuibhne is not robust, as it appears that only approximately 26% of the children are being socialised in Irish as the primary language of the home. This mirrors the earlier census figures suggesting that under 30% of people in Corca Dhuibhne use Irish as a home and community language.

These numbers follow from earlier indications of declining intergenerational transmission in the area; in his study conducted in 1983, for example, Ó Riagáin (1992) found that only 25% of those respondents under 45 years of age in the Corca Dhuibhne Gaeltacht would use 'all Irish' or 'mostly Irish' with their children if starting a family today. In Ó hIfearnáin's (2013: 356) study, he discusses how 'parents frequently remarked that there are no 'accidental' Irish speakers anymore' in Corca Dhuibhne, a sentiment which is encapsulated in this quote from second author Orlaith Ruiséal's interview as part of the public meeting of the language and community rights group *Misneach*:

> *go mbraitheadar go raibh níos mó tacaíochtaí ag teastáil ó na tuismitheoirí chun leanbh a thógáint le Gaolainn sa Ghaeltacht toisc ná raibh sé fé mar a bhí* y'know *daichead bliain ó shin nuair a raibh na haon duine ag labhairt Gaolainn agus go raibh sé ana nádúrtha mar rud ach anois go mbeadh saghas go mbeadh saghas cinneadh ag teastáilt chun é a dhéanamh toisc nach raibh b'fhéidir do chomharsan a' labhairt as Gaolainn agus ná raibh daoine ag bualadh le chéile fé mar a bhídís a' bualadh le chéile.*
> (they felt there were more supports needed for parents to rear children with Irish in the Gaeltacht because it was no longer as it had been y'know forty years ago when everyone was speaking Irish and it was very natural but now that a sort of decision was needed to do it as maybe your neighbour was not speaking Irish and that people were not meeting as they used to).

Orlaith's quote underscores how without widespread community use of the language, parents need more support in making the conscious decision to use Irish to their children in the first place and then further support in sustaining this decision through their language practices with the children. As a response to this understanding, Orlaith and other members of OChD set up the family language support programme, *Tús Maith* ('A Good Start'). The programme was modelled in part on the programme *Twf* ('Growth') in Wales (see Edwards and Newcombe 2005) and takes a multi-stranded approach to fostering intergenerational transmission and encouraging children's use of the language with their caregivers and with each other (see Ní Chathail 2003; Smith-Christmas and Ruiséal 2019). This includes assisting caregivers to make the decision to use Irish in the home in the first place through information booklets and then in providing complementary support for early years learning. These complementary supports include an Irish language parent-toddler group and two CDs of children's songs and rhymes as well as children's books (the *Orla Uan* series), all produced and published by OChD. For older children, complementary supports include a card game produced by OChD and a monthly Irish language Saturday family activity session as well as a weekly drama group. For all children, there are key seasonal events hosted by OChD, all through the medium of Irish: a visit with Santa, an Easter egg hunt and a games day on the beach.

In addition to these many and varied support activities, *Tús Maith* also set up the *Cuairteoirí Baile* (CB) scheme, where language assistants go into families' homes and work with them on integrating Irish in this private sphere for one hour per week. The CB scheme is state-funded through An Roinn Cultúir, Oidhreachta agus Gaeltachta (The Department of Culture, Heritage, and the Gaeltacht) and is designed to support a range of families with different linguistic needs, from families with extremely limited Irish to families where caregivers are fully fluent. There is no set programme for the families, and the individual CBs adapt each session to the family's, and especially to the children's, desires and expressed goals. This is in tandem with the *Cúntóirí Teanga* (CT) programme in the schools, which initially began in Corca Dhuibhne, but which is now available in all Gaeltacht areas, whereby CTs (language assistants) help foster children's linguistic skills through small-group sessions. The majority of the attendees at the CPD day that forms the locus of this paper worked for either the CT or CB schemes. The following analysis will examine how they construct their goals for intergenerational transmission in terms of *saibhreas* and the strategies they deploy to bring these goals to fruition.

Competent Language Use

One of the three aspects of *saibhreas* is competent language use. This aligns very much with 'linguistic competence' in the traditional sense—that is, the children's use of age-appropriate syntax, morphology, phonology and lexicon in accordance with caregivers' norms of use. This may seem a quite obvious goal of intergenerational transmission; after all, as discussed in the introduction, the underlying definition of successful intergenerational transmission or language maintenance has tended to operate an underlying notion of the child as an age-appropriate carbon copy of the caregivers' language use. Determining 'what counts' as age-appropriate use, however, is a complex—and due to the dynamic nature of language, some may argue unending—task, which forms the core of the field of child language acquisition, in terms of both monolingual language acquisition (see Fletcher and MacWhinney 1995 for an overview) and what is generally termed 'Bilingual First Language Acquisition' (de Houwer 1990). Work by Tina Hickey (1990, 1991) and other researchers (Nic Flannchadha and Hickey 2017; O'Toole and Hickey 2017; Müller, Muckley and Antonijevic-Elliot 2019) has advanced understanding of children's acquisition of the Irish language, especially in terms of lexical development and morphophonological processes. This work, along with other work on Irish (e.g. Péterváry et al. 2014) and other autochthonous minority languages such as Welsh (e.g. Gathercole and Thomas 2009), has illuminated the layered complexities in determining age-appropriate norms for children's language acquisition against the backdrop of societal language shift and long-standing language contact. Our goal in this discussion of competence is therefore not to determine what children's age-appropriate use of Irish should look like but rather, to explore how caregivers in Corca Dhuibhne discursively construct a notion of 'competence' vis-à-vis these realities, in particular, the dominance of English in Irish society, as well as the high degree of contact between Irish and English and how it manifests in the caregivers' speech (see Hickey 2009; also O'Malley-Madec 2007; Darcy 2014).

Our analysis centres primarily on the PowerPoint with accompanying handout and discussion around this material at the CPD day. The morning of the workshop centred on strategies to develop children's *cruinneas teanga*, which translates to 'linguistic accuracy'. The PowerPoint and handout list a number of linguistic *in*accuracies deemed by the workshop facilitator to be common among children. An example of these is given below. The correct form of many of these listed forms would be immediately known to caregivers, but the facilitator orally emphasised some of the correct forms for some of the inaccuracies (which is represented by Smith-Christmas's handwriting on the handout) (Image 1).

The listed examples given all represent either an aberration in terms of preposition or a synthetic prepositional form being levelled to a more analytical form. Irish, like the other Celtic languages, employs a prepositional pronoun system to convey meaning; for instance, in the first example, *cád faoi mise*, the correct form would be *cad fúmsa* 'what about me?', with the preposition *faoi* 'about' coalesced with the first person pronoun *mé*. However, what we see here is analytical levelling, which is generally understood to be an interlanguage or transfer feature where children are modelling forms on English structures (e.g. what is often referred to as 'calquing', as in this example they are literally saying 'what about me?' when using the form *cad faoi mise* in place of *cad fúmsa*). The analytical levelling of synthetic forms such as prepositional pronouns is not unique to children's use of Irish; for instance, first author Cassie Smith-Christmas has frequently heard *aig mise* rather than *agamsa* (literally 'at-me') from children who speak Scottish Gaelic. There seemed to be a clear consensus among the workshop practitioners that these examples constituted inaccurate forms and should be corrected in order to develop children's competent language use. From the discussion among the practitioners, the preferred method to address these inaccuracies was linguistic modelling of the accurate form rather than overt correction of

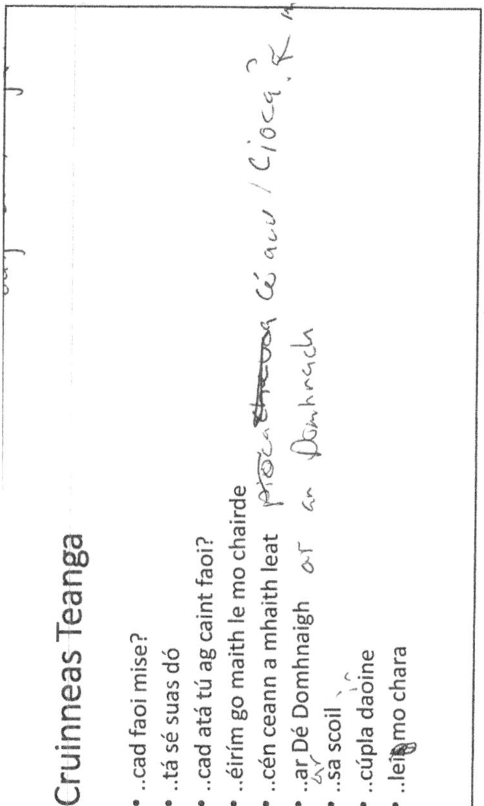

Image 1 Linguistic Accuracy Handout Example 1

the inaccurate form (see also Ó Duibhir 2018, for more of the challenges of addressing inaccuracies in Irish language pedagogy).

In contrast to the consensus on the previous list, the following list contained several items that caused some disagreement among the practitioners (Image 2).

Similar to the previous list, this list also contains items that evidence contact-induced aberrations, such as the literally rendered *sin cad a deir sé* 'that's what he says', where the superfluous *cad* takes the form of English language syntax. Whereas this appeared to be deemed an inaccuracy that would warrant correction, the items *níl clú agam* 'I don't have a clue' and *foirfe* 'perfect' were the source of debate among the practitioners. *Níl clú agam* is a calque of the English 'I don't have a clue' and employs the borrowing of the word 'clue' which in Irish orthography is written as *clú*. Some of the practitioners indicated they viewed categorising this item as 'inaccurate' as ascribing to a purist ideology and they indicated that they would most likely refrain from correcting a child should he or she utter that phrase. They defended this particular stance by highlighting the ubiquity of this phrase among fully competent adult Irish speakers and also within their own personal communicative practices. Similarly, some of the practitioners appeared to object to *foirfe* 'perfect' on the list. The workshop facilitator explained that she had placed the lexical item—which is a long-standing word in the Irish language and not a recent borrowing—on the list because it was simply being used in place of the English 'perfect', a common expression in English as spoken in Ireland to signal agreement, e.g. 'I'll come at ten, so'. 'Perfect'. Again, some of the practitioners seemed to indicate that they felt that this item, although it was indeed a calque due to this English language usage norm, did not undermine their perceived integrity of the language, or the competence of a speaker if he or she were to utter it. Rather, to them, it appeared to be an accepted facet of the long-standing contact between English and Irish, which they commonly employed in their everyday speech with other adults and also in their speech directed specifically towards children.

Although this illustration of 'competence' is limited to two examples, we hope to highlight how although the actual boundaries of competent Irish may be indeed negotiated, there is nonetheless an understanding of where these parameters lie, and how they should be enforced in order

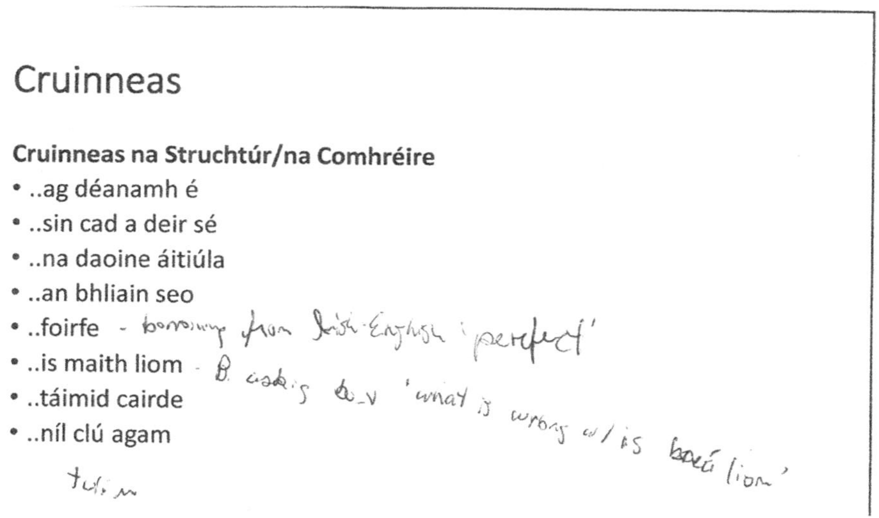

Cruinneas

Cruinneas na Struchtúr/na Comhréire

- ..ag déanamh é
- ..sin cad a deir sé
- ..na daoine áitiúla
- ..an bhliain seo
- ..foirfe - borrowing from Irish-English 'perfect'
- ..is maith liom
- ..táimid cairde
- ..níl clú agam

Image 2 Linguistic Accuracy Handout Example 2

to support children's linguistic development. Our analysis showed how calques and other aberrations that would violate grammatical norms of Irish would be considered 'inaccuracies' and therefore require correction; however, calques that did not violate grammatical norms could potentially pass under the radar, so to speak, especially if they were calques frequently employed by the practitioners themselves in everyday speech. This is not to imply that this rule stands for all such similar dichotomies, but rather, to show how a tacit agreement of what constitutes competent language use can co-exist with an understanding of a long-standing language contact situation and how this is negotiated by caregivers in language revitalisation efforts (see also McLeod [2004], for more on the challenges of purism in language revitalisation). In summary, it is clear that a main component of caregivers' goals in intergenerational transmission is that children speak competent Irish and that programmes such as the CB and CT schemes are designed to support this goal; however, competence is still subject to negotiation within an evolving sociocultural landscape.

Local Language Use

In addition to desiring children to speak Irish that is competent, we contend that caregivers also wish for their children to speak an Irish that is unequivocally 'local'—in this case meaning that children use speech forms associated with the Corca Dhuibhne Gaeltacht. As in the discussion of competence, our aim is not to provide an exhaustive inventory of what constitutes local Corca Dhuibhne Irish (see Ó Sé 2000), but rather to discuss how caregivers construct the importance of 'local' in terms of their goals for intergenerational language transmission and how they navigate the potential tensions arising from conceptions of 'local' versus 'non-local' and/ 'standard' (see Ó hIfearnáin and Ó Murchadha 2011). In many ways, this underlying tension mirrors the discussion of purism versus acceptance as discussed in the last section; in minority language contexts, 'local' often lies at the heart of how authenticity is constructed (see Woolard 2018), which in turn can potentially play a role in excluding certain speakers (see Ó Murchadha et al. 2018). In our discussion of *saibhreas*, we will examine how caregivers maintain a fine balance between drawing on the positive aspects of 'local', including engendering a sense of place among young children, and the potentially exclusionary aspects of 'local' alluded to in other research.

Although the focus of our analysis still lies in the CPD day, the concept of local language use as a *sine qua non* for *saibhreas* emerged across the interviews and ethnographic fieldwork in the SMiLE project (cf. Will's concept of *blas*, which literally means 'taste', but is also used to refer to someone's accent). Similarly, the importance of children speaking local Irish emerged as a key theme throughout the SMiLE project as well as Smith-Christmas's earlier IRC-funded project. Perhaps the most striking example is that in one of the families that Smith-Christmas worked with for the IRC project, she noticed in reading books to the children that the caregivers had gone through some of the books and written the local equivalents of certain lexical items. It was also clear from the interviews in the SMiLE project that caregivers desired for their children to have local models of language use; one grandparent—who had not been socialised in Irish in the home in the local area—for instance highly praised the *naíonra* leader not only for her pedagogical practices for the children, but for being a paragon of the local dialect, and he related with pride an incident in which his young grandchildren corrected his pronunciation of a particular lexical item.

During the CPD day, the importance of providing children with suitable models of the local dialect emerged as a central theme. This is illustrated, for example, by the following slide from the handout (Image 3).

The phrases here all serve to underscore the importance of one's own dialect and what particular aspects are embedded in dialectal use. The phrase in bold *dílseacht dod chanúint féin* can be translated as 'ownership of own dialect' which is followed by *saintréithe na canúna sin* (distinct characteristics of that dialect); *príomhthréithre na canúna sin* (main distinctions); *foghair na canúna* (dialectal pronunciation); and *saibhreas cainte / natha cainte na canúna* 'richness of speech/spoken idioms of the dialect'. This particular slide overtly encourages pride in one's own dialect and its inclusion in the workshop materials advocates

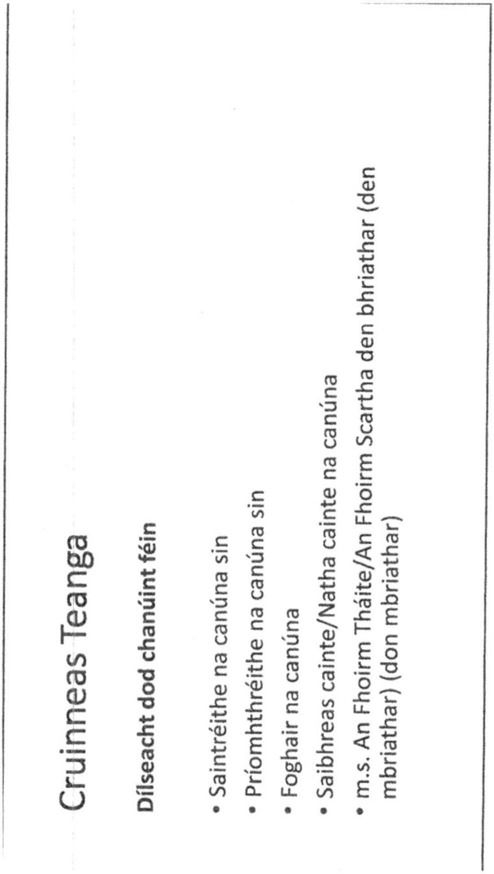

Image 3 Handout Example 3

that practitioners should use their own dialect when speaking to the children, a point which was further emphasised in other workshop materials as well as the discussion. This is illustrated in the following (Image 4).

On the left side, the form that is given is the one that is 'heard' (*cluas*) and on the right side, the written/standard form, i.e. the local form versus the non-local form. By explicitly pointing out these differences, the facilitator is able to foster practitioners' dialectal metalinguistic awareness and encourage them to use their own dialect when speaking to children. The slide also serves a dual purpose: by explicitly pointing out the 'non-local' variants, the slide enables practitioners to gain knowledge of forms other than those they habitually hear and use in their own communities. This means that they are less likely to mark a 'non-local' feature as inaccurate, thereby inadvertently, as Martín Rojo (2013) terms it, ' decapitalising' a child's particular linguistic repertoire. As described in detail in Sallabank and Marquis (2018), this decapitalisation can occur in other minority language contexts and can lead to certain speakers feeling excluded.

The facilitator further fostered a sense of effective pedagogy for inclusion by suggesting that practitioners use standard orthography when writing for children. This suggestion, however, was met with some debate; the facilitator, however, stressed that unless practitioners were able to use dialectal forms 100% consistently in their orthography, students' literacy could potentially be hampered by inconsistency. She further defended her point by drawing on an example of a local poet who used dialectal forms in her writing, specifically *cáil?* for *cá bhfuil?* 'where is', as in natural speech the two morphemes become coalesced. The practitioner emphasised that if practitioners wrote *cáil*, children would be unable to see how *bhfuil* would relate to other question phrases, such as *an bhfuil*? (present tense question construction). Therefore, a learning opportunity would be diminished, especially for children who were not socialised through Irish at home. (As also seen on the slide, the one exception to the facilitator's rule of using standard orthography when writing for children was in the epenthesis and lenition following the intensifier *an.*)

As in the discussion of competence, we have limited our discussion to a few examples. We hope, however, that we have achieved three main aims; first, that we have clarified what we mean by 'local' and how it is

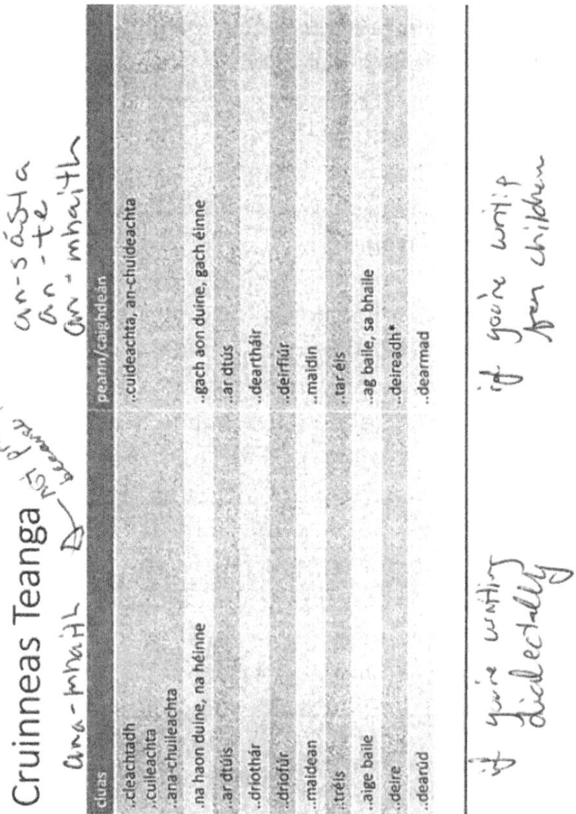

Cruinneas Teanga

cluas	peann/caighdeán
..cleachtadh ..cuileachta ..ana-chuileachta	..cuideachta, an-chuideachta
..na haon duine, na héinne	..gach aon duine, gach éinne
..ar dtúis	..ar dtús
..driothár	..deartháir
..driofúr	..deirfiúr
..maidean	..maidin
..tréis	..tar éis
..aige baile	..ag baile, sa bhaile
..deire	..deireadh*
..dearúd	..dearmad

Image 4 Handout Example 4

discursively constructed within the scope of our study; second, shown how it plays a constituent role in the *saibhreas* model; and finally, shown how practitioners navigate the complexities of valorising local language use while simultaneously minimising its exclusionary potential. We now turn to the final component of the *saibhreas* model: embodied language use.

Embodied Language Use

The final interrelated component of the *saibhreas* model is what we refer to as 'embodied' language use. In using this term, we are drawing on Csordas's (1995: 6) conception of embodiment as 'the existential ground of culture and self' as a way to understand how caregivers articulate and work towards achieving their goals in terms of the complex social and emotional dimensions of children's language use. We acknowledge that the particular term 'embodied' may entail different foci depending on one's particular field and that discussions of 'language' and 'embodiment' often centre on the relationship of the physical body to language, especially in terms of identity formation (Pennycook 2004). As will be explained throughout this section, our notion of 'embodied' views language as a 'way of being'. As Slavec (2019: 155) puts it, 'To *have* Irish in Corca Dhuibhne is a feeling and an experience, as well as an intimate commitment to *live* (through) Irish' (emphasis in original). The embodiment component of *saibhreas* is a means to articulate caregivers' desire that children both *can* and *do* navigate their social and emotional worlds through Irish and crucially, that Irish is not relegated to the status of an artefact (e.g. a 'school language' or a 'performance language').

Our discussion will begin with the concept that 'embodiment' involves children choosing to use Irish. The importance of 'choice' in language use is well established in the language policy literature: for example, Grin's (2003) tripartite model of successful language policy at the societal level consists of the capacity to use the language (cf. our conceptualisation of 'competence'), opportunity to use the language and the *desire* to use the language. Children may evidence a *lack* of desire to use the minority language for a number of reasons, including the influence of the majority culture on identity formation (e.g. Revis 2019); the dominance of the majority language in peer group language practices (e.g. Kopeliovich 2013); and the compounding effects of language shift, resulting in the child's higher competence in the majority language (e.g. Gafaranga 2010). Further, the language shift may contribute to the child's reluctance to use the minority language due to its association with elders and thereby with authority (e.g. Meek 2007). This residual authority of the language may be strengthened by its presence in the education system, especially in areas where community use of the language is weak (Hickey 2007; Kavanagh and Hickey 2013; Smith-Christmas 2016, 2017). In Hickey's (2007: 56) multi-sited *naíonra* study, for instance, she observes that one of the target children 'saw Irish as the appropriate choice when trying to manage the other children, but there was no evidence that she perceived Irish as a normal mode of communication with her peers'. This reality is echoed in the OChD *naíonra* leader's interview, in which she describes how although the children actively use Irish throughout the school day, they generally use English together in free play—*sin an áit is mó a bheadh Béarla* 'that's the place where English takes hold'.

Our conception of 'embodied' language use therefore centres on the idea that what caregivers want is for the children to actively *choose* to speak Irish and that the children do not limit their use of Irish to situations where the children feel they 'have' to speak the language, such as in the classroom. This was clear from the many observations of families, interviews with family members and observations of the CPD day as well as the subsequent observations of the CB and CT sessions, and it was clear that caregivers deployed multiple strategies so that, as the CB puts it in her interview, the children have 'the chance to use the language naturally as a social language' (*an deis acu é a dh'úsáid mar theanga sóisialta go nadúrtha*; cf. Hickey's quote discussed earlier). One way practitioners did this was through explicitly emphasising rhymes and games as the key components of facilitating children's language acquisition; while the first part of the CPD day was spent on linguistic accuracy, the second part was devoted to learning games and rhymes to teach and play with the children. The centrality of 'play' in practitioners' work and its role in fostering children's embodied use of language is highlighted in the *naíonra* practitioner's quote below:

> *an obair atá ar siúl againn, déanaimid í trí mheán an súgraidh. So is dócha nuair a dhéanann tú spraoi agus imirt tá sé i bhfad níos fusa an teanga a phiocadh suas. Tá sé an-difriúil leis an scoil.*
>
> (The work we do, we do through the medium of play. So perhaps when you do it [through] fun and play, it's much easier to pick up the language. It's very different from school).

Here, we see a very 'embodied' approach to language acquisition; the *naíonra* leader views her role as facilitating acquisition through the medium of play, rather than 'teaching' the language, which could have the potential for Irish to be seen as an 'object' rather than a 'way of being'. The *naíonra* leader's statement that 'it's very different from school' also underlines illustrates how practitioners try to foster the children's positive emotional relationship with the language from the child's initial entry to the *naíonra.* This sentiment is also echoed in the CB's interview, where she discusses how she consciously tries to disassociate the CB visits from a sense of school:

> *so thá siad tar éis an lá a chaitheamh ar scoil agus anois thá siad a' teacht isteach so ní – caithfidh tú é a dhéanamh i slí 'oh ní obair scoile é seo ní obair scoile é seo ní obair bhaile é seo' rud éigint 'tháimid chun cluichí a imirt'*
>
> (so they're just after spending a day at school and now they're coming in so – you have to do it [the CB session] in a way 'oh this is not school work, this is not homework' something [like] 'we're going to play games')

This quote also clearly illustrates how practitioners use play as a means to encourage children to use the language. In centring embodiment as a 'way of being', we also intend to highlight how caregivers actively desire for the children to *experience* the world through Irish and for children to articulate the psychological and physical sensations associated with emotions—both positive and negative—through Irish. The most striking example we encountered of this aspect of embodiment was through an interview with one of the two singers on the *Sicín Mise Go Sona Sásta* ('I'm a Happy Chicken') CD produced by OChD.

> *'Sicín mise go sona sásta táimse anseo insa an tuí im' luí. Féach anois ar mo dhá sciatháinín, eireabalaín álainn is goibín buí.' Agus raighfeá ar ais dtís na*

> *leanaí agus is maith leo é agus is maith leo ar an ngob agus mar shampla sona sásta agus bíonn na leanaí féin, leanaí beaga anois abair naíonáin bheaga agus naíonáin mhóra bíonn siad chomh sásta toisc go mbíonn an sicín sásta* you know. *Agus samhlaíocht atá acu mar agus tá sé ag múineadh saibhreas na Gaelainne dhóibh agus mar sin* do you know. *Mo dhá sciathháinín abair tá fhios agat agus eireaballaín álainn agus gobaín buí, tá sé chomh simplí ach fós nuair a chloiseann tú leanbh á rá déarfá ó tá sé sin go haoibhinn abair an Ghaelainn deas atá aici nó aige.* You know so *rudaí beaga mar sin atá ann a dtuigeas tú, rudaí beaga iad san a bheadh caillte mar mbeadh an an Oidhreacht anseo chomh maith.*
>
> ((Singing)) (I'm a happy chicken/Here I lay in the hay/Look now at my two little wings/A pretty little tail/And a little yellow beak)) And it goes back to the children and they like it and they like the mouth and for example happy and the children themselves – young children in pre-school or just in primary school – they're so happy because the chicken is happy you know. The imagination they have – and it teaches them the richness of the Irish language and things like that you know. 'My two little wings' you know and 'beautiful little tail' and 'yellow beak,' it's simple but still when you hear a child say that, you say, that's lovely the Irish he or she has. You know little things like that you understand little things that would be lost if Oidhreacht [Chorca Dhuibhne] wasn't here.)

Children's ability to experience empathy—that is, projecting another being's emotions onto themselves—is an important component of their developmental trajectory, in that it shows understanding not only of themselves as beings, but of other beings as separate from them (Simms 2008: 70). Here, the singer gives us a very simple but concrete example of this empathy: the children are happy because the chicken in the song is happy, and the singer highlights how the children are able to form this empathetic connection through their imagination. He also explicitly mentions *saibhreas* in this quote, and although his examples of *saibhreas* (relating to lenition and noun-adjective syntax) align more with the competence component discussed earlier, we argue that this quote also evidences the 'embodiment' that caregivers strive to facilitate in children: that children are able to experience emotion through Irish and in turn use language to relay this type of emotion; that Irish is part of their being, a way in which they experience the world.

Conclusion

In the opening of this chapter, we argued for the need for a concrete and holistic means to conceptualise 'successful' intergenerational language transmission. We hope that through this discussion of the *saibhreas* model and its three constituent components—competent language use; local language use; and embodied language use—we have provided a tangible means by which to understand how caregivers frame their visions of 'success' and how they go about bringing this success into being. We have hopefully shown how, although the constituent components themselves provide a concrete means to conceptualise 'success', the boundaries of the individual constituent components are malleable and may be negotiated by caregivers over space and time. Further, although the *saibhreas* model emerged from the specific context of language transmission in the Corca Dhuibhne Gaeltacht, we argue that this model can function as a lens to gauging and understanding 'success' in other language transmission contexts. As explained in our discussion of 'competence', linguistic competence is generally seen as a *sine qua non* to successful transmission, and our particular discussion centred on the boundary negotiation process in terms of the language contact, which naturally would be applicable to other contexts, but certainly, other language-specific features may take precedence in understanding how caregivers' view 'success' in other contexts. Similarly, although we have discussed the importance of 'local' in reference to the Corca Dhuibhne dialect, 'local' may take other forms in other contexts—for example, the child's sense of a particular national identity and use of culturally appropriate terms of address, for instance. Finally, given the discussion across various contexts about the child's propensity to prefer the majority language at the expense of the minority language, we argue that our notion of 'embodied' as meaning that not only does the child *want* to speak the minority language, but does so akin to a 'way of being' rather than an artefact, is applicable to other contexts. We hope that in the *saibhreas* model, we have provided researchers and caregivers alike with a useful conceptual tool in the challenging process of successfully transmitting a minoritised language to a child.

References

Altman, C., Z. Burstein Feldman, D. Yitzhaki, S. Armon Lotem, and J. Walters. 2014. Family Language Policies, Reported Language Use and Proficiency in Russian-Hebrew Bilingual Children in Israel. *Journal of Multilingual and Multicultural Development* 35 (3): 216–234.

Csordas, T.J. 1995. *Embodiment and Experience: The Existential Ground of Culture and Self*. Cambridge: Cambridge University Press.

Curdt-Christiansen, X.L. 2016. Conflicting Language Ideologies and Contradictory Language Practices in Singaporean Multilingual Families. *Journal of Multilingual and Multicultural Development* 37 (7): 694–709.

Darcy, G. 2014. Code-Mixing and Context: A Corca Dhuibhne Case Study. Unpublished PhD thesis, University of Limerick.

de Houwer, A. 1990. *Acquisition of Two Languages from Birth: A Case Study*. Cambridge: Cambridge University Press.

de Houwer, A. 2007. Parental Language Input Patterns and Children's Bilingual Use. *Applied Psycholinguistics* 28: 411–424.

Edwards, V., and L.P. Newcombe. 2005. When School Is Not Enough: New Initiatives in Intergenerational Language Transmission in Wales. *International Journal of Bilingual Education and Bilingualism* 8 (4): 298–312.

Fishman, J.A. 1991. *Reversing Language Shift: Theoretical and Empirical Foundations of Assistance to Threatened Languages*. Clevedon: Multilingual Matters.

Fletcher, P., and B. MacWhinney. 1995. *The Handbook of Child Language*. Oxford: Blackwell.

Grin, F. 2003. *Language Policy Evaluation and the European Charter for Regional or Minority Languages*. Basingstoke: Palgrave Macmillan.

Higgins, C. 2019. The Dynamics of Hawaiian Speakerhood in the Family. *International Journal of the Sociology of Language* 255: 45–72.

Gafaranga, J. 2010. Medium Request: Talking Language Shift into Being. *Language in Society* 39: 241–270.

Gathercole, V.C.M., and E.M. Thomas. 2009. Bilingual First-Language Development: Dominant Language Takeover, Threatened Minority Language Take-Up. *Bilingualism* 12 (2): 213–237.

Hornberger, N. 2015. Selecting Appropriate Research Methods in LPP Research: Methodological Rich Points. In *Research Methods in Language Policy and Planning*, ed. F. Hult and D.C. Johnson, 7–20. Oxford: Wiley Blackwell.

Hickey, T.M. 1990. The Acquisition of Irish: Word Order Development. *Journal of Child Language* 17 (1): 17–41.

Hickey, T.M. 1991. Mean Length of Utterance and the Acquisition of Irish. *Journal of Child Language* 18: 553–569.

Hickey, T.M. 2007. Children's Language Networks and Teachers' Input in Minority Language Immersion: What Goes in May Not Come Out. *Language and Education* 21 (1): 46–65.

Hickey, T.M. 2009. Codeswitching and Borrowing in Irish. *Journal of Sociolinguistics* 13 (5): 670–688.

Kavanagh, L., and T.M. Hickey. 2013. 'You're Looking at This Different Language and It Freezes You Out Straight Away': Identifying Challenges to Parental Involvement Among Immersion Parents. *Language and Education* 27 (5): 432–450.

King, K.A., L. Fogle, and A. Logan-Terry. 2008. Family Language Policy. *Language and Linguistics Compass* 2 (5): 907–922.

Kopeliovich, S. 2013. Happylingual: A Family Project for Enhancing and Balancing Multilingual Development. In *Successful Family Language Policy*, ed. M. Schwartz and A. Verschik, 249–276. Dordrecht: Springer.

Lanza, E. 1997. *Language Mixing in Infant Bilingualism: A Sociolinguistic Perspective*. Oxford: Oxford University Press.

Luykx, A. 2003. Weaving Languages Together: Family Language Policy and Gender Socialization in Bilingual Aymara Households. In *Language Socialization in Bilingual and Multilingual Societies*, ed. R. Bayley and S. Schecter, 25–43. Clevedon: Multilingual Matters.

Martín Rojo, L. 2013. (De)capitalising Students Through Linguistic Practices. A Comparative Analysis of New Educational Programmes in a Global Era. In *Language, Migration and Social Inequalities A Critical Sociolinguistic Perspective on Institutions and Work*, ed. A. Duchêne, M. Moyer, and C. Roberts, 118–146. Bristol: Multilingual Matters.

McLeod, W. 2004. "Feumaidh sinn a' Ghàidhlig a chumail pure": Problems of linguistic purism in Scottish Gaelic. In *Purism—Second Helping*, ed.

D. Ó Riagáin, and T. Stolz, 25–45. Bochum: Universitätsverlag Dr. N. Brockmeyer.
Meek, B.A. 2007. Respecting the Language of Elders: Ideological Shift and Linguistic Discontinuity in a Northern Athapascan Community. *Journal of Linguistic Anthropology* 17 (1): 23–43.
Müller, N., S.A. Muckley, and S. Antonijevic-Elliott. 2019. Where Phonology Meets Morphology in the Context of Rapid Language Change and Universal Bilingualism: Irish Initial Mutations in Child Language. *Clinical Linguistics and Phonetics* 33 (1–2): 3–19.
Ní Chathail, C. 2003. *Tógail Clainne le Gaeilge i nGaeltacht Chorca Dhuibhne.* Dublin: Institiúid Teangeolaíochta Éireann and Oidhreacht Chorca Dhuibhne.
Nic Fhlannchadha, S., and T.M. Hickey. 2017. Acquiring an Opaque Gender System in Irish, an Endangered Indigenous Language. *First Language* 37 (5): 475–499.
Ó Duibhir, P. 2018. *Immersion Education: Lessons from a Minority Language Context*. Bristol: Multilingual Matters.
Ó hIfearnáin, T. 2013. Family Language Policy, First Language Irish Speaker Attitudes and Community-Based Response to Language Shift. *Journal of Multilingual and Multicultural Development* 34 (4): 348–365.
Ó hIfearnáin, T. (2019). An dúchas, an anaithnideacht agus an seachadadh teanga/Nativeness, Anonymity and Language Transmission. Lecture Delivered at the New Professors' Inaugural Lecture Series. NUI Galway.
Ó hIfearnáin, T., and N.P. Ó Murchadha. 2011. The Perception of Standard Irish as a Prestige Target Variety. In *Standard Languages and Language Standards in a Changing Europe*, ed. T. Kristiansen and N. Coupland, 97–104. Oslo: Novus.
O'Malley-Madec, M. 2007. How One Word Borrows Another: The Process of Language-contact in Two Irish-speaking Communities. *International Journal of Bilingual Education and Bilingualism* 10 (4): 494–509.
Ó Murchadha et al. 2018. New Speakers, Familiar Concepts? In *New Speakers of Minority Languages: Linguistic Ideologies and Practices*, ed. C. Smith-Christmas, Ó Murchadha, M. Hornsby, and M. Moriarty, 1–22. Basingstoke: Palgrave MacMillan
Ó Riagáin, P. 1992. *Language Maintenance and Language Shift as Strategies of Social Reproduction: Irish in the Corca Dhuibhne Gaeltacht 1926–86*. Dublin: Institiúid Teangeolaíochta Éireann.
Ò Sé, D. 2000. *Gaeilge Chorca Dhuibhne*. Dublin: Institiúid Teangeolaíochta Éireann.

O'Toole, C., and T. Hickey. 2017. Bilingual Language Acquisition in a Minority Context: Using the Irish-English Communicative Development Inventory to Track Acquisition of an Endangered Language. *International Journal of Bilingual Education and Bilingualism* 20 (2): 146–162.

Plean Teanga LPT Chiarraí Thiar (PTCT). 2018. https://tobardhuibhne.ie/plean-teanga/. Accessed 18 December 2020.

Pennycook, A. 2004. Performativity and Language Studies, Critical Inquiry. *Language Studies: An International Journal* 1 (1): 1–19.

Pétervary, T., B. Ó Curnáin, C. Ó Giollagáin, and J. Sheahan. 2014. *Iniúchadh ar an gCumas Dátheangach: An sealbhú teanga i measc ghlúin óg na Gaeltachta / [ABC] Analysis of Bilingual Competence: Language acquisition among young people in the Gaeltacht*. Dublin: An Chomhairle um Oideachas Gaeltachta agus Gaelscolaíochta.

Revis, M. 2019. A Bourdieusian Perspective on Child Agency in Family Language Policy. *International Journal of Bilingual Education and Bilingualism* 22 (2): 177–191.

Sallabank, J., and Y. Marquis. 2018. 'We Don't Say It Like That': Language Ownership and (De)legitimising the New Speaker. In *New Speakers of Minority Languages: Linguistic Ideologies and Practices*, ed. C. Smith-Christmas, N.Ó. Murchadha, M. Hornsby, and M. Moriarty, 67–90. Basingstoke: Palgrave Macmillan.

Simms, E. 2008. *The Child in the World: Embodiment, Time, and Language in Early Childhood*. Detroit, MI: Wayne State University Press.

Slavec, N. 2019. 'To Have' Irish in Corca Dhuibhne: Language Ideologies and Practices in a Minority Language Community. Unpublished MA thesis, University of Ljubljana.

Smith-Christmas, C. 2017. 'Is It Really for Talking?': The Implications of Associating a Minority Language with the School. *Language, Culture and Curriculum* 30 (1): 32–47.

Smith-Christmas, C. 2016. *Family Language Policy: Maintaining an Endangered Language in the Home*. Basingstoke: Palgrave Macmillan.

Smith-Christmas, C., M. Bergroth, and I. Bezcioğlu-Göktolga. 2019. A Kind of Success Story: Family Language Policy in Three Different Sociopolitical Contexts. *International Multilingual Research Journal* 13 (2): 88–101.

Smith-Christmas, C., and O. Ruiséal. 2019. *An Nasc idir an teanga agus an pobal i gCorca Dhuibne/The intersection of language and community in Corca Dhuibhne*. Washington, DC: Smithsonian Institution.

Schwartz, M., and A. Verschik. 2013. *Successful Family Language Policy: Parents, Children, and Educators in Interaction*. Dordrecht: Springer.

Spolsky, B. 2004. *Language Policy*. Cambridge: Cambridge University Press.
Spolsky, B. 2012. Family Language Policy – The Critical Domain. *Journal of Multilingual and Multicultural Development* 33 (1): 3–11.
Will, V.K.A. 2012. Why Kenny Can't *Can*: The Language Socialization Experiences of Gaelic-Medium Educated Children in Scotland. Unpublished PhD thesis, University of Michigan.
Woolard, K.A. 2018. *Singular and Plural: Ideologies of Linguistic Authority in 21st Century Catalonia*. Oxford: Oxford University Press.

Family Language Policy in the Face of a Shrinking Community Language: Gaelic on the Isle of Lewis

Michelle Macleod

Introduction

This chapter is a tightly focussed study of five individual parents who are attempting to give Gaelic a place within their families. Each of the parents comes from the Isle of Lewis in northwest Scotland and is currently residing there; they all had two Gaelic-speaking parents, and some have Gaelic-speaking spouses: none were habitual fluent Gaelic speakers from childhood to adulthood and three currently use Gaelic on a regular basis. Based on data gathered from extensive interviews and self-penned diagrams of historical and current speaker networks, this chapter considers the motivations and the actions of the parents in attempting to bring their children up as Gaelic speakers. To explore this

M. Macleod (✉)
School of Language, Literature, Music and Visual Culture,
University of Aberdeen, Scotland, UK
e-mail: m.macleod@abdn.ac.uk

M. Hornsby and W. McLeod (eds.), *Transmitting Minority Languages*,
Palgrave Studies in Minority Languages and Communities,
https://doi.org/10.1007/978-3-030-87910-5_3

in detail, the following questions are considered: why is Gaelic important to the parents; what have the parents done to improve their own language competencies and those of their children; and how successfully have the parents renegotiated networks of interlocutors for themselves and their children.

Background

According to the 2011 UK census, of the 19,137 people over the age of three resident on the Isle of Lewis 58.1% of the population (11,111) had some skills in Gaelic: of this 58.1% not all are active speakers, with 8.5% claiming to understand the language only (Comhairle nan Eilean Siar n.d.: 9). Lewis still has one of the densest concentrations of Gaelic speakers in Scotland (Nance 2019) and is considered to be among the last remaining 'heartlands' of the language (Birnie 2018a, 2018b) and is included in Ó Giollagáin et al.'s (2020) study as one example of a 'remaining vernacular community'. While Lewis still has one of the densest concentrations of Gaelic speakers, it has experienced rapid decline in recent decades. Ó Giollagáin et al. summarise the decreases recorded in census data from three areas in Lewis thus: Stornoway suburbs were 61% Gaelic speaking in 1981 and 40% in 2011; Lewis East was 87% Gaelic speaking in 1981 and 51% in 2011; Lewis North & West was 93% Gaelic speaking in 1981 and 61% in 2011 (Ó Giollagáin et al. 2020: 41). The density of speaking practice today clearly depends to some degree on the location within the island, and recent studies on Gaelic usage in Lewis have helped us understand the nuances of usage in addition to what has traditionally been understood from census data. Birnie's recent work on language usage in Stornoway, the only town and the least Gaelic-speaking location on the island, has shown that out of 2,000 conversations in her linguistic soundscape survey of 10 public spaces, Gaelic was used in only 9.1% of them (Birnie 2018a: 223) suggesting that Gaelic 'has not been normalised as the language of public affairs' (Birnie 2018a: 228). Conversely, her work with language usage diaries by Gaelic language speakers showed that 'Gaelic was used in 45.1% of all private domain interactions' (Birnie

2018a: 230). The study by Munro, Taylor and Armstrong (2011) of the township of Shawbost, on the west coast of Lewis, showed the language to be at a tipping point in that community in terms of its sustainability as a community language, with 66% of residents being fluent Gaelic speakers 'but with this fluency being concentrated amongst those aged 50 and older'; they also noted 'an established and growing pattern of language shift to English' (Munro et al. 2011: 7). Ó Giollagáin et al. (2020) suggested that language shift was well established in the 'vernacular' community, pointing to numerous failures in the maintenance of Gaelic as a community language, including: 'societal weakness of the Gaelic-speaking group', 'an ongoing demographic crisis with a diminishing social density of Gaelic speakers' and 'marginal levels of societal and familial transmission of Gaelic' (Ó Giollagáin et al. 2020: 360).

The theoretical context for this study is within the discourse of heritage learners, learners who have a direct familial connection to the language (Valdés 2001; Van Deusen-Scholl 2003; Armstrong 2013) and their attempts to influence the language policy of their families. Family language policy (FLP) (King et al. 2008; Smith-Christmas 2016; Wilson 2020), as interpreted for this study, focuses on language ideologies and decisions taken within the family unit which impact on children's acquisition and use. Spolsky defines community language policy, and by extrapolation family language policy, as having three key components:

> its language practices – the habitual pattern of selecting among the varieties that make up its linguistic repertoire; its language beliefs or ideology – the beliefs about language and language use; and any specific efforts to modify or influence that practice by any kind of language intervention, planning or management. (Spolsky 2004: 5)

Smith-Christmas's long-term ethnographic study of Gaelic language management by one family (2016) has helped shape the way in which we understand how language use can shift and be impacted across generations. The current chapter does not have the benefit of longitudinality but explores issues of ideology and management in five families and in particular families of heritage learners. Armstrong's study (2014) of concepts of naturalism and ideology in mothers learning Gaelic alongside their young children demonstrated the tenacity required by these mothers to attempt to enact their FLPs. Armstrong noted that a couple of informants in his study were heritage learners and would thus benefit from extended family support in enacting their FLPs.

The potential role of the heritage learner has previously been considered in relation to Gaelic language revitalisation: it has been noted, for example, that this group was keen to become active speakers and may have more opportunities to use the language, although they could benefit from specifically focussed help in achieving fluency (Smith-Christmas and Armstrong 2014; Macleod and MacLeod 2021). However, Gaelic heritage learners do not always find it easy to unlock access to their potential networks (McEwan-Fujita 2010; Armstrong 2013; Macleod and MacLeod 2021) and in this respect share many experiences with 'new speakers' of Gaelic. Issues around second language acquisition and accessing networks have been problematised in recent years not only in relation to Gaelic (Armstrong 2013; Carty 2014; McLeod et al. 2017) but also in a broader context (e.g. O'Rourke and Pujolar 2015; Hornsby and Quentel 2013; Jaffe 2013; Smith-Christmas et al. 2018). Some of the themes considered in this study overlap with the new speaker discourse but are considered here through a heritage learner lens.

The Study

Method

A mixed methods approach of semi-structured interviews and participatory mapping was used to elicit data for this study, which is part of a bigger project looking at the experiences of heritage learners in Lewis (Macleod and MacLeod 2021). Emmel maintains that 'participatory social mapping is considered as an interactive approach using accessible and free-ranging visual methods in an individual or group interview setting to interrogate qualitative research questions' (Emmel 2008: 1). Five parents, all of whom were currently or had previously been actively involved in Gaelic learning at the same time as they were supporting their children's acquisition of the language, were interviewed about their experiences of establishing Gaelic as a family language. The small size of this cohort of course means that the experiences of the parents may not be representative: this was a self-selecting convenience sample who all met the criteria of (a) being from the Isle of Lewis, (b) not being a full Gaelic speaker from youth to adulthood and (c) attempting to use Gaelic as a family language. All participants had been exposed to Gaelic in their youths and had been raised in families where both parents were Gaelic speakers; they had all studied Gaelic as a subject at school to varying levels. They all used different labels to describe current competence, including 'learner', 'semi-speaker', 'heritage learner' and 'lapsed native speaker'. The in-depth interviews were all recorded and then transcribed and coded to identify key themes in their experiences. Themes which emerged through this coding exercise were parental language identity and ideology, issues surrounding adult (re)acquisition, language networks and supporting children's acquisition and experience of Gaelic.

Interviews were supplemented by the use of diagrams; each participant drew two diagrams to show how their Gaelic language networks had changed from the time of their youth to the present day. Participants drew maps of important people in their childhoods and were asked to indicate who spoke Gaelic; they were also asked to draw a map of Gaelic speakers in their contemporary lives and to indicate whether they used Gaelic or not with these individuals. All participants have been given pseudonyms to protect their anonymity.

Informants

The five informants range in age from 39 to 50 years old; there were four female participants and only one male participant. All but one of the informants had lived for some part of their life outside of Lewis; all had been at least partially educated in Lewis (two of them, sisters, having been born to Lewis parents on the mainland of Scotland, came to Lewis during their primary school years although they had spent much of their summer holidays prior to the move in Lewis). All of the informants attended state schools at the time of the local authority's bilingual education policy (see, e.g., Murray and Morrison 1984; O'Hanlon and Paterson 2014 for a discussion of local and national Gaelic education policy). All five informants had two Gaelic-speaking parents: only one remembers using some Gaelic with her parents in childhood but not consistently and not when she got older; all participants also had at least two living grandparents that they saw regularly in their youth who were also Gaelic speaking. All five participants raised their children as part of a two-parent family (Table 1).

Of the respondents in this chapter, two were brought up in Stornoway and now live in Stornoway (one after living for a period of time on mainland Scotland and in Asia); two (sisters) were largely brought up in Stornoway (having been born in Glasgow) but raised their own families outside of Stornoway and one was brought up in and was living at the time of the study in a village close to Shawbost (having lived on mainland Scotland for some time). The four who had been brought up in Stornoway as children all had connections with other parts of the island and reported extended Gaelic-speaking family networks in these areas.

In terms of current language practice, Dolina and Lily are habitual users of Gaelic although Lily identifies weaknesses in her language skills and had plans in place for improving. At the time of interview, Chrisella had only been engaged in actively learning Gaelic for a little over a year: she took as many opportunities as she could to use her Gaelic, even choosing to conduct her interview in Gaelic, switching to English when she struggled to express herself. Agnes is no longer engaged in learning Gaelic and does not use the language habitually: she has occasional

Table 1 Summary identities

				Gaelic-speaking ability of		
Identity	Age	Gender	Childhood residence	Mother	Father	Spouse
Agnes	40–49	F	Glasgow/Lewis	✔	✔	✔
Chrisella	40–49	F	Lewis	✔	✔	✔
Dolina	50–59	F	Glasgow/Lewis	✔	✔	✔
Lily	35–39	F	Lewis	✔	✔	X
Angus	40–49	M	Lewis	✔	✔	X

conversations at the workplace in Gaelic and even fewer conversations in Gaelic with her sons now they have grown up; she claims to understand everything that is said to her in Gaelic and is able to read Gaelic. At the time of interview, Angus had recently completed an advanced course in Gaelic and was keen to continue learning; he used his language skills occasionally both professionally and at home but was lacking in confidence in his ability.

It is not within the scope of this chapter to conduct a linguistic analysis of the Gaelic of Dolina, Lily and Chrisella, who all spoke at least some Gaelic during their interviews. However, it is clear even from the excerpts below that to varying extents their language differs from any concept of a standard form. They all, to different degrees, struggle for vocabulary, switching to English to fill gaps; their syntactic structures are on occasion deviant and while, for example, levelling in speech among native speakers in the use of the Gaelic nominal system has become common (Lamb 2003), this is especially pronounced here. Even Dolina, the most competent of this group of speakers, was aware of her own weakness in the language:

> *Bidh daoine ag ràdh gu bheil mi nas fileanta na tha mi a' smaoineachadh gu bheil,* so *tha mi a' smaoineachadh an-còmhnaidh tha seòrsa de chion-misneachd agam. Tha mi an-còmhnaidh a' faireachdainn mar gu bheil mi air deireadh . . . chan eil mi cho math 's a tha daoine eile a bha bruidhinn bhon toiseach.*
>
> (People tell me I am more fluent than I think I am, so I always think I have some kind of lack of confidence. I always feel like I am behind . . . I am not as good as other people who spoke from the beginning).

No further comment will be made about their output in respect of their willingness to conduct the research interviews in Gaelic.

Findings

Parental Language Identity and Ideology

All the parents in this study had taken the deliberate decision to support their children's acquisition of Gaelic: while the main aim of this chapter is to explore how this group of parents reintroduced Gaelic into their families, it is helpful to understand at the outset why they did this, in recognition of the fact that their decision is not now the norm in Lewis. Munro et al. (2011) found, for example, that even though 66% of adult residents of Shawbost are fluent Gaelic speakers, only one parent in five speaks mainly or only Gaelic to their children; they also noted that slightly less than half of the children attended Gaelic-medium education (GME). So, what were the ideologies of the cohort in this small study that led them to taking certain decisions affecting their family's language policy and then enacting this policy? The participants in this study all had very strong opinions about the language, about their perceived linguistic weaknesses and abilities and also about the values they attached to the language.

Perceptions of linguistic ability and badging began at a young age for this cohort. Growing up in Lewis, all of the informants were aware of Gaelic around them: when asked to reflect on who they knew in their youth who spoke Gaelic, this question caused some informants to speak about how they felt about their own language abilities and the abilities of others they knew in their youth. In secondary school, they would have been very aware of a distinction being made between Gaelic speakers and non-Gaelic speakers. Because of local authority policy, all of these informants would have been required to study Gaelic for at least two years in secondary school and there they would have been streamed into a 'native-speaking Gaelic class' or a 'learner Gaelic class'. At least two of the participants expressed how they felt both jealousy and admiration of their youthful peers who were fully fluent Gaelic speakers.

> I can remember even now aged 45 I was quite envious of Chrissie MacDonald because she had Gaelic and I thought that was really cool. (Agnes)

For Agnes's sister Dolina, the envy was mixed with shame at not being able to converse with friends who used Gaelic habitually even in school.

> *Tha cuimhne agam nuair a chaidh mi dhan àrd-sgoil gun robh mi beagan* frustrated, *tha mi a' creids' gun robh na* pals *seo cho fileanta agus bha mise mar seòrsa de* oddity *air sgàth 's nach robh mi cho fileanta.*
>
> (I remember when I went to secondary school that I was a little frustrated, I think because these pals were all so fluent and I was a kind of an oddity because I wasn't as fluent).

As noted by McEwan-Fujita in her earlier study of Gaelic learners in the nearby island of Uist, there is often a sense of shame present in non-speakers or heritage learners of Gaelic in Gaelic-speaking communities. She commented about a participant in her study thus:

> Her terse replies to my questions in this dance of disclosure enact the shame and other negative affect of intergenerational language transmission failure for one individual in her own social and familial context of language shift. (McEwan-Fujita 2010: 42)

McEwan-Fujita continued to suggest that these reactions to the linguistic environment have the ability to 'shape people's metalinguistic discourse and their language behavior more generally' (McEwan-Fujita 2010: 31). It is possible that for some of the participants in this study the reaction equated to a desire to make Gaelic a central part of their family life.

Only some of the informants spoke about friends in their youth as people of significance when it came to identifying with Gaelic; one theme which came through strongly in the analysis is the impact of the informants' parents on their attitude to the language. For Chrisella, there is frustration: why did her parents, who were both Gaelic speakers, not speak to her in Gaelic as a child?

> None. *Bha e brònach: tha Gàidhlig aig an dithis phàrant, ach chan eil iad a' bruidhinn Gàidhlig rium. Bha e seann-fhasanta.*

> (It was sad: both my parents speak Gaelic, but they don't speak Gaelic to me. It was old-fashioned).

Angus also noted that his mother identified Gaelic in his youth as something that was old-fashioned and had no value:

> So what I remember is, what my mother told me was that she didn't really teach me Gaelic but my grandpa, when I was a young kid, tried to teach me words in Gaelic so he probably saw the importance of learning our heritage, our Gaelic roots. But my mother, I think she was influenced by when she was growing up that Gaelic wasn't seen to be the language that was conducive to maybe a good career. She wanted me to concentrate on the English, I think that was the fashionable thing at the time, 60s, 70s.

Angus's statement about how it had become more 'fashionable' to focus on English in his youth concurs with the sociolinguistic evidence (e.g. MacKinnon 1977, 1993, 2006; NicAoidh 2006; Munro et. al 2011) that during the last three decades of the twentieth century the position of Lewis, and other islands in the Western Isles, as 'intact multi-generational Gaelic speaking communities' (Ó Giollagáin et al. 2020: 1) began to change, with dramatic decline in usage across domains and the breakdown of intergenerational transmission (Fishman 1964, 1991). This concept of language as a thing which either does or does not have an economic value is one that is used by some of the informants themselves when making their own parenting decisions as to why they want to introduce Gaelic as a family language and will be returned to later in the chapter.

In adulthood, there are also mixed emotions around the language: shame at not having the ability to speak it and not making more of an effort to learn the language. Angus takes the blame himself for failing to acquire the language:

> I think I'm maybe a bit too sensitive because maybe I see that, maybe I bring it on myself that I haven't learnt the language myself or I don't have that, so I'm probably more sensitive.

But one of the overriding reasons for wanting a better command of the language for themselves and for their families was to do with place and belonging. He identified the language as one way of connecting with his heritage:

> My grandparents were always speaking Gaelic. It was kind of like a tradition, the traditional language. I think when you're young you don't realise how important it is, you just think it's something not to do with yourself. But then when you grow up and you start maturing you think 'oh, I've lost something important here, I want to re-establish the link.'

Being or becoming a Gaelic speaker was seen as a way of expressing the local desired identity more visibly and connecting with the community past and present.

> *Agallaiche: Carson a tha e cudromach dhut a bhith ga faighinn air ais agus a bhith a' fàs nas fhileanta? Carson a tha Gidhlig cudromach dhut?*
>
> *Lily: em . . . uill . . . 's e . . . 's e a' chiad chànan a bh' agam ... um ... agus leis an obair an dèidh a bhith agam a' teagasg Beurla gu feadhainn bho thall thairis, tha fhios a'm cho cudromach 's a tha e a bhith a' cleachdadh an cànan agam. Tha mi a' smaoineachadh gu bheil ceangal ... 's e dòigh math a th' ann em ... chan eil fhios a'm tha thu a' bruidhinn saor ... le daoine timcheall ort ann an Gàidhlig. Ann an dòigh* you've got, you're an extra bit closer somehow. Does that make sense?
>
> (Interviewer: Why is it important for you to get it [Gaelic] back and to become more fluent? Why is Gaelic important to you?
>
> Lily: em ... well ... it's ... it was my first language ... um ... and with my job after teaching English to people from abroad, I know how important it is to use my language. I think that there is a link ... it's a good way em ... I don't know ... you speak freely ... with people around you in Gaelic. In a way you've got, you're an extra bit closer somehow. Does that make sense?)

Lily's expression that speaking Gaelic makes a person closer to the community is a central part of the shared ideology of this group of parents: in attempting to shape the linguistic pattern of their families, this group was also affirming their belonging to the place and its culture.

Adult (Re)Acquisition

Of the five participants in the study, only one participant remembers speaking Gaelic to any significant degree as a child: but even for this one there was an element of 'reactivating' the language in adulthood, and in particular to use the language with her own children. The table below summarises current language practices in the cohort; the detail of how the individuals arrived at this stage is discussed in relation to various acquisition themes. What did each of the individuals do to improve their language skills, and, in their opinions, what worked and what did not? It is perhaps of significance that three of the five informants chose to conduct their interviews through the medium of Gaelic, possibly indicating their own commitment to the language (Table 2).

As noted in the introduction, all the participants studied Gaelic to varying degrees in school. There was little value attached to Gaelic as a school subject: it was not seen as a means of achieving competency or as a reflection of ability. Agnes noted of her advanced school qualification: 'I've got a Learner Higher but it was dead easy to get a Learner Higher Gaelic in those days'. Angus, on the other hand, only studied Gaelic for a limited time at school: at the time he saw little value in the subject, although with the benefit of hindsight he realises that this judgement might have been erroneous:

> I did, yeah, 1st year and 2nd year and I didn't do it to O Grade level … I just did French. Again, I think it was this idea that French could take you further, although if we'd done Gaelic we could have got a job on the BBC!

Table 2 Current use of Gaelic

	Child(ren)	Spouse	Friends	Work	Community
Agnes	A little	X	X	A little	X
Chrisella	✔	✔	X	X	X
Dolina	✔	✔	✔	✔	✔
Lily	✔	✔	✔	X	✔
Angus	A little	X	X	A little	X

The concept of language as an object of instrumental value features both in relation to reasons for the previous generation's failure to uphold transmission and also as a reason for reintroducing the language into the family. For all, learning at school did not prepare any of those interviewed to become speakers in adulthood: each of them took different paths in their learning journeys and for the three who interviewed in Gaelic, there was clearly some success. As 'heritage speakers/learners', their learning journey was very different from that of someone approaching a language as a beginner. While the common desire for their children to be Gaelic speakers was an impetus for improving their linguistic competencies, there was never one 'critical juncture' (Walsh and O'Rourke 2014) where their linguistic practice changed. In this respect, the experiences of this cohort differ from a new speaker *muda*, as it would be difficult to point to a specific moment in their lives (Pujolar and Puigdevall 2015) when they became Gaelic speakers, and this was recognised by most of them, including Dolina below:

> *Tha mi an-còmhnaidh a' faireachdainn sin uabhasach duilich a freagairt.* Clearly, *chan e luchd-ionnsachaidh a th' annam, a thòisich a-mach le leabhraichean nuair a bha mi nam inbheach agus gun do rinn mi strì mòr. 'S e seòrsa de* cheat *sin ag ràdh air sgàth 's tha feadhainn eile a' dèanamh obair mòr, mòr a' fàs gu fileantas is cha robh an Gàidhlig aig an eanchainn ac' mar a bha agams'. Ach aig an aon àm, tha mi a' faireachdainn uaire-annan tha mi cho lapach agus cho* useless *bho àm gu àm nach eil e duilich ... tha e uabhasach duilich a ràdh gu bheil mi fileanta.*
>
> (I always feel it's really difficult to answer that. Clearly, I am not a learner who began with books in adulthood and who made a big effort. It would be cheating to say that because others have done an awful lot of work to become fluent and they didn't have Gaelic in their brains like I did. But at the same time, I sometimes feel I am so feeble and so useless that from time to time that isn't ... it's really difficult to say I am fluent).

Three of the informants spoke about formal classes they took and there was a mixed reaction to these as these were invariably designed for people who were not heritage learners. Agnes attended a college course in the evening: 'I didn't like it at all. It just wasn't for me. The group was really – I went to the college to do the course – the group was really disparate, too basic for me, really nice tutor, it just didn't bring me any further forward'. Chrisella, on the other hand, found attending classes helpful, although she noted that she used a variety of methods, including pushing family members to speak to her in Gaelic, to improve her language ability. Chrisella, who had been engaging with formal learning activities for a little over a year at the time of the interview, spoke about how important it was to her to have individuals supporting her as they offered a counterbalance to those who wished to detract from her efforts.

Chrisella: Uill , tha màthair aig Dàibhidh retired teacher *foghlam Gàidhlig. Tha ise – bha ise a' bruidhinn Gàidhlig rium ach chan eil fhios carson, stad i* – sometimes my mother will say …

Agallaiche: Cuin a thòisich màthair Dhàibhidh a' bruidhinn Gàidhlig riut?

Chrisella: An-uiridh nuair a thòisich mi le Ùlpan agus uill dìreach gach clas tha obair-dachaigh agus bha i a' cuideachadh le obair-dachaigh.

Agallaiche: An robh i toilichte gun robh thu ag ionnsachadh Gàidhlig?

Chrisella: Tha. Tha i texting *anns a' Ghàidhlig. Tha mi* spelling *wrong. … Chan eil mòran dhaoine ag iarraidh bruidhinn ann an Gàidhlig rium – ga h-àraid mo mhàthair. Tha mi an-còmhnaidh ag ràdh, carson, carson? An-còmhnaidh* excuses …

(Chrisella: Well, David [her husband]'s mother is a retired Gaelic medium teacher. She speaks … used to speak to me in Gaelic but I don't know, she stopped – sometimes my mother will say …

Interviewer: When did David's mother start speaking Gaelic to you?

Chrisella: Last year when I started the Ulpan course and well every class there is homework and she was helping with homework.

Interviewer: Was she happy that you were learning Gaelic?

Chrisella: Yes. She texts me in Gaelic. My spelling is wrong. … Not many people want to speak to me in Gaelic – especially my mother. She always says, why, why? Always excuses).

Angus, who also attended evening classes at the local college, expressed frustration around the fact that his mother would not help his learning:

Interviewer: Did you ever try and speak Gaelic to your mother?

Angus: A little bit, yeah, but she would correct me quite strongly and say 'oh that's not the proper pronunciation.' So it's quite difficult. That's

> why I think if there was a ... if you could take Gaelic learners out of that – I know it's terrible – out of the Gaelic environment and plonk them in with other people the same, with a few helpful people, that would do wonders.

Clearly for these informants the formal language options were not enough by themselves to help them progress to fluency: for those who were successful at breaking through to speaking, formal learning was only a small part, but gaining support from other speakers was crucial. One problem which has been identified previously (MacLeod et al. 2015) with regard to Gaelic learners making good progress in their learning journeys is the lack of opportunity to speak the language; perhaps surprisingly, this issue is not confined to learners without close family ties to the language who live in areas with few Gaelic speakers but also affects heritage learners in a 'heartland' community like Lewis.

It was noted above how Chrisella tried to use Gaelic with her mother and her mother-in-law to limited success. She had more success with her husband, who would sometimes use Gaelic with her but used Gaelic at home with their children. By and large, however, her network of speakers remains limited. Dolina, on the other hand, has managed to create a very diverse and large network in which she uses Gaelic on a regular basis. She created the diagram below of the people she habitually uses Gaelic with. Interestingly, although both Dolina's parents appear on the diagram, she admitted that she does not always speak to them both in Gaelic and that it can be dependent on the topic or location of their conversation. She acknowledged that changing the dynamic of that relationship was one of the hardest things in negotiating her speaker network (Fig. 1).

By applying Lo Bianco's (2008a, 2008b) COD (Capacity Development, Opportunity Creation and Desire) framework to Dolina's own diagram of her network of Gaelic interlocutors, we can see how she has been very successful in developing her capacity and creating opportunities.

> Capacity development is the development of personal language proficiency and language use, through both formal teaching and informal transmission of the language; opportunity creation is the development of

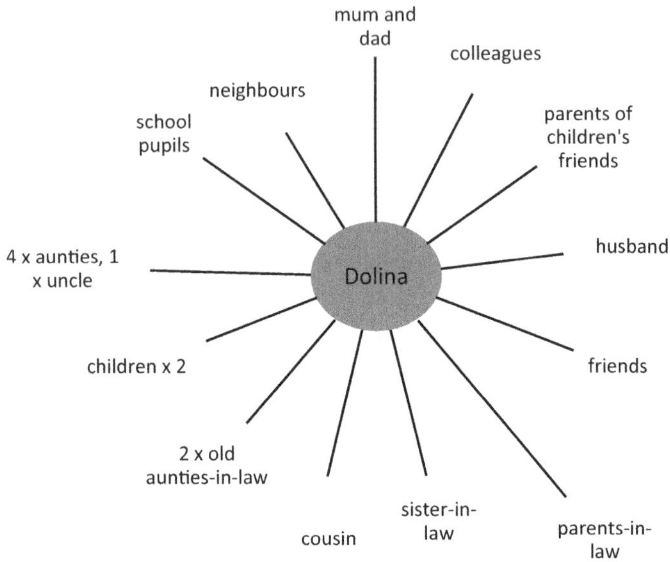

Fig. 1 Dolina's current Gaelic interlocutor network

> domains in which use of the language is natural, welcome, and expected; and desire involves creation of investment in learning the language, because proficiency in it brings certain rewards. (Lo Bianco and Peyton 2013: i)

Dolina's desire to become a Gaelic speaker was multi-faceted: she explained that she wanted to recapture something of her identity and she saw employment opportunities for herself; she has worked in Gaelic-related roles for more than twenty years. When she became a parent, it became more important than ever for her to use Gaelic as her language of family life and she spoke of how she and her husband began to use more Gaelic at home at that time.

> *Agallaiche: Agus am b' e Beurla a bha sibh a' cleachdadh an toiseach?*

Dollina: Chanainn, yeah. *Agus 's e nuair a bha clann againn agus rinn sinn an taghadh gun robh sinn a' dol a thogail a' chlann le Gàidhlig, tha mi a' smaoineachadh gun do dh'atharraich an cànan a bha sinn a' cleachdadh. Chan eil mi ag ràdh gu bheil sinn a' cleachdadh Gàidhlig a bharrachd na Beurla, 's dòcha nach eil, ach nuair a bha a' chlann beag bha sinn a' feuchainn air oidhirp mòr a dhèanamh agus a' bruidhinn Gàidhlig ac'.*
(Interviewer: And was it English you used to begin with?
Dolina: I would say so, yes. And then when we had children, we made the decision that we were going to raise the children with Gaelic, I think that changed the language we were using. I'm not saying we use Gaelic more than English, maybe we don't, but when the children were little, we made a big effort to speak Gaelic to them).

Becoming a parent and the desire to support children's acquisition was also one of the main motivators for improving ability in this cohort. Lily expresses this clearly:

Tha mi airson a bhith nas fileanta airson [na nighne agam] cuideachd. Tha mi airson gum bi Gàidhlig aicese. Agus 's e Gàidhlig a tha mi ... uill bidh i a' faighinn Beurla cuideachd airson chan eil Gàidhlig aig [mo dhuine] ach tha mi airson gum bi i fileanta. Em ... agus tha fhios agam em ... gun robh feum agams' air cuideachadh nuair a bha mi òg leis a' Ghàidhlig so *tha mi airson a bhith nas làidir gus an urrainn mi ga cuideachadh.*
(I want to be more fluent for [my daughter] too. I want her to speak Gaelic. And it's Gaelic that I ... well, she gets English too because [my husband] doesn't speak Gaelic but I want her to be fluent. Em ... and I know em ... that I needed help when I was young with Gaelic so I want to be better so that I can help her).

Again, using LoBianco's COD framework, her desire to support her daughter inspires her to improve her capacity in the varied opportunities she has available to her.

Children's Experience of Gaelic

As noted in the introduction, four out of the five parents here either have children who at the time of interview were participating in Gaelic-medium education (GME), or who had participated in GME; one informant's child was still too young to be involved in statutory education. The parents identified a number of reasons why it was important for them to support their children's acquisition of Gaelic.

As noted earlier, one of the reasons cited by Dolina for improving her own language competencies was the perception that Gaelic could now bring economic advantages to its speakers: the reverse of what was cited by Angus in relation to his explanation of why his mother did not speak to him in Gaelic as a child. Agnes, who as she notes below was working in economic development in the island at the time her children were born, was largely driven by the sense of language having an instrumental value as well as being a marker of identity and heritage.

> Agnes: I think the penny had dropped with me by then about opportunity … like, you know, the benefits of bilingualism and life opportunity. And a little, actually I wouldn't say a little bit, I would say a considerable dollop of doing the right thing by their language and by their island. I think by that point I was working in economic development myself and I'd seen the kind of trajectory and the stats were all a bit bleak at that point. I wanted to and I was a little bit, as I still am, a little bit frustrated that I wasn't better at it myself and I wanted to give them [her sons] every chance. Ross adopted it, Iain less so.
>
> Interviewer: And your partner at the time, was he in support? Was he a Gaelic speaker, is he a Gaelic speaker?
>
> Agnes: Yeah. Yes he is … but I would say it would be *my* decision for the boys rather than Calum's. Calum was a bit passive in that department, yeah.

Agnes does not just see the language as something which has an intrinsic value; she also judged that by enabling her sons to become Gaelic speakers she was reinforcing their connection to the place they came from. This concept of using the language to link the child to a place was also referred to by Angus.

Angus is attempting to bring his children up trilingually, with cultural and linguistic knowledge of Gaelic and equivalent elements from their mother's culture. For Angus, language is an important marker of identity and of maintaining a cultural connection: he is acutely aware of the loss of language in his generation. Angus's map of his language environment in his youth (Fig. 2) is striking (and not atypical of all the participants in this study). Angus was surrounded by Gaelic speakers in his youth, with nearly two-thirds of his closest associates in his primary school years being Gaelic-English bilingual.

Angus spoke emotively about wishing to reconnect with his heritage by attempting to learn the language himself and by helping his children to learn by enrolling his eldest daughter in GME:

> She's in preschool, aye. She'll be four in July. She's done very well. Of course she speaks English but she's now fluent in [mother's first language] and before she went away she'd be playing with her dolls and singing [mother's first language] songs and then she'd – she's got all the doctor toys – she'd put the thermometer under there and count to ten in Gaelic. So, I was thinking wow, this is brilliant! You get a bit emotional. I really want them to have, because you never know where you'll end up and you

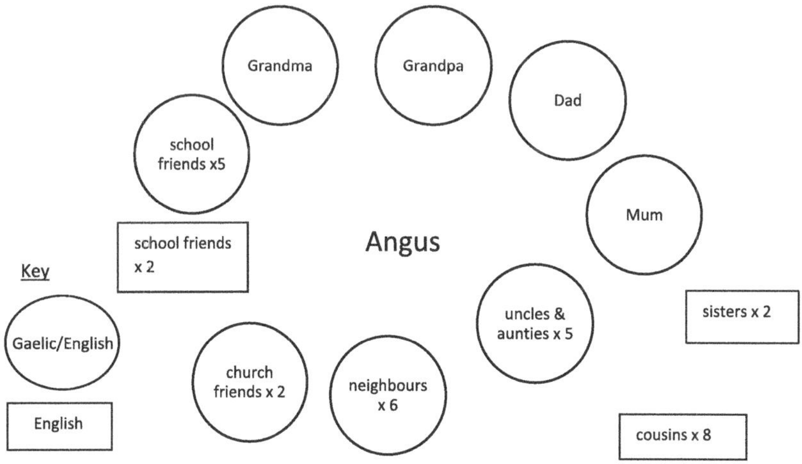

Fig. 2 Angus's childhood linguistic environment

> might move away and I really want her to have roots or to reconnect the line of the Gaelic that's gone up. I'm thinking of my grandparents and my aunties and uncles who all speak Gaelic but none of the cousins.

Angus struggles to get support from his family for his own learning and for his daughter: his wife does not speak Gaelic and his mother, a Gaelic speaker who has a significant presence in his daughter's life, questions his choice of his daughter being taught through Gaelic at school. It was noted above that Angus's mother was also not supportive of his own attempts to learn Gaelic. Angus's children were too young at the time of the study for him to be able to comment meaningfully on their linguistic competencies but he was confident that through the education system and his personal and professional commitment to the language, even though he himself had not managed to become an active speaker, his daughter's early success will continue and that his son (aged two at the time of the interview) will follow in her footsteps.

As noted above, Dolina and her husband made a conscious decision to use more Gaelic at home and with their daughters from a young age; they also elected to send their children to GME in a school approximately 15 miles from the family home. She spoke about how unpopular the decision was locally that she did not enrol her children in the village primary school, which only offered English-medium education at the time. She said some thought her decision to transport her children to a different location was a threat to the ongoing vitality of the very small rural school. Dolina's experience of feeling criticised for transporting her children is not unique and is one part of the discourse explaining why GME in the Western Isles has not succeeded in recruiting more children, as at the time of writing not every school in the local authority area offered that opportunity. The situation will change now with the decision that from 2020 all primary-aged pupils will automatically be educated in Gaelic medium in their local schools unless their parents opt out of GME; this should facilitate a bigger uptake from the 40% level in 2019–2020 (Bòrd na Gàidhlig 2020). As noted above, Dolina has created over time a very vibrant Gaelic network and she was able to ensure her children had access to this network of Gaelic-speaking grandparents and friends in addition to their experience in the school classroom. In terms of FLP, she has succeeded in managing both quantity and quality of input (Smith-Christmas 2018: 132): Dolina says of her children, who at the time of interview were older teenagers, that they are both competent and habitual Gaelic speakers.

Four of the five informants spoke about the role of their partners and children's grandparents in supporting their children's acquisition. Each of the five parents interviewed here identified themselves as the driving force behind their family's attempts to reintegrate Gaelic as a family language. Three of the interviewees were married to Gaelic speakers: of these three, Agnes's partner offered only limited support while Dolina and Chrisella both said their partners spoke Gaelic at home. Chrisella noted that while her husband habitually spoke Gaelic with the children, he was sometimes reluctant to speak to her in Gaelic, and she also noted that her parents needed to be reminded regularly to speak Gaelic to the children.

Agallaiche: A bheil do phàrantan a' bruidhinn Gàidhlig ri Teàrlach agus Aonghas?

Chrisella: Uill, uaireannan, feumaidh mi cur cuimhne orra: bruidhinn Gàidhlig, bruidhinn Gàidhlig ach chan eil fhios a'm dè trioblaid a th' aca. Ach an duine agam – tha Gàidhlig aige. Tha an duine agam, Dàibhidh, a' bruidhinn ri Teàrlach agus Aonghas gach latha an-còmhnaidh. A h-uile duine aig an teaghlach Dàibhidh a' bruidhinn Gàidhlig ri chèile. Tha mi a' faireachdainn mar an odd-one out.

Agallaiche: Am bi thu a' bruidhinn Gàidhlig ri Dàibhidh?

Chrisella: O tha, tha. Tha mi a' feuchainn. Ach 'tha thu ceàrr, feuch a-rithist. Och dìreach Beurla.' Agus cleachdaidh mi facail a dh'ionnsaich mi bho Radio nan Gàidheal agus tha Dàibhidh ag ràdh: chan eil mi cuala mi a-riamh sin. Dìreach Gàidhlig nàdarrach. Chan eil Gàidhlig airson facail ùra.

[Interviewer: Do your parents speak Gaelic to Charles and Angus?

Chrisella: Well sometimes. I have to remind them: speak Gaelic, speak Gaelic but I don't know what their problem is. But my husband – he speaks Gaelic. My husband, David, speaks to Charles and Angus every day always. Everyone in David's family speaks Gaelic to each other. I feel like an odd one out.

Interviewer: Do you speak Gaelic to David?

> Chrisella: Oh yes, yes. I try. But [he says] 'you are wrong, try again. Oh just [speak] English'. And I will use a word I learned from [Gaelic] radio and David says: I've never heard that. Just natural Gaelic. There isn't Gaelic for new words).

David's insistence on 'natural' language is not uncommon in some Gaelic speakers who, for a range of historic reasons, may only have a limited range of domains in Gaelic and are both unfamiliar with and hostile towards or suspicious of neologisms in the language (Bell and McConville 2018; McLeod 2017). At the time of interview, Chrisella's children were still in early primary school, but given that the language was in use at home and school there was a good likelihood that Chrisella's push for her two children to become active Gaelic speakers would be successful.

During the course of the interview with Agnes, she spoke about a number of different family members and their use of Gaelic with her sons. She notes that her husband and his brother, who were both fluent Gaelic speakers, did not speak in Gaelic to their children; she notes that her parents-in-law did use Gaelic with her children whereas her own parents (also Gaelic speakers) did not. Her sister, Dolina, speaks Gaelic to Agnes's children (Dolina refers to herself in this context as 'the mad Gaelic auntie'). Agnes's own language usage has changed with her children over the course of time: she reports how she tried to use Gaelic with them when they were young but that this changed.

> Interviewer: Do you speak Gaelic to the boys? Or did you?
> Agnes: Yes, I did.
> Interviewer: Do they speak Gaelic now?
> Agnes: They are both fluent Gaelic speakers.
> Interviewer: But *do* they?
> Agnes: No, not in practice. If spoken to they'll reply. Calum had a wee job before he went off to sea in the local petrol station in Lochs and I remember just standing in the queue listening to him speaking to customers ahead of me in the queue and I was thinking 'I'm amazed! You wee rascal'
> Interviewer: Is it English you would speak?
> Agnes: Yeah, absolutely, it would be English.

Agnes identifies the move to secondary school as the time when she and her sons stopped habitually using Gaelic with one another: 'that was partly at their behest and partly I drifted out of it. We live in an English world and that just became more dominant in the house than Gaelic did'. Perhaps her own lack of confidence and ability made her less proactive in pursuing the family language policy: 'I really wish I had better Gaelic. I think I understand nearly every word. I think I know how to say it but as soon as it comes out it comes out all rubbish. *(that's what I think to myself)* ... I've given Gaelic media interviews ... through Gaelic Medium school, homework never fazed me. I liked doing it'. Gaelic is still part of their life with the boys occasionally using Gaelic with other people but minimally with their mother.

It would be too soon to be sure about the linguistic future of Lily's daughter, given that she was very young at the time of interview. Lily herself has been able to build a successful network of Gaelic speakers around her since returning to the island after a period on mainland Scotland (Fig. 3).

Lily's network of Gaelic interlocutors is extensive and diverse: as noted above, she believes she needs to improve her language and to speak the language regularly so that her daughter has the opportunities she needs. Given Dolina's experience with her children who are older, this extensive network alongside the GME route already selected will give Lily's daughter the best possible chance at developing her capacity in the language and becoming an active Gaelic speaker.

Conclusion

Given the small-scale nature of this study, it is difficult to extrapolate a set of behaviours which could potentially point to a way in which a broken link in intergenerational transmission could be repaired, but the data certainly point to a set of shared experiences which help us further understand the complexities of this situation. Armstrong noted that being a heritage learner of Gaelic did not 'guarantee problem-free integration into local Gaelic networks' (Armstrong 2013: 352) and this finding was replicated here. However, what was noted was that, where

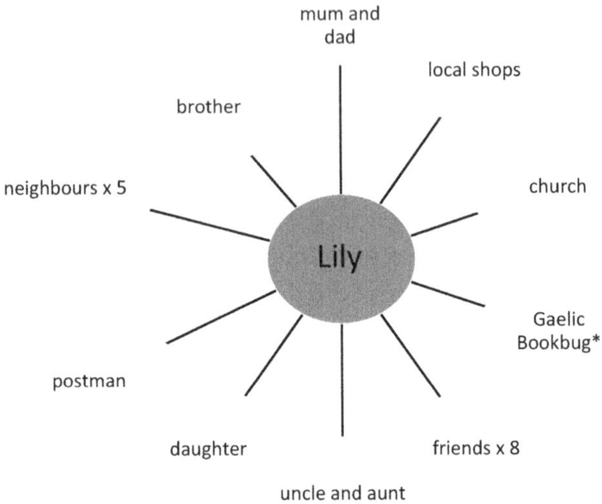

Fig. 3 Lily's network of Gaelic interlocutors (*Note* Bookbug is a group aimed at pre-school children to encourage storytelling and reading books; Gaelic Bookbug is a language intervention initiative aimed at encouraging Gaelic among families with young children)

the interviewee might have struggled to establish new language links with their parents, this was not the case for their children and that by and large the grandparent generation were supportive of the effort to have Gaelic as a family language. The implications for this finding are important in an area which has undergone significant language shift. All of the interviewees here either had, were currently using, or intended to use GME for their children: where this is supported even by minimal networks, as was the case for all the interviewees here, there was significant potential for these children to become active Gaelic speakers. Baker (2011) noted, in relation to creating new speakers through immersion education, that potential is not always achieved. Dunmore (2018) has shown through his extensive study of Gaelic-medium educated adults that language use in this group tends to be low except in instances where language socialisation also happens at home. Dunmore has already pointed to the implications of his findings for Gaelic language policy-makers: 'it is clear that the goal of strengthening Gaelic language socialisation in the home and community needs to be prioritised alongside developing GME as a policy objective' (Dunmore 2018: 74). The parents in this study have shown how they managed to strengthen language socialisation opportunities for their children: even Agnes's teenage sons who were no longer habitual Gaelic speakers were reported by both Agnes and Dolina to use Gaelic on occasion.

For the most part, these families have succeeded in re-establishing Gaelic in their families and repairing the broken intergenerational link. Beyond what was available from schools, this has been achieved with very little support in terms of targeted interventionist activity or support: it has been the individuals themselves that have recruited the assistance of grandparents and other family members to support them in their desire to influence the family language choice. This research shows that even when individuals have failed to become fully active speakers (like Agnes and Angus) their agency on behalf of their children in creating networks of practice can be successful. For policy-makers, the experiences of this group could be relatively easily supported and replicated in threatened 'heartland' areas by informing and supporting grandparents, and the extended family and community in general, to take an active role in supporting a Gaelic language choice and repairing the damaged intergenerational transmission.

Acknowledgements I would like to thank Marsaili MacLeod for her work on the data collection and for collaborating on an earlier project on heritage learners. I would like to acknowledge receipt of a small grant from Soillse for support with the fieldwork. Finally, I would also like to extend my gratitude to all the research participants who were so generous with their time and spoke about their experiences so openly.

References

Armstrong, T.C. 2013. Why Won't You Speak to me in Gaelic?': Authenticity, Integration and the Heritage Language Learning Project. *Journal of Language, Identity, and Education* 12 (5): 340–356.

Armstrong, T.C. 2014. Naturalism and Ideological Work: How is Family Language Policy Renegotiated as Both Parents and Children Learn a Threatened Minority Language? *International Journal of Bilingual Education and Bilingualism* 17 (5): 570–585.

Baker, C. 2011. *Foundations of Bilingual Education and Bilingualism*, 5th ed. Clevedon: Multilingual Matters.

Bell, S., and M. McConville. 2018. Dlùth is Inneach: Charting Language Ideology in the Contemporary Gaelic world. In *Gaelic in Contemporary Scotland: The Revitalisation of an Endangered Language*, ed. M. MacLeod and C. Smith-Christmas, 114–127. Edinburgh: Edinburgh University Press.

Birnie, I. 2018a. *'Gàidhlig ga bruidhinn an seo?' Linguistic practices and Gaelic language management initiatives in Stornoway, the Western Isles of Scotland*. Unpublished PhD thesis, University of Aberdeen.

Birnie, I. 2018. Gaelic Language Use in Public Domains. In *Gaelic in Contemporary Scotland: The Revitalisation of an Endangered Language*, ed. M. MacLeod and C. Smith-Christmas, 128–140. Edinburgh: Edinburgh University Press.

Bòrd na Gàidhlig. 2020. *Dàta Sgoile Gàidhlig 2019–20 Gaelic School Data*. https://www.gaidhlig.scot/wp-content/uploads/2020/11/D%C3%A0ta-Sgoile-POBLACH-2019-20-2.0-BnG-PUBLIC-Schools-Data.pdf. Accessed 17 November 2020.

Carty, N. 2014. The Adult Learner in Gaelic Language-in-Education Policy. *European Journal of Language Policy* 6 (2): 195–217.

Comhairle nan Eilean Siar. n.d. *2011 Census Statistics Lewis*. https://www.cne-siar.gov.uk/media/5560/lewis-profile.pdf. Accessed 9 November 2020.

Dunmore, S. 2018. When School is Over and Done With: Linguistic Practices and Socio-demographic Profiles of Gaelic-medium Educated Adults. In *Gaelic in Contemporary Scotland: The Revitalisation of an Endangered Language*, ed. M. MacLeod and C. Smith-Christmas, 62–78. Edinburgh: Edinburgh University Press.

Emmel, N. 2008. *Participatory Mapping: An Innovative Sociological Method*. Real Life Methods Toolkit. http://eprints.ncrm.ac.uk/540/2/2008-07-toolkit-participatory-map.pdf. Accessed 8 September 2020.

Fishman, J.A. 1964. Language Maintenance and Language Shift as a Field of Inquiry: A Definition of the Field and Suggestions for Its Further Development. *Linguistics* 2 (9): 32–70.

Fishman, J.A. 1991. *Reversing Language Shift: Theoretical and Empirical Foundations of Assistance to Threatened Languages*. Clevedon: Multilingual Matters.

Ó Giollagáin, C., G. Camshron, P. Moireach, B. Ó Curnáin, I. Caimbeul, B. MacDonald, and T. Péterváry. 2020. *The Gaelic Crisis in the Vernacular Community: A Comprehensive Sociolinguistic Survey of Scottish Gaelic*. Aberdeen: Aberdeen University Press.

Hornsby, M., and G. Quentel. 2013. Contested Varieties and Competing Authenticities: Neologisms in Revitalized Breton. *International Journal of the Sociology of Language* 223: 71–86.

Jaffe, A. 2013. Minority Language Learning and Communicative Competence: Models of Identity and Participation in Corsican Adult Language Courses. *Language and Communication* 33 (4): 450–462.

King, K., L. Fogle, and A. Logan-Terry. 2008. Family Language Policy. *Language and Linguistics Compass* 2 (5): 907–922.

Lamb, W. 2003. *Scottish Gaelic*, 2nd ed. Munich: Lincom Europa.

Lo Bianco, J. 2008a. Organizing for Multilingualism: Ecological and Sociological Perspectives. In *Keeping Language Diversity Alive: A TESOL Symposium*, 1–18. https://www.tesol.org/docs/default-source/new-resource-library/symposium-on-keeping-language-diversity-alive.pdf. Accessed 8 April 2021.

Lo Bianco, J. 2008b. Policy Activity for Heritage Languages: Connections with Representation and Citizenship. In *Heritage Language Education: A New Field Emerging*, ed. D.M. Brinton, O. Kagan, and S. Bauckus, 53–69. New York: Routledge.

Lo Bianco, J. and J.K. Peyton. 2013. Vitality of Heritage Languages in the United States: The Role of Capacity, Opportunity, and Desire. *Heritage Language Journal* 10(3): i–viii.

McEwan-Fujita, E. 2010. Ideology, Affect and Socialization in Language Shift and Revitalization: The Experiences of Adults Learning Gaelic in the Western Isles of Scotland. *Language in Society* 39 (1): 27–64.

Mac an Tàilleir, I. 2010. 1901–2001: A' Ghàidhlig anns a' chunntas-shluaigh. In *Coimhearsnachd na Gàidhlig an-Diugh*, ed. G. Munro and I. Mac an Tàilleir, 19–34. Edinburgh: Dunedin Academic Press.

MacKinnon, K. 1977. *Language, Education and Social Processes in a Gaelic Community*. London: Routledge.

MacKinnon, K. 1993. Scottish Gaelic Today: Social History and Contemporary Status. In *The Celtic Languages*, ed. M. J. Ball with J. Fife, 491–535. London and New York: Routledge.
MacKinnon, K. 2006. The Western Isles Language Plan: Gaelic to English Language Shift 1972–2001. In *Revitalising Gaelic in Scotland*, ed. W. McLeod, 49–72. Edinburgh: Dunedin Academic Press.
MacLeo, M., and C. Smith-Christmas, eds. 2018. *Gaelic in Contemporary Scotland: The Revitalisation of an Endangered Language*. Edinburgh: Edinburgh University Press.
Macleod, M., and M. MacLeod. 2021. Luchd-ionnsachaidh dualchasach: Innleachdan agus iarrtasan gu fileantas. In *Cànan is Cultar/Language and Culture: Rannsachadh na Gàidhlig 10*, ed. W. McLeod, A. Gunderloch, and R. Dunbar, 259–275. Aberdeen: Aberdeen University Press.
MacLeod, M., M. Macleod, L. Milligan Dombrowski, and K. Jones. 2015. *Lìbhrigeadh Gàidhlig do dh'Inbhich tro Ùlpan/Delivery of Gaelic to Adults through Ùlpan.* Inverness: Bòrd na Gaidhlig.
McLeod, W. 2017. Dialectal Diversity in Contemporary Gaelic: Perceptions, Discourses and Responses. In *Before the Storm: Papers from the Forum for Research on the Languages of Scotland and Ulster triennial meeting, Ayr 2015*, ed. J. Cruickshank and R. McColl Millar, 183–221. Aberdeen: Forum for Research on the Languages of Scotland and Ireland.
McLeod, W. 2020. *Gaelic in Scotland: Policies, Movements, Ideologies.* Edinburgh: Edinburgh University Press.
Milroy, L. 1987. *Language and Social Networks*, 2nd ed. Worcester: Billing & Sons.
Munro, G., Mac, I. Tàilleir, and T.C. Armstrong. 2011. *The State of Gaelic in Shawbost: Language Attitudes and Abilities in Shawbost*. Sleat, Isle of Skye: Sabhal Mòr Ostaig.
Murray, J., C. and Morrison. 1984. *Bilingual Primary Education in the Western Isles, Scotland: Report of the Bilingual Education Project, 1975–81.* Stornoway: Acair.
Nance, C., and R. Ó Maolalaigh. 2019. Scottish Gaelic. *Journal of the International Phonetic Association,* 1–15. https://doi.org/10.1017/S002510031900015X.
National Records of Scotland. 2015. *Scotland's Census 2011: Gaelic report (part 2).* Edinburgh: National Records of Scotland.

NicAoidh, M. 2006. Pròiseact Plana Cànain nan Eilean Siar: a' chiad ìre - rannsachadh air suidheachadh na Gàidhlig anns na h-Eilean Siar. In *Revitalising Gaelic in Scotland*, ed. W. McLeod, 73–86. Edinburgh: Dunedin Academic Press.

O'Hanlon, F., and L. Paterson. 2014. Gaelic Education Since 1872. In *The Edinburgh History of Education in Scotland*, ed. R.D. Anderson, M. Freeman, and L. Paterson, 304–325. Edinburgh: Edinburgh University Press.

Pujolar, J., and M. Puigdevall. 2015. How to Become a New Speaker in Catalonia. *International Journal of the Sociology of Language* 231: 167–187.

Smith-Christmas, C. 2016. *Family Language Policy: Maintaining an Endangered Language in the Home*. Basingstoke: Palgrave MacMillan.

Smith-Christmas, C., and T.C. Armstrong. 2014. Complementary RLS Strategies in Education: The Importance of Adult Heritage Learners of Threatened Minority Languages. *Current Issues in Language Planning* 15 (3): 312–326.

Smith-Christmas, C., N.P. Ó Murchadha, M. Hornsby, and M. Moriarty. eds. 2018. *New Speakers of Minority Languages: Linguistic Ideologies and Practices*. London: Palgrave Macmillan.

Smith-Christmas, C. 2018. 'One Cas, Two Cas': Exploring the Affective Dimensions of Family Language Policy. *Multilingua* 37 (2): 131–152.

Spolsky, B. 2004. *Language Policy*. Cambridge: Cambridge University Press.

Valdés, G. 2001. Heritage Language Students: Profiles and Possibilities. In *Heritage Languages in America: Preserving a National Resource*, eds. J.K. Peyton, D.A. Ranard and S. McGinnis, 37–77. McHenry, IL: Center for Applied Linguistics and Delta Systems.

Van Deusen, N. 2003. Toward a Definition of Heritage Language: Sociopolitical and Pedagogical Considerations. *Journal of Language, Identity, and Education* 2 (3): 211–230.

Walsh, J., and O' Rourke, B. 2014. Becoming a New Speaker of Irish: Linguistic Mudes Throughout the Life Cycle. *Digithum* 16: 67–74.

Wilson, S. 2020. *Family Language Policy: Children's Perspectives*. Basingstoke: Palgrave Macmillan.

Transmission in Post-traditional Families

The Transmission of Breton in the Family: The Effect of Family Rupture and Recomposition

Katell Chantreau and Stefan Moal

Introduction

This chapter is based on research which is currently underway on 450 Breton-speaking parents born between 1970 and 1995.[1] The first results highlight the fluctuating nature of Breton family transmission. This transmission can take place at the time of the birth of the first child or later, and it can be weakened or strengthened or even abandoned, according to disruptions in life circumstances and the attitudes of the different actors in the transmission process.

K. Chantreau (✉)
CREAD, University Rennes 2, Rennes, France
e-mail: katell.chantreau@univ-rennes2.fr

S. Moal
CELTIC-BLM, University Rennes 2, Rennes, France
e-mail: stefan.moal@univ-rennes2.fr

M. Hornsby and W. McLeod (eds.), *Transmitting Minority Languages*, Palgrave Studies in Minority Languages and Communities,
https://doi.org/10.1007/978-3-030-87910-5_4

In this chapter, we are particularly interested in the influence of family separations and recomposition on the transmission of Breton from parent to child. How does separation modify the transmission process? How can family recomposition prepare and facilitate transmission or, in contrast, make it more difficult? Can the transmission of Breton be a significant point of tension for the couple? The quantitative and qualitative data from a questionnaire to which 450 parents responded, as well as interview data from a dozen parents, form the basis of this study.

Sociolinguistic Situation of the Breton Language

Breton, a Minoritised Celtic Language

Breton is an Indo-European language belonging to the Celtic group and the Brittonic sub-group, more precisely to south-western Brittonic together with Cornish—Welsh being closer to the Brittonic variety once spoken in northern Britain. Coming mainly from Dumnonia (today's Cornwall and Devon) and to a lesser extent from Wales, Bretons arrived in Armorica in successive waves from the third to the seventh century. Their language assimilated whatever was left of Gaulish in the peninsula, as the two varieties had remained very close in any event, due to uninterrupted relations across the Channel since Antiquity. From the twelfth century onwards, as the links with Britain weakened, the various Brittonic dialects became distinct languages. Brittany was increasingly in the political orbit of western continental Europe, particularly that of the neighbouring Frankish kingdoms, which explains why Breton is today the Celtic language with the most romanised lexicon, under the influence of Latin, Romance (in its Gallo form in Upper Brittany) and finally French.

Until the ninth century, Breton was spoken almost as far east as Nantes and Rennes, before losing ground both geographically—a gradual reduction to the western half, known as Lower Brittany—and socially—a gradual abandonment by the elites in favour of Romance, then French (see Kennard, this volume). Like all languages, Breton presents diatopic variations affecting mainly its phonology and to a lesser extent its lexicon, while morphosyntax generally remains more homogeneous. The traditional dialectal division aligned on former bishoprics (Kerne, Leon, Treger and Gwened) appears too simplistic. Historically, two distinct areas can be discerned in Lower Brittany, one in the West, the other in the East, mostly Gwened/Vannes. Moreover, the Breton-speaking area is formed of two linguistically conservative poles, Leon (NW) and Gwened-Uhel (SE) separated by a wide diagonal area of linguistic innovation, from Kerne-Izel (SW) to Treger-Goueloù (NE).

The National Statistics Office (Institut national de la statistique et des études économiques, INSEE) has examined only once, in 1999, the dynamics of all the languages spoken in France in the twentieth century (Héran et al. 2002). The break in family transmission is most frequent for regional languages, and among these, the situation is most critical for Franco-Provençal, Flemish, langue d'oc and Breton, which, nine times out of ten, have ceased to be used habitually with the next generation. As far as Breton is concerned, 'conventional' intergenerational transmission broke down almost completely in the immediate post-World War II period. Consequently, family language use has been very largely—though not exclusively—a revivalist phenomenon since the 1960s (TMO Régions, Région Bretagne 2018).

The Situation as of 2018

A sociolinguistic survey (TMO Régions, Région Bretagne 2018) of unprecedented scope in Brittany was carried out in 2018 among 8,162 people aged 15 and over, surveyed by telephone using the quota method by gender, age and socio-professional profile in each of the 25 administrative units of the five Breton départments. With less than 6% of the total population claiming to be able to speak Breton—around 207,000 people—the language situation remains extremely unfavourable. Unsurprisingly, the rate of speakers is much higher in Lower Brittany (12.5%) than in Upper Brittany (1%). Similarly, the rate of understanding Breton is much higher in Lower Brittany (20%) than in Upper Brittany (2%).

One speaker in five speaks Breton every day, but one in five never does. The rate and number of speakers who never speak Breton have been increasing steadily over the last two decades, which can be explained by widowhood, old age depriving the speakers of friends and relatives of their age group, and isolation, particularly in urban areas. In such cases, the language is no longer vernacular or vehicular and traditional speakers are no longer a potential resource for learners and new speakers. Eight out of ten Brittophones are aged 60 or over, an extremely unbalanced age pyramid which, however, now shows at its base an embryonic generational resurgence. The youngest speakers are the ones who use their Breton most often: at least weekly for six out of ten speakers aged 25 to 39 and for seven out of ten speakers aged 15 to 24. The mode of transmission of Breton has been completely reversed between the younger and older generations: nine out of ten of those over 70 acquired it from their parents, while nine out of ten of those under 24 learned it in an educational setting. Evening classes, six- or nine-month full-time training courses, university courses, etc. appear in 12% of responses, indicating the importance of acquisition in adulthood as a 'second chance' after adolescence and secondary education. Nevertheless, immersion in the immediate locality (10%) remains a significant mode of transmission.

When asked about their wish to know (or to have known) Breton, for themselves and for their children, one-third of non-speakers and one-third of parents of non-speakers express this wish. Whether one's place of residence is in Upper or Lower Brittany, or whether one is of Breton origin or not has very little influence on the percentage of parents who wish their children knew Breton. The younger and the more qualified the parents are, the more this wish is expressed, and slightly more in urban and peri-urban areas than in rural areas.

In the context of a near-total break in intergenerational transmission, some young parents, frustrated by this situation, decided to resort to formal education to help them pass on Breton to their children, hence the creation of the Diwan immersive associative schools as early as 1977, followed by semi-immersive classes in public and Catholic education in the 1980s and 1990s. Their growth has been continuous but very slow ever since, as still only 3% of Brittany's school-age population attend bilingual Breton-French education in 2020.[2] There are no statistics indicating the proportion of Breton speakers among the parents concerned; however, empirical observation in primary schools indicates percentages between 5 and 10% of mothers or fathers, a great majority being themselves new speakers or children of new speakers. Parents make plans for their children, in terms of both bi-/multilingual academic attainments and the development of bi-/multilingual social and relational skills, and therefore, they deploy various strategies (educational, linguistic, identity-based, utilitarian, etc.) to achieve the goals they set, consciously or unconsciously, for their children and for themselves. The roles attributed to Breton-French education (Adam and Larvol 2019) are multiple: safeguarding the language, transmission of a cultural heritage, cognitive development, general education, external support of family language policy, personal development of the child, etc.

Research on the Family Transmission of Breton

The fact that the Breton language has undergone an almost complete interruption of its family transmission makes the resumption of this transmission, even if only on a very small scale, particularly interesting, as it has been observed since the turn of the twenty-first century. The research discussed here is structured around three main axes. The first revolves around the factors that influence the linguistic choices of Breton parents. The second focuses on family language policies, that is, the strategic and pedagogical forces mobilised by parents to transmit Breton to their children. Finally, the third axis concerns the links between language transmission and the parental educational project, and the meaning of the transmission of Breton for parents.

Theoretical References

All Breton-speaking parents are at least bilingual. Whenever they speak to their child, they, therefore, use one repertoire rather than another, unless they mix several repertoires (Deprez 1994). Parents may decide to speak a particular language to their children from the moment they choose their spouse or from the birth of their first child, but this choice is often renewed and modified several times, hence changing a parenting style which no longer sits comfortably with them (Prigent 2016: 51–52). Language choices and language practices are 'part of an ever-changing family history, the dynamics of interpersonal relationships, and the evolution of experiences according to age, time and space' (Deprez-de Heredia and Varro 1991: 300). The dynamic nature of language transmission is noted by many authors. Changes in family structure, schooling, work, relocation and 'biographical crises' in general can bring about linguistic changes (Deprez 1994; Darmon 2006; Pentecouteau 2002).

Some researchers have attempted to construct general models of linguistic behaviour in minority contexts: for example, Landry based on the experience of minority Francophones in Canada (Landry et al. 2005), or Coyos and Martinez de Luna based on the Basque experience (Coyos 2007). Landry's model highlights the importance of language socialisation, particularly the empowering experience that nurtures the speaker's self-confidence, and the consciousness-raising experience that invites speakers to reflect on their history, the history of their group and on the situation of their language. Martinez de Luna's work emphasises the importance of the Basque-speaking exchange network into which the speaker is inserted. As for Coyos, he emphasises the dialogical relationship between the potential speaker and his interlocutor.

Other researchers have attempted to identify the various factors that influence language choices in minority situations. It is common to distinguish between internal factors, concerning the speaker herself or himself, and external factors, concerning her or his immediate or more distant environment. The internal factors frequently identified are: the feeling of language competence (Chrisp 2005; Salaün et al. 2016), socio-demographic factors such as gender or level of education (Forrest 2018; Kahn 2004; King 2000; Morris 2012; Pungier 2005), biographical factors such as language socialisation and life trajectories (Pentecouteau 2002), psycho-affective factors such as emotions, self-confidence or agency (De Houwer 2006; Okita 2002; Ortega et al. 2017; Pavlenko 2005) and finally ideological factors, i.e. parents' beliefs, norms and representations of bilingualism, of languages in general and their minority language in particular (Chrisp 2005; King 2000). External factors include the immediate family, i.e. the spouse and children. The latter, through their language proficiency and their attitude towards the minority language (whether positive or negative), participate in family language negotiations and influence the choices of the parents (Filhon 2009; Morris 2012; Mueller-Gathercole et al. 2007; Smith-Christmas 2018). The presence of a third party also influences the dialogical situation and the choice of language (Lüdi and Py 2003; Morris 2012). External factors also include the support network, i.e. the local language community that can support family transmission: school, friends, family, neighbours and leisure activities (Chrisp 2005; Fishman 2001; Prigent 2016), and finally the general prestige of the minority language, including the proportion of speakers, the attitude of the majority population towards the minority language, the legal status of the language, its use by the mainstream media, economic prestige and so on (Moreau 1997; Ramallo Fernández 2012).

Methodology

The research in progress has the aim of cross-referencing quantitative and qualitative data. In 2018, an online questionnaire written in Breton was distributed by e-mail and on the internet. It was aimed at each parent involved as opposed to family units as a whole. Both spouses of the same couple sometimes replied, but separately.

450 parents answered the questionnaire, out of a speaker population of mothers estimated at 7,000 people.[3] Although the sample is relatively large, it nonetheless remains a voluntary sample and therefore not representative. Parents most motivated by the transmission of Breton are over-represented and parents who speak Breton but do not read it were de facto excluded. In 2019 and 2020, semi-structured interviews were carried out with around fifty parents who responded to the questionnaire, selected on the basis of several criteria such as gender, place of residence, transmission practices, age and mode of learning Breton.

The Population Surveyed

This research concerns parents born between 1970 and 1995 who spoke Breton fluently at the time of the birth of their first child. When the questionnaire was distributed, it was specified that 'fluent' meant 'able to have a conversation in Breton with a friend for an hour without feeling the need to change language in order to express oneself'. This assessment was left to the subjectivity of the parents, and, in fact, the respondents had varying levels of language proficiency. A series of questions inserted in the questionnaire allowed us to assess each parent's sense of language proficiency.

The choice of the generation selected was motivated by two reasons: on the one hand, this is a generation that is experiencing the transmission of Breton in the present day and on a daily basis, since most of the children of parents born between 1970 and 1995 are between 0 and 15 years old and still live with their parents; on the other hand, this generation has been influenced by the language activism of the Breton revival of the 1960s and 1970s, which allows us to investigate the issue of the reclaiming of this heritage.

Some Characteristics of the Sample

Gender: 57% mothers and 43% fathers. The over-representation of women in the sample corresponds to the reality of the Breton speaker group: for this age group, there are more Breton-speaking women than Breton-speaking men, even though there are slightly more men in the overall population (TMO 2018 survey, INSEE Bretagne 2018).

Place of residence: 78% in Lower Brittany (a traditionally Breton-speaking area), 16% in Upper Brittany (a traditionally Gallo-speaking area), 6% outside Brittany (elsewhere in France and abroad).

Level of education: 9% have a high school diploma or less, 6% have had 2 years of higher education, 85% have had three years or more of higher education. The parents in the sample are much more highly educated than the Breton average (among parents in this age group,

22% have had three or more years of higher education (TMO 2018 survey)).

Age and method of learning Breton: 60% of respondents learned Breton in adulthood (evening classes, university, long-term training, internships, etc.) and 40% learned it in childhood (including 5% in their family, 14% in their family and at school and 21% at school only). 35% of respondents were educated in Breton.

Language Transmission Practices

We have distinguished four degrees of direct transmission[4] of Breton:

- strong: parents who speak Breton to their children all (or almost all) the time,
- intermediate: parents who speak to their children in Breton as well as in another language,
- low: parents who speak Breton to their children from time to time,
- non-existent: parents who do not speak Breton to their children or very rarely.

A degree of direct transmission was attributed to each parent, based on their answers to the following questions:

- frequency of use of Breton with each of the children: always or almost always, 50% Breton, occasionally, never,
- frequency of use of Breton in eight particular speech situations (during meals, for homework, when angry, etc.): always or almost always, 50% Breton, occasionally, never (Table 1).

Statistical cross-tabulations show that certain variables strongly influence the practices of direct language transmission, among them gender (59% of fathers and 32% of mothers strongly transmit Breton), the feeling of language competence (62% of parents who feel they have a good level of Breton strongly transmit Breton to their children, compared with 24% of those who feel their level is too low), the mode of learning (54% of parents who learned Breton within their family pass it on

Table 1 Intensity of parent–child transmission of Breton (Treuzkas scale)

Direct transmission	Number of parents	Percentage
Strong	196	44
Intermediate	91	20
Weak	116	26
Non-existent	47	10
Total	450	100

strongly to their children, compared to 28% of parents who learned it at school), the language skills of the spouse (68% of parents whose spouse speaks good Breton pass it on strongly, compared to 23% of parents whose spouse does not speak Breton at all). This leads us to the question: Does the family structure therefore influence transmission practices?

Some Clues for Studying the Effect of Family Breakups and Recomposition

There is no specific study on the family structure of households in which there is at least one Breton-speaking parent. There is no reason to believe a priori that households with Breton-speaking parents are less diverse than in the population as a whole, so that they may encompass traditional families, single-parent families, families with alternating childcare systems, blended families, families with same-sex parents, families with several cohabiting generations, etc. (Table 2).

Our sample is composed as follows:

It can be seen that parents living apart or in a reconstituted family are older than the parents as a whole (56% born between 1970 and 1979 compared to 42% on average). The average age of the first divorce is 42 in France (INSEE 2014). Younger parents have simply had less time to separate. We also note that women are over-represented in the population of separated parents (65% of separated parents are mothers), which is in line with national trends indicating that women who separate from their spouse remain alone more often than men (Vivas quoted by Segalen and Martial 2013: 137).

As for language transmission, it is slightly lower than average in the population of separated parents, mainly on account of women (37%

Table 2 Parental types of family (Treuzkas scale)

Parents living…	Number of parents	Percentage	Parents cited in the following paragraphs
In a traditional family	360	80	
Separated	43	9	Gwendal*, Marie*, Yoann, Gurvan*, Stéphanie, Bleuenn, Fanny*, Morgan*
In a reconstructed family	47	11	Tinaig*, Janig*, Katell*, Aziliz*, Tudual*, Sébastien*, Franck*, Nolwenn
Total	450	100	

Note Asterisks denote those who were interviewed. The other parents cited provided their responses through responses to open-ended questions on the questionnaire. First names have been changed.

strong transmitters and 23% intermediate transmitters), and is average for mothers living in reconstructed families, but higher for fathers experiencing family recomposition.

The Influence of Separation on Transmission

This part of the investigation posed the questions, 'Today, do you speak more or less Breton to your child than before? If there have been changes, can you explain the cause(s)?' Among the 43 parents living apart, only five (three mothers and two fathers) mentioned separation as the cause of changes in their transmission practices, with four reporting a decrease in transmission and one reporting an increase. A few parents interviewed also mentioned this influence. Two points will be discussed here to better understand the effects of marital separation on language transmission: the influence of ex-spouses and the influence of child custody time.

The Influence of Ex-spouses

The overall analysis of the responses of the 450 parents shows the strong influence of spouses on the language choices of Breton-speaking parents. An index combining the linguistic competence of the spouse, his or her commitment towards Breton and the use of the language in the couple allows us to measure the willingness of the (ex-)spouse to transmit Breton in the family.

Looking at the 43 separated parents in our sample, it appears that fathers' former partners were much more favourable to Breton than mothers' former partners. For example, 60% of the fathers' ex-spouses were fluent in Breton, and in 20% of cases, Breton was the language of the couple, but only 25% of mothers' ex-spouses spoke Breton, and Breton was the language of the couple in only 7% of cases. We see here that fathers, before separation, were in conjugal situations much more favourable to transmission than mothers. At the time of separation, the pattern of transmission, or of non-transmission, is already taken. Gwendal summarises as follows:

> Now that I live separated from the mother of my children, I no longer have any reason to speak French with them. Yet I continue to do so: the habit has been established…

However, in some cases of strong transmission of Breton by only one of the parents, the Breton-speaking parent may feel that transmission is now facilitated, that it is no longer 'hindered' by bilingual interference. Thus, Marie had chosen to always speak Breton to her children. Her former spouse understood Breton well and expressed a positive attitude towards the language, but despite this, in family conversations, Marie often switched to French to integrate her partner. Today, her daughters are in alternating custody, but a little more often with their mother than with their father. Marie has lost the habit of switching to French, and as a result, she feels that her daughters' exposure to Breton is more intense. In this case, the separation simplifies the dialogical situation by reducing the number of people involved in the conversation and the linguistic influence of the former spouse fades away.

The Influence of Child Custody Time

The amount of time the child is in custody after separation can also affect the outcome. The figures show large disparities between fathers and mothers regarding the influence of the amount of time spent in childcare. Even though they represent very small numbers, it seems useful to give them here (Table 3).

Unsurprisingly, and despite the progression of alternating custody, we see that mothers assume more responsibility for childcare after marital separation. When they have their children full time or almost full time, they transmit Breton more strongly than the average. They find themselves in a way as the sole decision-makers and, in some cases, this encourages the transmission of Breton. Fathers in alternating custody transmit Breton more strongly than the average of the 450 parents. Among fathers whose children are only occasionally in their custody, two-thirds continue to transmit Breton, while mothers who have their children half-time or occasionally transmit Breton much less than the average. For these fathers, we theorise that linguistic investment is perhaps a way of expressing their desire to assume their fatherhood and their educational role.

Qualitative data allow us to go further in the analysis of the relationship between custody time and language transmission by looking at the unique situations of some parents. Sometimes, the briefness of custody time and the geographical distance make transmission difficult or even impossible.[5] Yoann grew up in Breton. Breton was the language of communication with his parents and with his brothers, and he attended school in Breton until the very end of his secondary education. He went to work in Germany and met a German woman with whom he had a child. He now lives in Brittany separated from his child and the mother of his child. He discusses the evolution of his language practices with his son as follows:

08/2013: birth of my son in Germany. I speak only in Breton, or almost (family language and language of love, obviously).
08/2014: separation from the mother. I see my son every day. One day in French, every other day in Breton.

Table 3 Influence of child custody time on the level of intensity of the parental transmission of Breton (Treuzkas scale)

Transmission of Breton	Permanent custody			Alternating custody			Occasional custody		
	Fathers (2) (%)	Mothers (16) (%)	Total (18) (%)	Fathers (7) (%)	Mothers (10) (%)	Total (17) (%)	Fathers (6) (%)	Mothers (2) (%)	Total (8) (%)
Strong	50	38	39	71	10	35	50		38
Intermediary	50	31	33		30	18	17		13
Weak		13	11	29	30	29		100	25
Non-existent		19	17		30	18	33		25

08/2015: relocation of my son. I only see him at the weekend. One day in French, one day in Breton. I'm not allowed to take him with me to Brittany when on holidays.
01/2018: my son is four and a half. He speaks a lot but only in German. He says a few words in Breton and French but he's not able to make sentences. He understands some of what I say to him, but actually very little. He finds even simple items difficult. I address him in German more and more.
04/2018: I'm back in Brittany. I will see my son only every month or every two months. He will speak neither French nor Breton and he doesn't understand either, unfortunately. He will learn French in primary or secondary school.

Yoann's child has little exposure to the Breton language due to the distance from his father. His production capacities and even his comprehension of Breton are weak, which could lead Yoann to abandon his project of linguistic transmission.

Gurvan also does not live with his daughter on a daily basis (he separated from the mother before the birth of the child). He takes care of her about one weekend a month and part of the school holidays. However, the short time spent with her does not prevent transmission, as he manages to mobilise other resources. Gurvan has chosen to speak almost exclusively Breton to his daughter, which made exchanges complicated when she was very young, knowing that the mother, although having been educated in Breton, does not speak Breton at all to her daughter. But Gurvan is supported in his transmission project by his parents and brothers, who help him to create a total immersion environment around his daughter when she is on holidays with her father at her grandparents' house. The schooling of the child in Diwan from the age of three has also made it possible to create more favourable conditions for family language transmission.

In Stéphanie's case, we see how the mother adapts her strategies to the new family situation. She has three children and their father has chosen a strict Breton monolingual strategy and requires his children to speak to him in Breton. Stéphanie, for her part, had adopted a bilingual strategy to balance the father's contribution. Now separated from the father and having the children in her care most of the time, she has revised her strategy to ensure that her youngest child has sufficient exposure to Breton:

> I make sure to use more Breton at home again because the little one does not live permanently with his father (who always speaks Breton). I want my children to be bilingual, so she has to be exposed to a lot of Breton from birth. I've asked my two elder children for help and they usually speak Breton to their sister, especially the eldest, who wouldn't utter one word of Breton at home when her father was with us. The little one is two years old and her first words are half in Breton and half in French.

It is not possible to establish a general rule on the link between child custody time and language transmission. Each case is individual. But through these different experiences, we can see the different influences that custody time can have on the parents' language choices.

Having seen the links between marital separation and language transmission, we will now look at another form of family restructuring: reconstituted families.

The Influence of Family Recomposition on Transmission

Family recomposition can take many forms. In our sample, we have parents who live with the father or mother of their child(ren) and a child or children who are not theirs (most often from an earlier relationship) (20 parents out of 47), parents who live with the father or mother of some of their children and sometimes other children (8 parents out of 47), parents who live with a spouse who is not the father or mother of their child(ren) and sometimes other children (19 parents out of 47).

The Influence of the New Spouse

Two questions interest us in this section: Do Breton parents who are separated from their first spouse choose a new spouse who makes roughly equivalent provision for the Breton language? Can the introduction of a

Table 4 Attitude of the new partner towards Breton compared to that of the previous partner (Treuzkas scale)

Attitude of the new spouse	Fathers (9)		Mothers (16)	
More favourable	3	33%	5	31%
Less favourable	2	22%	9	56%
Equivalent	4	45%	2	13%

new spouse change the system of parent/child language practices already in place, sometimes for many years?

Of the 47 parents living in a reconstituted family, 25 live with a spouse who is not the father or mother of their child(ren) or of all their children. Comparing the index of attitude towards the Breton language of spouse 1 and spouse 2, we find (Table 4).

The majority of the parents in our sample chose a new partner who was either more or less favourable to Breton than the first. Many mothers chose new partners who were less favourable to Breton, which probably led to renewed negotiations between the partners on the language issue. However, no general trends can be drawn from this observation due to the small size of the sample. On the other hand, the parents' testimonies clearly show the impact of the new spouses' disposition on the family transmission of Breton.

Tinaig has a first child with a man who is favourable to Breton (good understanding and interest in the language). She speaks Breton and French to her baby, sings songs to him in Breton and the child is educated in a bilingual class. The couple separates. Tinaig takes up with a new partner who is not very Breton-friendly. Soon enough, the new couple moves to a neighbourhood where there is no bilingual school. Tinaig's eldest daughter now attends a French school and Tinaig stops speaking Breton to her. Two other children are born to whom she does not speak Breton.

Janig has a child with a Breton-speaking partner. She speaks a lot of Breton to her baby, and this is made easier by the exclusive use of Breton in the couple. After the separation from the father of her child, she meets a new companion who is not very favourable to Breton. Today she speaks little Breton to her child and only outside the home. Perhaps without being aware of it, the new partner has changed Janig's strategy:

Is the fact that Breton is only used outside home linked to your spouse not knowing Breton?

Yes. It's true that when the three of us are together, most certainly there won't be any Breton, because this concern for not leaving out anyone applies everywhere, in my opinion.

Did you discuss with J. the place of Breton at home?

Not much, no, because he's not against Breton but he doesn't speak it, doesn't want to speak it and has no interest in it, so I felt straight away that it would have been a major struggle to impose . . . to make him turn to Breton, and at the time I probably needed to distance myself too, like I was already immersed in Breton, and I am, 200%, so it doesn't bother me to take a little break, so I didn't push him at all. But . . . well he's not interested in Breton . . . but . . . he doesn't care.

Do you think he realized the place of Breton at home had shrunk?

I don't think so, he hasn't noticed, no. He doesn't pay attention.

In the case of Katell, the situation is opposite; her new husband motivates her in her practice of Breton. Katell grew up in a Breton-speaking family. She raised her two children alone, outside Brittany, all in Breton at first. But feeling limited in her expression in Breton, when they were four or five years old, she started to use French as well, and the Breton language gradually faded between Katell and her children. A few years ago she returned to Brittany. Her children are now grown-up teenagers. For some time now, she has been sharing her life with a Breton speaker who himself has three children with whom he speaks only Breton. Katell's youngest daughter learned a little Breton at secondary school and high school, as an optional subject, and understands it better and better by being immersed in a strongly Breton-speaking environment (everyone in the house speaks Breton except her). This situation reminds Katell of the interrupted transmission and has revived her desire to speak Breton to her daughter. Her new partner offers her a favourable environment and a role model. But how to tackle this after so many years spent living in French?

The Influence of Stepchildren

As far as stepchildren are concerned, several factors come into play, first and foremost the proportion of time they spend in the reconstituted family (full-time, alternating custody, presence during weekends and holidays) and their knowledge and use of Breton.

The first observation is that stepchildren, whether voluntarily or involuntarily, may force their stepmother or stepfather to use French more than they would with their own children, for the sake of integration. This constraint comes into play when the stepchildren do not speak Breton, when their proficiency is too limited or when they express a lack of interest or even a degree of rejection of the language.

The presence of stepchildren who speak little or no Breton can destabilise monolingual strategies for transmitting Breton. Aziliz explains that the presence of her husband's first children, slightly older than her own and not Breton speakers, brought French into the house at weekends and during the holidays:

> With my husband's children there were intricate conversations in French, so it was harder to bring in Breton whenever they'd be with us.

Tudual reports that when he met his girlfriend's son, she encouraged him to speak Breton to her son, aged five, since the latter was in a bilingual stream:

> I spoke to the little boy in Breton and he was puzzled, yes, completely puzzled because he couldn't say . . . because I wouldn't just ask 'go and fetch pencils', 'go and get scissors', 'let's go to the canteen' . . . but rather 'what did you do today? What do you think? How did you feel?' And he couldn't. He was able to say: 'je sais, un loup on dit ur bleiz, un renard on dit ul louarn' [I know, for a wolf you say *ur bleiz*, for a fox you say *ul louarn*'), but at the end of the day he wasn't able to make sentences . . .

The child then refused Breton and forced Tudual to speak to him in French. Today, he has made great progress by dint of hearing his stepfather speak Breton, but it is French that dominates the relationship between the two of them, which leaves his stepbrother wondering:

> My son asked me to speak French one day a week because he wanted to hear his father speak French. He didn't understand why his older brother would be allowed to hear French from me, and he wouldn't. So I thought, all right let's go, let's do it . . . and I didn't manage. The first Monday it lasted 5 minutes, the second Monday we forgot, and finally we ended up never doing it. He still asks me every now and then: it would be good to speak a bit of French together . . .

Stepchildren may be willing to learn Breton at the same time as their younger siblings, but this depends very much on their age and schooling. We have not heard of any cases of stepchildren aged six and over not learning Breton at school, and becoming speakers through the practice of Breton by a stepfather or stepmother at home. On the other hand, their daily exposure to intense practice enables them, if they are willing, to acquire words, phrases and even a fairly good understanding of the language. Aziliz reports that the youngest of her stepchildren, who was four years old when she got married to his father and would come to their house on weekends and holidays, understands Breton well and is able to formulate simple sentences because he has heard her speak it for more than ten years.

The second finding is that stepchildren can allow one to test future strategies before the birth of one's own children. Three examples help us to better understand this phenomenon.

When he met his future wife and son, both non-Breton speaking, Sébastien was a bilingual school teacher. Spontaneously, because he was used to doing it at school, he taught his stepson a few words of Breton through play. But he did not keep it up. When his first child was born, Sébastien did not speak Breton to him and later the child went to school in French.

Franck, also a bilingual school teacher, set up a household with a partner who was not a Breton speaker but whose daughters went to a Diwan school. He speaks in French to his stepdaughters, with a bit of Breton from time to time. Later, when his child was born, Franck spoke to her in French, even though he also uses a few occasional words in Breton. His son now goes to school at Diwan and there is more Breton between them, especially on the way to school and for homework.

Nolwenn, who is also a bilingual school teacher, met a man with two children who were being educated in a bilingual stream. Spontaneously, Nolwenn speaks to them in Breton, and the children accept it well. She says that when she was pregnant, encouraged by her, the two children spoke Breton to the baby while caressing her belly. When the baby was born, Nolwenn chose to speak Breton to the child. She was prepared for this because Breton was already part of everyday family life with her stepchildren, even though they were only present every second week.

Through the examples of Franck and Nolwenn, we can see that stepchildren who already speak a little Breton can serve as a revelation of future transmission choices. It is also interesting to compare the cases of Nolwenn and Tudual. Both of them met their partner's children, who were educated in a bilingual school or stream. One succeeded in establishing Breton as the language of interaction with them, while the other met refusal. Several elements can play a part in these different ways of welcoming the Breton of the step-parent: the linguistic competence of each different stepchild, their appetite for Breton, their age, their openness or closeness of mind regarding their father or mother forming a new couple, the pedagogical abilities of the step-parent and so on.

The Breton Language: A Bone of Contention in the Couple

We have discussed above an overview of the possible effects of marital separation and family recomposition on the linguistic transmission of Breton. Before concluding this chapter, we would like to turn the question around and ask whether Breton and the transmission of Breton can be factors that create conflict within the couple or even of family restructuring? During our field survey, we identified two types of conflict: conflicts concerning the strategies of linguistic transmission to children and those concerning the language(s) of the couple.

Conflicts Over Language Transmission Strategies

Stéphanie and Bleuenn both live and had children with a Breton-speaking partner. These two fathers have opted for a strict monolingual strategy: they only speak Breton to their children and demand that their children speak to them in this language. Stéphanie chose a bilingual strategy and got into the habit of answering the child in the language of the question. Solenn, for her part, always speaks Breton to her children but accepts that they speak in French if they wish to do so. They blame their former companions for an overly strict strategy that infringes on the children's freedom and pushes them to take a stance. This strategic disagreement, highlighting different attitudes towards the education of their children, was the source of arguments within these couples.

Conflicts Concerning the Language(s) Used by the Couple

For a long time, Fanny suffered from Morgan's lack of involvement in the linguistic transmission of Breton to their child, and, to put it mildly, his refusal to make Breton the language of the couple and the family. Morgan learned Breton at school and works in Breton on a daily basis. Fanny learnt Breton when she was 25 years old, following a long training course. When they met, she had just finished her training and the meeting took place in French. Fanny, out of personal taste and in a search for coherence, would have liked Breton to have taken its place in their relationship, but Morgan did not want this because he felt that Fanny did not have the same personality in Breton and in French and because he did not like her learner's Breton, which was too bland according to him. Fanny, despite her lack of fluency in Breton, chose to speak Breton to her child all the time. She continued to ask Morgan to make room for Breton in the family. Had he accepted, it would have been a sign that he was endorsing her transmission project and she would no longer be alone in this project. The sign did not come but Morgan ended up requiring Fanny to take part in the family language transmission project. Fanny then gradually relieved herself of a burden that was too heavy for her.

Tudual, for his part, ardently desires that his children become active speakers, at ease with Breton. To do this, he is convinced that Breton must be the language of the family and therefore of the couple:

> I told my girlfriend: all right, you can speak French to your son, this is your choice, but if you could speak to me in Breton then the baby could see or hear that it's a language for conversation, between adults, not just for her or him.

His partner, who is pregnant, is very enthusiastic about this project of immersive transmission. But Breton is still a recent discovery for her (a year-long intensive course a few years ago) and, after the birth of the child, putting it into practice is difficult and painful. Tudual reproaches her for not speaking Breton enough. After a year, she no longer wants to hear the language. Today, the practices are quite distinct: Breton with the father, French with the mother and little Breton within the couple. For Tudual, making Breton the language of the couple was a transmission issue to give her children the image of a living language spoken by children and adults. But the different levels of use of Breton, in-depth by Tudual and more superficial for his partner, made it impossible for both parents to adopt an identical transmission strategy.

Language transmission practices can be an important issue, even a source of conflict in the couple, revealing different relationships to the language, different personalities and different views on matters involving education. They can thus contribute to the many tensions that may arise in the life of a couple.

Conclusion

It is not possible to identify a homogeneous influence of family separation or recomposition on the family transmission of Breton. Each case is particular. When a parent separates from the father or mother of their child(ren), it is rare for them to review their transmission strategy in depth, unless they are forced to do so by residential distance. In cases of family recomposition, the influence of stepchildren is undeniable. It depends on how long they are present in the home and on their linguistic competence in Breton, but also on whether or not they welcome the linguistic proposals of their stepmother or stepfather. The influence of the new spouse is just as obvious. More often than not, the formation of a new couple leads to new negotiations between the partners and the use of languages in the family is part of this, consciously or unconsciously.

Language transmission is a multi-actor game that takes place in a particular environment. A separation or a new union modifies the game of the actors and the environment: the negotiations between the partners, the dialogic situation and the living environment also sometimes (relocation, change of school and so on). Parents find themselves having to reposition themselves, adapt their strategies and sometimes even abandon the transmission project.

Notes

1. PhD in educational science on the family transmission of Breton, Katell Chantreau, University Rennes 2, CREAD, supervised by Hugues Pentecouteau and Stefan Moal.
2. The calculation of the percentage of 30%, out of the total school-age population, is a compilation of recent statistics (http://www.fr.brezhoneg.bzh/evenement/2181/50-actualite.htm) from the *académie de Rennes* on the one hand and the *département de Loire-Atlantique* on the other.
3. In 2018, TMO Régions interviewed 8,132 people by telephone. 651 of them stated they spoke Breton well or fairly well, including 24 parents born between 1970 and 1995. From the survey, TMO estimated the number of Breton speakers at 207,000, all ages combined, in the whole of historical Brittany. By extrapolation, we estimated that the share of speakers corresponding to the mother population of this study was around 7000 people. This number should be used with caution because of the small number of respondents allowing for this estimation.

4. By direct transmission we mean the language that parents speak to their children. It differs from indirect transmission linked to the choice of schooling the children in a bilingual stream. A parent may not speak Breton to his or her children (no direct transmission) but choose for them a bilingual Breton-French formal education (strong or medium indirect transmission, depending on the stream chosen).
5. Situations of impossible transmission are not anecdotal, especially in the case of separated fathers. In 2005 in France, 40% of children under the age of 25 rarely saw their father or never saw their father again after their parents' separation (Segalen and Martial 2013: 127).

References

Adam, C. and G. Larvol. 2019. Scolarisation bilingue et appropriation d'une langue (minoritaire). *Revue TDFLE*, 1. https://doi.org/10.34745/numerev_1339. Accessed 20 December 2020.

Chantreau, K. 2017. *Treuzkas ar brezhoneg d'ar vugale? Choazoù ha pleustroù ar gerent vrezhonek yaouank/Transmettre le breton à ses enfants? Les choix et les pratiques linguistiques des jeunes parents bretonnants.* Unpublished Masters thesis, Université Rennes 2.

Chrisp, S. 2005. Māori Intergenerational Language Transmission. *International Journal of the Sociology of Language* 172: 149–181.

Coyos, J.-B. 2007. Ecart entre connaissance et usage d'une langue minoritaire: modèles théoriques et cas de la langue basque. In *Variable territoriale et promotion des langues minoritaires*, ed. A. Viaut and X. Lamuela, 411–427. Bordeaux, Maison des Sciences de l'Homme d'Aquitaine.

Darmon, M. 2006. *La socialisation.* Paris: Armand Colin.

De Houwer, A. 2006. Le développement harmonieux ou non harmonieux du bilinguisme de l'enfant au sein de la famille. *Langage Et Société* 116 (2): 29–49.

Deprez, C. 1994. *Les enfants bilingues: Langues et familles*. Paris: Didier/Credif.

Deprez-de Heredia, C., and G. Varro. 1991. Le bilinguisme dans les familles. *Enfance* 44 (4): 297–304.

Filhon, A. 2009. *Langues d'ici et d'ailleurs: Transmettre l'arabe et le berbère en France*. Paris: INED.

Fishman, J., ed. 2001. *Can Threatened Languages Be Saved?* Reversing Language shift Revisited, Clevedon: Multilingual Matters.

Forrest, W. 2018. The Intergenerational Transmission of Australian Indigenous Languages: Why Language Maintenance Programmes Should be Family-focused. *Ethnic and Racial Studies* 41 (2): 303–323.

Heran, F., A. Filhon, and C. Deprez. 2002. La dynamique des langues en France au fil du XXe siècle. *Population Et Société* 376: 1–4.

INSEE. 2014. https://www.justifit.fr/b/guides/droit-famille/divorce/combien-de-couples-divorcent-en-france/.

INSEE Bretagne. 2018. https://www.insee.fr/fr/statistiques/2011101?geo=REG-53#chiffre-cle-1.

Kahn, E. 2004. *Perspectives de parents en union mixte sur la transmission linguistique intergénérationnelle*. Unpublished doctoral thesis, Université de Montréal.

King, K. 2000. Language Ideologies and Heritage Language Education. *International Journal of Bilingual Education and Bilingualism* 3: 167–184.

Landry, R., R. Allard, K. Deveau, and N. Bourgeois. 2005. Autodétermination du comportement langagier en milieu minoritaire : Un modèle conceptuel. *Francophonies D'amérique* 20: 63–78.

Lüdi, G., and B. Py. 2003. *Être bilingue*, 3rd ed. Bern: Lang.

Moreau, M.-L., ed. 1997. *Sociolinguistique: les concepts de base*. Liège: Mardaga (Psychologie et sciences humaines).

Morris, D. 2012. The Role of the Family in the Revitalization of a Minority Language. *Caplletra: revista internacional de filología* 53: 149–165.

Mueller-Gathercole, V., E.M. Thomas, E. Williams, and M. Deuchar. 2007. *Language Transmission in Bilingual Families in Wales*. Cardiff: Welsh Language Board.

Okita, T. 2002. *Invisible Work: Bilingualism, Language Choice, and Childrearing in Intermarried Families*. Amsterdam: John Benjamins.

Ortega, A., E. Amorrortu, J. Goirigolzarri, and J. Urla. 2017. *Los nuevos hablantes de euskera: Experiencias, actitudes e identidades*. Bilbao: Universidad de Deusto/BizkaiLab.

Pavlenko, A. 2005. *Emotions and Multilingualism*. Cambridge: Cambridge University Press.

Pentecouteau, H. 2002. *Devenir bretonnant*. Rennes: Presses Universitaires de Rennes.

Prigent, M. 2016. *Enjeux de la transmission des langues pour des parents plurilingues*. Unpublished Master's thesis, University of Utrecht.
Pungier, M.-F. 2005. Expériences d'appropriation de la langue bretonne chez des jeunes de 15 à 25 ans: Modes, usages, motivations. *Language and Culture* 4: 255–279.
Ramallo Fernández, F. 2012. El gallego en la familia: entre la producción y la reproducción. *Caplletra: revista internacional de filología* 53: 167–191.
Région Bretagne, and TMO-Régions. 2018. *Enquête sociolinguistique « Langues de Bretagne », rapport final*.
Salaün, M., J. Vernaudon, and M. Paia. 2016. Le tahitien, c'est pour dire bonjour et au revoir : Paroles d'enfants sur une langue autochtone en sursis. *Enfances Familles Générations* 25: 1–23.
Segalen, M., and A. Martial. 2013. *Sociologie de la famille*. Paris: Armand Colin.
Smith-Christmas, C. 2018. 'One Cas, Two Cas': Exploring the Affective Dimensions of Family Language Policy. *Multilingua* 37 (2): 131–152.

Wider Community Stance and Irish-Speaking Families in the Gaeltacht

Tadhg Ó hIfearnáin

Perceptions of Decline and Resilience in Home and Community Language Use

The decline of Irish as the majority language in Ireland has been well-documented, from the start of the societal language shift to English after the seventeenth-century conquest to the substantial body of research focussing on the huge political, economic, social and consequent linguistic change in the nineteenth century, and the continuing dynamics of marginalisation from then until the present. Although slowed, this degeneration of Irish as a community language has persisted despite the efforts of organised movements and the intervention of the independent Irish state since the early twentieth century in what Zuckermann (2020: 200) calls *reinvigoration*, to differentiate policies aimed at an endangered

T. Ó hIfearnáin (✉)
School of Languages, Literatures and Cultures, NUI Galway, Galway, Ireland
e-mail: tadhg.ohifearnain@oegaillimh.ie

M. Hornsby and W. McLeod (eds.), *Transmitting Minority Languages*, Palgrave Studies in Minority Languages and Communities,
https://doi.org/10.1007/978-3-030-87910-5_5

language that still has many child speakers from *revitalisation*, which aims to breathe life into severely endangered languages such as Cornish (Dunmore 2002) or Gallo (Nolan 2018). Irish is still spoken as a home language by a minority of the population throughout the country, but the main areas of speaker density are the officially defined Gaeltacht areas (see Map 1). The status of the language in the community and as a home language in those areas is extremely complex. While the majority of Gaeltacht residents have an ability to speak Irish, which still distinguishes the Gaeltacht from the rest of the country, the numbers who speak Irish

Map 1 Gaeltacht areas mentioned in the text

on a regular, daily basis outside the education system and who bring up their children as Irish speakers have been shown to be weakening, as has the depth and range of the Irish that many of those speakers employ as a spoken and written medium. Informed by ethnographic observation, but largely based on an analysis of census data and of the returns from *Scéim Labhairt na Gaeilge*, a grant scheme for Irish-speaking Gaeltacht households that ran continuously, though in several different forms, from 1933 to 2011 (Ó Gliasáin 1990; Ó Bróithe 2012), Ó Giollagáin and Charlton (2015: 141) suggest that no Gaeltacht area will survive beyond 2025 in a cultural and social sense because the people of the Gaeltacht are 'falling off the cliff of minority language viability' ('ag titim thar fhána aill na hinmharthanachta mionteanga') (2015: 142). They predict that some thin networks of speakers, particularly among the grandparent generation, might survive a little longer, but such groups would not be sufficiently strong or dynamic enough to set a linguistic example or lead their communities. They set this linguistic viability threshold at approximately 70% of active speakers, determined through a statistical analysis of the available census returns and *Scéim Labhairt na Gaeilge* data. This interpretation, which is an update of an earlier study (Ó Giollagáin et al. 2007), has played a considerable role in the debate about language policy and planning in the Gaeltacht, both for those who agree with its vision and those who reject it, especially since the Gaeltacht language planning areas were introduced under the *Gaeltacht Act 2012*.

The conclusion that a language cannot survive as a community language when only practised by a minority within that community is problematic. While it would certainly be easier for individuals and families who speak Irish as their home language and for the wider population to use the language in a socially unmarked, normalised way if it were not a minoritised language, the fact that Irish is a minority language both nationally and locally does not preclude its continuing use as a language of family and community. Indeed, we know that there are small numbers of families bringing up their children through Irish in every part of Ireland. Using data extracted by the Central Statistics Office from the 2016 Census of Ireland, discussed in more detail below, we can estimate that there are approximately 15,000 children being brought up as Irish speakers in over 6,000 different Irish-speaking households in the state (a little over 4,000 of those children in about 1,800 households in the Gaeltacht areas). About half of those households are in urban areas, but there is little evidence of any remarkable density in any setting outside the larger Gaeltacht areas (Seoighe et al. 2021). Irish-speaking families are present throughout the country, but the continued concentration of Irish-speaking families in designated Gaeltacht areas owes much to the role of Irish in those rural communities, a phenomenon which differentiates them from wider Irish society.

Surveys and qualitative fieldwork in many Gaeltacht regions consistently reveal contradictory perceptions about the quantity and quality of Irish being spoken in families, in schooling and in the wider community setting. The prevailing discourse among fluent and habitual Irish speakers, and that in most academic analysis, is that Irish is perceived to be declining. However, at the same time, much quantitative and qualitative data sampling the whole local population consistently reports a perception that Irish continues to be maintained in families and that in many cases more Irish is believed to be in use than in the recent past. This perception is often strongest in Gaeltacht areas where Irish is demonstrably weaker, and among research participants whose own Irish is not fluent, though not in all cases. For example, in 2008, Údarás na Gaeltachta (the Gaeltacht development agency) and the government's Department of Community, Rural and Gaeltacht Affairs undertook a language survey in 28 Gaeltacht areas as part of the *Gaeilge 2010* initiative. It was hoped that the act of undertaking the survey work would motivate local groups in subsequent language planning initiatives, envisaged as part of the *20–Year Strategy for the Irish Language 2010–2030* (Government of Ireland 2010) and later given a statutory footing by the *Gaeltacht Act 2012*. The areas chosen were mostly those which had not thus far undertaken community-based research on language practices and attitudes. The Múscraí Gaeltacht area in west Cork, which informs much of the discussion below, was not included because Údarás na Gaeltachta had recently commissioned research on employment, education and the Irish language which had surveyed 870 households in 2006–2007 (Mortell et al. 2008). A standard questionnaire was used in all areas for the *Gaeilge 2010* initiative, in Irish and English versions. A huge amount of data was collected from a total of 4,454 households.

The results were not published but were collated and made available to each of the community groups concerned. A more detailed discussion of the nature of the research and analysis of findings focussing on English-speakers in Gaeltacht areas where fluent Irish speakers were in the minority (according to the findings of the local fieldwork) are in Ó hIfearnáin 2014. The following are some examples of qualitative responses from the survey on the state of Irish in two south-western Gaeltacht areas in the same province as Múscraí; An Clochán-Bréanainn and Uíbh Ráthach (see Map 1), where community Irish usage is generally regarded as very weak. An Clochán-Bréanainn is a small area in Kerry on the eastern side of a mountain that separates it from the larger and more strongly Irish-speaking Corca Dhuibhne Gaeltacht area and was added to the official Gaeltacht in 1974. It only has about 25% fluent speakers according to the 2008 research.

> Tá a lán daoine ag déanamh an-iarracht chun an Ghaoluinn a labhairt sa cheantar. (Lots of people are making a great effort to speak Irish in the area.)

> Tá mé an-sásta leis an nGaeilge atá san áit seo. Tá súil agam go mbeidh an Ghaeilge níos tábhachtaí i gcéad bliain ná mar atá sí anois.
> (I am happy with Irish in this place. I hope that Irish will be more important in a hundred years than it is now.)

> Tá Gaeilge ag gach duine san áit. Tá an scoil náisiúnta agus an naíonra trí Ghaeilge.
> (Everybody in the place speaks Irish. The primary school and pre-school are in Irish.)

> Tá an Ghaoluinn ag treisiú an t-am ar fad.
> (Irish is strengthening all the time.)

In the south Kerry Gaeltacht of Uíbh Ráthach, a large area but with a population of only 1,808 in 2016, the new local language planning initiative reports research showing a lot of passive ability in Irish but only some 3% who use Irish as a home language and very few other habitual speakers (Comhchoiste Ghaeltacht Uíbh Ráthaigh 2017). Despite this, the following opinions were expressed in 2008:

> Tá feabhas mór tagtha ar an nGaeilge sa cheantar seo le roinnt blianta anuas. Tá suim mhór ag na daoine bheith ag comhrá trí Ghaeilge anois. (There is great improvement in Irish in the area in recent years. People have great interest in conversing in Irish now.)
>
> A lot of the local people outside the regular speakers are well able to converse *as Gaeilge*.
>
> Tá an-bháidh leis an nGaeilge sa cheantar.
> (People are very sympathetic to Irish in the area.)
>
> I think that there is quite a lot of Irish in the area.
>
> The true Irish is in this area.
>
> There is a lot of Irish in my work place – answering phone etc.

It would be easy to dismiss these perceptions as erroneous or misinformed, but they are important parts of the stance towards Irish in the wider local community and play a role in the way that Irish speakers and families within the areas are received and perceived by their neighbours. The discussion here will show that Irish has continued to be spoken for decades as the main language of some homes in Gaeltacht communities where such families are in the minority and seeks to present a nuanced interpretation of the perception in the wider community of the amount and frequency of Irish being spoken. It seeks to reconcile and explain the ways in which the language can be paradoxically regarded by local people as simultaneously in terminal decline and stable or even strengthening in the community. Further, it sees these discursive constructions as both beneficial and challenging for families for whom Irish is a main or a major language and for other speakers in such Gaeltacht areas.

This discussion draws principally on research that informed the language planning process undertaken in the Múscraí Gaeltacht region in

Co. Cork, in the south-west of Ireland, in response to the requirements of the *Gaeltacht Act 2012*. The locally led initiative was coordinated by Rosaí Nic Chárthaigh, a member of the local community, and undertaken from October 2016 until June 2017. The main findings are reported in the published language plan (Meitheal Pleanála Teanga Mhúscraí 2017; English summary pp. 182–202). A starting point for research planning in all the Gaeltacht language planning areas, and one which echoes the work of Ó Giollagáin et al. (2007), is an analysis of the available census data. However, despite its widespread currency, the census data is not immediately transparent regarding language ability, home use nor frequency of usage.

The Problematic Use of the Irish Census Data on Language

The census has been one of the most enduring tools to count the number of people who speak Irish since a language question was asked for the first time in 1851. We have a series of information provided by the Central Statistics Office (CSO) on the Irish language in the state from the first Free State census in 1926 until today, although the question has differed slightly over time and there are certain gaps in the information series.

The CSO has always been in doubt about the usefulness of the questions on the Irish language (e.g. see Central Statistics Office 1956: 32, 1966: vi–vii), believing that the language data is most valuable in comparing different places in one year or in looking at variations in the data series from census to census. They highlight that what the data actually means is subjective because no definition of what it means to be an Irish speaker has been offered on the questionnaire. However, even regarding the data as a series is a little challenging because of gaps at crucial times. The State's language policy took several turns in the mid-twentieth century, leading to the omission of the language question in 1951 and 1956. Those were critical years for the Gaeltacht, which was designated by statute in 1956 in order to define the geographical area under the jurisdiction of the new Department of the Gaeltacht. A special inquiry into the knowledge and use of Irish in those areas which were defined by the Gaeltacht Commission in 1926 was undertake by the Gardaí, as census enumerators in 1956. (Central Statistics Office 1956). Since 1961, we have access to census information gathered at ten year intervals since 1961 and at five year intervals since 1986. There have been slight disruptions to the regularity of the period between censuses because of measures to prevent foot and mouth disease in 2001 which led to the census being taken in 2002, and the 2021 census was postponed until 2022 because of the coronavirus pandemic.

The census question is often claimed to be a self-assessment, unlike in some other jurisdictions, which offer examples or explanations of what is meant by the category of speaker for which data is required. It may be surprising that the number of people who say that they speak Irish in the census returns is not actually higher than that reported given that the vast majority will have learnt Irish for 12 years at school, where it is compulsory. Indeed, in studies where more nuanced guidance about levels of Irish competence is given, the number of people who claim ability does increase (see Ó Riagáin 2018; Ó Gliasáin 1996: 9–12). In the national surveys carried out in 1973, 1982 and 1993, for example, approximately 80% claimed that they had some ability in Irish (Ó Riagáin 2018: 54–75). According to the national survey carried out by Mac Gréil and Rhatigan (2009), only 16% of Irish-born people said they had no Irish.

For the purposes of discussing family language usage, there is another difficulty regarding 'self-assessment' in the census returns that must be taken into account when discussing the number of children and teenagers who speak Irish and their language habits, whether in the Gaeltacht or in the rest of the country. The census return is usually the opinion of one member of the household. It is the 'head of household' that fills in the form for herself/ himself and for every person under the age of 18 years in the household. As such, it is an assessment of the ability and language habits of family members by one of the parents/adults in the family, not necessarily a report from the perspective of the young speakers themselves.

The Numbers of People Who Speak Irish as a Home Language in the Census

The language question in the State's first census (1926) differed from the previous and subsequent censuses in the context of this discussion because it sought to ascertain the number of native Irish speakers, i.e. people raised with Irish at home. However, responses were difficult to interpret in a reliable way (Lyon 1932), and it was concluded that a very large proportion of the population did not understand the difference between a 'native' and a 'fluent' speaker of Irish, a fact which has come to the fore in many research projects since, including *Gaeilge 2010*. In the end, the only figures published were for monolingual Irish speakers, those who could speak both languages and those who had no Irish. The question of 'native' language is asked in some other jurisdictions because citizens who are native speakers, rather than those who learned the language, have defined language rights, for schooling and public services, for example. This is ultimately an ethnolinguistic question, rather than a question of language proficiency. The fundamental belief that Irish is the native language of the whole Irish nation is enshrined in the language ideology that came to the fore during the Revival in the late nineteenth century, under the influence of the Gaelic League, and remains a strong political and cultural discourse on language in Ireland, where Irish is defined in Article 8.1 of the Constitution as the primary official language *because* it is the national language. ('Ós í an Ghaeilge an teanga náisiúnta is í an phríomhtheanga oifigiúil í': Bunreacht na hÉireann 1937, Article 8.1).

Despite the problem of defining a speaker for census purposes, certain state agencies and Irish language organisations, particularly in the Gaeltacht, feel that it would be beneficial to get information from the census on the number of people raised in Irish and raised through Irish. Between October and November 2017, the CSO carried out a consultation process on questions to be introduced in the next census questionnaire (to be undertaken in 2022). More than 400 submissions were received and a subcommittee made up of representatives from government departments and organisations drafted new census questions for a pilot survey, completed in September 2018. The pilot questions from the two versions of the pilot survey included the following:

13. Is Irish the main spoken language of your household?
14. Can you speak Irish?
    If 'yes' do you speak Irish?

1. Daily, within the education system
2. Daily, outside the education system
3. Weekly
4. Less often
5. Never

If 'Yes', how well do you speak Irish?

1. Very well
2. Well
3. Not well

15. Did you grow up in a household where Irish was the main spoken language?

Unfortunately for our purposes, the report on the pilot explains (Central Statistics Office 2018: 11) that the answers to Q13 on Irish being the main household language were not reliable. When the question was cross-tabulated against the ability to speak Irish by all family members, some 59% of the people living in families in which Irish was reported as the main spoken language said that they were not able to speak Irish. In addition, 76% of those families had at least one family member who could not speak Irish at all. Q15 in the pilot survey was not successful either because the number of positive responses was too low to render them useful. The CSO (2018: 17) found that the number of people aged 18 or over who indicated that they had grown up in a household which spoke Irish (1.1%) was less than the number of people who did not answer this question (2.5%). Replicating these numbers in a full census would not allow significant small area statistics or cross-tabulation to be conducted on people who have grown up in Irish-speaking families while keeping the information anonymous. In addition, it was felt that asking a question to which up to 99% of the population would have a similar answer would not be an efficient use of resources. In contrast, pilot question 14 was statistically successful and will provide useful information in the future on how well those who describe themselves as speakers of Irish believe they can speak the language.

Thus, because the census currently does not provide reliable data on home language usage nor on whether people were brought up as Irish speakers, language planning initiatives in the Gaeltacht have tried to use the available information on frequency of usage as a proxy for both language ability and use in the home. Those who claimed to speak Irish in the 2016 census were asked to say how frequently they did so and could tick all valid boxes:

1. Daily, in the education system
2. Daily, outside the education system
3. Weekly
4. Less often
5. Never.

The number of daily speakers outside the education system is often considered as the 'real' number of Irish speakers. The variable is broadly useful, but the frequency does not definitely reflect ability to speak well, as discussed in the data below. In addition, because of the way in which statistics are administered, two data rows need to be combined in order to calculate the exact number of daily speakers: people who speak Irish daily outside of the education system + people who speak Irish daily outside and within the education system. There are a number of other difficulties in the combination of frequency options. Schooling is overtly mentioned in 1 and 2, for example, and sets something of an agenda. Options 3, 4 and 5 are not related to schooling but do not offer any other contextual choices for settings where usage could be envisaged.

Calculating the number of households with children that use Irish regularly is still problematic when using the available census data on frequency of usage because the data was gathered and processed for individuals. In order to try to arrive at an approximation, it is necessary to first define an Irish-speaking family or household and then extract information for the individuals within those households from the census data. For this discussion, the CSO was able to provide data for households in which there was at least one adult (defined as 19 years old and older in the census data) and at least one child (18 years or younger) who were returned as speaking Irish daily outside the education system (or inside and outside the education system). Although a useful proxy, there are still some problems with the data. The figures cover all families made up of parents and children who speak Irish regularly, but we cannot be sure about the frequency they speak it at home, nor about the ability of every other person in the household to speak Irish, the frequency with which they do so, nor how much English or any other language is used. It is also possible to imagine a few examples where adult children of the household who are over 19 years old would speak Irish on a daily basis, but not their parents, or a mix between children who are now adults and children who are still under 18. We cannot verify the relationship between family members from the statistics, but nevertheless, whatever the household composition, we can say that these family members are speaking Irish daily and that it is likely that they do this at home. Table 1 presents the

Table 1 Numbers of Irish speaking households with children in Gaeltacht counties (2016)

State	Number of households 6,254	Gaeltacht 1,796	Outside Gaeltacht 4,458
Meath	233	37	196
Cork	491	85	406
Kerry	263	161	102
Waterford city and county	166	60	106
Galway city	128	40	88
Galway county	1,005	842	163
Mayo	155	51	104
Donegal	714	520	194

Source CSO calculation from 2016 census data based on at least one adult and one child returned as daily speakers of Irish outside + inside and outside the education system estimated number of Irish-speaking households in the Gaeltacht areas in each county.

This gives an estimation of there being some 85 households in the Gaeltacht areas of Co. Cork where children are being bought up speaking Irish. The majority of these are in the Múscraí region. There is a second Gaeltacht area in Cork, the island of Cléire off the southern coast (See Map 1). To protect anonymity, the CSO was not able to provide the breakdown of figures for the island, but according to the 2016 census there were 147 people living in Cléire, of whom 24.8% (over the age of 3) spoke Irish daily outside the education system and *Scéim Labhairt na Gaeilge* returns from 1993 to 2011 reveal that between 2 and 6 families in any one year were awarded the grant. It is likely that there are only a very few households in Cléire that would meet the criteria as set out. It is therefore reasonable to take the estimated number of Irish-speaking homes with children in Múscraí to be a little over 80 according to the 2016 census and this method.

Identifying Irish-Speaking Families with Children in Múscraí

The team conducting the background research for the Múscraí language plan undertook extensive fieldwork, including public meetings, targeted meetings and surveys of parents and pupils at all schooling levels. For the purpose of this discussion, we will concentrate on the survey data from questionnaires and meetings with parents of school-going children, and the questionnaires filled in by the primary and secondary school students themselves. The questionnaires to parents were distributed via their school-going children and contained 34 questions about their linguistic background, skills and habits in a mixture of multiple choice and Likert scale replies, many allowing spaces for open, qualitative responses. All the questionnaires are available in the appendices to the published language plan (Meitheal Pleanála Teanga Mhúscraí 2017).

The data collected was informed by 620 parents in 326 households, 186 of which declared that they spoke Irish to some degree at home with their children. This data only includes information from those households that returned their questionnaire and must by necessity only include those who had children in primary or secondary level, not those who only had children in pre-school or who had left school before the Leaving Certificate, typically taken by those who are 17 to 18 years old. Although substantial in quantity, it therefore represents a minimum number of the possible households targeted. The data reveals elements that challenge the reliability of using the census data in linguistic viability studies, but does provide valuable refinement to our understanding of the number and nature of Irish-speaking households and their sociolinguistic context.

Figures 1 and 2 contrast the skill sets in Irish of the parents with the frequency with which they use the language. The frequency question was purposely modelled on that from the Census to help elucidate whether being a daily speaker of the language corresponded to a high level of fluency, as often assumed. Here we see that 43% of parents say that they speak Irish every day, but that only 21% claim to be fully fluent in the language. A further 21% did report being able to speak Irish 'well' although not fluently, but the overall conclusion is that there is no direct correspondence between daily usage and full fluency.

186 households (57%) of the 326 in the study reported using some Irish at home with their children. Parents were asked to say what

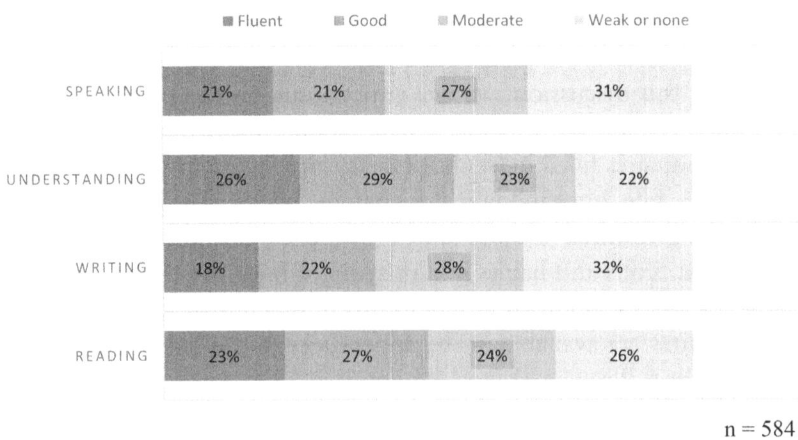

Fig. 1 Irish language skills of parents of school pupils in Múscraí (2017)

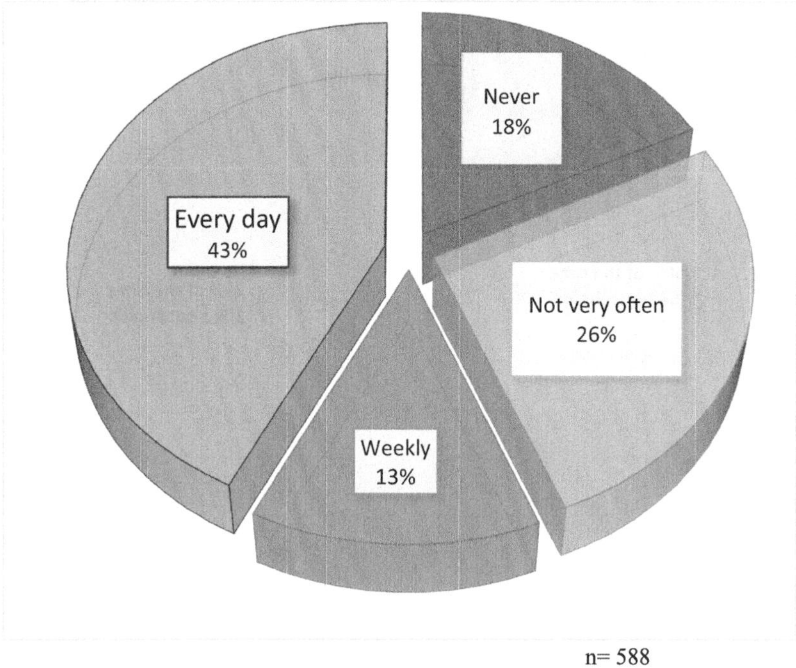

Fig. 2 Parents' frequency of speaking Irish

percentage of the time Irish was spoken in their households. This form of questioning builds on a long research tradition of approximating the number of households where Irish is the main language by the proportion of time spent speaking it. Figure 3 shows that of the 186 households, 9 said that Irish was used all the time while a further 17 said that Irish was used at least three-quarters of the time, giving a total of 26 homes where Irish was the main language, or about 8% of the total households in the survey. In ethnographic follow-up conversations with some of these parents, the general difficulty of estimating the relative quantity and frequency of Irish used came to the fore. Even for those households which declared themselves wholly Irish speaking, English (and in some cases another language) were also present to some degree. It was felt that saying that one's home was wholly or predominantly Irish speaking was at once taking a linguistic stance and reflecting whether or not

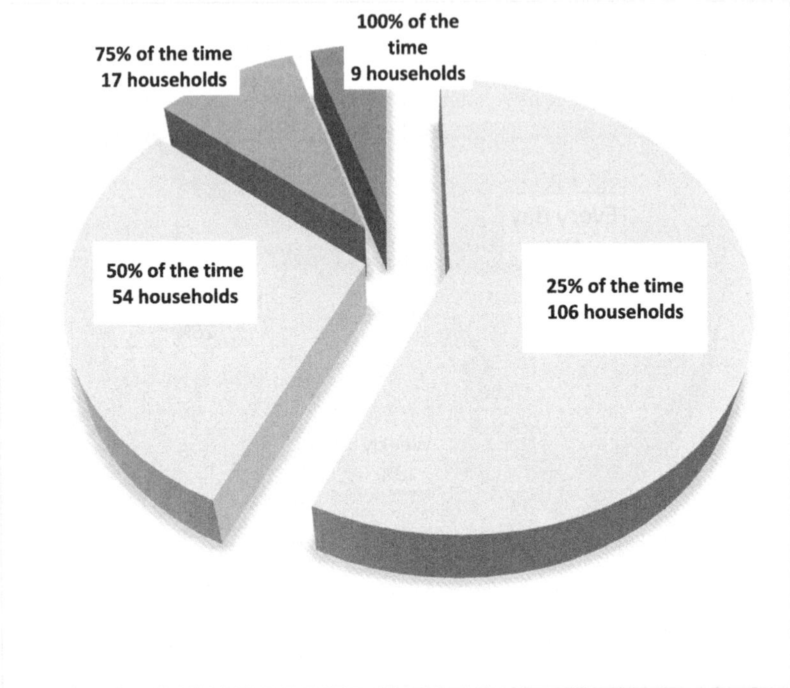

Fig. 3 Frequency of Irish usage at home according to parents

such a family language policy was succeeding. This underlines the reality that bringing up children in an Irish-speaking household requires active engagement, extra effort and thoughtful application. As reflected in an earlier study in Múscraí and in Corca Dhuibhne (Ó hIfearnáin 2013), a recurring comment among parents was that there are no longer any 'accidental Irish speakers' in the younger age groups; children no longer become competent speakers unselfconsciously without the deliberate input of parents, other family and community members and institutional supports, particularly from educators. A secondary observation was made that not all homes where the children are proficient and high frequency speakers of Irish actually speak Irish from 75 to 100% of the time because another language is also spoken, sometimes a language other than English and in some cases more than one other language. This challenges the binary nature of the dominant discourse in Irish language policy that sees Irish and English on a closed graduated scale where if families are using 40% Irish, they are understood to be using 60% English or vice versa. This linear interpretation of household bilingualism is deeply engrained, most clearly in initiatives such as *Scéim Labhairt na Gaeilge*, which encouraged sole use of Irish at home and have been the backdrop to the state's Gaeltacht family language policy since the 1930s. A monolingual strategy in favour of Irish that measured its success in how much English had been resisted had a certain inherent logic in a situation defined as a conflict between Irish and English for family language dominance, in which the stakes were very high for Irish. It remains clearly logical that for a minority language to be passed on to the younger generation, the input in that language must be as strong as possible, at home and supported by school and the wider community. However, not all families in the study agreed that the application of an Irish-only home policy stance necessarily precludes other languages being used on occasion or even regularly, despite the seeming contradiction. The population of Múscraí, like all of Ireland, has become increasingly linguistically diverse, the small Gaeltacht area now home to several hundred people from a variety of non-English speaking backgrounds from around Europe and beyond. Several parents claimed that their children have high linguistic skills in Irish and in English and/or in another language, which they use *all the time* at home, having 'full' linguistic identities in each language rather than a mixed language background that could be described on a linear scale of success or shortfall in intergenerational transmission of Irish. The current data does not enable us to test the degree to which these children master their different languages, but the increasingly multilingual nature of Irish society in both urban and rural settings will require further research into understanding the ways in which individuals, families and the Gaeltacht communities mobilise their language repertoire and what effect this will have on their Irish skills and usage.

When the findings of the pre-language planning research were made public in Múscraí, there was some consternation that the number of families who claimed to use predominantly Irish at home was so small. Many had believed that it would be much higher because of the positive image that they had formed of Irish language practices (discussed above and further below), because of the indications from the widely publicised 2016 census data that 23.1% of the population in Múscraí were daily speakers of Irish (nearly 900 people), and above all that the last returns for *Scéim Labhairt na Gaeilge* in the area in 2011 showed that the grant for Irish-speaking families was awarded to 101 households. There seemed to have been a catastrophic decline in just six or seven years.

Scéim Labhairt na Gaeilge was an award to Irish-speaking households of €260 per year. Replacing an earlier version of the scheme that started in 1933, which identified individual children for the grant rather than households, it operated from 1993 until 2011. It was framed as an incentive scheme to encourage families to keep speaking Irish as their only home language and to attend a Gaeltacht Irish-medium school. There was also a reduced grant which could be awarded to families who were deemed by the inspectors to be potentially fully Irish speaking and who might be encouraged to make an additional effort to work towards the full grant. The understanding in Múscraí, and doubtless in other Gaeltacht regions, had long been that the full grant was awarded by the inspectors to Irish-speaking households; typically, where the parents were Irish speakers and the children were fluent in the language. It was also understood that the reduced grant was given to households where one parent spoke Irish or where the children clearly spoke some Irish at home but were not fully fluent at the age-appropriate level. There is, of course, a difference between that local 'folk' interpretation and the sophisticated analysis by Ó Bróithe (2008, 2012) of the dynamics of the grant and how it was awarded. That analysis includes the differences between the language skills of elder and younger siblings and the estimate to what degree the numbers of grants made corresponded to the actual role of the language in the home. As it was intended to incentivise the partially Irish-speaking households to strengthen the place of Irish in their home, the reduced grant was time-limited and could not be awarded indefinitely while the children were still in full-time education, as was the case for the full grant. In the latter years of the scheme, a decision was made (Ó Bróithe 2012 and personal communication) that rather than stopping the reduced grant for families who remained partially Irish speaking at the end of its term, it would be more equitable and more in keeping with the aim of the scheme to award those families the full grant instead of cancelling it and classing them as no different to the non-Irish-speaking families in the area. Figure 4 shows the *Scéim Labhairt na Gaeilge* full and reduced grants in the Múscraí Gaeltacht from the school years 1993–1994 until 2010–2011 and Table 2 the grants made in the last year of the scheme (2010–2011) and the average number of awards annually for the period 1993 until 2005, when the switch from reduced to full grants for those families came into effect.

The *Scéim Labhairt na Gaeilge* data and the information from the language planning initiative research in 2017 point to an unexpected finding. There is little or no evidence of any change in the number or proportion of households that use Irish as their main home language in

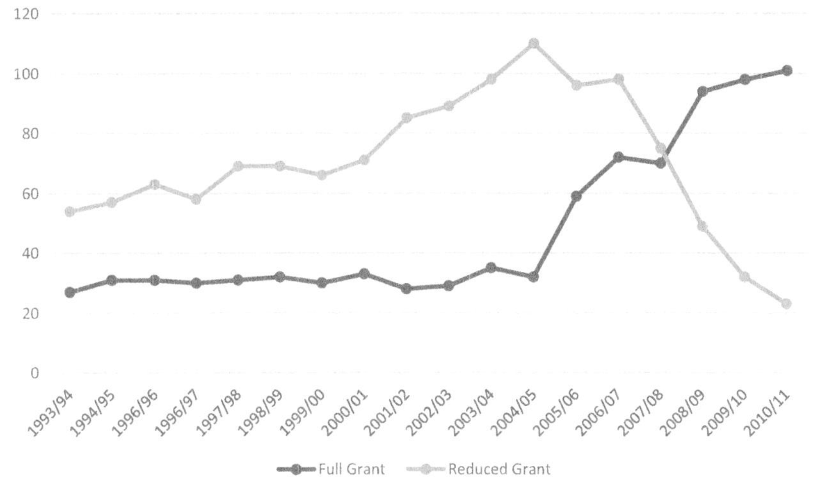

Fig. 4 Numbers of full and reduced grants to households under Scéim Labhairt na Gaeilge from school year 1993–1994 until 2010–2011

Table 2 Household grants under *Scéim Labhairt na Gaeilge* in Múscraí in school year 2010–2011 and averages for the award in the periods 1993–1994 to 2004–2005 and 2005–2006 to 2010–2011

	Full grants awarded	Reduced grants awarded
School year 2010–2011	101	23
Average 1993/4–2004/5	30	74

Source Department of Tourism, Culture, Arts, Gaeltacht, Sport and Media the Múscraí Gaeltacht since at least the early 1990s. Raising children in an Irish-speaking home is certainly a minority pursuit in the area, undertaken by some 25 to 30 families at any one time, which is less than 10% of the families in the area with school-going children, but the stability in the numbers is nevertheless remarkable. Given the time span of at least 30 years, these cannot be the same families, although qualitative inquiry does point to core kindred groups among these families through the generations, families being concentrated in Cúil Aodha in the centre-north of Múscraí and a smaller hub in the Béal Átha an Ghaorthaidh area to the south. The Irish-speaking families in the other areas within Múscraí and those who speak Irish to a greater extent than most in the area do, in the majority, also have family connections to one of those two core areas. Further supporting this pattern, the data on Irish-speaking households calculated from the 2016 census points to a similar number of households now as those recognised by the full and reduced *Scéim Labhairt na Gaeilge* grant in the 1990s (ranging between 81 and 100 grants in total per year).

The apparent stability in the numbers of families who speak predominantly Irish at home cannot, however, mask the differences that contemporary parents of young families see in the linguistic environment when compared to their own youth. In discussions about the findings of the 2017 research, one father had the impression that the current situation was nothing like it was in his youth, some thirty years ago, when it seemed to him that much more Irish was spoken in his own local area and around Múscraí. Even allowing for the possible interpretation offered by another parent that when one is young one tends to spend a lot of time with family, family friends and neighbours and that for the more strongly Irish-speaking families those would also be more Irish speaking than the average, there is clearly a change in habitual Irish speakers' perceptions of language use in their local community. Current research participants observe that there were more interlocutors in the past who may not have spoken Irish all the time at home but who would speak Irish to the more regular Irish speakers, and we can see from the 2017 qualitative responses that many of those who are habitual speakers and also those who are less fluent in Irish, or who use it infrequently, both perceive a widening gap in linguistic practices between them.

Fluent speakers regarding less fluent speakers:

Níl muinín ann gurbh fhiú an beagán Gaolainne a úsáid agus tógáil diaidh ar ndiaidh. (There is not enough confidence that it is worth speaking a little Irish and gradually building it up.)

Ní mór an misneach a thabhairt do gach éinne í a labhairt.
(We should encourage everyone to to speak it.)

... rá leo bheith cróga agus an méid atá acu a labhairt le daoine fásta eile agus le gach éinne.
(Tell them to be brave and use the amount they have with other adults and everyone else.)

Ní fheadar. Tá níos mó Gaolainne ag daoine máguaird ná cheapfá, ach fós, leisc orthu [í a úsáid] agus is é an Béarla atá le clos go formhór.

(I do not know. There is much more Irish in the area than you might think, but they are reluctant to use it and it is English that is heard the most.)

Less Fluent Speakers Regarding Their Relations with Fluent Speakers:

Ní bhíonn an deis agam labhairt le cainteoirí maithe.
(I do not get the opportunity to converse with good speakers.)

Caithfimid níos mó Gaeilge a labhairt sa bhaile agus iarracht a dhéanamh le daoine eile.

(We have to speak more Irish at home an make the effort to speak to others.)

It would be good if the fluent speakers would be more patient.

It is hard to talk easily. I hear adults using it and if people meet outside the school, they speak it.

> It would be good if the community encouraged and helped those who don't have as good Irish.

We are fortunate to be able to make a longitudinal comparison of the current perceptions of Irish-speaking parents with quantitative and qualitative research conducted among fluent Irish speakers in Múscraí from November 2000 through January 2003 (Ó hIfearnáin 2006, 2007, 2013). At that time, participants were asked if they felt if the amount of Irish being used in the community was similar to ten years previously, or if more or less Irish was being spoken. Overall, the fluent speakers interviewed believed that the situation was fairly stable or even improving at the time, with 170 of the 230 participants saying that Irish was being used with similar frequency (89 participants) or more frequently (81 people). However, despite the overall impression of resilience to language change, there was already a nuanced difference between the perception of the younger and older participants. Whereas over 80% of those in all age groups over 30 believed that similar amounts or more Irish were being used, only half those under 29 believed this to be the case. Similarly, although a large majority of those over 30 did not believe that Irish was dying out in the Gaeltacht, the under 30s were even split on the question. Once again, the qualitative work in the community was able to offer insights into why the habitual fluent speakers saw less of a change. Regarding their use of Irish in their local shopping habits, for example, an area most noted as a contrast in the 2017 research, older people in 2000–2003 had fairly set patterns of where and to whom they spoke Irish. Indeed, only one in five of the fluent Irish speakers over 30 years old (regardless of if they regarded Irish as their first or as acquired language) spoke Irish 'rarely' or 'never' when shopping locally. This reflects both the language ability of the retailers at the time and the overall linguistic reality for those generations. The younger fluent speakers' more pessimistic view of Irish in wider society doubtless reflects their own experience of their peer-group, a pattern which is further advanced in the 2017 research.

The Múscraí language planning initiative questionnaires for both parents and secondary pupils gathered information on Irish and English usage in a wide variety of social settings. The picture that emerges from the secondary school pupils (around 13 to 18 years old in the Irish education system), presented in Fig. 6, is one where Irish has a fairly strong hold in a core group of families, is used by the vast majority of the teenagers in school—including higher usage in the schoolyard than in general society—and is fairly well-anchored in organised clubs and societies, but where the peer-group uses mostly or only English in most other physical and online social settings, regardless of their linguistic ability and background. Figure 5 shows that of the 135 secondary pupils who speak Irish fluently, around 35 speak mostly or at least half of the time to both their parents and their siblings in Irish. The parental survey allows us to identify 23 secondary school children from the households where Irish is the main language, so we can hypothesise that this figure includes them and some of the 56 other children from households returned as speaking Irish half of the time, often with one of the parents (Fig. 6).

The data clearly points to increasingly visible core groups of families whose speak Irish at home and whose children continue to use the language among their inner peer-group. Nearly all secondary pupils have strong competencies in Irish and although this data is only a snapshot

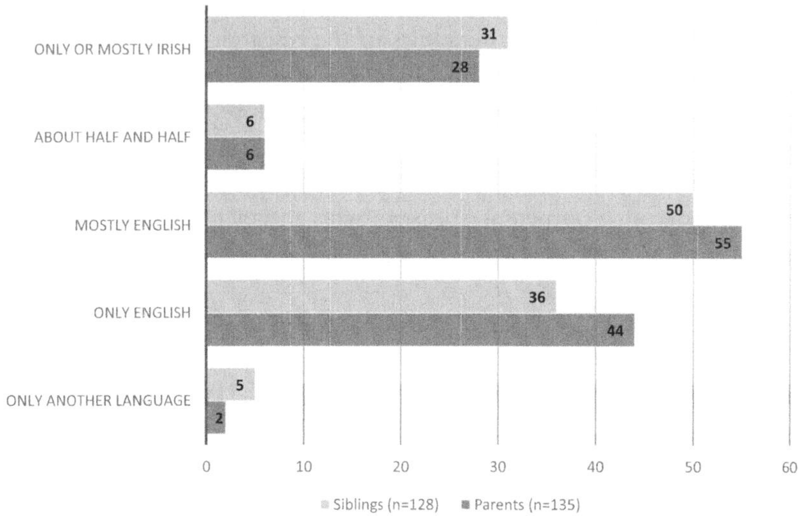

Fig. 5 Language use with parents and siblings of secondary school pupils who claim fluent Irish

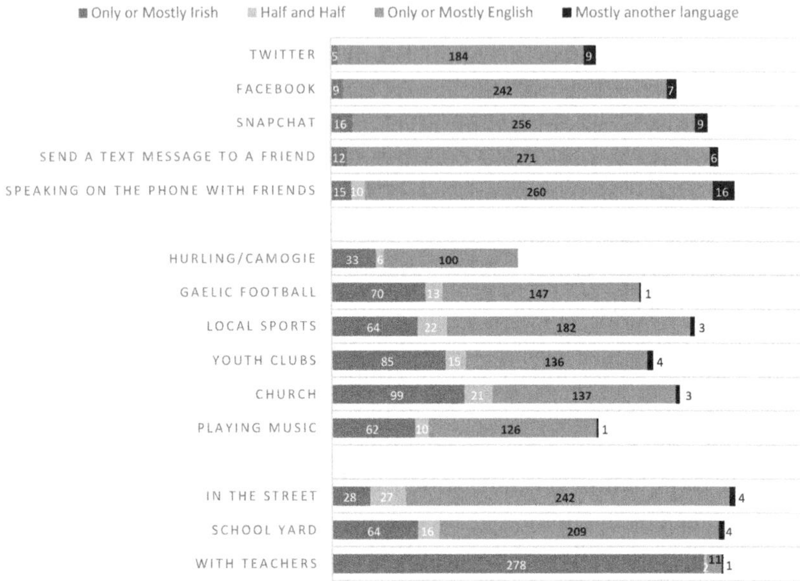

Fig. 6 Use of Irish ouside the home by secondary school pupils (all language abilities)

in time, the experience of the adults in the research projects shows that once children leave school and organised activities, their contact with Irish reduces rapidly unless they are from or close to one of the more strongly Irish-speaking kin groups. We can thus see that although the core appears to be holding for the time being, the outer circles of those less frequent but competent speakers who interact regularly with that core, and who over time before now might have joined it, is increasingly compromised.

Perceptions from the Periphery of the Core Language Group

In a series of essays published over an extended period, Nancy Dorian (2014: 135–202) has repeatedly emphasised the importance of including the working margins of the language group as a central consideration, both linguistically and socially, in understanding the linguistic dynamics of the core, fluent, active speakers and of their view of their linguistic community. Such an understanding is important for successful language planning intervention in favour of Irish. The Múscraí language plan draws attention to the very strong community spirit in Múscraí (2017: 60–62, inter alia). Language is a core element in what defines the local identity, but bonds of family and neighbourhood loyalty transcend language ability and usage in many instances. The emphasis here is on language use in the home and the striking resilience of a relatively stable minority within the community who continue to speak Irish at home and raise their children as speakers. Such home or first language speakers have been shown to have a set of beliefs and ideologies about Irish which are different in nuance both to other fluent speakers of Irish (Ó hIfearnáin 2013) and to the wider community. The needs of the children from this core group of families are clearly different to second language speakers from a linguistic perspective despite their cultural similarities to the wider community (Ó Duibhir 2019). Early education, medical and developmental services stand out in the fieldwork. However, within this and many other Gaeltacht communities, they are a small proportion of the local population. Further, policies which focus only on maintaining the core group without addressing the context of the wider community can only, at best, preserve the current state of linguistic affairs. Indeed, the 1956 language Inquiry (Central Statistics Office 1956: 21) identified some 41 Irish-speaking households in Múscraí, which is similar to the number in the current discussion in that it also included households without school-age children. However, it also reported some 823 households that spoke both Irish and English, which highlights the main area of decline since that time.

The positive perception of the strength of the Irish language in this area, and in other areas where Irish remains a language of the home but very much in a minoritised context, is important in understanding the overall view of the community and requires more discussion in the language planning context. The data gathered on home and family use of Irish in the Múscraí language planning research provides some glimpses and explanations of how, despite the very low numbers of Irish-speaking families and the view among the core speaker groups that the use of Irish outside their homes is declining, many in the 'linguistic periphery' see a contrary trend. A high number of the most fluent Irish-speaking parents occupy professions which are in the public eye. Over half of them work in education, health care and public administration, while 18 and 17%, respectively, work in a professional trade (plumbers, electricians) and in local shops and restaurants. To many in the area who do not speak Irish regularly or even not at all, it may well appear that a great many of their daily contacts are fluent Irish speakers, and they will know that many of them speak Irish with their families at home. As in many parts of Ireland, schooling is the key area where non-speakers come into contact with the Irish language. In this Gaeltacht region, as we have seen, the schools are Irish-medium and the pupils speak Irish with their teachers. Pupils are quite confident of their ability in spoken Irish, only 2 of the 298 in the survey saying that their Irish was 'weak'. An analysis of the data for all adult fluent Irish speakers included in the survey shows that more than half of them work professionally with the language or use the language in their professional lives (Fig. 7) During the 2001–2003 fieldwork, the remarkably high number of fluent speakers in Múscraí who worked in education, often travelling daily outside of the area to neighbouring districts and towns sometimes quite far away, solicited further enquiry. The general conclusion of discussions was that for those who were brought up as Irish speakers, professional use of the language was often an extension of their stance on the language. As in many rural areas, positions within education and other areas of public service had always been respected and encouraged by parents, but the opportunities for Irish speakers to make meaningful contributions enhanced the attraction. As such, using Irish in one's profession was generally an extension of one's use of Irish at home and community, not that one had become a regular speaker because of the profession.

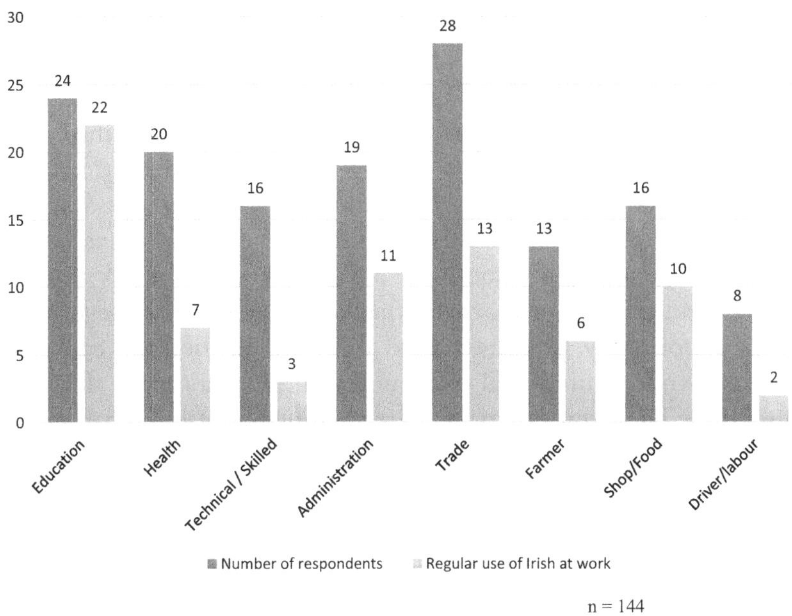

Fig. 7 Employment of fluent Irish speakers and language use at work

Conclusion

Irish society is changing very rapidly, socially and linguistically, but these changes are more complex than the simple replacement of Irish by English as the main language of home and community. The case of the Múscraí Gaeltacht area highlights some unexpected findings regarding the ability for linguistic regeneration in the family over an extended period. Habitual users of Irish as a main home language have been in the minority for several generations in the area, yet the absolute numbers of such families have remained relatively stable for several decades. Parents who are the most fluent and regular speakers of Irish do indeed believe that there is much less Irish spoken around them than in their own youth and worry about sustainability in the longer term. The research highlights certain key elements in the sustainability of Irish as a home language in such a minority setting. A parent, or ideally parents having strong language skills, is the first key factor, but is not enough on its own for children to acquire and successfully continue to use the language among their siblings and to any extend beyond their immediate family networks. The active decision and determination of parents to bring up their children as Irish speakers was identified as the second key factor by the parents in the research and is supported by the findings. The local community institutions that support the linguistic endeavours of families, particularly the schools and social outlets for children in the younger age groups are a third key contributory factor in Múscraí. Indeed, key members of that core group of language practitioners perform key language-related functions in the local education, voluntary work, professional and public administration for the whole community. These three elements were identified by research participants as the very minimum requirements. Where all parties see a decline in Irish usage is among those who have relatively high skills in the language but who do not have the daily connections at home or otherwise with the most fluent speakers, constant contact that was more common in the recent past. The lack of regular usage itself can lead to a circle of attrition where speakers become out of practice and sometimes reluctant to speak the language with more fluent interlocutors.

The language planning initiatives in this and other Gaeltacht regions have identified the need for efforts and resources in supporting those who have consciously chosen to continue to use Irish as their home language, but the sustenance of that core group requires investment in what Dorian (2014: 156, 167) has called their 'working margins' because that wider community is not completely culturally separate from the active linguistic minority and its desire to maintain itself. The members of that linguistic 'periphery' are, of course, deserving of attention in their own right and not simply as a support to the 'core'. Although there is no reason to assume that Irish could not continue as a home language in Múscraí and other Gaeltacht areas even if the wider community loses the language, making it little different to the rest of the country outside the Gaeltacht, where more isolated families continue to speak Irish, it is the sustenance dynamic of the interactions between the most fluent habitual speakers, the less frequent speakers and the wider community who have passive (or even no) knowledge of the language that make

Gaeltacht areas, even the 'weaker' of them, socially different from the scattered and isolated families of Irish speakers throughout the country.

References

Bunreacht na hÉireann/Constitution of Ireland. 1937. http://www.irishstatutebook.ie/pdf/en.cons.pdf. Accessed 10 April 2021.

Central Statistics Office. 2018. *Report on the Public Consultation on Content of Census 2021 and the Census Pilot Survey 2018.* Dublin: Central Statistics Office.

Central Statistics Office. 1956. *Census of Population, 1956*. Irish Language Inquiry: Unpublished report.

Central Statistics Office. 1966. *Census of Population of Ireland 1961. Irish Language with special tables for the Gaeltacht areas.* Dublin: The Stationery Office.

Comhchoiste Ghaeltacht Uíbh Ráthaigh. 2017. *Plean Teanga do Ghaeltacht Chiarraí Theas. 2018–2024.* Ceann Eich: Comhchoiste Ghaeltacht Uíbh Ráthaigh.

Dorian, N. 2014. Defining the Speech Community to Include its Working Margins. In N. Dorian, *Small-Language Fates and Prospects: Lessons of Persistence and Change from Endangered Languages. Collected Essays*, 156–166. Leiden and Boston: Brill.

Dunmore, S. 2002. A Cornish Revival? The Nascent Iconization of a Post-obsolescent Language. *Journal of Historical Sociolinguistics* 6: 1–26.

Gaeltacht Act 2012. No. 34 of 2012. http://www.irishstatutebook.ie/eli/2012/act/34/enacted/en/html. Accessed 10 April 2021.

Government of Ireland. 2010. *20-Year Strategy for the Irish Language 2010–2030.* Dublin: Government of Ireland.

Lyon, S. 1932. Explanatory Notes. *Census of Population, 1926. Volume VIII—Irish Language.* Dublin: The Stationery Office.

Mac Gréil, M., and R. Fergal. 2009. *The Irish Language and the Irish People: Report on the Attitudes towards, Competence in and Use of the Irish Language in the Republic of Ireland in 2007–08.* Maynooth: Department of Sociology, National University of Ireland, Maynooth.

Meitheal Pleanála Teanga Mhúscraí. 2017. *Plean Teanga do Limistéar Pleanála Teanga Mhúscraí.* Béal Átha an Ghaorthaidh: Comharchumann Forbartha Mhúscraí.

Mortell, P., R. Lane, A. de Róiste, V. Murphy, and T. O'Connor. 2008. *Gaeltacht Mhúscraí. Anailís Riachtanas Socheacnamaíoch agus Cultúrtha. A Socio-economic and Cultural Needs Analysis.* Cork: Cork Institute of Technology.

Nolan, J.S. 2018. Maintenance and Revitalization of Gallo. In *The Routledge Handbook of Language Revitalization*, ed. L. Hinton, L. Huss, and G. Roche, 289–296. Abingdon: Routledge.

Ó Bróithe, E. 2008. *Scéim Labhairt na Gaeilge: Staidéar cróineolaíoch ar theaghlaigh faoin Scéim.* Unpublished MA dissertation, National University of Ireland, Galway.

Ó Bróithe, E. 2012. Scéim Labhairt na Gaeilge: Feidhm agus mífheidhm. In *An Chonair Chaoch: An Mionteangachas sa Dátheangachas*, ed. C. Lenoach, C. Ó Giollagáin, and B. Ó Curnáin, 237–268. Indreabhán: Leabhar Breac.

Ó Duibhir, P. 2019. Bilingual Education in Minority Language Contexts: When a High Level of Linguistic Competence is Not Enough. *ELIA: Estudios de Lingüística Inglesa Aplicada* 1, 39–64.

Ó Giollagáin, C., and M. Charlton. 2015. *Nuashonrú ar an Staidéar Cuimsitheach ar Úsáid na Gaeilge sa Ghaeltacht: 2006–2011.* Na Forbacha: Údarás na Gaeltachta.

Ó Giollagáin, C., S. Mac Donnacha, F. Ní Chualáin, A. Ní Shéaghdha, and M. O'Brien. 2007. *Comprehensive Linguistic Study of the Use of Irish in the Gaeltacht: Principal Findings and Recommendations.* Dublin: Department of Community, Rural and Gaeltacht Affairs.

Ó Gliasáin, M. 1990. *Language Shift Among Schoolchildren in Gaeltacht Areas 1974–1984: An Analysis of the Distribution of £10 Grant Qualifiers.* Dublin: Institiúid Teangeolaíochta Éireann.

Ó Gliasáin, M. 1996. *The Language Question in the Census of Population.* Dublin: Institiúid Teangeolaíochta Éireann.

Ó hIfearnáin, T. 2006. *Beartas Teanga.* An Aimsir Óg, Páipéar Ócáideach 7. Dublin: Coiscéim.

Ó hIfearnáin, T. 2007. Raising Children to be Bilingual in the Gaeltacht: Language Preference and Practice. *International Journal of Bilingual Education and Bilingualism* 10 (4): 510–528.

Ó hIfearnáin, T. 2013. Family Language Policy, First Language Irish Speaker Attitudes and Community-based Response to Language Shift. *Journal of Multilingual and Multicultural Development* 34: 348–365.

Ó hIfearnáin, T. 2014. Paradoxes of Engagement with Irish Language Community Management, Practice and Ideology. In *Endangered Languages: Beliefs and Ideologies in Language Documentation and Revitalization*, ed. Peter K. Austin and Julia Sallabank, 29–51. Oxford: Oxford University Press/British Academy.
Ó Riagáin, P. 2018. *Measures of Language Proficiency in Censuses and Surveys: A Comparative Assessment.* Cham: Palgrave Macmillan.
Seoighe, S., C. Smith-Christmas, and T. Ó hIfearnáin. 2021. *Teaghlaigh atá ag tógáil clainne le Gaeilge lasmuigh den Ghaeltacht.* Dublin: Glór na nGael.
Zuckermann, Ghil'ad. 2020. *Revivalistics. From the Genesis of Israeli to Language Reclamation in Australia and Beyond.* Oxford: Oxford University Press.

Alternatives to 'Traditional' Transmission

Native and Non-native Speakers' School Language Practices and Transmission in Upper Lusatia

Nicole Dołowy-Rybińska

This chapter provides insights into language practices and strategies of minority language transmission in a situation of contact between native and non-native speakers of a minority language who learn together in a bilingual school. The particularity of the described situation lies in the way both communities function, their mutual relations and their language ideologies. The minority language community in question, Upper Sorbian, is traditionally oriented towards native speaker and intergenerational transmission stances. Their strategy of language maintenance lies in protecting it against non-Sorbian speakers, namely Germans. Concurrently, attitudes towards the Sorbs and their language in the region on the part of the wider community are strained, if not hostile. As a result of these conditions, those non-native Sorbs who are

N. Dołowy-Rybińska (✉)
Polish Academy of Sciences, Institute of Slavic Studies, Warszawa, Poland

M. Hornsby and W. McLeod (eds.), *Transmitting Minority Languages*, Palgrave Studies in Minority Languages and Communities,
https://doi.org/10.1007/978-3-030-87910-5_6

learning Upper Sorbian through formal education face different obstacles in becoming new speakers of a minority language.

Some of these problems are linked to the way minority language education functions. It separates Sorbian native speakers and learners, giving the latter little chance to practise Sorbian. Yet, as is presented in this chapter, immersion of non-native individuals into Sorbian and allowing them to acquire the language with their native-speaking friends can produce positive results. Other obstacles in becoming a new speaker of Sorbian are connected to the traditionalist character of the Sorbian community and its strong connection with Catholicism. On this basis, those Sorbian learners who are Catholics have better chances to become accepted as part of the community. Sorbian is transmitted to them through Catholic community life, which takes place mainly in Sorbian. Another difficulty for learners is that provision in the Sorbian language that is not school-related, traditional or community-based is very limited. As a consequence, learners have few opportunities to have contact with Sorbian and to practise it. However rare, situations in which Sorbian learners engage in activities in Sorbian and cooperate with Sorbian native speakers do happen. Minority language transmission through a community of practice gives learners the chance to speak Sorbian and become recognised as a part of the group.

The Upper Sorbs: Sociolinguistic Context and Sorbian-German Relationships

The Sorbs are a Slavic minority living in eastern Germany near the borders with Poland and the Czech Republic. Although the Sorb population is relatively small, with about 60,000 members, they are internally divided into two communities that speak two separate Slavic languages: Upper Sorbs living in the Free State of Saxony, in the area historically known as Upper Lusatia, roughly comprising the Bautzen and Görlitz districts (with approximately 40,000 people who identify themselves as Upper Sorbs and 10,000–15,000 Upper Sorbian speakers) (Elle 2010), and Lower Sorbs (with approximately 20,000 members and up to 4,000 speakers, with intergenerational transmission almost entirely interrupted between the 1930s and 1950s) (Norberg 1996; Jodlbauer et al. 2001) inhabiting the Land of Brandenburg. As the sociolinguistic and cultural situations of these two communities vary significantly, as do the strategies used in contacts with Germans, this chapter focuses only on Upper Sorbs. Consequently, henceforth, when referring to 'the Sorbs', this will mean 'Upper Sorbs' and 'Sorbian', 'Upper Sorbian'.

The Upper Sorbian community is also internally diverse. The core of this group is the Catholic Sorbs—the only Sorbian community where intergenerational transmission of the language has been maintained, and where the youngest generation is still raised in Sorbian as the first language (Walde 2004). In Catholic Upper Lusatia, the ideal of a monolingual Sorbian household has been maintained even if many Sorbian children are now raised bilingually. In the Catholic territory, in about 70 villages, the Sorbs constitute the majority or a significant proportion of the inhabitants (Jaenecke 2003; Elle 2014), and it is possible to use Sorbian there on a daily basis. This is also the only Sorbian community where the Sorbian identity is linked to the use of Sorbian. Among the Catholic Sorbs, the division between the 'Sorbs' and the 'Germans' is important. The 'Sorbs' are those who speak Sorbian, participate in Sorbian village life and preferably are members of the Catholic community. The 'Germans' are thus those who are not Sorbian native speakers, who live outside of the Sorbian-speaking territory and who are not Catholics. The notion of 'Germans' thus includes both those who have no connection with the Sorbian community and those who are of Sorbian descent, who often have double Sorbian and German identity, but are not directly connected to the Catholic Sorbian community and are not (native) Sorbian speakers. Because of their particular sociolinguistic situation, language maintenance and the existence of a strong language-based community, the Catholic Sorbs perceive themselves as the 'authentic' Sorbs, the only ones who are able to preserve the language, and often take the role of language guardians. As a consequence, the path to becoming a new speaker of Sorbian, and a part of the 'Sorbian club' is not obvious either for non-Catholic Sorbs or for German speakers (Dołowy-Rybińska and Ratajczak 2019a).

The Catholic Sorbian community is surrounded by Protestant Germans and other Sorbs who converted to Protestantism in the sixteenth century and have to a large extent assimilated linguistically and culturally with the Germans. The group of German (and German-speaking) Catholics is small, often consisting of people of Sorbian origin, and for that reason Catholics are often associated with the Sorbs and Sorbian language speakers. The Catholics' connection to the Sorbian language is deeply related to their faith and the practising of the Sorbian language religious and ethnic celebrations throughout the whole year. Catholic Sorbs protected in the past and still protect today their identity and language by constructing and enforcing a threefold boundary: religious (Catholics vs Protestants), ethnic (Sorbs vs Germans) and linguistic (Sorbian vs German) (see Schön and Scholze 2014). Even today, when the traditional Catholic bans and orders preventing marriages with non-Catholics are no longer definitive, and with the freedom of residence and lifestyle after the political change and the unification of Germany in 1990, the division between Catholic Sorbs and Germans remains strong and is maintained by both groups.

The strategy of 'parallel biculturalism' (Ratajczak 1998) practised for centuries by the Sorbs is based on the assumption: no language contact—no cultural conflict. Therefore, whenever Sorbs enter the German world they make their Sorbianness indiscernible and inaudible (Ratajczak 1998: 144). On the one hand, the separation of Sorbian and German worlds is designed to support the distinctiveness of the Sorbian community and not to expose it to assimilation. In the past, cultural and linguistic contact between the Sorbs and the Germans always ended up with language shift on the part of the minority language speakers. On the other hand, this attitude is enforced by German speakers who do not wish to hear the Sorbian language and claim openly that in Germany all people should speak German (Ratajczak 2011).

German-Sorbian relations may be understood in terms of the 'paradox of acceptance' (Ratajczak 2011: 35–39): the German inhabitants of Lusatia, in general, accept Sorbs and their language but on condition that it is not used in their presence. We often hear in Lusatia (and this concerns both German and Sorbian speakers) that it is 'not polite' to speak Sorbian when it cannot be understood by everyone, even those who are not directly involved in the conversation (Dołowy-Rybińska 2020). The discourse and related language ideology that the Sorbian language should not be used in the presence of Germans determines people's language practices: the Sorbs use Sorbian among themselves and switch to German when in mixed-language groups. The tactic of separating Sorbian and German worlds and avoiding speaking Sorbian in the presence of Germans has major consequences for potential new speakers of Sorbian. Non-native Sorbian speakers are classified by the Sorbian Catholics as 'Germans' regardless of their ethnic background and motivation to learn Sorbian and are excluded from Sorbian language conversations. This tactic has significant implications for the Sorbian language schooling system, which is now open to native-German-speaking pupils who are supposed to learn Sorbian alongside Sorbian native speakers.

The Upper Sorbian Schooling System and the Research Methodology

Upper Sorbian language teaching was introduced in Lusatia as early as 1945, just after the end of World War II (Pech 2001). Since 1952, a division between form 'A' (lessons conducted almost entirely in Upper Sorbian for pupils from Sorbian-speaking families) and form 'B' (in which Upper Sorbian was taught as a second language to German-speaking children) was established and applied in the schools within the Sorbian administrative settlement area, attended both by Sorbs and by German speakers. Teaching Sorbian in 'B' classes was a political compromise and, in general, was not effective. This system of dividing the 'native' Sorbs from 'non-natives' and enforcing the boundaries between the Sorbs and the Germans remained until its recent change in the first decade of the twenty-first century.

By the time of the political changes in Germany in 1990, the Sorbs realised that due to, among other things, the mixed-language marriages and migration of the Sorbs, the number of children brought up in the Sorbian language had started to decline even among the Catholic Sorbs. For the first time, Sorbian internal discourse opened up to the necessity of creating new speakers from among Sorbian learners. Labelled as 'Germans' despite their ethnic origin and expressed identity, there were among them both children from linguistically assimilated Sorbian families and Germans with no Sorbian background. The idea was to give students from German-speaking families the opportunity to integrate linguistically with the Sorbian speech community and become proficient in the language.

In the 1990s, the Sorbs initiated—at first only in the pre-school classes—the Witaj [Welcome] programme, a type of education (mainly) in the Sorbian language. Kindergartens that participated in the programme were attended by children of Sorbian-speaking and German-speaking families whose parents, for various reasons, wanted their children to learn Sorbian (Kaulfürstwowa 2008; Budarjowa 2009). However, the intensity of Sorbian language use depended on many factors: from the location of the establishment to the attitudes of the teacher and the parents (Menzel and Šołćina 2018). For the immersion education to bring results, the programme '2 plus' for primary and post-primary schools was established. The programme was based on the educational concept recommended by the European Union known as 'native language +2' (Gazsi 2005; Rindler-Schjerve and Vetter 2012). In the case of Lusatia, the programme consists of instruction in two languages (German and Upper Sorbian) and learning of a third language. However, due to the very differentiated level of the Sorbian language competences of pupils, this resulted in a different language policy in Witaj establishments (from full immersion to the use of Sorbian only for performances), as well as in the conviction, deeply rooted in the minds of many Germans, that they should not be forced to hear and speak Sorbian, bilingual teaching became an issue in the wider community.

At the beginning of grammar school education, at the fifth grade, students—depending on their family language, the extent of their Sorbian language education in kindergarten and primary school, and the competences gained there—are allocated to one of the language groups. The first is for students with 'native-like' Sorbian. This group is attended mainly by Sorbian native speakers from the Catholic community. They have many courses in the Sorbian language. The second group is for students who have developed Sorbian language competence. Here, we mainly find children from German-speaking homes who participated in the Witaj pre-school and primary school education. It is often attended by students from linguistically assimilated Sorbian homes, sometimes students from mixed Sorbian-German language families and rarely by Sorbian native speakers. This group has some bilingual lessons with two teachers and, additionally, lessons in Sorbian. In practice, the use of Sorbian depends on student language competence and attitudes and these vary from year to year. The third group is for students with poor Sorbian language competence: children from German-speaking homes who had only some Sorbian language lessons in primary school. Although they also have some lessons in Sorbian and some bilingual lessons with two teachers, their Sorbian language level is low,[1] and they are not expected to understand Sorbian or to speak it. The language groups division lasts to the end of the tenth grade. From the eleventh grade to the baccalaureate, the teaching system changes and for the two last years of their education students have a system of courses chosen on the basis of their individual interests and plans. However, because of the very differentiated language competences of students, the common courses are mainly in German.

The research presented in this chapter relates to the language practices of young people and the way the Sorbian language is transmitted among native and non-native students. The research was carried out between 2017 and 2019 at the Upper Sorbian Grammar School in Bautzen/Budyšin. This is a special place as it is the only Upper Sorbian grammar school. The method used consisted of anthropological research based on participant observations of the students' language practices at school and some after-school activities and in-depth interviews with students in the eleventh grade as well as focus group discussions with students in the tenth and eleventh grades. Excerpts from these recordings are used as the basis of the analysis and serve as an illustration of the issues presented.

Intra-School Relations Between Sorbian- and German Speakers: Towards Immersion

The strategy of separating the Sorbian and German linguistic worlds has important consequences for language transmission at school. Participant observation at school and during after-school activities revealed that while together in their group, Sorbs use local varieties of Upper Sorbian (Scholze 2008), but when they enter in contact with Sorbian learners who do not belong to their close community, they use mainly German. Only rarely are native Sorbian speakers and Sorbian language learners encouraged by individual teachers to use Sorbian and German in the same classroom space, and sometimes to engage in translanguaging (Dołowy-Rybińska 2020).

For Sorbian language learners, this situation is simultaneously comfortable and difficult. On the one hand, when everything is in German, they can easily participate in the conversation and not have the feeling of antagonism from the Sorbian first-language speakers.[2] On the other hand, as a consequence, they have no contact with Sorbian as a language of everyday life and spontaneous conversation. This makes it really difficult for them to improve their language skills (Dołowy-Rybińska 2018). It is also difficult for those who learned Sorbian to become legitimised as Upper Sorbian language speakers. This concerns those situations when language transmission takes place not only through school but also through participation in Sorbian religious and cultural life, as set out in the subsequent parts of this chapter.

From this perspective, individual students from German-speaking families who are learning in the Upper Sorbian 'native-language' group are the most interesting to investigate as far as language transmission at school is concerned. These few students represent a positive example of how language-acquisition-through-immersion works. Yet, it is not obvious how non-native Sorbs can be accepted into the first group. The criterion of being assigned to one of the groups is based on the different levels of Sorbian language competence pupils get in kindergarten and primary school. They have to be able to follow Sorbian language courses. However, competence is not a sufficient criterion for studying in the first group. Such a decision has to be strongly supported by these children's parents, as it goes against the principles accepted by the Sorbs and the 'Germans' in separating their linguistic worlds. These two sentences from a student express her path to becoming an active Sorbian speaker:

> *Naše staršі su to derje namakali a su prajili, zo dyrbimy to w maćernorěčnej rjadowni spytać. (…) A ja sym potom naraz serbsce móhła, dokelž sym dyrbjała.*
>
> (Our parents recognised it [that it is possible to learn Sorbian only in the first group] and said that we need to be in the native-speaking group. […] And suddenly I could speak Sorbian, because I had to.)
>
> (NF19, girl from a German-language family who is learning Sorbian in the first type of class of the eleventh grade)

This short quotation also points to the role of parents who were persuaded that the only way for their child to become fluent in Sorbian is through being immersed in the language, hence to be in the Sorbian native-speaking group. Such a decision was found to be 'strange' by the Sorbian teachers, who tried to discourage the parents and persuade them to send their daughter to the second group, explaining that it would be too difficult for their child to be in the Sorbian class. The parents did not give way on this point because of their background in education and their strong conviction that multilingualism was positive and possible to achieve only through immersion. Nevertheless, such attitudes among parents are rare, due to the habits of separating Sorbian and German, the low prestige of Sorbian and the lack of institutional support.

Another important aspect touched upon in this extract concerns the nature of immersion, with its forcible dimension of language use. The girl states that she had no problem with learning Sorbian because she had to communicate in this language: in her class, apart from one other student, all were Sorbian native speakers. This disproportion was too high to make the minority language speakers switch to the dominant language (see Baker and Wright 2017: 296), which usually happens when there are more German speakers in the classroom, and which actually happens in the second group. Yet, putting the dominant language speakers in the situation where they actually have to use a minority language is perceived by the Sorbs and the Germans as something extremely inappropriate. Therefore, immersion in Upper Sorbian through school education may be a way of becoming a new speaker only for a chosen few. This process is well described in the group discussion carried out among native speakers of Upper Sorbian.

LF: *Woni su za to, zo so wšo němsce čini.*

TF: *To ja tež rozumju, za nich je to ćežke, woni hewak sobu njepřińdu. Woni potom tón maćiznu njerozumja a to je škoda, hdyž dyrbja woni pod tym ćerpjeć. Snano pak by lěpje było, hdyž bychmy porjadnje dźěleni byli [...]*

KM: *To je wjetšina, ale dawaja tež młodostni kotřiž přińdu tu do našich rjadownjow z ryzy němskich swójbow, kotrež su wot pěstowarnje sem serbsce wuknyli a su přeco w serbskich rjadownjach byli a nětko tež sobu w serbskich kursach sedźa. Pola tych to njeje žadyn problem, te su to nawuknyli.*

TF: *Woni tež jara derje serbsce rěča.*

[...]

NDR: *Potajkim móže to fungować?*

LF: *Haj, hdyž su woni zwólniwe.*

JF: *Hdyž su woni ze Serbami w jednej rjadowni a Serbja z nimi tež serbsce rěča.*

TF: *Pola nas w zakładnej šuli běše tak, zo smy jednu holcu z ryzy němskeje swójby a jedneho hólca ze serbskim nanom a němskej maćerju w rjadowni měli. Dokelž my jako dźěći njejsmy němsce móhli běchu woni dwejo přećiwo dwacećom abo tak a woni su so potom takrjec dyrbjeli nam kłonić a tohodla nětko tež tak derje serbsce rěča, dokelž su to wot dźěćatstwa sem tak nawuknyli.*

KM: *A wot tutych njejsu tež wšitcy katolikojo! Ta šula je tajki medium kotryž je cyle njewotwisny wot nabožiny. Tak woni tež serbšćinu nawuknu a su tež integrowani. Te prašenje je, što po šuli budźe.*

(LF[3]: They [German students] prefer that everything is in German.

TF: Which I can understand, it is difficult for them, otherwise they would not participate. Then they don't understand the content and it is a pity, because afterwards they suffer. Probably, it would be better if we were well divided [...]

KM: That's the case for the majority, but there are also students who come to our classrooms from purely German families, who did learn Sorbian from kindergarten and thereafter in the Sorbian groups and now they participate in Sorbian courses. For them it is not a problem, they have learned it.

TF: They also speak very good Sorbian.

[...]

NDR: So, it can work?

LF: Yes, if they are willing.

JF: If they are in one classroom with Sorbs and the Sorbs also want to talk with them in Sorbian.

TF: In my primary school, we had one girl in our classroom from a purely German family and one boy who had a Sorbian dad and German mother. As children we could not speak German, so they were two against us twenty and they, how can I say, needed to bow down to us and therefore now they speak Sorbian so well because they learned it from their childhood.

KM: And they are not all Catholics! The school is an institution totally separated from matters of faith. Therefore, they can learn Sorbian and can integrate. The question is what will be like after school.)

This quite lengthy excerpt is an observation on language transmission through formal education in Lusatia. The immersion system in the case of the dominant language children (demanding students to speak in their non-native language) is perceived as negative. Young Sorbs imagine their German-speaking classmates as 'suffering' when they are exposed to Sorbian. Therefore, they think it would be better for students to separate the language groups fully, as was the case in former times when learners had no contact with native speakers of Sorbian. Furthermore, this concern extends in two directions: it is not only to protect German speakers from Sorbian, but also—and perhaps mainly—to protect the Sorbian community and its language. The two perspectives—those of the native Sorbian speakers and the learners—are contradictory. Participant observations, interviews and focus group discussions with students of the second and third language group have shown that students from German-speaking families are not actively encouraged to speak Sorbian and are learning Sorbian through grammar and translations into German, and not through practice (Dołowy-Rybińska 2018). Therefore, Sorbian becomes a symbolic language for most of these learners, which does not help in relation to communication. As most learners are not integrated through other activities with the Sorbs, the division of the Sorbian and German worlds remains constant for them.

It is different in the case of the German speakers who are learning in the first group.[4] Yet, the necessary condition to immerse non-native speakers into a language group is their limited number (Hickey 2001). In any other situation, these Sorbian native-speaking students would switch into the dominant language. This process is well illustrated by the metaphor used by one of the focus group participants quoted above, of the German speakers 'bowing down' to Sorbs (which is the reverse of the power relations in real life). In addition, the non-natives need to have a 'willingness' to learn the language and to become a part of the group: this takes time (a few years of education in the native-speaking group) and necessitates consistency in language use by both native and non-native students. Apart from the selected few who are learning in a single class with native speakers and immersed in Sorbian, the process of becoming a new speaker of Sorbian demands additional motivation and non-formal ways of language and culture transmission. In the case of the Upper Sorbian language, this is mainly through Catholicism. Although one of the students notes that not all 'new speakers' in their grade are Catholics and they can still integrate with the Sorbian group, it concerns only those students who are immersed in Sorbian through being a part of a native-speaking group and achieved 'native-speaking-like' Sorbian language competence. For others, participation in Sorbian Catholic life allows them to integrate with native speakers and learn Sorbian. This leads us to the next type of Sorbian language transmission in Lusatia: through the Catholic faith and Church-related practices.

Language Transmission Through Catholicism

Most of the students who are in the 'Sorbian' class belong to the Catholic community, know each other from childhood and participate in the same cultural and religious events during the year. They share the same cultural and linguistic repertoire. Therefore, language transmission in Lusatia within the speech community goes simultaneously in two directions: through family transmission and through Church-related community life. The background of these relations as well as their influence on the Upper Sorbian community was touched upon in the introductory part of this chapter. It is important to underline that this religious aspect remains a determinant for language practices and identity in the young generation as well. Most of the Sorbian learners come from non-Catholic families and live outside of the cohesive Sorbian language and Catholic area, and it is difficult for them to integrate with the Sorbian community. Young Catholic Upper Sorbs in the focus group discussion explain how faith, language and Sorbian identity (culture) are perceived by them as inseparably interrelated:

KM: Ja sej to druhdy každ jedyn třiróžk předstaju, hdźež serbska rěč, kultura a nabožina hromadźe zwisuja. Wjetšina tych nałožkow ma jedyn nabožny pozadk, to je bjez nabožiny bjez zmysła. [...] Ja sej myslu, zo hdyž Serbja woprawdźe nabožinu zhubja, zo potom serbska rěč tež wjac njefunguje, dokelž potom tutón třiróžk njeje wjac dospołny a wšitke swjedźenje a tak z tym zwisuja.

NDR: Potajkim je to za němskich, kotřiž serbsce wuknu tež tajka hranica z tym katólskim? Hdyž woni to nimaja, je ćežko, so integrować, abo?

TF: By prajiła, zo je tež bjez teje nabožiny móžno, so integrować, to je jenož tróšku ćešo. Dokelž jen te samsne swjedźenje njeswěći, respektiwnje woni nimaja tón samsny woznam a přez to so jen z tymi tamnymi njemóže tak derje identifikować. Ta zhromadnosć tróšku pod tym ćerpi, sej ja myslu.

(KM: I perceive it as a triangle, where the Sorbian language, culture and religion are interrelated. Most of our customs have religious backgrounds, and therefore, without religion they have no meaning. [...] I think that if Sorbs really lose their faith, then the Sorbian language would not function any longer, because then the triangle is not completed and all celebrations are related to this.

NDR: So Catholicism is also a boundary for the Germans? If they are not Catholics, it is difficult for them to integrate, then?

TF: I'd say that it is possible to integrate without this faith but it is a little bit difficult. Because they do not celebrate the same events, or they do not have the same meaning for them and therefore they cannot identify with it that well. The Upper Sorbian community suffers a bit because of this missed opportunity, I think).

The Catholic religion binds the Upper Sorbs together and separates them from the outside German and Protestant worlds. According to Pauline Jaenecke, the way of life in a Sorbian village is characterised by 'merging religion and social life' (Jaenecke 2003: 313). The Catholic Church in Lusatia offered a protected space for the Sorbian language in the German macrocosm. This Sorbian universe separated by linguistic, ethnic and religious boundaries was—to a large extent—free from German institutions, language and power. To be a recognised member of such a community, a person is socially 'obliged' to speak Sorbian. Jaenecke demonstrates that the motivation to speak Sorbian in the villages results from the power of the Catholic Church in this area (Jaenecke 2003: 343). While Catholicism restricts German speakers' access to the Sorbian world and delegitimises non-Catholics, principally Germans, as possible members of the Upper Sorbian community, it also works the other way: the German-speaking Catholics who live in the Upper Sorbian Catholic area have a higher chance of becoming recognised as new speakers (see Kimura 2015). Language transmission passes through the communal celebrations and masses and participation in Catholic community life. To illustrate this, a story from a new speaker, a girl who has been integrated into the Sorbian community through the Church, is presented here.

NF2: Sym mnohich hižo ze serbskeje młodźiny, etc. znała a woni su wot započatka sem serbsce ze mnu rěčeli. Mam tón začišć, zo so tu wjac wažnosće na to kładźe. A tež hdyž jónu něchtó němsce ze mnu rěči někotři hnydom praja, zo móžu ja serbsce a zo móža ze mnu tež serbsce rěčeć. Poprawom tu jenož serbsce rěču, němsku rěč ja tu lědma wužiju.

CR: A čuješ so ty nětko poprawom jako serbowka?

NF2: Poprawom haj, wosebje tež přez cyrkej a te cyłe tradicije, kaž družka abo wuslěkana hić. Tež jako njejsym hišće tak prawje serbsce móhła sym hižo te cyłe tradicije sobučiniła a sym so poprawom tež hižo tak čuła. Dokelž wosebje tu we wokolinje jen wšak tež wjele z tymi tradicijemi do kontakta přindźe.

CR: Ty sy prajiła, zo tradicije při tym ważnu rólu hraja. Měniš zo je rozdźěl mjez noworěčnymi kotřiž tež wot pěstowarnje abo šule sem serbsce wuknu, ale njejsu katólscy?

NF2: Haj, małki rozdźěl tam po mojim měnjenju je. Dokelž hakle přez tute tradicije móže jen to wšo do cyłkowneho zwiska stajić, wšako rěč a tradicije někak hromadźe zwisujetaj. Hdyž jen serbsce rěči a tute cyłe tradicije w Serbach sobučini ta to tež pomha, so do tuteho serbskeho žiwjenja zažiwić.

(NF2: I already knew many Sorbian Catholic young people and they spoke Sorbian with me from the beginning. I have a feeling that more emphasis is put on it here. And even when someone talks to me in German, some immediately say that I speak Sorbian and that it is possible to speak with me in Sorbian. I really speak only Sorbian here, I barely use any German.

CR: *And do you already feel like a Sorb?*

NF2: To be honest, yes, also through the Church and all these traditions, as bridesmaid or when I am dressed in costume. Also when I could not yet speak Sorbian well I already participated actively in all the traditions and I already felt like that. Because in this area you have a lot of contacts with these traditions.

CR: *You said that these traditions play an important role here. Do you see a difference between those 'new speakers' who learned the language at kindergarten or at school and who are not Catholic?*

NF2: Yes, I think there is a difference. Because already through these traditions you can relate all of these, as the language and traditions somehow are connected together. When someone is speaking Sorbian and participates in all these Sorbian traditions then it really helps to settle in this Sorbian life.)

(interview with NF2, the Upper Sorbian female new speaker of the second group in eleventh grade; CR—interviewer)

The quoted girl participated in Sorbian Catholic life well before she started to speak Sorbian herself. Unlike her German-speaking friends from school who had limited access to non-school-related transmission of Upper Sorbian due to their lack of interest in Sorbian language events and who were not Catholic and never participated in the Sorbian village customs, she was constantly exposed to it. To understand how the flow of language transmission through the Catholic way of life works, it is necessary to look at the structure of Sorbian Catholic life in the area and over the course of a lifetime.

The Upper Sorbian language area today covers Catholic territory. There and only there, in the 'Catholic Sorbian triangle' (Walde 2004), are the Upper Sorbs still in the majority or at least constitute a substantial community. Their everyday life, as well as their whole life trajectory, is established by the main Catholic sacraments and related customs from birth to death. Children are also expected to serve as ministrants during masses and participate in the children's religious week. Teenagers meet regularly in the Deanery Youth organisations and participate in different activities, including pilgrimages. Most of the Upper Sorbian boys from the age of fourteen take part in the Easter horse-riding processions, while the girls have a role as 'bridesmaids' (*družka*) after their first communion. From this time on, the girls accompany brides from their families and participate in processions wearing a distinctive dress and speak Sorbian during all the ceremonies. Girls wear the traditional Sorbian Catholic costumes not only on religious occasions and other village celebrations, but also during village festivities such as the Maypole. Young people join the services (not only on Sundays), acquire the impressive (religious) Sorbian singing repertoire and participate in religious festivities. They establish relationships with each other and with potential life partners during the bigger meetings such as the Pentecost pilgrimage to Róžant/Rosenthal. In this way, the entire year is structured around events where the larger Sorbian speech community meets. Even non-religious activities, such as dancing events for the young people and Sorbian band concerts, are planned according to the Catholic calendar, and it is inconceivable that they would take place during a period of fasting.

The main language of communication in the Catholic church is Sorbian. Children from German-speaking families are encouraged to speak Sorbian (Kimura 2015). As the quoted girl expressed it, 'they spoke Sorbian with me from the beginning' even before she was able to answer in this language. This means that the Catholic Sorbian community is that very rare sphere in the Sorbian-German world where bilingual communication is possible and learners are encouraged to speak Sorbian.

Language transmission which includes non-natives is, therefore, one of the important aspects of Catholicism. The second is the full integration of new speakers into the Sorbian community. This goes hand in hand with the legitimisation of these persons as members of the community. Let us go back to the excerpt from the interview. Not only does this girl say she feels 'like a Sorb' herself through celebrating the same events, and by having her own costume that marks her out as a member of the community (Feng-fang 2009), but also because of being able to understand and internalise Sorbian culture as her own. Language competence is important but for becoming a legitimised speaker in the community based on strong cultural and religious bonds, intercultural competences are essential. These are the cross-cultural capacities that give learners a sense of belonging to a group as well as motivating them to use the language. It is one thing to learn the language of a minority. It is another to learn a culture that can 'be accomplished only through direct, sustained, and deep involvement with it' (Valdiviezo and Nieto 2015: 94). What serves as an advantage for the non-Sorbian-speaking Catholics can be an insurmountable barrier for those who do not belong to the religious community. In this context, it can be stated that the main obstacles for teenagers from German-speaking families in becoming new speakers of the Upper Sorbian language is that they do not have many opportunities to use the language they are learning outside the classroom. This is due both to the cultural and spatial separation of the Sorbian Catholic community and to religion. To facilitate them in this process of becoming new speakers, other forms of transmission of the Sorbian language, secular in nature and separated from traditional Sorbian life, are needed. Such transmission is an exception in Lusatia, and it may be related to the notion of the 'communities of practice'.

Transmission Through the 'Community of Practice'

The separation of Sorbian and German students at school and during after-school activities is almost total up to the end of the tenth grade. There are just a few common activities (not classroom-related) where both groups could meet and establish friendships and language contacts. As a consequence, Sorbian learners are to a large extent deprived of opportunities to practise their Sorbian as a language of daily communication and not just of the classroom. Not only do Sorbian and German-speaking students have different cultural backgrounds, they do not form a school community as such that influences German speakers' motivation to participate in the Sorbian community life outside of the school and to speak Sorbian. If we adopt the theory of situated learning, we perceive the process of learning as acquiring skills connected with living in a particular community and sharing common practices (Lave and Wenger 1991). Through this process, participants may become conscious members of a specific group, called a 'community of practice' (Wenger 1998). Such a community is a social construct, and in this way 'is different from the traditional community, primarily because it is defined simultaneously by its membership and by the practice in which that membership engages' (Eckert and McConnell-Ginet 1992: 464). Therefore, creating a community of practice gives young people who identify with the dominant language and culture a much better possibility of adopting a minority language as a language of communication within such a group than any other form of teaching. As Wenger explained, members of a community of practice interact at different levels, and personal engagement is formed through these interactions. All members of such a group, regardless of their ethnic identification, share common activities and practices while being together, and this is referred to as a joint enterprise. Moreover, all participants share a repertoire of resources, such as language, through which they express their identity as group members (Wenger 1998: 72–85).

The school itself does not really provide opportunities to create these types of communities which combine Sorbian and German speakers. Instead, such opportunities as do exist are organised by individual Sorbian activists on the basis of their personal commitment to the language. A very particular example is SAEK (Sächsischer Ausbildungs- und Erprobungskanal / Saxon training and rehearsal channel) which has been led for many years by the Sorbian activist Michał Cyž. Even if SAEK is not a Sorbian institution, there are many activities provided in Sorbian or bilingually. This is possible thanks to its leader's personal engagement and conviction (which goes against prevailing understandings) that Sorbian-German bilingualism is possible.[5] SAEK offers, among other things, dubbing and production of films for young people in Upper Sorbian (called video krušk), live-streaming of Sorbian events and internal Sorbian school radio. As the use of Sorbian is important for the SAEK leader, there are many Sorbian learners who thanks to this institution had their first contact with Sorbian outside of the classroom and the possibility of using it actively. Below is an excerpt from an interview with one of the students of the second group of the tenth grade at the Sorbian Grammar School:

CR: Und die reden dann auch mit dir Sorbisch? In diesem Video Krušk?
AF: *Ja.*
CR: Und das hat dich auch nicht abgeschreckt oder so?
AF: *No, ich verstehe es ja. Kann halt nur nicht reden. Da ist halt diese Hemmung dahinter. Dann muss ich immer dreimal überlegen, was ich überhaupt sagen will und ehe, dann ist schon wieder ein anderes Thema und dann ist das alles schon wieder vorbei.*
CR: Und hast du das Gefühl, dass sie dich zum Sorbisch sprechen ermuntern?
AF: *In welchem Sinn?*
CR: Dass das auch gern gesehen wird, wenn du Sorbisch redest.
AF: *Ja, von unserem Leiter ja. Und die Jungs nehmen es mir nicht so übel, wenn ich mal Deutsch mit ihnen rede, die wissen dass das nicht so leicht ist. [...] Aber irgendwie habe ich mich an Sorbisch gewöhnt. Ich war bei Europeada mit in Südtirol, ich habe Passion mitgemacht in Crostwitz, ich mache Brigada immer mit. Festival mal in Crostwitz. Alles Mögliche eigentlich. Ich versuche alles mitzunehmen. Und ich war eine Woche mit dem Mannschaftsbus mit der wubranka.*
CR: Ich schätze das ganze lief dann schon nur Sorbischsprachig ab?
AF: *Wenn du nur unter Sorben bist, dann hast du keine andere Wahl mehr.*
CR: Und das funktioniert dann.
AF: Ja.

(*CR*: *And do they talk to you in Sorbian also? In this video krušk?*
AF: Yes.
CR: *And does it scare you or something?*
AF: Nope, I understand it. I just cannot speak. There is this embarrassment behind it. Then I always have to think three times what I want to say and then the topic has moved on and it starts all over again.
CR: *And do you feel that they are encouraging you to speak Sorbian?*
AF: In what sense?
CR: *That it is welcome when you're talking in Sorbian.*

AF: Yes, by our leader, yes. And the boys do not mind if I speak German with them, they know it's not that easy [to speak Sorbian]. [...] But I somehow got used to Sorbian. I was at Europeada[6] in South Tyrol, I took part in Passion in Crostwitz,[7] I always participate in Brigada.[8] Sometimes in the Festival in Crostwitz.[9] Everything is actually possible. I try to take part in everything. And I was a week in the team bus with the *wubranka*.[10]

CR: *I guess the whole thing was just Sorbian-speaking?*

AF: If you are the only one who is not a Sorb, then you have no choice.

CR: *And that works.*

AF: Yes.)

The rest of the people who participated in this focus group discussion stated that they did not have any opportunities to speak Sorbian. AF. was a member of the 'video krušk' lead by Michał Cyž and thanks to this, the language was transmitted to her by this community of practice's co-members. Not only was she immersed in Sorbian by the Sorbian-speaking group but she also felt encouraged to actively speak Sorbian, at least by the team leader. She also felt she was a member of a group. Overcoming inhibitions to start speaking the language a person is learning is often tedious: it is related to the embarrassment of making mistakes, inability to express ideas properly and not being recognised by the group (see also Jaffe 1999; Costa 2015). It may be the moment of giving up. AF. managed to overcome these difficulties and to 'get used to Sorbian', and it was thanks to the Sorbian-speaking community of practice into which she was accepted as a member despite her language competences. Nevertheless, she was expected to speak Sorbian. She also had to participate in the Sorbian cultural and Sorbian-speaking life. As a result she got to know Sorbs, participate in Sorbian community-building activities and be accepted as a member of the group and be a legitimate Sorbian new speaker.

Such an informal way of transmitting the Upper Sorbian language is not common. First of all, it is founded on the individual decision and conviction of the particular Sorbian language activist, which in itself is not a stable basis. Secondly, being a member of the community of practice requires the existence of these communities (which are very rare in Lusatia) and a willingness to participate in them. When a Sorbian community is a closed one, this is not obvious for young people. Thirdly, this also demands that all the community members contravene the deeply rooted habit of not speaking Sorbian in the presence of Germans. When all these conditions are met, immersion in Sorbian becomes possible for learners.

Conclusion

Upper Sorbian language transmission in the young generation depends mainly on family ethnic and linguistic background. In the Catholic community the language, as well as Sorbian customs and traditions, are transmitted from generation to generation by the family and the community. However, once intergenerational transmission is broken, it is difficult to be re-integrated linguistically and culturally into the Upper Sorbian community.

Becoming a new speaker of a minority language not only demands an effort on the part of those who are willing to learn and to use this language but also from the community who 'owns' it (see O'Rourke 2011). Formal school education is not enough to acquire a language, especially when it is a language that is not used widely by the immediate society. Its efficacy depends on the chosen model of language learning (immersion, bilingual, teaching a minority language as a second/foreign language) and of the contact learners may have with the speakers of the language. In the case of Upper Sorbian, learning the language at school is based mostly on the acquisition of the rules of grammar rather than on practising it as a living language. In addition, it is not easy for learners to practise Sorbian with native speakers because first-language German speakers and non-Catholics are hardly recognised as legitimate speakers of this language. This was supposed to be changed by classes in school which connect native and non-native speakers.

In the Upper Sorbian context, the new education system opened to non-Sorbian native children the opportunity to become familiar with the minority language. But it does not structurally provide them with the chance to practise it because of the lack of the personal bonds created between native and non-native students. Only those rare students who are in the classroom with Sorbian native speakers—contrary to the conventional and accepted practice—become bilingual and feel fluent in Sorbian as they had to immerse themselves in the language. As a consequence of the long-established practice of separating the Sorbian and German worlds and languages, new Upper Sorbian speakers created through the educational system are the exception rather than the rule. Moreover, they do not constitute a community as such, and are not integrated well enough with the Sorbs to ensure the sustainability of their language competences and practices in the future.

Among young Sorbian learners in Upper Lusatia, there is no 'new speaker community' which would allow them to use their Sorbian and not be judged (or not having the feeling of being judged) by the native speakers (see McEwan-Fujita 2010). In the Upper Sorbian community, apart from native speakers of Sorbian, there is a place mainly for individuals who acquire the language through informal transmission that is connected to involvement in cultural practices. This involves some partners of the Sorbs who were open enough not to ignore Sorbian and who managed to integrate into the community. For young people, this process becomes easier in the case of Catholics because among them Sorbian is the dominant language, used in both casual conversation and Sorbian ceremonies. The linguistic appropriation of the whole 'Catholic space' is accepted by the Sorbian community, and consequently it is even demanded that non-Sorbs at least understand the language.

Such an attitude is not commonly found in different Sorbian-related after-school activities and for communities of practice created in Upper Lusatia. In most cases, non-natives are not welcome there at all, and they therefore do not try to participate or gain access to them.[11] Only rarely, as in the SAEK example, there are activities not related to the school and which are attractive to young people held in Sorbian. Nevertheless, this requires changing the tradition of not imposing a minority language on the dominant language speakers. For Upper Sorbian language transmission at school and through school-related activities for non-native speakers to be effective a change in the educational system is not enough.

The structural problems involved in the lack of acceptance of bilingualism in Lusatia, the negative attitudes towards Sorbian and related language ideologies, and the separation of the Sorbian and German worlds should all be resolved at the same time.

Funding Details This article presents research which has been funded by a grant from the National Science Centre, Poland entitled "Language contact and culture conflict. Acquiring linguistic competence and cultural identity creation—the case of pupils in the Sorbian Grammar School in Bautzen (Upper Lusatia)" (UMO-2016/21/B/HS2/00001).

Notes

1. The language tests with some students from the second and third group at the beginning of the eleventh grade were part of the research project carried out by Nicole Dołowy-Rybińska and Cordula Ratajczak. The results of these tests demonstrated that students from the third group have poor Sorbian language competence.
2. This feeling that any time Sorbs speak Sorbian in the presence of Germans, they are saying something against the Germans is common among Sorbian learners in particular, but also the German inhabitants of Lusatia in general (Ratajczak 2011). It is related, among others, to the lack of exposure to Sorbian, which in turn is the result of the strategy of separating the Sorbian and German worlds.
3. L/T/K/J—symbols given to a person; NDR—interviewer; F/M—gender.
4. It is also different for the few non-Sorbian native students who belong to the Sorbian-related communities of practice described above.
5. The strategy of separating Sorbian and German worlds is common in Lusatia, and it results in perceiving receptive bilingualism—the use of two languages at the same time—as impossible in practice. Therefore, people who can understand Sorbian but are not active Sorbian speakers are not exposed to this language. In SAEK, when

there is a group of mixed languages, where German speakers have at least the basis of Sorbian, every activity is bilingual with Sorbian as the major language.

6. The European football championship of the autochthonous national minorities organised by the Federal Union of European Nationalities (FUEN).
7. Performed annually since the end of the nineteenth century.
8. The school's choir, which sings in Sorbian and is attended mainly by Sorbian native speakers.
9. International Folklore Festival in Chróśćicy/Crostwitz that takes place every other year, attracting participants from all over the world and many thousands of visitors.
10. Sorbian football team.
11. A good example of such enclosed Upper Sorbian 'community of practice' is the school's choir (see Dołowy-Rybińska and Ratajczak 2019b).

References

Baker, C., and W.E. Wright. 2017. *Foundations of Bilingual Education and Bilingualism*, 6th ed. Bristol: Multilingual Matters.

Budarjowa, L., ed. 2009. *Witaj a 2plus – wužadanje za přichod / Witaj und 2plus – eine Herausforderung für die Zukunft*. Budyšin: Serbske šulske towarstwo.

Costa, J. 2015. New Speakers, New Language: On Being a Legitimate Speaker of a Minority Language in Provence. *International Journal of the Sociology of Language* 231: 127–145.

Dołowy-Rybińska, N. 2018. Learning Upper Sorbian: The Problems with Minority Language Education for Non-native Pupils in the Upper Sorbian Grammar School in Bautzen/Budyšin. *International Journal of Bilingual Education and Bilingualism* 21: 1–16.

Dołowy-Rybińska, N. 2020. Informal Bilingual Teachers' Language Practices and the Consequences on Pupils' Language Choices in a Situation of

Unequal Bilingualism: The Case of an Upper Sorbian Education System. *Multilingua* 39 (2): 169–191.

Dołowy-Rybińska, N., and C. Ratajczak. 2019a. Languages and Cultures in Contact. The Place of New Speakers in the Education System in Upper Lusatia. *Cognitive Studies | Études cognitives* 19: 1–17.

Dołowy-Rybińska, N., and C. Ratajczak. 2019. Upper Sorbian Language Education: When Community Language Maintenance Practices Disregard Top-Down Revitalisation Strategies. *Language, Culture and Curriculum* 34 (1): 65–79.

Eckert, P., and S. McConnell-Ginet. 1992. Think Practically and Look Locally: Language and Gender as Community-Based Practice. *Annual Review of Anthropology* 21: 461–490.

Elle, L. 2010. Sorben – demographische und statistische Aspekte. In *Minderheiten als Mehrwert*, ed. M.T. Vogt, J. Neyer, D. Bingen, and J. Sokol, 9–18. Frankfurt am Main: Peter Lang.

Elle, L. 2014. *Sprachenpolitik in der Lausitz. Sprachenpolitik und Sprachenrecht im deutsch-sorbischen Gebiet 1990 bis 2014*. Bautzen: Domowina Verlag.

Feng-fang, T. 2009. Gendered Ethnicity – Ethnicized Gender: Traditional Costumes as an Expression of Ethnic Identity? Three Case Studies of Sorbian Women. In *Trachten als Phänomen der Gegenwart*, ed. I. Keller and L. Scholze-Irritz, 33–41. Bautzen: Domowina-Verlag.

Gazsi, O. 2005. *2plus. Schulartübergreifendes Konzept. Die zweisprachige sorbisch-deutsche Schule für allgemeinbildende Schulen im sorbischen Siedlungsgebiet*. Radebeul: Sächsisches Staatsinstitut für Bildung und Schulentwicklung.

Hickey, T. 2001. Mixing Beginners and Native Speakers in Minority Language Immersion: Who Is Immersing Whom? *Canadian Modern Language Review* 57 (3): 443–474.

Jaenecke, P. 2003. *Religiosität und Spracherhalt bei den katholischen Sorben*. Berlin: Weiβensee Verlag.

Jaffe, A. 1999. *Ideologies in Action: Language Politics on Corsica*. Berlin: Mouton de Gruyter.

Jodlbauer, R., G. Spiess, and H. Steenwijk. 2001. *Die aktuelle Situation der niedersorbischen Sprache. Ergebnisse einer soziolinguistischen Untersuchung der Jahre 1993–1995*. Bautzen: Domowina Verlag.

Kaulfürstowa, J., ed. 2008. *Das WITAJ-Projekt in Kindertagesstätten im Freistaat Sachsen – Zwischenbilanz und Ausblick in die Zukunft*. Bautzen: WITAJ-Sprachzentrum.

Kimura, G.C. 2015. Spracherhalt als Prozess. Elemente des kirchlichen Sprachmanagements bei den katholischen Sorben. *International Journal of the Sociology of Language* 232: 13–32.
Lave, J., and E. Wenger. 1991. *Situated Learning: Legitimate Peripheral Participation*. Cambridge: Cambridge University Press.
McEwan-Fujita, E. 2010. Ideology, Affect, and Socialization in Language Shift and Revitalization: The Experiences of Adults Learning Gaelic in the Western Isles of Scotland. *Language in Society* 39: 27–64.
Menzel, T., and J. Šołćina. 2018. Przedszkola serbołużyckie w różnych konstelacjach językowych i etnokulturowych. *Zeszyty Łużyckie* 52: 25–43.
Norberg, M. 1996. *Sprachwechselprozeß in der Niederlausitz: Soziolinguistische Fallstudie der deutsch-sorbischen Gemeinde Drachhausen/Hochoza*. Uppsala: Studia Slavica Uppsalensia.
O'Rourke, B. 2011. Whose Language is It? Struggles for Language Ownership in an Irish Language Classroom. *Journal of Language, Identity, and Education* 10: 327–345.
Pech, E. 2001. The Sorbian School System in Germany 1945–2000. *Education Et Sociétés Plurilingues* 10: 39–48.
Ratajczak, C. 1998. Zwischen sorbischer Innen- und deutscher Außenperspektive. Grenz-Werte einer Mischkultur im Lausitzer Braunkohletagebaugebiet. In *Grenzgänger*, ed. R. Schneider, 135–146. Saarbrücken: Saarbrücker Druckerei und Verlag.
Ratajczak, C. 2011. Vom Image einer Minderheitensprache – Erfahrungen und Einstellungen Bautzener Schüler zum Sorbischen. *Lětopis – Zeitschrift für sorbische Sprache, Geschichte und Kultur* (special issue).
Rindler-Schjerve, R., and E. Vetter. 2012. *European Multilingualism – Challenges and Perspectives*. Clevedon: Multilingual Matters.
Scholze, L. 2008. *Das grammatische System der obersorbischen Umgangssprache im Sprachkontakt*. Bautzen: Domowina-Verlag.
Schön, F., and D. Scholze, eds. 2014. *Sorbisches Kulturlexikon*. Bautzen: Domowina Verlag.
Valdiviezo, L., and S. Nieto. 2015. Culture in Bilingual and Multilingual Education. In *Handbook of Bilingual and Multilingual Education*, ed. W. E. Wright, S. Boun, and O. García, 92–108. Malden, MA: Wiley-Blackwell.
Walde, M. 2004. Demographisch-statistische Betrachtungen im Oberlausitzer Gemeindeverband „Am Klosterwasser". *Lětopis – Zeitschrift für sorbische Sprache. Geschichte Und Kultur* 51: 3–27.
Wenger, E. 1998. *Communities of Practice. Learning, Meaning, and Identity*. Cambridge: Cambridge University Press.

Creating Language Shift: Factors Behind the Language Choices of Māori Speakers

Vincent Ieni Olsen-Reeder

Introduction

Reversing language shift (RLS) has always been centred on the family home as a critical domain. A key reason for this is intergenerational transmission, the transfer of language from one generation to another, over successive generations. As a privately controlled domain, away from the influence of macro-level policy and language planners, the family domain also appears to be one of the most difficult spaces in which to effect change (Spolsky 2012).

V. I. Olsen-Reeder (✉)
Ngā Pōtiki a Tamapahore, Wainuiōmata, New Zealand
e-mail: Vini.Olsen-Reeder@vuw.ac.nz

Te Kawa a Māui, Te Herenga Waka—Victoria University of Wellington, Wellington, New Zealand

M. Hornsby and W. McLeod (eds.), *Transmitting Minority Languages*, Palgrave Studies in Minority Languages and Communities,
https://doi.org/10.1007/978-3-030-87910-5_7

When 'people establish a regular relationship, one of the features governing their normal practices is the choice of a language variety' (Spolsky 2009: 14). For communities engaging in language revitalisation, the RLS process will undoubtedly include changing the language variety used in the home from a dominant variety in society, to the one undergoing revitalisation. This is the case for te reo Māori (the Māori language) in Aotearoa New Zealand. Of the total homes that could be primarily Māori-speaking, just 2.6% of them actually are (Māori Language Advisory Group 2015). Understanding the language choices of Māori speakers is thus a critical contribution to scholarly work in the area.

This chapter presents the findings of the author's doctoral research, completed in 2017.[1] The research examines the myriad of choices made by Māori language speakers either towards English or towards Māori use, or away from either of those languages. International research is further used to support how these language choices might play out within the walls of the family domain, to give insights into how the dynamics of the home might affect language choices. This chapter firstly provides context to the language situation in Aotearoa New Zealand, including an interrogation of speaker population statistics. The language choice factors of Māori speakers are then presented, with discussions around the implications of those choices for our speaker community. It is hoped that understanding these choices will act as a catalyst for micro-level language policy within the homes of Māori speakers and provide insight for other language communities around the world who may experience similar events.

Context

For an international readership, it might be useful at the outset to provide some context to the Māori language. The Austronesian language family, of which Māori is a part, covers a larger area of the world than any other family (Biggs 1968). The Māori language is Indigenous to Aotearoa New Zealand, and structurally syntactically close to the Indigenous languages of Tuamotu, Rarotonga and Tahiti (Otsuka 2005). Distinct isolation and colonisation histories have meant that these languages share lexical and grammatical similarities that allow the speakers of these languages to communicate with each other to a certain degree, but they are not mutually intelligible. The Māori language itself contains several dialects spanning across the islands of New Zealand, with the most significant differences occurring between the North and South Islands (White and Rewi 2014).

The colonisation and consequential destruction of Māori land, people and language have been discussed at length elsewhere, and need not be restated here. It is enough to say in this chapter that those unfounded Eurocentric ideals of superiority and dominance left a devastating mark on the land in which Māori people call home, and the resulting language shift to English has left many generations bereft of a wealth of knowledge that many, such as the United Nations, assert is a human right. In the author's experience, it seems Aotearoa New Zealand is often regarded as a forerunner in Indigenous rights and language revival, but I wish to present quickly here some opposing thoughts. New Zealand initially voted against the United Nations Declaration on the Rights of Indigenous Peoples in 2007, a document its citizens helped create.[2] It only signed the Declaration in 2010 (New Zealand Parliament 2010), and only sought to start responding to the document in 2019 (Te Puni Kōkiri 2019). Contained within Article 13 of that document is the assertion that Indigenous communities have a right to access their languages. Therefore, while gains have certainly been made here, the overall macro context in which RLS is operating at the time of writing is, arguably, rather incoherent.

The Data on Māori Speakers

According to some treatments of the data we have, te reo Māori still faces 'certain extinction' (Barrett-Walker et al. 2020). However, it is incredibly difficult to assert confidence in the data we have with regard to the Māori language, and its speaker population.[3] The number of Māori speakers is a complex topic to debate (Lane 2020). The primary reason the numbers are so difficult to navigate is the manner in which data are collected—methods change too frequently to have faith in them (Bauer 2008). Therefore, it is difficult to discern how many speakers are actively contributing to the reinstatement of intergenerational transmission in the home, and therefore difficult to contribute to increasing this number. As we will see below, increasing this number is integral to revival of the Māori language.

National census data collected by Statistics New Zealand, our national entity for official data collection, offers one example. A table of these figures from the 2018 census report (Statistics New Zealand 2020a, b) shows the usual trend produced by these census data over time (Table 1).

At first glance, these numbers do not seem all that unusual. The Māori population continues to grow over time and speaker numbers fluctuate a little. Each national census though seems to bring a new question type—'do you speak Māori', 'how well do you speak Māori', 'do you know a few words or phrases, or more'. When question types are not held consistently over the years, they are not valid enough to draw trends from and produce a range of different results. These discrepancies in methodology have even been noted by Statistics New Zealand (2014a), but as yet, have not been corrected. For this reason, it is not possible to have confidence in the census data.

Further peculiarities arise when considered alongside data gathered by Statistics New Zealand via other sampling methods. Through random sampling, a dedicated 2013 study (the same year as the national census) inferred in 2013 that 'an estimated 55 per cent [of] Māori adults reported they could speak more than a few words or phrases', and '50,000 (11 per cent) could speak te reo very well, or well' (Statistics New Zealand 2014b). These numbers are both outliers to the census

Table 1 Census Data for Māori speakers, by Māori ethnicity and total population (from Statistics NZ, 2020)

Census year	2006	2013	2018
Māori speakers of Māori descent	131,613 (23.3%)	125,532 (20.9%)	159,645 (20.6%)
-Total Māori population	565,329	598,602	775,836
All Māori speakers, NZ	157,113 (3.9%)	148,395 (3.5%)	185,955 (4.0%)
-Total population, NZ	4,027,947	4,242,048	4,699,755

data, one to either extreme. Given that the questions are all different as well, it is difficult to place much faith in them.

Lastly, to add to the complexity of the situation, this same random sampling study was repeated again in 2018, the same time as the national census. It was reported that 8.1% of the Māori population could speak Māori 'very well' or 'well' (Statistics New Zealand 2020a, b). At least here, one conclusion might be drawn—a drop in those who can speak Māori 'well or very well' occurred here, from 11% in 2013 to 8.1% in 2020. This may be the most reliable trend we can glean from all of this data. However, there are still issues with the question types, which undermines the faith we can have in them. In the 2018 survey, the question was changed from asking who spoke 'more than a few words of phrases' to who spoke 'no more than a few words of phrases'—these are polar opposites. Furthermore, categories around understanding and reading te reo Māori were added. This could have affected the way participants differentiated speaking Māori (as *knowing* Māori) and speaking Māori (as opposed to other communicative modes, such as understanding and reading).

Although there is so little known about our speaker population, Bauer (2008) argues that what is more important is how people actually use the language. It makes sense to observe how many people actually use the language as the primary language of a household, and how they make those decisions. The Māori Language Advisory Group (2015: 75) note that only 2.6% of households that could use te reo Māori as a main language of communication do so. We do not have data yet concerning where those households are. If the 2018 Census numbers above are correct, it can be estimated that approximately 4,835 people use te reo Māori as the primary home language. With a national average of 2.7 people in any given household (Statistics New Zealand 2014c), there are potentially 1,791 households choosing to speak te reo Māori. This is an absolute guess. However, these would be the most likely homes in which intergenerational transmission could occur, provided there were children present occurs, and the bastions of micro Māori language policy. As well as continuing efforts in education, broadcasting and the like, one overall objective of RLS, then, would be to try to increase this number.

All Māori Speakers Are Bilingual

There is one more layer of complexity to the context of RLS in the home. All Māori speakers are probably bilingual in Māori and English. As we will see below, this could affect greatly the language choices Māori speakers make—every time we open our mouths to speak to another Māori speaker, we are choosing between at least Māori and English. There is not monolingual Māori-language space controlled by people who do not know English.

To give some context to this, a great deal of language shift had occurred here in Aotearoa before the 1970s, when Māori communities started to consciously see generations of Māori growing up unable to speak Māori (Tawhiwhirangi 2014). Because of this reality, some fifty years later, as far as we can tell, all Māori speakers speak English as well as Māori. Figure 1 shows the number of self-reported monolingual speakers of Māori, as reported in the 2013 National Census.

Here, it can be seen that the largest group of monolingual Māori speakers reported are babies, or under the age of 15. Under this age, according to New Zealand law the parents must complete the survey on the behalf of children. Therefore, it is possible that some children are monolingual speakers, but as they age, they will become bilingual. There is a sharp decline in the numbers from age 15 to 16. One explanation for this is that non-speaker parents are filling out the census on behalf of their children and are over-estimating their child's Māori proficiency. As

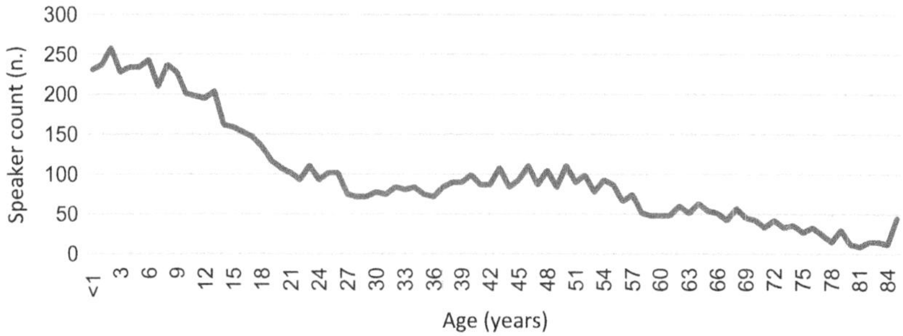

Fig. 1 Self-reported monolingual Māori speakers (2013 National Census)

a last thought, prior to 2018, the census could not be filled out in Māori and needed to be completed entirely in English. Anyone completing the survey would thus have needed some English proficiency in order to complete it and thus would not have been totally monolingual.

Every time a Māori speaker uses a language in their repertoire, there is a certain linguistic response, that is, a choice. What affects those choices are therefore critical in language revitalisation. In short, we should try to promote choices that support the use of Māori and reduce or limit the limitations that do not support the use of Māori. Simultaneously, we might like to better understand what factors support the use of English and see if any of those can be affected to provide more opportunities to use Māori, especially in the home. As explained above, most speakers who could speak Māori in the home simply do not. If the home domain is as important as is suggested, raising the number of home speakers thus relies not just on learning the language, but learning to change the language of the home.

Do Bilinguals Really 'Choose' a Language, and Are They Bilingual?

In the many research fields where multiple languages and their speakers are examined, bilingualism is not necessarily an apt term. As many scholars have noted, it has supported unhelpful theories around how people access a wide linguistic repertoire (Grosjean 2008; Mackey 2000; Li 2000). In the main, bilinguals are still often pitched as deficient in a language, incomplete in their language capacity, and are commonly compared to monolingual counterparts as if monolingualism is the apex of 'correct' language behaviour (McCardle 2015). The author is not aligned with these views. However, in order to make sense of the relationship between Māori and English use, it is necessary to allow both languages to hold space in scholarly discussions and name the process of language choice. If avenues of research can examine bilingualism without applying deficit modes of thinking to the work, it still has a place. The author very much requires that room here, so the term bilingualism is used.

There is a systematic series of language choices bilinguals make when they speak. However, it should be understood that 'choice' is not altogether appropriate for describing decision-making around language. Choice seems to imply that a minimal amount of consideration might be involved in language decisions. As this chapter suggests, the considerations are complex—some are socio-politically induced over time, others are rapid responses. Language choice is not random, but a response to complex internal and external power occurrences of the moment. Therefore, choice may be an inadequate term, but is applied here for lack of better descriptors. Practitioners and communities may be able to identify more appropriate ones.

Language Choices

As mentioned above, language choices are complex. The literature seems to agree that in any given speech act, there is generally a 'better' choice of language over another. Myers-Scotton (1983: 118) notes that 'while [rights and obligations of a speech act] do not determine code[4] choice, they do determine the markedness of code choices. A range of choices is possible, but some choices are more unmarked than others'. While there is always a 'choice' to use any language in a given situation, there is generally one that makes more sense—this might be the one that is more commonly understood by all involved, or the one the speaker if more proficient in, for example. There are, undoubtedly, a range of factors that present in these situations that tips the balance between a marked choices, but it makes sense that one language seems less marked than another. The primary function of language is communication, therefore, acceptance by target listeners is paramount when making a choice. '[T]he more a person desires another's approval, the more that individual will converge his or her speech in the direction of the other' (Giles et al. 1977: 322). Therefore, it makes sense that a bilingual will opt for the one they understand as less marked when they speak, that is, the one that is deemed most acceptable, for whatever reason. That understanding, while generally true, is probably too superficial to account for all language choices. As is seen below, some Māori speakers make socio-political decisions to use the marked language in their speech acts, such as taking a stance for the status of the language in typically English spaces. Nevertheless, it is a useful starting point in discussions around choice, and the fact that there does seem to be a less marked language in any given speech act, and one that is more marked.

To get closer to the complex factors that induce choice, Herman (1961) notes in his research on bilingual speakers that there are three categories which account for language choice: personal, immediate and background. Personal choices are driven by the speaker's own internal feelings. Immediate choices are driven by those in the immediate vicinity, that is to say, the listeners involved in the speech act. Lastly, background inhibitors are those imposed by other external people in the vicinity of the speaker, but not participating in the speech act. These factors may exist in isolation, or a combination of such. The strongest element wins, as it where, as the most prevalent factor dictates the choice of language—except in cases where the speaker consciously chooses to ignore it.

Language Choice in the Home

Language choices in the home have even more added complexity. There is a more interpersonal relationship in speech acts that share a more connected, intimate or enduring nature. If homes can be considered social networks, or connected to social networks, then social network theory has much to offer in adding to our understanding of these complexities. Milroy (in Sachdev and Giles 2006: 364) asserts that normative patterns exist within such networks: 'Patterns of language use are deeply embedded in the social networks of interlocutors and networks play an important role in reinforcing normative behaviour'. In a family, the normative behaviour is decided by interlocutors who are indelibly linked together. Milroy and Milroy (1985: 359) further note that 'the closer the individual's ties to a local community network, the more likely he[5] is to approximate to vernacular norms'. Therefore, family members are indeed going to share linguistic choice norms between them, and this seems to be a relatively concrete act that contributes to the language choices made in the home.

It makes sense to question who makes the language choice decision in the home. Jernudd and Thuan (1983: 72) state that 'partners in communication need to find out what norms of implementation the other person has, need to express each his own norms, and between them find a way to agree on what norms shall be used for a particular act of speaking'. Piller (2002: 140) takes this further, noting that '[spouses] stick to the language of their first meeting because they might lose the sense of knowing each other, the sense of connectedness and the rapport derived from being able to anticipate what the partner might be about to say if they switched'. If this is true for spousal relationships, it will also be true for their children. All adults are going to establish relationships and power dynamics in the home with their children. If those are set up through one language, it makes sense to infer that is going to be as difficult as it is across spousal relationships—re-meeting your father in another language is surely going to feel strange.

Doctoral Research Study

As mentioned above, there are a range of factors which affect the language choices of Māori speakers. To draw these together cohesively was the intention of the author's doctoral thesis, completed in 2017. The data collected was an amalgamation of two research projects. The first was the author's small-scale Master's research, which was later upgraded to a doctoral study. The second was Te Kura Roa, a much larger nationwide language study into the lives of active Māori language speakers (Higgins et al. 2017). In total, around 800 people were surveyed by these projects. Some 80,000 cells of data were categorised for the language choice themes they represent, in a quasi-societal treatment fashion. Once categorised, they were organised into the internal, external or immediate language choice type they represent, and which language they geared the speaker towards. Together, those themes convey the reasons Māori learners and speakers use, or do not use, te reo Māori.

In the following sections, discussions are situated around participant responses that gesture towards a language choice of either English or Māori. These are then broken down into internal, external or listener-based choices. This is not necessarily an exhaustive list, but is what was presented in the 80,000 cells of captured data.

English Language Choices

The reasons a bilingual Māori speaker chooses English are varied. Table 2 presents the overall classifications of factors promoting the use of English among Māori speakers. Following the table, each factor is explicated in more detail.

Internal Factors

Internally within the individual, speakers choose English when they feel their own proficiency is not high enough to sustain conversation in Māori. They may not feel they have enough vocabulary or sentence structure to communicate. While this is understandable, it does present some issues. High proficiency in Māori is not an indicator of high use, and lower proficiency speakers are more likely to engage in the language (Ormsby-Teki et al. 2011). While we do not understand yet exactly why this is the case, this suggests lower proficiency users contribute greatly to the life of the language through actual use. Since lower proficiency speakers are more likely to be inhibited by this fear, it is rather detrimental to language health on the whole to have this fear within an active

Table 2 English language choices of Māori speakers

	Factor promoting English use
Internal	Speaker is affected by proficiency
	Speaker is affected by anxiety
External	English is the dominant language of the context
	Family actively dissuades Māori language use
Listener	Listener Is affected by anxiety
	English is the language of first encounter

community of speakers. Lower proficiency speakers can contribute much to language revitalisation if they are using what they know, as much as they can, as soon as they possibly can.

Secondly, it is possible this language choice may result from speakers comparing their Māori proficiency to their English. If people feel their proficiency in Māori is not adequate, it is natural to assume they will revert to English. Remember, all Māori speakers are bilingual, so all Māori speakers know they can speak English to another Māori speaker, and be completely understood. People may believe they need to be equally bilingual in English and Māori before speaking Māori to a great extent. This has two implications worth considering. Firstly, as noted above, not many people learn Māori as their first, or only, language, to any great extent. So, we are all bilingual. Furthermore, most Māori speakers are L2 learners of Māori (Te Kura Roa 2017a). A natural question to ask is whether speakers are ever going to achieve a native-like competency in their second language, and if this is even a reasonable expectation. As has long been pointed out, equal proficiency in multiple languages is incredibly rare, and it is entirely normal bilingual behaviour to have varying proficiencies of those languages depending on the domains in which those languages are needed (Beardsmore 1986; Grosjean 2008; McCarty and Wyman 2009). If comparisons are occurring, speakers may never feel equipped enough to carry on conversation in Māori, even though they actually are. The idea of achieving native-like proficiency is one that should be treated with more care in language revitalisation discussions, especially within the community, since it is so rare, and unnecessary to be a successful bilingual who contributes positively to revitalisation. As one final thought here, the time it takes to achieve this goal is considerable, and time is something languages undergoing revitalisation cannot afford.

The second internal factor identified that promotes a shift to English is language anxiety. While some believe knowing te reo Māori makes one feel more Māori, engaging with the language for the first time can be challenging for Māori, because of the intense internal identity attachment that comes with the task (Te Huia 2015). Many Māori have been raised outside Māori cultural contexts and may know very little about their culture (Statistics New Zealand 2013). They may have had no exposure to their identity at home, and there is no national adoption of language or culture in the mainstream education system—a system that caters to 90.4% of Māori children (Education Central 2019). Growing up this way is incredibly normal, and so, is a primary context in which language learning operates—it is the first time in which many Māori people have done anything remotely Māori. It also means the bulk of our speakers, as learners themselves, have experienced this anxiety at some point.

To feel deficient in one's heritage, language can negatively affect one's internal identity as a Māori person, and this is the basis of language anxiety. According to Te Huia (2013: 87), anxiety was a reason 'individuals would not initiate language use or engage with language-learning settings'. Additionally, language is also how we fix stress, as it is 'a means of getting rid of our nervous energy when we are under stress' (Crystal 2006: 465). It is easy to see then, why anxiety of any form can trigger a shift away from the anxiety-inducing language, to the safer option. One reason the safer option is English is that Māori people can comfortably exercise their Māori identity in English (Holmes 2005). This may sound like a categorical statement that may be contested by some, but it is not. It is entirely acceptable in Aotearoa to be Māori without ever learning the language. The key marker of Māori identity is whakapapa, ancestry, not language (Kukutai and Callister 2009). If a Māori person feels anxiety from learning or speaking Māori, they can comfortably and safely navigate their Māori identity in English.

I want to state here unequivocally I detest the view that Māori people must learn Māori in order to be Māori, or that knowing the language makes some Māori more Māori than others. I am unwilling to entertain either view—to be Māori is to have Māori ancestry, whether that ancestry is consciously known by a Māori descendant or not. However, there are two implications that identity anxiety brings to new Māori learners of Māori and they also deserve attention. Firstly, one does not need the language in order to be Māori, and learning Māori challenges that person's identity. Therefore, I understand how it can seem much easier to just not learn or use the language. Part of the RLS efforts needs to show people the identity benefits that come with learning the language—pride in communicating as our ancestors did, taking part in the operations and rituals of Māori spaces and participating in strengthening our communities. We also need to address the anxiety head-on in our classes and teaching spaces and show learners that it is possible to move beyond that language anxiety.

Further to the point, there are unhelpful opinions present within the speaker community that encourage learner anxiety—and speakers must do better to correct their attitudes. Once learners come into contact with the language, and its community, some of those unhelpful opinions are internalised as identity rejection. One such opinion is an adage that you must speak Māori in order to be Māori (Rewi 2012; King 2007). When new learners encounter this opinion, they may internalise that they're not 'Māori enough' to even bother learning in the first place. Remember too, these people may be able to comfortably negotiate their identity entirely in English. It makes sense then, that this internal struggle would be difficult to overcome—there is little reason to enter into an uncomfortable negotiation of one's identity in Māori, if the same is unquestioned in English. The speaker community, as a whole, needs to understand and see this attitude as altogether unhelpful and remove that attitude from its people.

External Factors

External factors also exist that promote a shift to English. These are both societal and family-based. If English is the primary language of any given situation, it makes sense that bilinguals would accommodate to English. Since so much of Aotearoa society promotes the de facto use of English, this factor is simply a response to normal bilingual behaviour.

Family dissuasion of Māori language use is potentially more problematic, especially for the home domain. The effects of being beaten as children for using the language has promoted long-lasting traumatic effects that exist to this day (Wirihana and Smith 2014), and trauma of all kinds can be transferred to younger generations (Byers-Brown 2015). Even if perpetrators do not know what they are doing, family members who are politically against the normalisation of Māori in the home can covertly or overtly voice that feeling (Te Kura Roa 2017b: 11).

As explained at the start of this chapter, changing attitudes in the home is difficult, and such negative attitudes would have a significant effect on the language choice in this domain.

Listener Factors

As discussed above with relation to speaker anxiety, the same is true for a listener. If a speaker predicts that a listener will feel some anxiety around Māori language use, or if that anxiety is visible, the conversation may take place in English when it does not actually need to be. This is part of a considerate response to communication with people. Another critical factor presented here is the language of first encounters. As already pointed out, Piller (2002) notes that if two bilinguals meet in one language, they will navigate their communicative rules and personalities in that language. Changing that language of interaction feels ingenuine, as those rules and personalities have to be renegotiated. Therefore, if that language is English for two bilinguals, that language will be difficult to change. This has implications for the home, given that some English-speaking families can know each other well, and they essentially have to meet each other again as strangers in order to change that language. This would undoubtedly be awkward, since families are the mainstay of intimate language, and the people within the home would know each other so well. To date, while there are anecdotal instances of families successfully changing their communicative norms in favour of the Māori language, no thorough studies have been completed on the topic.

Māori Language Choices

Having presented the array of themes the author identifies that promote an English language choice, it is necessary to do the same for Māori language choices, adopting the same internal, external and listener categories. Table 3 shows the myriad of factors Māori speakers make Māori language choices.

Table 3 Māori language choices of Māori speakers

	Factor promoting Māori language use
Internal	Speaker adopts a political stance that Māori should be used at all times
	Māori is the dominant language of the context
	Māori is used as a private language
	Māori is used only for simple greetings
External	Speaker privileges Māori language contexts in life, or avoids English ones
Listener	Children are present
	A listener is Māori-presenting
	Māori is the language of a community of practise

Internal Factors

Politically, some learners and speakers adopt the internal ideal that Māori should be spoken and used at all times. Indeed, the adage 'speak Māori at all times, in all places' has long been part of the macro-level policy intentions for the language (see Te Taura Whiri 1990). This has culminated in Mahuru Māori, a groundswell of speakers who commit to speaking only Māori for the month of September every year, regardless of who they are speaking to (Te Taura Whiri, n.d.). This practice is good in theory, because it takes a political standpoint to use a marginalised language in each and every space around the country, and thus contributes greatly to challenging the status quo which privileges English as a language for the nation.

Taking this standpoint is likely to be a marked language choice in some spaces, however. For example, the speaker may not be understood by a listener who does not speak Māori. It can be accepted that Māori is a politicised language in Aotearoa, and speaking Māori in public has received negative attention over the years (Wright 2015). Listeners sometimes feel uncomfortable in these situations as they try to navigate forced miscommunication. However, it is also somewhat necessary to pursue this avenue for the normalisation of the language, as majority populations need to encounter this discomfort—tourists and residents of New Zealand who do not speak English are still able to live lives in New

Zealand. Because of this, the author is not prepared to assert that the discomfort of a monolingual English speaker is unjustified.

Secondly, when a speaker has the understanding that Māori will be the dominant language of a particular context, it creates an internal notion that Māori should be used. This seems, at first, an ideal belief and one that has immense potential for revitalisation. On closer inspection, however, the researcher found these contexts were few and far between, and mostly limited to rote-learnt behaviours such as prayer, whaikōrero and karanga.[6] Because these contexts are mostly very short, relegated to very few people of status and not related to spontaneous conversation, this does suggest the opportunity to have this particular internal factor occur is quite slim. Given that such exemplary behaviour is restricted to older members of the community, it also has little impact on language change among younger generations. Lastly, these occurrences happen mostly on marae,[7] and not within homes. It is therefore likely that these kinds of speech acts bear no weight upon language use among the family.

Māori is, on occasion, used as a private language to avoid others understanding. While this factor was reasonably prevalent, the author has reservations about its ability to affect positively on language use. The author recalls a situation at a protest where Māori speakers were talking about him negatively in Māori, behind his back. That party were not aware the author could speak Māori. It was an uncomfortable affair, and the author had to correct those people—who turned out to be relations of his. Therefore, while a positive language choice is made, exclusion of others can have an equally negative outcome for all involved.

Lastly, some speakers maintain a use of Māori automatically in any situation, but that is restricted to simple greetings only. This has some potential for normalisation, but its ability to affect positive language change for intergenerational transmission is probably limited. This is not unlike discussions in the international literature around post-vernacularity. Glaser (2008: 162), for example, comments that 'a language [can be] capable of making a social statement, devoid of its vernacular use. This statement can be made through commodification, performativity, translation, and sometimes the act of learning to speak the Yiddish language'. Closer to home, Harlow (2005: 145) has raised similar concerns about the Māori language being symbolic, arguing that these kinds of 'measures serve to increase the visibility and distinctiveness of Māori as an element within an English-speaking environment, not as a language in its own right'. If simple greetings serve us in this regard, there is likely a disconnection between what speakers want to achieve and what we are actually achieving.

External Factors

There was just one external factor identified that promoted a Māori language choice. When a Māori speaker privileges Māori-speaking contexts, or avoids English ones, there is more ability for the external factors at play to support a Māori language choice. There are no data to quantify this, but it is possible that some speakers of Māori have a greater capacity in Māori than English, and so try to arrange their lives to situate themselves in contexts where they can use the language they are more comfortable in. However, this would be somewhat limiting free movement around the country, because one could only take part in the very few Māori-speaking parts of society—on rural marae, for example. However, it does raise another thought—a natural idea to positively enhance the use of Māori is to expend resources into creating more of those spaces for people to enjoy.

Listener Factors

Three listener-induced factors were identified in the research. Firstly, when children are being spoken to, many speakers will choose to use Māori. This can be a proficiency factor—adults feel more comfortable using the Māori they know to children. This is also possibly related to an understanding of intergenerational transmission, and the idea that children need to speak and hear Māori. This seems like a positive move for language movement in the home, as it is the space in which intergenerational transmission occurs.

There are two insights to be wary of here, however. Firstly, it seems relatively common that if the presence of children promotes language shift, it is possible that the Māori language use here is structured around communicating orders and discipline. There is a negative relationship between discipline and linguistic development (Del Vecchio et al. 2014). Therefore, if children are only receiving orders and discipline in Māori, they will attach negativity to the language, although no immediately relevant research can substantiate that claim.

Secondly, if children are spoken to in Māori, and expected to engage in the language, but adults are communicating English, the child will inevitably adopt the understanding that adults do not speak Māori to each other, and therefore the language is not something worth valuing in adult life later on. Intragenerational transmission, the visible exchange of languages between generations, is just as important as intergenerational transmission. In the *Te Kura Roa* findings, the same research for which this data was collected found that intragenerational transmission is not widely occurring among our speakers (Higgins et al. 2017: 13). This is also supported by other research projects (Hutchings et. al. 2017). The power dynamics of this point have been touched on above—if the parents are requiring children to speak a language they do not speak among themselves, there is no real reason the children should want to use that language. This is something that must be overtly corrected among Māori-speaking adults. It should be mentioned too that this is different from One Parent One Language theories, as the power dynamics in these situations are different.

Secondly, if a Māori person is Māori-presenting, that is, if they appear visibly Māori to a speaker, speakers are more likely to speak Māori to them. This is good, as long as speakers are cognisant of the fact that many Māori speakers are not necessarily Māori-presenting, and that Māori-presenting monolingual English speakers may induce feelings of shame if they cannot speak Māori. Attaching that identity to them would be anxiety-inducing for the listener.

Lastly, Māori speakers are more likely to use Māori if they have a connected, established community of practice that engages in Māori. This community may have been established during a language class, another class related to the Māori world where the language is used or a social group. The group lasts beyond the confines of a single physical location, and so does the language of choice. Indeed, it seems feasible that establishing one's own community of practice where Māori is the language of choice is a positive way of supporting language use. For a family, it seems to make sense to establish such a cluster of like-minded people, to co-exist with other families. Such initiatives do exist in Aotearoa. In the South Island, *Kotahi Mano Kāika, Kotahi Mano Wawata* is one such programme, which has enjoyed some success since its inception over a decade ago (White and Rewi 2014). The initiative, from the South Island's largest tribe Ngāi Tahi, aspires to create one thousand Māori-speaking homes by 2025. While little public information is available to illustrate its success so far, there is no doubt that the movement has enjoyed some success, with 2,000 families currently participating in the exercise to make Māori the primary language of the home, and within that, the reinstatement of the tribe's first generation of native speakers in some time (Kotahi Mano Kāika, n.d.).

Conclusions

There are many complex factors that inhibit the language choices of Māori speakers, and this chapter has aimed to identify those factors and organise them in a cohesive way. Of course, the study is not without limitations relevant to this book—in the main, it was not a study connected explicitly to the home. There is also little research to substantiate some of the claims this chapter makes. However, the language choices shown paint an overall picture as to how these decisions are made, from which inferences that affect language use in the home are also made, as a micro-environment of society at large.

Māori language revitalisation has been occurring for over forty years, and one key question is whether that period of time is long enough to observe some kind of trend in intergenerational transmission. If it is deemed long enough, the trend does not seem so high. However, it is also fair to posit the theory that intergenerational transmission involves three complete generations (grandparent, to parent, to child). This is perhaps not aligned to the conventional definition, but it does make sense to think about transmission in this way, as it solidifies language transmission across the generations. Therefore, success may not be quantifiable by any secure means until the arrival of the fourth generation—if those children are being raised with te reo Māori as the primary language of the home, success would be quite clear.

While intergenerational transmission is important, one significant and less researched component of family language policy identified; here is intragenerational transmission. The amount each individual generation is talking to each other has not been subject to study yet. If children are not observing their parents or grandparents talking Māori to each other, it makes sense to infer that they will be less likely to do the same when they reach that same age. This chapter suggests a phenomenon whereby te reo Māori use is geared towards children only, and not necessarily towards adult use. If this is the case, children may adopt the idea that te reo Māori is not really for adults to speak. As they age, they may cease speaking Māori, and perpetuate a cycle of adult-to-child communication, but not adult-to-adult communication. If this cycle is solidified, intergenerational transmission is probably not going to be possible. This inference, of course, comes without consideration of many other factors that are valid and real. One Language One Parent policies, for example, can be very successful. However, it does at least make sense to examine how intragenerational transmission affects intergenerational transmission, and it seems reasonable to suggest that we need to make a more concerted effort to convince adult Māori speakers to communicate in the language among themselves, if we are going to succeed.

Notes

1. Readers should therefore be aware that this content has been also collated elsewhere, in the Māori language (see Olsen-Reeder 2017).
2. Such as Aroha Mead, Dr Moana Jackson and Dame Ngāneko Minhinnick.
3. It is the feeling of this author too, that there is also an overall fascination with language death in the Māori language world, and this almost certainly ensures conversations hover at the bleaker end of the spectrum (see Olsen-Reeder 2018).
4. Code is an umbrella term for languages, dialects and sociolects. The author uses language choice in this chapter, to denote that

two distinct languages (rather than dialects or sociolects) are being discussed.
5. The author is altogether uncomfortable with gendered pronouns as they are used here; however, they must remain in order to preserve academic integrity of the paper.
6. Whaikōrero and karanga are traditional modes of welcome to traditionally Māori spaces.
7. Marae are traditional communal places for a tribe, or sub-tribe.

References

Barrett-Walker, T., Plank, M., Ka'ai-Mahuta, R., Hikuroa, D., and James, A. 2020. Kia kaua te reo e rite ki te moa, ka ngaro: Do Not Let the Language Suffer the Same Fate as the moa. *Journal of the Royal Society* 17. https://doi.org/10.1098/rsif.2019.0526.

Bauer, W. 2008. Is the Health of Te Reo Māori Improving? *Te Reo* 51: 33–73.

Beardsmore, H. 1986. *Bilingualism: Basic Principles*. Clevedon: Multilingual Matters.

Biggs, B. 1968. The Maori Language: Past and Present. In *The Maori People in the Nineteen-Sixties*, ed. E. Schwimmer, 65–84. Auckland: Blackwood & Janet Paul.

Byers-Brown, T. 2015. 'He Reached Across the River and Healed the Generations of Hara': Structural Violence, Historical Trauma, and Healing Among Contemporary Whanganui Māori. Unpublished Master's Thesis, Victoria University of Wellington.

Crystal, D. 2006. *How Language Works*. London: Penguin.

Del Vecchio, T., R. Pochtar, and K. Rhoades. 2014. The Impact of Children's Language Ability on Parent Cognitions and Harsh Discipline Practices. *Infant & Child Development* 23: 388–401.

Education Central. 2019. *Three Ways to Promote Positive Outcomes for Māori in English-Medium Education*. https://educationcentral.co.nz/three-ways-to-promote-positive-outcomes-for-maori-in-mainstream-education/. Accessed 24 September 2020.

Giles, H., R. Bourhis, and D. Taylor. 1977. Towards a Theory of Language in Ethnic Group Relations. In *Language, Ethnicity and Intergroup Relations*, ed. H. Giles, 307–348. London: Academic Press.

Glaser, A. 2008. From Polylingual to Postvernacular: Imagining Yiddish in the Twenty-First Century. *Jewish Social Studies* 14 (3): 150–164.

Grosjean, F. 2008. *Studying Bilinguals*. Oxford: Oxford University Press.

Harlow, R. 2005. Covert Attitudes to Māori. *International Journal of the Sociology of Language* 172: 133–147.

Herman, S. 1961. Explorations in the Social Psychology of Language Choice. *Human Relations* 14: 149–164.

Higgins, R., Rewi, P., and Olsen-Reeder, V. 2017. *Ngā Whakakitenga a Te Kura Roa*. Auckland: Ngā Pae o Te Māramatanga.

Holmes, J. 2005. Using Māori English in New Zealand. *International Journal of the Sociology of Language* 172: 95–115.

Hutchings, J., Higgins, R., Bright, N., Keane, B., Olsen-Reeder, V., and Hunia, M. 2017. *Te Ahu o te reo Māori: Overview Report*. Wellington: Te Wāhanga, New Zealand Council for Educational Research.

Jernudd, B., and E. Thuan. 1983. Control of Language Through Correction in Speaking. *International Journal of the Sociology of Language* 44: 71–98.

King, J. 2007. Eke ki runga i te waka: The Use of Dominant Metaphors by Newly Fluent Māori Speakers in Historical Perspective. Unpublished PhD Thesis, Canterbury University, Christchurch.

Kukutai, T., and P. Callister. 2009. A 'Main' Ethnic Group?: Ethnic Self-Prioritisation among New Zealand Youth. *Social Policy Journal of New Zealand* 36: 16–31.

Lane, C. 2020. Contrasting Statistical Indicators of Māori Language Revitalization: Conversational Ability, Speaking Proficiency, and First Language. http://hdl.handle.net/10125/24924. Accessed 17 June 2020.

Li, W. 2000. Dimensions of Bilingualism. In *The Bilingualism Reader*, ed. W. Li, 3–25. London: Routledge.

McCardle, P. 2015. Bilingualism: Research and Policy. *The Global Context for New Directions for Child and Adolescent Development* 147: 41–48.

McCarty, T., and L. Wyman. 2009. Indigenous Youth and Bilingualism—Theory, Research, Praxis. *Journal of Language, Identity and Education* 8 (5): 279–290.

Mackey, W. 2000. The Description of Bilingualism. In *The Bilingualism Reader*, ed. W. Li, 26–54.

Māori Language Advisory Group. 2015. *Te Whare o te Reo Mauriora*. Wellington: Te Puni Kōkiri.

Milroy, J., and M. Milroy. 1985. Linguistic Change, Social Network and Speaker Innovation. *Journal of Linguistics* 21 (2): 339–384.

Myers-Scotton, C. 1983. The Negotiation of Identities in Conversation: A Theory of Markedness and Code Choice. *International Journal of the Sociology of Language* 44: 115–136.

New Zealand Parliament. 2010. *Ministerial Statements—UN Declaration on the Rights of Indigenous Peoples—Government Support*. https://www.parliament.nz/en/pb/hansard-debates/rhr/document/49HansD_20100420_00000071/ministerial-statements-un-declaration-on-the-rights-of. Accessed 17 June 2020.

Olsen-Reeder, V. 2017. Kia Tomokia Te Kākahu o te reo Māori. Unpublished PhD Thesis, Victoria University of Wellington.

Olsen-Reeder, V. 2018. Deathly Narratives: Theorising "Reo-rientation" for Language Revitalisation Discourses. *MAI Journal* 7 (2): 203–214.

Ormsby-Teki, T., Timutimu, N., Palmer, H., Ellis, R., and Johnston, P. 2011. *Reo o te Kainga: A Ngāi Te Rangi Tribal Response to Advancing Māori Language in the Home.* Auckland: Ngā Pae o te Māramatanga.

Otsuka, T. 2005. *History of Polynesian Languages*. http://citeseerx.ist.psu.edu/viewdoc/download?doi=10.1.1.403.8742&rep=rep1&type=pdf. Accessed 17 June 2020.

Piller, I. 2002. *Bilingual Couples Talk: The Discursive Construction of Hybridity.* Amsterdam and Philadelphia: John Benjamins.

Rewi, P. 2012. An Active and Functional Language: Te Reo in the Early Contact Period. In *Huia Histories of Māori: Ngā Tāhuhu Kōrero*, ed. D. Keenan, 73–92. Wellington: Huia.

Sachdev, I., and H. Giles. 2006. Bilingual Accommodation. In *The Handbook of Bilingualism*, ed. T. Bhatia and W. Ritchie, 353–378. Malden, MA: Blackwell.

Spolsky, B. 2009. *Language Management*. Cambridge: Cambridge University Press.

Spolsky, B. 2012. Family Language Policy—The Critical Domain. *Journal of Multilingual and Multicultural Development* 33 (1): 3–11.

Statistics New Zealand. 2013. Taku Mara E: Connecting to ancestral marae 2013. http://archive.stats.govt.nz/~/media/Statistics/browse-categories/people-and-communities/maori/te-kupenga/taku-marae-e-2013-english/takumarae2013-english.pdf. Accessed 18 December 2020.

Statistics New Zealand. 2014a. *Measuring te reo Māori Speakers: A Guide to Different Data Sources*. http://archive.stats.govt.nz/browse_for_stats/people_

and_communities/maori/measuring-te-reo-maori-speakers.aspx. Accessed 18 December 2020.

Statistics New Zealand. 2014b. *Ka mārō te aho tapu, ka tau te korowai: Te reo Māori Findings from Te Kupenga 2013*. http://archive.stats.govt.nz/browse_for_stats/people_and_communities/maori/te-reo-report-2013.aspx#gsc.tab=0. Accessed 18 December 2020.

Statistics New Zealand. 2014c. *2013 Census QuickStats about Families and Households*. http://archive.stats.govt.nz/Census/2013-census/profile-and-summary-reports/qstats-families-households/households.aspx#gsc.tab=0. Accessed 18 December 2020.

Statistics New Zealand. 2020a. *Te Kupenga: 2018 (Provisional)—English*. https://www.stats.govt.nz/information-releases/te-kupenga-2018-provisional-english. Accessed 18 December 2020.

Statistics New Zealand. 2020b. 2018 Census Totals by Topic—National Highlights (updated). https://www.stats.govt.nz/information-releases/2018-census-totals-by-topic-national-highlights-updated. Accessed 18 December 2020.

Tawhiwhirangi, I. 2014. Kua Tū Tāngata E! Moving a Critical Mass. In Higgins, Rewi & Olsen-Reeder (eds). *Te Hua o Te Reo Māori: The Value of The Māori Language*. 33–52. Wellington: Huia.

Te Kura Roa. 2017a. *Pūrongo 1: He Whenua Haumako – Te Kōhanga Reo, Te Ataarangi*. http://www.maramatanga.ac.nz/sites/default/files/project-reports/Purongo%201LR.pdf. Accessed 18 December 2020.

Te Kura Roa. 2017b. *Pūrongo 3: Te Reo Māori me te Whānau*. http://www.maramatanga.ac.nz/sites/default/files/project-reports/Purongo%203LR.pdf. Accessed 18 December 2020.

Te Huia, A. 2013. Whāia te Iti Kahurangi, ki te Tuohu koe, me Maunga Teitei: Establishing Psychological Foundations for Higher Levels of Māori Language Proficiency. Unpublished PhD Thesis, Victoria University of Wellington.

Te Huia, A. 2015. Kia aha te Māori kia Māori ai? Perspectives Towards Māori Identity by Māori Heritage Language Learners. *New Zealand Journal of Psychology* 44 (3): 18–28.

Te Puni Kōkiri. 2019. *UN Declaration on the Rights of Indigenous Peoples*. https://www.tpk.govt.nz/en/whakamahia/un-declaration-on-the-rights-of-indigenous-peoples. Accessed 17 June 2020.

Te Taura Whiri. 1990. *Me pēhea te reo Māori e ora ai?*. https://www.tetaurawhiri.govt.nz/en/he-muka/he-muka/me-pehea-te-reo-maori-e-ora-ai/. Accessed 25 September 2020.

Te Taura Whiri. N.d.. *Mahuru Māori*. https://www.tetaurawhiri.govt.nz/en/he-muka/he-muka/mahuru-maori/. Accessed 24 September 2020.

White, T., and P. Rewi. 2014. The Value of Dialect amongst Kāi Tahu: Kā puananī o Tahu Pōtiki, he Manawa Reo, he Manawa Kāi Tahu. *Psychology and Developing Societies* 26 (2): 213–232.

Wirihana, R., and C. Smith. 2014. Historical Trauma, Healing and Well-being in Māori Communities. *MAI Journal* 3 (3): 197–210.

Wright, K. 2015. *Ugly Attitudes Towards Maori Language*. https://www.nzherald.co.nz/rotorua-daily-post/news/news/article.cfm?c_id=1503437&objectid=11465489. Accessed 25 September 2020.

Peer-to-Peer Endangered Language Transmission Among Adults

Julia Sallabank

Introduction and Literature Review

Measures of language vitality usually focus on intergenerational transmission as their key descriptor. According to the most influential assessment scales (Fishman 1991; Moseley 2010; Lewis and Simons 2010), languages are described as endangered when the parental generation—especially young adults—does not use the language in the home or community. Thus, a common definition of an endangered language is that it is not being passed on to children in the home or community.

Given this disciplinary emphasis on intergenerational transmission, it is hardly surprising that the majority of language revitalisation programmes foreground the teaching of languages to children, usually

J. Sallabank (✉)
School of Languages, Cultures and Linguistics,
SOAS University of London, London, UK
e-mail: js72@soas.ac.uk

M. Hornsby and W. McLeod (eds.), *Transmitting Minority Languages*,
Palgrave Studies in Minority Languages and Communities,
https://doi.org/10.1007/978-3-030-87910-5_8

via formal education. Immersion education is a frequently chosen model (Pine and Turin 2017), but it requires teachers who are proficient in both language and curriculum content. In a highly endangered language context, where the language is used only by the (great-)grandparent generation, such teachers may not be readily available. Fishman (1991, 2001) identifies the 'home-family-neighbourhood-community' nexus as crucial for language maintenance. For this too, proficient adults are essential: 'if there are no efforts undertaken to teach parents of child-bearing age the threatened language as an active [threatened language as a second language], then parents [...] will not be able to transmit that language as a mother tongue to their children' (Fishman 2001: 15). Baker et al. (2011: 56) agree that 'given that language planning [...] requires the acquisition of a threatened language by children, [...] adult language learning enables such acquisition'. Thus, without proficient adult speakers, there can be no intergenerational language transmission, either in schools or in the family. It follows that development of proficient new speakers, together with language teaching skills, should be a priority for language planning in endangered language contexts. Regarding Scottish Gaelic, Smith-Christmas and Armstrong (2014: 312) argue that 'in order to best maximise Gaelic education as means to RLS [reversing language shift], the education of adult heritage learners needs to be seen as a complementary strategy to childhood education, not as a secondary (and often lower priority) tactic to ensuring the vitality of the language'.

In contrast, this chapter argues that children are not necessarily the most effective target population sector for language revitalisation to succeed. Romaine (2006) points out that many language planners ignore Fishman's advice to focus on the home and community, and instead invest in the relatively resource-heavy strategy of teaching minority languages through schools to each cohort afresh. In several parts of the world, endangered languages, such as Welsh, Breton or Māori, have been taught in language nests and immersion schools since the 1950s, but this has not secured the widespread re-establishment of intergenerational transmission in the family or the community (Edwards and Newcombe 2005; Pacific Policy Research Centre 2010).

The substantial financial and human resources needed for immersion education are not available for the revitalisation of Guernesiais, the local language of Guernsey, Channel Islands. As will be described in the section "Becoming a New Speaker of Guernesiais", Guernesiais has very low vitality, i.e. few speakers below the age of 80. Delays in political recognition have meant that there are no schoolteachers trained to teach Guernesiais; in order for revitalisation to progress, it is therefore necessary to develop proficient adult speakers and teachers.

This chapter will examine the experiences of adult learners of Guernesiais, as they seek to move beyond beginner and elementary levels. It will also discuss and evaluate some initiatives that encourage peer-to-peer language transmission among adults: both individual efforts and organised activities. I will argue that, for highly endangered languages at least, peer-to-peer adult transmission, as a crucial element of developing new speakers, may be a more realistic strategy for revitalisation than the traditional focus on intergenerational transmission through the schools or family.

Many so-called language revitalisation activities such as festivals or signage are effectively emblematic in nature, since they focus on language promotion rather than acquisition (e.g. Shandler 2006; Sallabank 2011). If such activities are to form part of integrated language planning for revitalisation, they need to be linked to effective language acquisition and status planning strategies. In order to produce, for example, signage in a local language, or learning materials, there needs to be a core of proficient speakers with enough skills to provide the required resource (e.g. literacy in the local language; translation skills; digital expertise; pedagogical knowledge). As argued in a blog post on Scottish Gaelic: 'Just seeing a language pictured [on road signs] does little to help us learn it; we need to actively use a language to accomplish this and, perhaps more importantly, continue to use it' (Mattschey 2020).

Learning and teaching a small, highly endangered language differ in many ways to a major national or international language. An endangered language has lower visibility and audibility than a major one. There are often few learning resources. Standard descriptors and goals designed for larger languages (e.g. in the Common European Framework of Reference for Languages 2020) are not applicable when there is very little target language in the media or linguistic landscape. Where most fluent speakers are aged 80 or over and their number is declining rapidly, there are few interlocutors for prospective new speakers, and the traditional speaker community is fragmenting. For many minority languages, there is no full language description, standardised writing system or reliable pedagogical/reference materials. As will be seen in the section "Learners' Experiences and Needs", Guernesiais learners would particularly welcome more opportunities to hear and speak in a non-formal environment. This echoes the findings of Mitchell (2020) regarding adult learners of Inuktitut as a second language: whether in a classroom setting or not, the most effective learning activity was practice in speaking Inuktitut, especially with Elders and advanced learners as interlocutors: the latter were seen as effective mentors and a source of inspiration. Keegan (2020) examined the effect of the COVID-19 lockdown on Māori language learning; a key finding was the realisation that one-to-one interaction was a fundamental need for learners—the provision of online content was not sufficient. Prospective new speakers of Guernesiais find it difficult to progress beyond beginner level because of the lack of opportunities and resources, including a shortage of teachers and of lessons beyond low-intermediate level. But the key hindrance to developing fluency identified by participants in the research reported in this chapter was a lack of opportunities to practise outside formal classes. As noted in a blog post on learning minority languages, 'if you're learning a minority language your main problem may not be the grammar and vocab but finding some native speakers to practise with' (Popkins 2020).

Nguyen and Hamid (2020) link individuals' minority language use to language policy outcomes using Grin's (2003) framework, which outlines three key conditions for language use:

1. *capacity*—people's competence and ability to use the language
2. *opportunity*—their chances for language use in a favourable environment
3. *desire*—their willingness or motivation to use the language.

Nguyen and Hamid go on to stress that

> Grin argues that policies aiming to maintain regional or minority languages need to consider enhancing people's linguistic capacity, facilitating their language use opportunities and motivating their desire to use these languages for language maintenance and revitalisation to occur (Nguyen and Hamid 2020: 4).

In this framework, peer interaction in a minority language is key for language maintenance, and therefore, capacity and opportunity to do so should be promoted through language policies. These conclusions are supported by a review of adult learning of Welsh; moreover, 'language acquisition planning depends on such learners moving to fluency in the language, and thereby to daily language use' (Baker et al. 2011: 41).

As many endangered languages are under-described and not taught in mainstream education, there is rarely an official measure of language proficiency. As noted above, 'can-do' descriptors such as those used in the Common European Framework of Reference for Languages are not applicable when many of the 'can-do' activities are unavailable in the target language. This chapter uses a provisional descriptor to assess conversational fluency in a lesser-used language: 'able to hold a *sustained*, *impromptu* conversation on a *range of topics*'. These criteria enable a researcher to distinguish proficient speakers from people who can understand but not reply at length, or whose language is largely formulaic, or who use a restricted range of structures and vocabulary, or who use the language mainly in rehearsed situations such as recitals—or even classrooms.

New Speakers and the *Muda*

In a highly endangered language context, the heritage language is no longer the main language of the wider community: it is *post*-vernacular (Shandler 2006). Most fluent speakers are from the great-grandparent generation; fewer and fewer native speakers are active outside their homes, and their numbers are reducing due to age and attrition. In such contexts, language survival depends on the emergence of a new speaker community, which learners need to build for themselves through proactive effort and peer interaction. In doing so they may invest time, energy and part of their identity into the target heritage/minority language (Norton 2013; Ayres-Bennett and Fisher 2021). The research discussed in this chapter benefited from participation in a network of researchers focusing on the dynamics involved in becoming a *new speaker* of a language in the context of a multilingual Europe.[1] Researchers active in this network developed not only the concept of new speaker, but also that of *muda*: 'a critical juncture in the life cycle where a speaker changes linguistic practice in favour of the target language' (Walsh and O'Rourke 2014: 68). Walsh and O'Rourke identify a number of stages at which learners may develop a *muda*, based on experience in minoritised languages such as Catalan, Galician or Irish, where there are several opportunities for linguistic *mudes* throughout the lifespan (Walsh and O'Rourke 2014; Pujolar and Puigdevall 2015; Puigdevall et al. 2018). But in the case study in this chapter, Guernesiais is less widely spoken and has even less institutional support than these 'medium-sized' minority languages. Given the small size of both the speaker and general populations in Guernsey, it can be difficult for prospective new speakers to make a conscious change to their language practices to use Guernesiais as their main language of communication. There are nevertheless examples of individuals and small groups who have decided consciously to use Guernesiais to converse with other speakers/learners, both informally and at organised activities. As noted by Pujolar and Puigdevall (2015: 167), the study of linguistic *mudes* provides 'a new and productive perspective on how people develop their linguistic repertoire, their attachment to specific languages and the significance of these aspects for social identity'. This chapter interprets *muda* not only in terms of language proficiency, but extends the concept to encompass a mindset indicating identification with, and attachment to, the heritage language, and a commitment to take active measures to develop fluency.

Adult Learning of a Minority Language

Many adult language learners are hampered by the belief that adults cannot learn languages well. Research into age factors in second language acquisition generally recognises the existence of a 'critical period', although this has recently been found to last considerably longer than previously thought: 'grammar-learning ability [...] is preserved almost to the crux of adulthood (17.4 years old)' (Hartshorne et al. 2018: 263), while learners who start after the age of 20 can attain 'native-like' levels.[2] There is no age limit on vocabulary learning, and adults bring increased life experience and analytical skills, as well as self-motivation, to the task of language learning (Singleton and Ryan 2003). As recognised by Andrew (2012), age is a social construct, and learners' beliefs and expectations play an important role in how they construct their identities as language learners.

In Guernsey, as with many other minority-language contexts, many learners have learnt other languages previously: often French at school, sometimes Spanish, and occasionally German during the Second World War when Guernsey was occupied. Guernesiais is therefore often their third or more language, so they bring experience and memories (positive and negative) of prior language learning (Cenoz 2019).

Very few studies deal specifically with adult learning of minoritised and endangered languages. Belmar et al. (2019) investigate the motivations of learners of West Frisian in the Netherlands. Flynn (2020) discusses affective factors (attitude, motivation and identity) that shape the learning of Irish, which include the social and psychological distance between Irish language learners/new speakers and 'traditional' or 'native' Irish speakers, an issue that also affects learners of Guernesiais (see the section "Learners' Experiences and Needs"). Flynn makes the valuable points that language attainment goals should be based on learners' own aspirations rather than on native-speaker models or on what researchers or pedagogues have deemed the ultimate goal of language learning. However, these studies do not investigate learners' strategies to accomplish their goals. Basham and Fathman (2008) asked the question 'What factors contribute to successful language learning by latent speakers?' (see the section "Latent Speakers and Language Reactivation"), but they too focused on motivation; from their two case studies, it is impossible to tell whether formal or informal learning was more effective in developing fluency. Cordella and Huang (2016) recommend interaction between older speakers and younger learners of migrant minority languages, akin to Hinton et al.'s (2002, 2018) Master–Apprentice method for endangered languages (see the section "Learners' Experiences and Needs").

Latent Speakers and Language Reactivation

Many gradations of speaker proficiency and characteristics have been identified in endangered languages research (Grinevald and Bert 2011; Flores Farfán and Olko 2020). Those who call themselves native speakers of an endangered language are not necessarily fully fluent. Under the definitions provided by Grinevald and Bert (2011) and Dorian (1977), many 'native speakers' of Guernesiais could be categorised as 'semi-speakers', who 'have not had and do not have regular conversation partners in the endangered language, and operate most of their socio-linguistic lives in the dominant language rather than the endangered language' (Grinevald and Bert 2011: 50). As an 'engaged researcher' (Grinevald, personal communication 2009) I avoid using the term 'semi-speaker', which can be perceived as insulting and which has overtones of the discredited notion of 'semilingualism' (Edelsky et al. 1983). Basham and Fathman (2008: 578) use the term 'latent speaker' to denote 'an adult raised in an environment where a heritage language is spoken who did not become a fluent speaker of that language'. This describes a cohort who developed receptive competence: they can understand the language and make appropriate responses (often non-verbal) in some contexts, but they did not develop productive proficiency. This is a very common phenomenon in language shift contexts, in some cases covering an entire generation. In Guernsey, latent speakers are typically aged approximately 55–75 at the time of writing.

Basham and Fathman (2008) stress the potential of latent speakers to re-learn their heritage language. Grinevald and Bert use the term 'rememberer' for people with a lower level of language knowledge: those who heard the language when young but did not acquire receptive competence. Nevertheless, the term 'rememberer' 'evokes the possibility that such speakers may regain or reacquire some partial active use of the language' (Grinevald and Bert 2011: 51). As will be seen in section "Rememberers", some Guernesiais language supporters from this cohort have re-appropriated the term 'rememberer' and are making efforts to reactivate their language knowledge as part of their identity construction: in effect, a *muda.* In language acquisition or psycholinguistic research terms (e.g. Scovel 1998), this involves converting ability to understand a language, or 'competence' (sometimes called passive knowledge) into active 'performance' (overt production) and requires careful encouragement and support as well as commitment and opportunity.

Language attrition and latency are not confined to native speakers (i.e. those who were brought up in a home where the language in question was (one of) the language(s) of socialisation). Dunmore (2019) points out that it is not uncommon among alumni of immersion education. As immersion pupils do not generally make the decision themselves to be educated through a minority language (Costa 2014), they need both opportunities to use the language and motivation or commitment, to continue speaking it into adulthood—one of the categories of *muda* described by Walsh and O'Rourke (2014).

Becoming a New Speaker of Guernesiais

The Research Context

Guernsey is the second largest of the Channel Islands, an archipelago close to the coast of Normandy, France, but with political ties with the UK.[3] The traditional heritage vernacular language is Guernesiais, a variety of Norman which has been spoken there for over a thousand years. Gradual shift to English has been underway since the eighteenth century, but has accelerated since the end of the Second World War. According to recent research by local language teacher and researcher Yan Marquis (Guernsey Museums and Galleries 2020), there are now fewer than 100 fluent speakers of Guernesiais; most are aged 80 or over. The author estimates that there are fewer than ten people under the age of 65 who fulfil the definition of fluency in the section "Introduction and Literature Review" above. The UNESCO Atlas of Endangered Languages (Moseley 2010) categorised the languages of the

Channel Islands as 'severely endangered', i.e. intergenerational transmission has ceased. However, according to current estimates a more accurate UNESCO classification for Guernesiais would be 'critically endangered': 'the youngest speakers are grandparents and older, and they speak the language partially and infrequently' (Moseley 2010).

At the time of writing, there is no training for teachers specifically to teach Guernesiais; as noted, there are very few proficient adults of working age. Guernesiais is not part of the mainstream school curriculum, although there are extra-curricular language clubs in some primary schools, run mainly by retired native or latent speakers. There are evening or lunchtime language classes for adults, with capacity for 30–40 learners at any one time. The lessons are mainly aimed at beginners, and there are none above lower-intermediate level.

On 20 August 2020, the Guernsey parliament (States) voted to support Guernesiais through a Language Commission with a small budget and to recognise Guernesiais as an official language alongside English and French. The Commission's remit is broad and policy details remain to be seen. Previous language revitalisation and support activities have remained largely at the symbolic level (Sallabank 2011), e.g. language festivals and some public signage. A Guernesiais translation service is sponsored by a local jewellery firm; its popularity indicates widespread interest in Guernesiais as an identity marker.

Learners' Experiences and Needs

This chapter reports on interviews carried out in 2020[4] with nine 'new speakers' of Guernesiais, both second language (L2) learners and latent (reactivating) speakers, aged 25–80, and participant observation of language activities over the previous ten years. It also builds and draws on earlier research (other aspects of which were reported in Sallabank and Marquis 2018) to investigate the motivations, goals and needs of adult learners of Guernesiais,[5] which included interviews with 30 current and former learners. It also draws on the author's PhD research (Sallabank 2007).

It is relevant to note the demographics of the participants. An effort was made to seek out younger adults and women, as initially the sample was dominated by middle-aged men (40–60 years). Men outnumbered women in language classes by approximately two to one, and middle-aged male learners demonstrated longer-term commitment than women or younger learners, and were attaining higher levels, while more women than men had given up learning Guernesiais. This may reflect gender issues such as caregiving commitments, but may also be related to views on legitimacy (Sallabank and Marquis 2018). During my PhD research some older people, especially men, expressed surprise that I, as a younger woman, would want to speak a low-status language variety such as Guernesiais. It is a common finding in sociolinguistic studies for women to aspire to higher-status ways of speaking (e.g. Gal 1978; Lindgren 1984; Williamson 1991). Gender issues can also impede language practice: women are more constrained by domestic responsibilities, and female language learners can feel uncomfortable meeting male classmates in informal settings.

Key themes which emerged from the interviews with L2 learners centred on ways to achieve more fluency, resources needed, language and identity, and issues of authenticity and legitimacy in language. The theme of language and identity is the subject of a separate paper (Sallabank and King 2021), while authenticity and legitimacy have been discussed in detail elsewhere (Sallabank 2017; Sallabank and Marquis 2018), so these will only be touched on here where relevant. Approximately a third of the learners attending lessons were not of local origin, but still expressed a desire to (re)connect with Guernsey culture. Beliefs about the supposed inherent difficulty of adult language learning (see section "Adult Learning of a Minority Language") were compounded by an ideological view that Guernesiais is 'too hard' for L2 learners; this is reinforced by, and in turn influences, lack of effectiveness in learning and teaching Guernesiais.

Adult learners of working and parental age have busy lives, and many find it difficult to fit in language learning, especially in the daytime:

> It's difficult to concentrate after 11 hours at work – I hit a brick wall, I'm frazzled.

> It's important to speak with people at the same stage, but I can't meet every day.

Both less proficient L2 learners and some Rememberers (see section "Rememberers") report finding it tiring to speak Guernesiais for more than 45–60 minutes, as they need to concentrate to speak Guernesiais, especially at the end of a day.

Many prospective new speakers expressed a desire to experience more Guernesiais, especially as used by native speakers:

> I would love to just sit and listen and be completely immersed.
> I'd like to be able to have a conversation and understand what comes back … get past hello and the weather.
> I've done the beginners' class a couple of times but there's no opportunity to use it, I never get beyond beginner stage.

Learners would like to become fluent enough to join a speaker community for social interaction:

> to be able to have a conversation and understand replies
> to talk about everyday things
> to converse on all types of subjects
> to exchange pleasantries
> to be able to generate language spontaneously
> to get to the stage where lots of people have a grounding [i.e. a critical mass of proficient speakers for social interaction to be facilitated].

One interviewee commented that lessons provided a good foundation and provided inspiration to continue learning independently. However, due to language endangerment, natural opportunities for immersion are decreasing, and the perception of the vitality of Guernesiais is higher than it is in reality. Several learners mentioned that they wanted 'to be able to talk to old guys on the shore / leaning on the sea wall'; but these older men, who epitomise a stereotype of Guernesiais speakers, are no longer there (as noted at the beginning of this section, few native speakers are now socially active). Several learners expressed a desire for more opportunities to practise ('We need a support structure with mentors or a network of support'), but it has to be said that few had actually taken steps to find interlocutors themselves. A frequent complaint of L2 learners is that they do not know any native speakers and are unable to find fluent interlocutors. Paradoxically, loneliness and boredom are increasingly common among elderly speakers as their family and friends are passing away. One learner had put their name down for an initiative to find language buddies with native speakers, 'but nothing came of it'.

Organised activities to promote interaction in Guernesiais are available. They are usually held in informal locations such as pubs or community centres and attempt to bring together newer and older speakers. One of the most popular is 'Speed Patois',[6] informal sessions held every couple of months, based on a 'speed dating' format of short interactions, which are well attended by speakers and learners of all ages and abilities (Guernsey Language Commission 2016). Due to this format conversations rarely extend beyond basic phrases, although at one session in which I participated, where more sustained conversations developed, it was noticeable that after half an hour or so, less fluent latent speakers gained appreciably in confidence. Meanwhile, some more fluent speakers find these sessions frustrating, so the organisers added a supplementary initiative, 'Pure Patois', to provide an opportunity to socialise in Guernesiais for people who consider themselves fluent. This too is popular, but in practice few L2 learners attend the Pure Patois sessions due to (self-) perceived lack of proficiency; one interviewee also complained that they are not frequent enough to support sustained learning. The organiser commented that venues have to be chosen with care: good acoustics are necessary for older speakers who may have hearing issues. A female interviewee noted that the majority of people attending were male (especially at first) and wondered why.

The Guernsey Song Project in 2014 was an initiative which brought together singer-songwriters and speakers of Guernesiais. A database of speakers who volunteered to be contacted was set up to enable songwriters to meet up with speakers to help write and translate songs. This network was called 'Ley Bouti', 'the buddies', and a secondary aim was to encourage mentoring partnerships along the lines of 'Master–Apprentice' schemes in other endangered language communities (epitomised by Hinton et al. 2002). According to the Guernsey Song Project guidelines:

> These 'buddy systems' have worked well in other minority languages and we would be delighted if these friendships through Ley Bouti were extended through the project and beyond. (p. 3)

While the project was successful in raising awareness and in creating new language content in non-traditional musical genres, ultimately no mentoring partnerships were sustained long-term. Nevertheless, there have been examples of productive private, informal mentoring relationships, which have been particularly effective in improving new speakers' proficiency and fluency. One interviewee mentioned that 'it's handy to have a boyfriend who speaks Guernesiais', noting that there is a generational gap in both age and attitudes between learners and native speakers. Peer interaction, especially on a day-to-day basis, is recognised as ideal for developing language skills; additionally, 'pillow talk' or intimate language is not only motivating but also essential if family language use is to be re-established.

Almost all the learners expressed a desire for more practice, but many found that more fluent speakers were unable, or unwilling, to adapt or slow down their speech for comprehensible input (Krashen 1982).

> No-one knows how to talk at a level a learner can manage. Normal conversation goes way over my head.
> Nobody [at Speed Patois] said 'you're a learner, can I help you?'
> They're pleased to see us there, but they don't have the skills to 'dumb down' the conversation.

In return for participation in this research, I have found myself providing conversation practice for learners in this situation. A Rememberer pointed out that a mentor or buddy does not have to be completely fluent to help or teach; latent speakers can help each other with words that others have forgotten.

Several learners and Rememberers expressed a lack of confidence in using Guernesiais, especially with more fluent speakers.

> I need more conversation sessions with native speakers, but helpful ones.
> I find people too quick to correct – as learners we're only at toddler stage.

> I don't like speaking in front of people who are really good for fear of making mistakes.

Older speakers are frequently critical of learners' output: they find it difficult to encourage fluency rather than accuracy. Some former learners reported having given up because of such discouragement and criticism (see also Sallabank and Marquis 2018). One new speaker who does interact with several older speakers noted that speakers do not all agree on usage, and that it is necessary to learn to accommodate to the preferences of different interlocutors.

Learners would therefore prefer opportunities for peer interaction/buddying, more frequent than 'Speed Patois' and 'Pure Patois' mentioned above, where learners can converse 'without worrying about making mistakes' 'because we're all in the same situation':

> I almost need a conversation partner for coffee to practise what we've done in class.

Unfortunately, the small number of learners, especially those who have reached a level where they can construct sentences and express ideas, means that it has not been possible to organise such groups yet. Small group or one-to-one conversations are preferred by some learners, as group dynamics mean that 'stronger characters' can dominate the conversation.

Some learners have boosted their confidence, and absorbed more advanced language, by learning passages for recitation at festivals (and in some cases, getting involved in the organisation, which adds legitimacy to their participation). One commented that learners can be creative with language, even if they are not so good at it. Taking part in such events can also be enjoyable, as the atmosphere is supportive.

Current teaching methods favour a communicative approach, but some more analytical learners find explanations of patterns in language helpful. As found by Mitchell (2020), more advanced learners and Rememberers would welcome reference materials which explain grammar points (verb tables were mentioned most frequently). There are very few pedagogically oriented materials available for Guernesiais, and no language course with built-in progression. Most materials available give no help with pronunciation, which learners find one of the most difficult aspects. One new speaker reported that in the absence of learner-oriented materials, language documentary resources such as those deposited by the author and Yan Marquis in the Endangered Languages Archive (Marquis and Sallabank, n.d.) had been beneficial: listening practice was more useful than books or dictionaries that have no pronunciation guidance. Several interviewees expressed the desire for a multimedia language app to remedy these gaps, but the expertise and resources to build one are lacking.[7]

Rememberers

The concept of latent speakers was described in the section "Adult Learning of a Minority Language" above. It is common in language shift contexts for a generational cohort to develop receptive competence but not productive proficiency in a heritage language. In Guernsey, latent speakers are typically aged approximately 55–75 at the time of writing. As mentioned in "Adult Learning of a Minority Language", some call themselves 'The Rememberers'.

Some of the interviewees in this research were raised in families where adults spoke Guernesiais among themselves but not to the children. Predominant language ideologies, along with their own unhappy experiences at school, led parents to encourage children to speak English at the time, even if they regret this decision later in life:

> My parents' generation were ashamed of Guernsey French. My parents' first language is Guernesiais. They wanted the children to speak English when they were young, but now they will only speak Guernesiais.

Other participants reported that they spoke Guernesiais at home until starting school, at which point the schools' monolingual ideology made them switch to English. Some reported getting out of practice after marriage, if spouses did not speak Guernesiais (so children were not brought up bilingually); widowhood had prompted some to reconnect with other Guernesiais speakers. Some interviewees had moved to the UK for education or work, and recovering/reclaiming Guernesiais language was part of their general reconnection with the island and their local roots:

> I've got back into the group of people I knew before I went away ... and then I got drawn into the group *La Gaine du Vouest* ... It's a lot of fun – when we've been practising a play and as a group of people we jell very well together and it's very – we have a lot of laughs you know, it's really good fun.

Another interviewee said they had not spoken Guernesiais for fifty years, but were now making considerable efforts to find conversation partners; after a couple of years, they were able to converse easily and even run basic lessons. Their *muda* has reached the stage where most social interaction is in Guernesiais (although formal interactions are unavoidably in English, given its societally dominant position).

Another interviewee, who had become a leader in some revitalisation activities, recognised their own role in halting intergenerational transmission:

> As a teenager I rejected the microcosmic culture that my parents represented – the baby went out with the bathwater ... my rebellion included despising Guernsey French – 'it's so Guernsey'.

Rememberers are usually keen to establish their own authenticity and legitimacy as speakers, stressing that their family had a history of speaking Guernesiais, and that it was spoken in the neighbourhood. At the same time, many express a lack of confidence, stating that they forget words or are not as fluent as 'true' native speakers. It is indeed possible to identify differences in usage between speakers in their 80s and those in their 70s or below (see Sallabank and Marquis 2018), but Rememberers have access to cultural knowledge, traditions and idioms that L2 learners have to be taught or discover, and have a more 'authentic' accent. Some Rememberers attend Guernesiais lessons, but the teacher found that it was difficult to teach them in the same class as L2 learners, as Rememberers had a tendency to recall linguistic features unexpectedly, to remember or reactivate receptive knowledge rather than to learn new language, and sometimes to show off in front of other learners (stressing legitimacy through inherited linguistic competence). A separate class was therefore started.

In a concurrent initiative, an informal group calling itself 'The Rememberers' meets on a weekly basis to chat in Guernesiais, with the overt goal of reactivating receptive or latent competence into active use. The sessions are held in informal locations and involve mainly conversation, with some discussion of language points, especially vocabulary and traditional (remembered) usage.

An unexpected finding in this research was that many of the Rememberers and older speakers interviewed seemed to be unaware of the existence of L2 learners of Guernesiais. One had thought they were the youngest speaker until they met a younger language supporter (also a latent speaker/reactivator).[8] Several Rememberers expressed surprise that people who did not grow up with Guernesiais in their background would want to learn it. For Rememberers, links to family and community are key motivators, so they don't understand the motivations of people without these links:

> I can't imagine anyone who would want to learn Guernesiais; it's only for people who live in Guernsey, or who are interested in the local dialect.

On the other hand, some expressed optimism at increased interest among younger people:

> We're like dinosaurs but Guernsey's language won't die since younger people are interested.

'The Rememberers' sessions are generally held on weekday afternoons, which it has been pointed out can preclude people of working age (including some Rememberers). This may go some way towards explaining the disconnect between Rememberers and younger new speakers aspiring to a *muda*.

Several Rememberers expressed strong feelings of personal empowerment and identification through recovering their heritage language.

Some felt that a part of themselves was missing if they did not have access to Guernesiais:

> Without the language I wouldn't be complete.
> When I speak to my brother in Guernesiais I feel a contact ... it's a different feeling to when we speak in English. I never felt this way all my life before speaking in Guernesiais ... There's a lightness when we talk that isn't there in English – it's *mognifique* [wonderful] – it's worth all the work to read and study.

Discussion

As well as resource-related obstacles and a lack of capacity and opportunity to use their target language, minority-language learners also encounter ideological issues such as ongoing negative attitudes towards the indigenous language (both among majority-language speakers and internalised by the minority-language speaker community). In this research, older speakers frequently expressed surprise that younger people would be interested in learning their language. There is also a pervasive ideology of legitimacy and authenticity in the speech community (not only among native speakers), which holds that new speakers are not necessarily a 'good thing': they can never attain native-like proficiency and will change the language for the worse (Hinton and Ahlers 1999; Hornsby 2005; Sallabank 2017; Sallabank and Marquis 2018). Participants in this study are aware of societal attitudes towards their language and wish to challenge discourses of deficit and strengthen heritage culture. Given the scale of challenges they encounter, it is difficult for learners to achieve high levels of proficiency; some show remarkable tenacity and resilience (which successful learning can reinforce).

The disconnect between latent/reactivated and L2 new speakers is all the more poignant since there is overlap in age range between the majority of L2 learners (40–60) and Rememberers (55–80). There is also overlap in their proficiency in Guernesiais: especially at the start of their reactivation journey, latent speakers may well be at a lower level than more advanced L2 learners (though their gaps in knowledge are different). When asked about their motivation, Rememberers stressed that enjoyment is central, combined with socialisation with peers. Some learners also mentioned that they enjoyed meeting 'friendly and endearing' people, and becoming 'part of a unique club'. Both types of new speaker aspire to a *muda* in Guernesiais. Given these commonalities, it is worth asking what keeps the groups apart, what is meant by 'peer', and despite the difficulties encountered in formal classes, to encourage interaction between the two groups. As with Master–Apprentice initiatives, a degree of organised training might be necessary to show more fluent speakers how to support learners. As noted by Nguyen and Hamid (2020), capacity and opportunity to facilitate peer interaction—and the resources needed to support it—need to be prioritised by language policy bodies such as the newly reconstituted Guernsey Language Commission.

In Guernsey, despite the vote to support Guernesiais in August 2020, language revitalisation is very low down the political agenda. As well as combating attrition, in such a context adult learners, Rememberers and new speakers have to create their own opportunities for a new speaker community and a *muda*, and it is mainly middle-aged and retired people who have the time and resources to do so. The age range of the majority of participants in this research illustrates that even people who learn a heritage language when young (either at school or in the home) may have to wait until middle age to have the time and leisure to devote to language, culture, personal growth and lifelong learning. A radical solution might be to 'cut out the middleman' of schools and promote direct peer-to-peer acquisition among adults as a more reliable route to language maintenance. Armstrong (2020) and Costa (2016) view language revitalisation as a social movement; it is adults who are at the forefront of this movement, which is experienced in terms of both social and individual identity (Ayres-Bennett and Fisher 2021). Researchers such as Skrodzka et al. (2020) and Whalen et al. (2016) are finding correlations between endangered/heritage language maintenance, mental health and well-being, and King (2009, 2014) has found that learners of a minority language expect the language to revitalise them as much as they are revitalising the language. Armstrong

(2020) asserts that it takes active effort to create new speaker communities, so adults driving language revitalisation are not just hobbyists but network-activists. The motivation of 'enjoyment' can thus be seen not just as learning a 'hobby language', but as a keystone of building a new speaker community, and as contributing to personal and community revitalisation and empowerment.

In conclusion, this chapter has argued that for the maintenance of highly endangered languages such as Guernesiais, peer-to-peer adult transmission is a crucial element of developing proficient new speakers. Furthermore, it may be a more effective strategy than the traditional focus on intergenerational transmission through schools or family as essential for language vitality. As noted above, adult language acquisition is vital for transmission of a highly endangered language to children. Practice with other learners can improve fluency and support this aim. In addition, peer-to-peer transmission is a valid aim in its own right to further community use of endangered languages.

Acknowledgements The author is very grateful to all those who agreed to be interviewed for this research and especially to Yan Marquis and Jo Dowding for contacts and advice. All interpretations of interviews and data are my own. The writing of this chapter has benefitted from discussions on the themes of 'new speakers' as part of the COST EU Action IS1306 entitled, 'New Speakers in a Multilingual Europe: Opportunities and Challenges'.

Notes

1. Funded by European Cooperation in Science and Technology (COST) Action IS1306 on New Speakers.
2. However, this study focuses on knowledge of syntax rather than fluency.
3. The islands are Crown Dependencies: they are semi-autonomous with their own parliaments and are not part of the UK, but have the British monarch as head of state. They control their own internal policies but are dependent on the UK for defence.

4. Because of COVID-19 the interviews were conducted via video link or telephone.
5. Sallabank and Marquis are grateful for support from British Academy Small Grant SG112592.
6. The term 'patois' is controversial and some language supporters dislike it, since it is French for 'dialect', with negative connotations. However, many Guernsey people do not see *patois* as derogatory or know its connotations in French; for many, it is simply how the language is referred to.
7. There is also frequently a gap between perceptions of what is desired from an app and what apps can actually provide; Keegan (2020) comments that many Māori language apps are poorly designed.
8. 'Younger' is relative—the younger one is now aged 60.

References

Andrew, P. 2012. *The Social Construction of Age: Adult Foreign Language Learners*. Bristol: Multilingual Matters.

Armstrong, T.C. 2020. Not Enough Words: Language Acquisition and Identity Work in Tertiary-Level Gaelic-Medium Education. Presentation at Foundation for Endangered Languages Conference, 23–25 September.

Ayres-Bennett, W., and L. Fisher, eds. 2021. *Multilingualism and Identity: Interdisciplinary Perspectives*. Cambridge: Cambridge University Press.

Baker, C., H. Andrews, I. Gruffydd, and G. Lewis. 2011. Adult Language Learning: A Survey of Welsh for Adults in the Context of Language Planning. *Evaluation and Research in Education* 24 (1): 41–59.

Basham, C., and A. Fathman. 2008. The Latent Speaker: Attaining Adult Fluency in an Endangered Language. *International Journal of Bilingual Education and Bilingualism* 11: 577–597.

Belmar, G., C. van Boven, and S. Pinho. 2019. Why Do Adults Decide to Learn a Minority Language? A Study of the Motivation(s) of Potential New Speakers of West Frisian. *Sustainable Multilingualism* 14 (1): 138–159.

Cenoz, J. 2019. Third Language Acquisition. In *Encyclopedia of Applied Linguistics*, ed. C. Chapelle. Wiley Online Library. https://doi.org/10.1002/9781405198431.wbeal1214.pub2. Accessed 19 November 2020.

Cordella, M., and H. Huang, eds. 2016. *Rethinking Second Language Learning: Using Intergenerational Community Resources*. Bristol: Multilingual Matters.

Common European Framework of Reference for Languages (CEFR). 2020. *The CEFR Levels*. Strasbourg: Council of Europe. www.coe.int/en/web/common-european-framework-reference-languages/level-descriptions. Accessed 29 September 2020.

Costa, J. 2014. Must We Save the Language? Children's Discourse on Language and Community in Provençal and Scottish Language Revitalization Movements. In *Endangered Languages: Beliefs and Ideologies in Language Documentation and Revitalization*, ed. P.K. Austin and J. Sallabank, 195–212. Oxford: Oxford University Press/British Academy.

Costa, J. 2016. *Revitalising Language in Provence: A Critical Approach*. Oxford: Blackwell & Philological Society.

Dorian, N.C. 1977. The Problem of the Semi-Speaker in Language Death. *Linguistics* 191: 23–32.

Dunmore, S. 2019. *Language Revitalisation in Gaelic Scotland: Linguistic Practice and Ideology*. Edinburgh: Edinburgh University Press.

Edelsky, C., S. Hudelson, B. Flores, F. Barkin, B. Altwerger, and K. Jilbert. 1983. Semilingualism and Language Deficit. *Applied Linguistics* 4 (1): 1–22.

Edwards, V., and L.P. Newcombe. 2005. When School Is Not Enough: New Initiatives in Intergenerational Language Transmission in Wales. *International Journal of Bilingual Education and Bilingualism* 8 (4): 298–312.

Fishman, J.A. 1991. *Reversing Language Shift: Theoretical and Empirical Foundations of Assistance to Threatened Languages*. Clevedon: Multilingual Matters.

Fishman, J.A., ed. 2001. *Can Threatened Languages Be Saved? Reversing Language Shift, Revisited: A 21st Century Perspective*. Clevedon: Multilingual Matters.

Flores Farfán, A., and J. Olko. 2020. Types of Communities and Speakers in Language Revitalization. In *Revitalizing Endangered Languages: A Practical Guide*, ed. J. Olko and J. Sallabank, 75–87. Cambridge: Cambridge University Press.

Flynn, C.J. 2020. *Adult Minority Language Learning: Motivation, Identity and Target Variety*. Bristol: Multilingual Matters.

Gal, S. 1978. Peasant Men Can't Get Wives: Language Change and Sex Roles in a Bilingual Community. *Language in Society* 7 (1): 1–16.

Grin, F. 2003. *Language Policy Evaluation and the European Charter for Regional or Minority Languages*. Basingstoke: Palgrave Macmillan.

Grinevald, C., and M. Bert. 2011. Speakers and Communities. In *The Cambridge Handbook of Endangered Languages*, ed. P.K. Austin and J. Sallabank, 45–65. Cambridge: Cambridge University Press.

Guernsey Language Commission. 2016. What Is Speed Patois? https://www.youtube.com/watch?v=epa4yzC8GZQ. Accessed 29 September 2020.

Guernsey Museums and Galleries. 2020. Voice–Vouaïe Project. http://museums.gov.gg/voice. Accessed 29 September 2020.

Guernsey Song Project. 2014. http://www.guernseysongproject.org.gg/. Accessed 30 September 2020.

Hartshorne, J.K., J.B. Tenenbaum, and S. Pinker. 2018. A Critical Period for Second Language Acquisition: Evidence from 2/3 Million English Speakers. *Cognition* 177: 263–277.

Hinton, L., and J. Ahlers. 1999. The Issue of 'Authenticity' in Californian Language Restoration. *Anthropology and Education Quarterly* 30 (1): 56–67.

Hinton, L., M. Florey, S. Gessner, and J. Manatowa-Bailey. 2018. The Master-Apprentice Language Learning Programme. In *The Routledge Handbook of Language Revitalization*, ed. L. Hinton, L. Huss, and G. Roche, 127–136. New York: Routledge.

Hinton, L., with M. Vera, N. Steele, and the Advocates for Indigenous California Language Survival. 2002. *How to Keep Your Language Alive: A Common Sense Approach to One-on-One Language Learning*. Berkeley, CA: Heyday Books.

Hornsby, M. 2005. Néo-breton and Questions of Authenticity. *Estudios de Sociolingüística* 6 (2): 191–218.

Keegan, P.J. 2020. A Stocktake of Māori Language Teaching and Learning Resources in 2020: Coping with an Event Horizon. Presentation at Foundation for Endangered Languages Conference, 23–25 September.

King, J. 2009. Language Is Life: The Worldview of Second Language Speakers of Māori. In *Indigenous Language Revitalization: Encouragement, Guidance & Lessons Learned*, ed. J. Reyhner and L. Lockard, 97–108. Flagstaff, AZ: Northern Arizona University.

King, J. 2014. Revitalizing the Maori language? In *Endangered Languages: Beliefs and Ideologies in Language Documentation and Revitalisation*, ed. P.K. Austin and J. Sallabank, 213–228. Oxford: Oxford University Press/British Academy.

Krashen, S.D. 1982. *Principles and Practice in Second Language Acquisition*. Upper Saddle River, NJ: Prentice-Hall International.

Lewis, M.P., and G.F. Simons. 2010. Assessing Endangerment: Expanding Fishman's GIDS. *Revue roumaine de Linguistique* 55 (2): 103–120.

Lindgren, A.-R. 1984. What Can We Do When a Language Is Dying? *Journal of Multilingual and Multicultural Development* 5: 293–300.

Marquis, Y., and J. Sallabank. n.d. *Documentation of Guernesiais, the Indigenous Language of Guernsey, Channel Islands*. London: Endangered Languages Archive. https://elar.soas.ac.uk/Collection/MPI928986. Accessed 2 October 2020.

Mattschey, J. 2020. Bilingualism: Why Boosting the Rights of Minority Language Speakers Could Help Save Gaelic in Scotland. *The Conversation*, September 15. https://theconversation.com/bilingualism-why-boosting-the-rights-of-minority-language-speakers-could-help-save-gaelic-in-scotland-143767. Accessed 22 September 2020.

Mitchell, J. 2020. Qallunaat Learners of Inuktitut: A Qualitative Investigation of How and Why Non-Inuit Learn Inuktitut as a Second Language. Presentation at Foundation for Endangered Languages Conference, 23–25 September.

Moseley, C., ed. 2010. *Atlas of the World's Languages in Danger*. Paris: UNESCO.

New Speakers Network. 2017. Edinburgh: Heriot-Watt University. http://www.nspk.org.uk/. Accessed 2 September 2020.

Nguyen, T.T.T., and M.O. Hamid. 2020. Language Choice in Peer Interactions and the Role of Peers in Minority Language Maintenance: A Case Study from Vietnam. *Language Problems and Language Planning* 44 (2): 123–145.

Norton, B. 2013. *Identity and Language Learning: Extending the Conversation*. Bristol: Multilingual Matters.

Pacific Policy Research Center. 2010. *Successful Bilingual and Immersion Education Models/Programs*. Honolulu, HI: Kamehameha Schools, Research & Evaluation Division.

Pine, A., and M. Turin. 2017. Language Revitalization. *Oxford Research Encyclopedia of Linguistics*. https://doi.org/10.1093/acrefore/9780199384655.013.8.

Popkins, G. 2020. How to Find Minority Language Native Speakers. https://howtogetfluent.com/finding-minority-language-native-speakers/. Accessed 19 November 2020.

Puigdevall, M., J. Walsh, E. Amorrortu, and A. Ortega. 2018. 'I'll Be One of Them': Linguistic Mudes and New Speakers in Three Minority Language Contexts. *Journal of Multilingual and Multicultural Development* 39 (5): 445–457.

Pujolar, J., and M. Puigdevall. 2015. Linguistic Mudes: How to Become a New Speaker in Catalonia. *International Journal of the Sociology of Language* 231: 167–187.
Romaine, S. 2006. Planning for the Survival of Linguistic Diversity. *Language Policy* 5 (4): 441–473.
Sallabank, J. 2007. Attitude Shift: Identity and Language Maintenance in Guernsey Norman French. Unpublished PhD thesis, Lancaster University.
Sallabank, J. 2011. Norman Languages of the Channel Islands: Current Situation, Language Maintenance and Revitalisation. *Shima: The International Journal of Research into Island Cultures* 5 (2): 16–41.
Sallabank, Julia. 2017. Purism, Variation, Change and 'Authenticity': Ideological Challenges to Language Revitalisation. *European Review* 26 (1): 164–178.
Sallabank, J., and J. King. 2021. Language, Identity and Empowerment. In *Multilingualism and Identity: Interdisciplinary Perspectives*, ed. W. Ayres-Bennett and L. Fisher. Cambridge: Cambridge University Press.
Sallabank, J., and Y. Marquis. 2018. 'We Don't Say It Like That': Language Ownership and (De)Legitimising the New Speaker. In *Ideologies and Practices of New Speakers of Minority Languages*, ed. C. Smith-Christmas and M. Hornsby, 67–90. Basingstoke: Palgrave Macmillan.
Scovel, T. 1998. *Psycholinguistics*. Oxford: Oxford University Press.
Shandler, J. 2006. *Adventures in Yiddishland: Postvernacular Language and Culture*. Berkeley and Los Angeles: University of California Press.
Singleton, D., and L. Ryan. 2003. *Language Acquisition: The Age Factor*. Bristol: Multilingual Matters.
Skrodzka, M., K. Hansen, J. Olko, and M. Bilewicz. 2020. The Twofold Role of a Minority Language in Historical Trauma: The Case of Lemko Minority in Poland. *Journal of Language and Social Psychology* 39 (4): 551–566.
Smith-Christmas, C., and T.C. Armstrong. 2014. Complementary Reversing Language Shift Strategies in Education: The Importance of Adult Heritage Learners of Threatened Minority Languages. *Current Issues in Language Planning* 15 (3): 312–326.
Walsh, J., and B. O'Rourke. 2014. Becoming a New Speaker of Irish: Linguistic Mudes Throughout the Life Cycle. *Digithum* 16: 67–74.
Whalen, D. H., M. Moss, and D. Baldwin. 2016. Healing Through Language: Positive Physical Health Effects of Indigenous Language Use. *F1000Research* 5: 852.
Williamson, R.C. 1991. *Minority Languages and Bilingualism: Case Studies in Maintenance and Shift*. Norwood, NJ: Ablex.

Basque Intergenerational Transmission from a Language Socialisation Perspective

Paula Kasares, Ane Ortega, and Estibaliz Amorrortu

Introduction

The Basque language has undergone a significant increase in the number of speakers during the last decades, due to the consolidation of family transmission and to the increasing number of new speakers, namely those who learnt Basque outside the family, mostly in early childhood at school in the case of the younger generations. As a result, the way by which Basque speakers acquire the language has diversified and new and

P. Kasares
Public University of Navarre, Pamplona, Spain

A. Ortega (✉)
Begoñako Andra Mari Teacher Training University College, Bilbao, Spain
e-mail: aortega@bam.edu.es

E. Amorrortu
University of Deusto, Bilbao, Spain

M. Hornsby and W. McLeod (eds.), *Transmitting Minority Languages*, Palgrave Studies in Minority Languages and Communities,
https://doi.org/10.1007/978-3-030-87910-5_9

different speaker profiles have emerged. The paradigm of language socialisation (Ochs and Schieffelin 1992 [1984]; Schieffelin and Ochs 1986) that we present in the section "The Language Socialisation Paradigm" of this chapter allows us to integrate in a single model all sociolinguistic types of Basque speakers and different kinds of families who raise Basque-speaking children, all of them contributing directly to the above-mentioned increase in the number of speakers.

In this chapter, we focus on agents and spaces of socialisation that contribute to the process of becoming Basque speakers. In order to do this, we draw on data gathered in three different studies carried out in the Autonomous Community of Navarre (henceforth Navarre) and in the Basque Autonomous Community (henceforth BAC), the two regions where there has been more success in the revitalisation of Basque. The first study, *Growing up Bilingual in Navarre: Intergenerational Continuity of Basque and Language Socialization in Basque-speaking families* (Kasares 2014), researched the conditions under which Navarrese children from different sociolinguistic types of families become Basque speakers in two different sociolinguistic contexts: that of highly Basque-speaking Irurita (where 80% of the population is Basque speaking) in the Western Pyrenees and that of highly Spanish-speaking Pamplona (around 15% Basque-speaking). Paula Kasares, who used the paradigm of language socialisation in her study, followed 20 families belonging to the two communities, using ethnographic techniques such as participant observation and linguistic biographies.

Secondly, data from the study *New Speakers of Basque* (Ortega et al. 2016) will be discussed. New speakers, who have learned Basque by means other than family transmission, give an interesting insight into our topic, precisely because they challenge the Mother-Tongue ideology (Skutnabb-Kangas and Phillipson 1989) and the traditional transmission model based on parent competence. Ortega and her associates used both qualitative and quantitative techniques to examine the experiences, attitudes and identities of different profiles of new speakers in the BAC. The qualitative study, which comprised nine focus groups and nine in-depth individual interviews, was followed by a questionnaire designed to measure quantitatively the most important results of the qualitative study.

Parents who are not Basque speakers themselves can also be important agents in the intergenerational continuity of minority languages, since they make decisions regarding the languages their offspring learn at school, often themselves taking action towards a greater use of Basque in the family. The third set of data comes from the *Attitudes and Prejudies of Non-Basque Speakers* project (Amorrortu et al. 2009), which addressed this strategic group and carried out a mixed methods study, based on 10 focus groups in the BAC and Navarre, and a survey to quantify some of the data in the qualitative part.

Although the sociolinguistic situation and language policy and planning in favour of Basque are different in Navarre and the BAC, which has resulted in greater progress being made in the BAC, both contexts share some characteristics that make the data of the different studies comparable and complementary. The two regions have experienced: (a) an increase in the number of Basque speakers in the last decades; (b) a very small increase in the use of Basque, which is seen as a matter of great concern to Basque advocates; (c) a change in the profiles of Basque speakers, with increasing importance of the above-mentioned new speakers; and (d) a diversity of sociolinguistic situations within the two regions, ranging from areas with high percentages of Basque speakers (80%+) to highly Spanish-speaking areas where Basque speakers are but few.

Progress in the recovery of the language is shown by the increase in Basque speakers in both regions: in Navarre, from 9.6% in 1996 to 12.9% in 2016 among the 16+-year-old population, and in the BAC from 27.7 to 33.9% in the same period and same age group; this is an increase of 27,000 and 137,000 Basque speakers, respectively (Gobierno Vasco 2019). Notably, the greatest growth has taken place in the under 25 group, thanks to an increase in Basque-medium education: in the 16–25 age group 25.8% in Navarre and as much as 71.4% in the BAC are Basque speakers today.

The spread of Basque immersion education and Basque adult education have been instrumental in the increase of speakers who have learned Basque outside the family, especially in the 16–34 age group, where around 50% are new speakers (Gobierno Vasco 2019), with this percentage increasing as the age of speakers decreases. The second factor affecting the increasing numbers of Basque speakers is the family transmission of Basque, which has also improved in the last four decades. The latest survey data gathered in 2016 (Gobierno Vasco 2019) asked subjects about the language they had learned at home before the age of three and whether their parents were Basque speakers. The answers show the following information on Basque transmission: when both parents are Basque speakers, they tend to transmit only Basque in the family (70% in Navarre and 80%+ in the BAC), whilst some transmit both Basque and Spanish (about 12% in Navarre and 7% in the BAC). In the case of mixed couples, where one of the parents does not know Basque, Basque—together with Spanish—is also transmitted to a high level: of those in the 16–34 age group who had just one parent who spoke Basque, as much as 42% in Navarre and almost 62% in the BAC had learnt Basque in the family.

In the context of these positive results, in this chapter we address the intergenerational continuity of Basque from the language socialisation paradigm, one which we believe is best suited to explain the complexity of factors and diversity of agents that contribute to the intergenerational recovery of minority languages such as Basque. We first review the limitations and biases of the traditional transmission paradigm in Basque studies and then present the language socialisation paradigm, as defined by Schieffelin and Ochs (1986) and applied by Kasares (2014, 2017, 2020) to the Basque case. By drawing on data from the three studies mentioned above, we then show how the agents and spaces revealed by the new language socialisation paradigm have had an impact on the revitalisation of Basque.

The Study of Intergenerational Transmission in the Basque Context

For minority languages undergoing processes of language revitalisation, boosting intergenerational transmission of the language is a fundamental area of action (Fishman 1991). At the start of the Basque revitalisation process, when the percentage of Basque speakers was very low (21.9% of the total population of the BAC in 1981 (Gobierno Vasco 2005) and a mere 9.9% in Navarre even a decade later (Gobierno de Navarra 2011), this goal was indeed a clear objective of civil society organisations, as well as of the Language Policy of the newly created Basque Government. A large speaker base was also seen as one of the conditions for an ultimate goal: Basque *normalisation* (Zalbide 1998: 365). This term is commonly used by Basque sociolinguists instead of *revitalisation.* It captures better the concept that the objective is not to avoid the death of the language and make its health better, but to make Basque the language of *normal* use, by increasing and consolidating its use in all domains of Basque society. In this sense, language transmission is also a strategy and a tool (Hernández 2015).

Language maintenance and shift have mostly been approached from the disciplines of sociolinguistics and anthropology. In Basque research on the intergenerational transmission of the language, these two approaches are present, but with a much greater amount of macro-quantitative studies focusing on transmission and use in the family. Among them, the most important ones are the Sociolinguistic Surveys and Maps, which have been carried out in the BAC and in Navarre every four years since 1991. Although these studies are useful in measuring the percentages of parents who transmit Basque to their children and lately the speaker-type configuration of parents (whether they are Basque speakers or not, whether they are new speakers or Basque L1, etc.), they give no information on the qualitative aspects related to the process by which children become speakers of the language. This question has been more successfully addressed in micro-qualitative studies, especially those following an ethnographic perspective (e.g. Hernández 2007). However, this type of study has started to be more widespread only in the last 15 years.

The intergenerational continuity of minority languages has traditionally been studied from the point of view of *transmission*—as *transfer* of the language from parents—and *reproduction*—of language forms and norms of use being adopted by the offspring. The same model has been followed in Basque studies, as a review carried out by Kasares (2014, 2017) has shown. However, this paradigm is being increasingly seen as inadequate, particularly by authors working in the field of Basque anthropology (cf. Hernández 2015). We will refer to this approach as the 'transmission model'. Its most important biases, consequences and limitations have been summarised in Kasares (2017: 136–37):

a. The focus of Basque studies on *transmission*, understood as linguistic *transfer* from parents to offspring, places the onus on the learning of the *mother tongue* and on the period in early childhood when that first language is acquired, with no regard for the life trajectory of the speakers. This conceptual framework has a number of implications, as described in points (b), (c) and (d).
b. The parents' linguistic competence becomes the main criterion in defining research subjects, and thus only families where one of the parents speaks Basque (well) are studied. Parents who do not speak Basque—or have only limited competence—but who may deploy a number of strategies to support their children's learning are never included in these studies.
c. Moreover, parents' linguistic competence is viewed as static, disregarding the fact that the process of parenthood may bring about relevant changes, such as learning or recovering Basque.
d. A further consequence of the transmission model is that all agency is placed on parents—and, by extension, adults—and, therefore, only the linguistic practices and strategies of the parents are researched; the agency of children and the interactions between children are not considered. Children are viewed as passive recipients of language as well as of the ideologies transmitted by adults. Generally speaking, children are often the *objects* of Basque revitalisation projects, but rarely *objects* (and *subjects*) of research studies.
e. In Basque sociolinguistics, a clear distinction is made between two ways in which a language is learned: by natural transmission, primary, informal, which happens mainly in the family, but also through close community relationships; and formal, secondary learning, in institutionalised settings, the most important one being school (Zinkunegi 1995: 76; Sánchez Carrión 1987). These two modes are studied independently from each other, without addressing the relationship between them. As a consequence, studies focus on the home and the family in isolation from other crucial domains, such as the school.

f. Macro-quantitative studies are not usually followed up by micro-qualitative data. In fact, in this field of enquiry studies from these two perspectives are seldom put into dialogue with each other.

The conceptual framework described above shows clear limitations in explaining how Basque and indeed other minority languages are being maintained socially and how the new generations become speakers. Such a family-based transmission model, often with full-competence native-speaker parents at the core, offers little hope for languages that have low numbers of such ideal language 'transmitters'. Moreover, this model fails to accommodate the changes that revitalisation processes bring about, such as new speaker profiles, more linguistically diverse family types, new linguistic identities, and changing values attached to the minority language (Hernández 2015: 55).

A further problem is that parental competence is most often viewed as static, disregarding the fact that life histories are dynamic, and that parents go through changes such as learning a language, abandoning it or starting to use a language that has been abandoned or never used. The relationship that speakers have with language—including their own linguistic competence—is a process, not an a priori condition, and it should be considered a dynamic variable of the language socialisation of children (Kasares 2020). As in other minority languages, there is a high proportion of Basque families where parents do not speak or have limited competence in Basque, but whose role has nevertheless been crucial in the process of Basque revitalisation. It is necessary to build a framework that embraces them, as well as other agents in the social universe where Basque children grow up to become Basque speakers.

The limitations of the traditional way of viewing Basque and its transmission have been noted and challenged in the last decade. Jone Miren Hernández (2007, 2015) has pointed out some of the problems outlined above and prefers the Family Language Policy framework (FLP) as an alternative conceptual and methodological model that can efficiently encompass the diversity of family types, strategies and practices, as well as ideologies, found in the Basque context (Hernández 2015: 55–60). This framework has been applied in other minority language contexts with interesting results (Smith-Christmas 2016; Nandi 2017, 2018).

However, by definition, FLP focuses on the family and this can be seen as a limitation, although admittedly decisions, strategies and practices are not constrained to the home and family and do include domains such as school and leisure, among others.

In Basque sociolinguistics, another model has been put forward, one which from a holistic view examines the life itineraries of speakers, their linguistic choices and how these relate to the social context. This model takes into account all agents and factors involved in the process by which children become speakers and includes parents who are not themselves speakers of the minority language. Such an alternative conceptual and epistemological framework is the one based on the notion of *language socialisation* (Schieffelin and Ochs 1986), which has been applied to the Basque case by Paula Kasares (2014, 2017). This model is discussed in the next section.

The Language Socialisation Paradigm

The language socialisation paradigm was first formulated in the early 1980s by American linguistic anthropologists who felt that the field of language acquisition did not capture adequately the social and cultural aspects involved in the process of becoming a speaker of a language, and thus proposed looking at the process from an interdisciplinary perspective in a holistic and integrative manner. For Bambi B. Schieffelin and Elinor Ochs (1986: 167), this research field aims at understanding how people become competent members of a social group and the role that language has in this process. Language socialisation focuses on how children are *socialised through the use of language*, as well as on how they are *socialised to use language* (Schieffelin and Ochs 1986: 184). In this sense, language socialisation goes beyond the mere learning of a language, as it includes the cultural influences that affect all aspects of human development.

For these authors language socialisation is a continuous, lifespan process (Ochs and Schieffelin 1992) and therefore not limited to childhood. It starts in babyhood well before babies can talk and can span across the whole adult life of individuals. In this paradigm language socialisation is a holistic process—and therefore not limited to family—since it is dynamic, interactional and situated in its context, that is, it develops when speakers engage in situated interactions.

The interactional nature of language socialisation rejects the top-down unidirectionality (from parents to offspring, from adults to novices) that the notions of *transfer* or *transmission* embed. Therefore, children are not considered passive recipients, as they can in turn socialise the adults in their families as well (Schieffelin and Ochs 1986: 184) and be active agents of socialisation of other children. For this reason, the process is characterised by its *bidirectionality* and *multidirectionality* (Garrett and Baquedano-López 2002: 346; He 2012) and *multiagency* (He 2012): the language socialisation of children is viewed as a dynamic web of interactions in the family. Parents do promote specific linguistic practices and attitudes in their children, but in the linguistic ecology of the family children too are *agents*, not just *objects*, and 'for this reason, socialisation should be viewed in terms of "participation", rather than merely "transmission"' (Luykx 2003: 41).

Since the beginning, scholars working in the field of language socialisation have criticised the research tradition that studied *language acquisition* and *socialisation through language* as two separate processes, as it did not consider that language acquisition was fundamentally affected by cultural values and by contextual factors during the learning process, and saw context as extra-linguistic, and therefore separate from language learning and usage. Authors such as Ochs and Schieffelin (1992) showed the tight relationship between the two processes and proposed the framework for a more integrative field of inquiry. For these authors, however, this does not mean that socialisation is determined by its context. In fact, this paradigm views individuals as flexible, capable of adapting to changes and to transform. Socialisation is not a deterministic and mechanical process, and thus it transcends the idea of *reproduction* of social structures. On the contrary, it acknowledges the deviations that happen in the process of adaptation to the context and defends the agency of individuals to act freely, adapt to linguistic and social changes and even to transgress (Ochs and Schieffelin 2008: 11).

In their concern to understand the process of *socialisation to use language*, the authors studied the linguistic practices that children display in order to participate appropriately in social life. Research on monolingual and multilingual contexts in different social domains (including the home and school, but many others as well) has shown that children become aware of the social norms for appropriate language use by observing how language is used in social activities and indeed participating in them themselves (Schieffelin and Ochs 1986: 171). Therefore, together with the language 'code', children acquire a whole set of social norms and values related to the hierarchies between languages. Children who have been socialised bilingually learn two codes but also learn how to use each, where, who with and what for, as well as when it is permissible to mix languages, and when it is not (Luykx 2003: 41).

One of the most interesting contributions of the language socialisation perspective is the importance given to everyday life and to the linguistic practices that take place there (Schieffelin and Ochs 1986; Garrett and Baquedano-López 2002): 'The focus of language socialisation research on socializing routines—recurrent, situated routines that provide structured opportunities for children to engage with caregivers and other community members—has been highly productive' (Garrett and Baquedano-López 2002: 343).

Another significant contribution of language socialisation has been its problematisation of the relationship among the individual, the group and the social order, by challenging a deterministic and void-of-conflict view (Garrett and Baquedano-López 2002: 352). In bilingual and multilingual contexts, factors such as ethnic and cultural identity affect language socialisation. Bi- and multilingual communities (re)constitute and (re)define themselves, and researchers in language socialisation are interested in how individuals assert and negotiate their often-changing identities in these heterogeneous contexts.

Therefore, language socialisation is not monolithic and does not assume a homogeneous use of language; on the contrary, it acknowledges that models for language use can change over time. For instance, parents make decisions about what language to transmit to their children, but their decision is not just taken before or when the baby is born, but is revisited at different times during their children's childhood (Chrisp 2005). This happens because language socialisation takes place in a given socio-historical context which influences how languages are perceived, as well as their social value. The ideas speakers have about their languages affect their linguistic behaviour, and those ideas—about the nature of language itself and its relationship with cultural and individual identity—change between communities and even within the same community (Garrett and Baquedano-López 2002: 354–355).

Language socialisation is interested in the history of individuals and tries to access the ideologies and power relationships that underline socialisation interactions. Therefore, this field of enquiry uses ethnographic methodology, and even though observations and interviews focus mainly on the home and the family, they are not limited to these. Studies tend to be long-term and longitudinal.

Some authors (e.g. Duranti et al. 2012) have argued that the language socialisation paradigm can make an important contribution to understanding processes of language minorisation and shift, language maintenance and language revitalisation. However, studies in this area are scarce, especially for European languages (e.g. Fellin 2002). In Spain, the first application of the language socialisation paradigm is Paula Kasares's (2014, 2017) work on the intergenerational continuity of Basque.

Agents and Spaces of Language Socialisation in the Basque Context

For the study of the process by which children become speakers of Basque, applying the language socialisation perspective allows us to make visible aspects and agents that had before been overlooked or hidden, despite their fundamental role in such processes.

In the traditional model of transmission, the home and school are the key domains for language acquisition. In the home *natural* transmission—informal, primary—takes place, whilst at school *formal* and secondary transmission takes place. The agents of transmission are parents and teachers—always Basque speakers obviously—in a model where language is 'transferred' top-down in a unidirectional way from adults to novices (Kasares 2017: 143–45).

From the language socialisation perspective, the agents and factors that contribute to the linguistic upbringing of children, and indeed to the development of intra-generational practices in the minority language, spread beyond school and family. Other domains of social life are taken into account, and language socialisation is viewed in a holistic way, where the notions of *multidirectionality* and *multiagency* characteristic of this perspective are extended to the community as a whole.

We will next unpick who or what can be considered as *agents* of minority-language socialisation in the Basque context, be they people, spaces or activities.

Parents: Much More Than Language Transmitters

Without any doubt, bi-/multilingual parents are key agents in the minority-language socialisation of their children, as they choose what language(s) to use with their children and the transmission model they intend to adopt (e.g. Minority Language Only, One Parent-One Language, One Language-One Environment [Romaine 1995]). But, as well as the fundamental decisions in this area, they take many other decisions regarding their children's use of language in other domains and activities outside the home, the choice of school being one of the most important ones (discussed next in the section "The Basque-medium School as an Ecosystem for Language Socialisation"), but not the only one. In this section, we will review the different forms in which parental agency is exercised, not only by Basque-speaking parents, but also by parents with limited or no competence in Basque. According to our data, whether they are themselves Basque speakers or not, Basque parents take decisions that consciously take into account the minority-language situation of Basque, and many approach the bilingual upbringing of their children in a holistic way that seeks to include as many support strategies as they can possibly manage.

We will start by looking at the transmission of Basque in the home. Sociolinguistic surveys show that this has recovered and is indeed consolidating in favour of Basque-only or Basque and Spanish when one or both parents are L1 Basque speakers, as seen in the introduction. Acknowledging that parents' linguistic profiles have changed in the last forty years, the latest survey of 2016 (Gobierno Vasco 2019) included data not only on parents' knowledge of Basque but also on whether one or both were new speakers. Data showed that new speakers are indeed transmitting Basque to their children, especially when the other parent is also a Basque speaker. Ortega et al.'s (2016) study showed similar results for the BAC: among those new speakers who had children (35.2% of the sample), 48.3% declared that they used 'only Basque' with their children and 16% that they used 'both Basque and Spanish' (35.6% said that they used mostly Spanish). Those who had no children (54.8% of the sample) were also asked what language they would use with their children if or when they had them. Interestingly, whilst the percentage of those who declared they would use Basque only (49.2%) was similar to actual parents, only 12.9% stated the intention to use Spanish-only (12.9%), whilst a substantial percentage favoured bilingual transmission (34.6%), that is, both Basque and Spanish as home languages. We are fully aware of the fact that intention is not the same as practice in a real situation but, bearing in mind that this latter sample includes mainly younger-generation subjects, we can make a positive interpretation: data suggest that most young new speakers are not nowadays considering *not* using Basque with their children. From the point of view of intergenerational transmission, this is good news indeed, if intentions do materialise.

It should be noted that new speakers who choose to use Basque with their children have actually chosen to use a language in which they themselves were not socialised by their own parents. This shows a great sense of commitment and effort, often involving a deep process of reflection. These parents want their children to have Basque as their L1 and choose a Basque-only family-policy so that their children develop an emotional attachment to the language as well as enough competence and linguistic habits to counter the pressure of Spanish in society. Consider Maribel's rationale, a new speaker mother from Bilbao who married an L1 speaker from Bermeo and went to live in this highly Basque-speaking town:

(1) I have a son and a daughter, and our relationship is in Basque, my children's mother tongue is Basque. / I am convinced, and even more so since I had my children, I am convinced that if Basque is not prioritised, they would tend to use Spanish. And I think that when they are children, the less contact they have with Spanish, the better;

the better it is for them. (BE–C, 17/453) (Ortega et al. 2016: 136, original in Basque)

Strategies like these are aimed at what Schieffelin and Ochs termed (1986: 184) 'socialisation to use language', common in the Basque context among L1 and L2 Basque-speaking parents (Kasares 2014: 192–193), and linked to the objective of developing in children the habit of speaking in Basque and develop usage-norms favourable towards Basque. To develop this habit and these norms, parents actively monitor and encourage the use of the language in the home, in a family policy that is accompanied by awareness-raising strategies and explicit transmission of values of identity and love for Basque. As Basque is a minority not-yet-*normalised* language (cf. the section "The Study of Intergenerational Transmission in the Basque Context"), these strategies within the home and the family are very important, especially in highly Spanish-speaking areas:

(2) Father used to get really angry if he heard us play in Spanish. 'You don't know how to talk, or what?'. School was in Spanish, you see. But my father used to get really mad when he heard us talking in Spanish. 'Don't you know Basque, or what?' Yes, yes, I remember this well. (Nikolas, FG3) (Kasares 2014: 193, original in Basque)

Developing positive attitudes and emotional attachment to the minority language is an often-overlooked crucial factor. Parents tap into different factors to develop them, Basque identity being a major one, as Miren below reports:

(3) You cannot imagine how much I give them an earful for it: that we are Basque, that we have to look after our language.... What they [subject's daughters] have seen at home is that we have to respect it, maintain it, and look after it. At the end of the day, we are our children's reference. (Miren, FG3) (Kasares 2014: 213, original in Basque)

In the case of new speakers, the motivation of recovering the language is also an important one, as this speaker explains. He lives in the highly Spanish-speaking city of Vitoria; he and his partner are new speakers but they have made Basque the family language, even in the extended family, as his sister and her family have also learned the language:

(4) For me it was the most important thing. I did not have Basque when I was a child, I did not speak it, and for me the most important thing was that my children had Basque in the family, that Basque was their mother tongue. That we recovered that language that my grandmother had, but my mother didn't. (GA-A, 13) (Ortega et al. 2016: 140, original in Basque.)

So far we have reported on families in which at least one parent is a Basque speaker, whether they are L1 or L2 Basque speakers. In the traditional transmission model, these are the only families that count. We have tried to show that in minority-language contexts, transmission does not happen by default, and that parents make conscious decisions that are unequivocally linked to the minority status of the language; transmitting Basque is by no means like transmitting Spanish. But intergenerational transmission is not just in the hands of these Basque-speaking parents: parents who do not speak the language can also do a lot to support Basque and indeed do so. As mentioned above, these families are invisible for the traditional transmission model but we wish to stress their strategic importance in minority-language contexts such as that of Basque, where they indeed are a majority. We will next review some of the crucial ways in which non-speaking parents have a positive impact on the revitalisation and normalisation of the minority language.

One key decision is, of course, the linguistic model of their children's school. In the BAC, in the school year 2021–2022, more than 90% of the students in pre-primary, primary and secondary schools were enrolled in Basque-medium schools, either in the so-called D modality—Basque as the only language of instruction—(roughly 3 out of 4 students), or B modality (with a minimum of 50% of the curriculum in Basque) (Gobierno Vasco 2021). A different scenario is evident in Navarre, with more modest, albeit rising, numbers in Basque-medium education enrolment: in the 2018–2019 school year 27.3% of pre-primary and primary children attended Basque-medium schools and 19.9% attended the Spanish-medium education model where Basque is a subject, whilst 52.8% attended Spanish-medium schools with no Basque in the curriculum (an option that is not available in the BAC) (Gobierno de Navarra 2019).

The study on attitudes to Basque on the part of non-Basque speakers (Amorrortu et al. 2009) confirmed the support for Basque education among those who do not speak the language, especially in the BAC: when informants were asked to position themselves in relation to a number of actions to support Basque, the ones that gathered most support were: 'I would make sure that my children learn Basque correctly' (3.47 on an agreement scale of 1–4) and 'I would find opportunities so that my children get to know the cultural world in Basque, by taking them to extracurricular activities, theatre, clowns […] in Basque' (3.35 on a scale of 1–4).

A very important way in which non-Basque-speaking parents can have a great impact on their children's attitudes towards the minority language is by welcoming the language in the family. This is done in many ways, such as learning the songs their children bring home, or by incorporating *emblematic* use of the language in their daily practices: *Egun on* (Good morning), *Zelan eskola gaur?* (How was school today?). It may be the children who introduce the language into the home (discussed below in the section "Children as Socialisation Agents"), but what the parents do with it is crucial for the child.

In this vein, parents who encourage their children to speak Basque among themselves, even if they cannot do it, transmit a strong message of support for the language:

(5) I have a younger brother and since we were little our parents have told us to speak in Basque between ourselves. They say that we both know Basque, and why don't we use it at home. (Gazte-BI-C, 114) (Ortega et al. 2016: 174, original in Basque)

Finally, parents can do much more to support the minority language beyond the home with the decisions they take in relation to the language of extracurricular and leisure activities and the consumption of cultural products, such as books, television or music.

The role of parents from this new perspective needs to be brought more into the awareness of parents of school-aged children. Whilst many parents have understood and embraced their important role in the process of their children becoming speakers of the minority language, many others are not that aware of how important their attitudes and day-to-day decisions are in relation to what more they can do to support their children. This is especially important in the case of parents who cannot speak Basque. In fact, the study on non-Basque speakers (Amorrortu et al. 2009) showed a certain naïveté among non-Basque speakers about the results the school system alone can achieve, assuming that their children become full speakers of Basque just by attending an immersion school, 'they speak perfectly', as they put it. However, data on new speakers of Basque (Ortega et al. 2015) have shown that many Basque speakers who have learned solely at school feel their competence to be inadequate and confess not feeling legitimate speakers of the language and not fit to use it in everyday life. These feelings by new speakers from the Basque context seem to prove Fishman's (1991) assertion that 'school is not enough' and that other types of exposure to and experiences with the minority language are needed to enrich and reinforce these speakers whose main language input is the school. And parents need to be aware of the limits of school and know what more they can do.

The Basque-Medium School as an Ecosystem for Language Socialisation

The role of school as a determining factor in increasing the prestige of a minority language as well as the number of its speakers is well known. Indeed, it has played a key part in Basque revitalisation and has been a key policy area in Basque language policy and planning since the beginning of democratic Spain in the early 1980s. Its positive achievements have already been discussed in the introduction and the section "Parents: Much More than Language Transmitters". The aspect we would like to stress here is one that is often overlooked: the fact that school can be—and has been—much more than an institution of formal language transmission. School can also be an agent actively involved in the language practices of the students, in the 'sociolinguistic' education of parents, and ultimately, a space and institution that triggers and brings together activities and communication networks in the minority language.

Let us listen to the words of the following teacher from a Basque-medium school in highly Spanish-speaking Pamplona. She tells us how she encourages Basque-speaking parents to speak to their children in Basque as much as they can and to non-Basque-speaking parents to learn a bit:

(6) I tease them. I ask them what language they use with their child, and what language their child uses with them. If one of the parents is a Basque speaker, I always ask them. You see, the idea that 'they will learn at the *ikastola*' [Basque-medium school] is quite widespread. My attitude is first to encourage parents: 'you speak well!' And I always tell them: 'Think of the effort this is for your child: their life is in Spanish, Spanish at home as well, it's an effort for him/her'. I know it's easier for the parents to speak in Spanish, it's an effort, I know, but I tell them, 'make a bit of an effort, yes? Give it a try!' 'Yes but I know very little Basque…' 'Well, your child knew even less when s/he first came here! Do it together with them', I tell them. 'It's a lovely age to start learning and speaking in Basque with your child. Don't be ashamed if you make mistakes, just reading stories you can do a lot. And you build your relationship [in Basque] at the same time… S/he'll teach you'. And some do go for it. 'You have brought Basque into the house, and that is… wow!' We always encourage them to join in the Basque classes we have for parents in the afternoon. (LE) (Kasares 2014: 302, original in Basque)

Many Basque-medium schools offer Basque lessons to non-speaking parents, as well as advice on strategies to support their children, as shown in the next quote. In this way, home and school work in partnership in the process of Basque socialisation.

(7) Two weeks ago they gave us a letter telling us that they had noticed that the children were using more and more Spanish among themselves, or that they were mixing the languages more. And, please, to get them to watch TV in Basque, internet programmes in Basque, cartoons… (Ixa, FG9) (Kasares 2014: 223, original in Basque)

When the minority-language-medium school is viewed as a whole ecosystem of institutional and informal activities involving the whole community (teachers, parents, children, administrators, ancillary workers, etc.), other socialisation agents, spaces and opportunities are revealed. Typically, schools create opportunities for Basque use and learning in informal settings through extracurricular activities and projects involving parents. Other schools go further and create a whole project for parental involvement, such as the one led by Karmelo ikastola of Bilbao, with a positive impact on the use of Basque by students inside and outside the classroom, and on attitudes towards Basque (Ciriza 2019).

But not all is organised by the school. It is often parents who organise themselves in what turn out to be effective communities of practice to support the language, getting together for cultural or nature outings, for instance, as this mother says: 'We try to get together in activities now and then so that they [the children] can be together' (Susana FG19, in Kasares 2014: 303). Especially (but not only) in places with a low social presence of Basque, the Basque-medium school becomes the point of reference for the language, a true active agent of Basque socialisation beyond the classroom by providing opportunities for social organisation and cultural activity whose axis is Basque. This favours Basque, but, as Hernández (2007: 386–387, our translation) notes, this also brings the community together: 'Schools play an important role in the increasing socio-cultural and linguistic regeneration of the community'.

Children as Socialisation Agents

We have argued that one of the most interesting repercussions of adopting the language socialisation paradigm is the recognition of multiagency—with the displacement of sole agency from parents—in a process that is not just top-down and unidirectional from adults to children. The process needs to be seen as bottom-up as well, acknowledging the close and multi-directional interaction between generations. In this light, children are not mere and passive receivers of a language; on the contrary, they themselves have an impact on their own and others' language socialisation processes in a number of interesting ways. In this section, we review some of these.

(a) **Children introducing the minority language into the home**

Children who attend Basque-medium schools bring the language with them into the home and are often the introducers of the language in homes where parents do not speak it. By means of their books, their songs, their stories, their experiences, the Basque words they bring in, Basque has made its way into many homes where the language did not previously have a place. Parents with a keen interest in supporting their children's bilingualism engage with the new language, often adopting some linguistic practices in Basque. However, symbolic these may seem, it is an important step. This is the experience of Raquel, a mother living in Pamplona, whose family came from Castille in Spain, and who does not speak Basque:

(8) I often tell her, 'Teach me, Helena, you teach me!' I don't know and I often tell them to teach me. With Basque this has been a real discovery for me. (Raquel, FG20) (Kasares 2014: 287, original in Spanish)

(b) **Children as motivators to learn the minority language and as triggers of processes of *muda* in parents and other family members**

In the Basque context, there are many cases of non-Basque-speaking parents who have decided to learn the language in order to support their children's learning process. That is the case of this mother:

(9) I had never really had any contact with Basque until we took them [her twin son and daughter] to the *ikastola* [Basque-medium school] [...], they started at the age of 3. And I started going to adult classes myself, 'at least to learn a bit so I can understand', I said to myself. (Susana, FG19) (Kasares 2014: 286, original in Spanish)

Amorrortu et al.'s (2009) study of non-Basque speakers' attitudes towards Basque showed children to be one of the greatest motivators for their parents to learn the language. In a questionnaire designed to measure attitudes and practices, among those who replied that they were learning Basque or would like to learn Basque, 23.1% gave as the first reason 'because they wanted to help their children with their studies' (this being the second most popular reason, just behind 'because it's our language', chosen by 23.7%). In the same vein, among those who were not learning Basque at the time of the survey, 76% said they would be ready to do it 'if it were in activities related to their children's' (Amorrortu et al. 2009: 262–263).

In their study of *muda* moments in Catalan (*muda* as key life moments when new speakers adopt Catalan as an active language in everyday life), Pujolar and his associates (Pujolar and Gonzàlez 2013) identified starting a family and having children as one of the most potent *muda* triggers. The same has been found for Basque. An example of this is the testimony of a mother from Pamplona, who decided to recover her previously abandoned Basque when her daughter was born:

(10) And now my Basque is coming back to me thanks to her: with her school work, by talking to her teacher, I do it in Basque now. And I say to myself, 'I'm going to make the effort', to recover it, use it again... And, sure thing, I am much more confident now. (Amelia, FG18) (Kasares 2014: 285, original in Spanish)

It is often the case that other family members such as grandparents make a *muda* or recover the language. Many Basque-speaking grandparents who did not speak to their children in Basque when they were themselves parents in the 1960s or 1970s speak to their grandchildren in Basque now. The socio-political situation then was not favourable to socialising children in Basque, but 50–60 years on the situation is very different and different practices take place. This proves to be one of the most important tenets of the language socialisation paradigm, namely, that socialisation is socio-historically situated (Schieffelin and Ochs 1986; Garrett and Baquedano-López 2002).

However, children's impact is not just as motivators for adults; they also exercise agency, as illustrated in the next points.

(c) **Children as gate-keepers**

It has often been the case that in the minority language's last domain—the family and the home—the hegemonic language has inexorably entered through children. Children observe and internalise social norms—often conflicting norms—and to a great extent make their own choices, for instance, to speak the hegemonic language, despite parents' efforts. The following example, however, shows children displaying adherence to the 'Basque-in-the-home' norm and working as gate-keepers of it. This mother reports that their children resent it when they hear their parents breaking this rule, for instance, by talking in Spanish to each other:

(11) They [their children] often… when they hear us talking in Spanish they get angry and tell us off: 'Speak in Basque!' 'Yes, you are right'. And we change back to Basque. (Laura, FG7) (Kasares 2014: 220, original in Basque)

In the process of 'socialisation to use language' (Schieffelin and Ochs 1986: 184), children internalise the social norms of use. In Basque society, family norms to use Basque often conflict with societal norms in favour of the hegemonic language, and no doubt children and teenagers can—and indeed do—challenge and renegotiate rules, but in this example we can see how children, despite possibly great pressure from Spanish in society, can strengthen the minority language.

(iv) **Children as socialisation agents for other children**

Seldom do studies reflect on the impact of children on other children, and yet peer influence is far from negligible. In the case of new speakers of Basque talking about their process to become Basque speakers, many have stressed the influence of their friends and of being part of a Basque-speaking social network. This has been described mostly in Basque-speaking contexts, but not exclusively so.

The example below shows how this is done: child H, age 8, who does not have full competence in Basque, and has a clear tendency to use Spanish, is helped by the group when playing a game of dice:

(12) Child H says in Spanish: *¡Que me toque dos! Ahora repito, ¡que me toque dos!* [And now I throw again. Let it be a 2! Let it be a 2!]
The group repeats the same expression in Basque: *Tokatzea bi! Tokatzea bi!* [Let it be a 2!]
Child H with the group repeats in Basque: *Tokatzea bi! Tokatzea bi!* [Let it be a 2!] (Kasares, LK 2011-2-3)

We would like to stress the important role children have in their own language socialisation process, but also in others' language learning and *muda* processes. As they would do with other languages, children can help socialise other children in the minority language and teach them the way they talk (and therefore, socially productive ways that are not necessarily learned in institutionalised school settings). The traditional transmission model does not study or value the impact children can have, even when there is evidence that children do learn languages from other children and, in fact, that they tend to model more their peers' speech rather than their parents' (Barron-Hauwaert 2004: 57–59). By stressing the 'interactive nature of the process' (Ochs and Schieffelin 1992; Schieffelin and Ochs 1986; Friedman 2012), as well as its multiagency and multidirectionality (He 2012), the language socialisation perspective makes visible the impact of children's agency.

The Community as an Agent of Socialisation

Multiagency in language socialisation allows us to look beyond the usual domains studied according to the transmission model, but also by the Family Language Policy framework. Our data clearly show that 'the community', as it is often referred to, and spaces and activities provided by and in the community, also have an impact on the processes of minority-language socialisation. Indeed, in many Basque-speaking areas, it is the whole community that contributes to raising children in Basque. Evidence of this is most clearly seen in the many cases of new speakers who, despite Basque not having been 'transmitted' by their parents, consider themselves good Basque speakers. Eunate, aged 21, is a case in point:

(13) My parents came here [highly Basque speaking village] four years before I was born. [...] So I learned Basque as a child, I did all my studies in Basque.... With my friends in Basque, everything in Basque. / I do not consider myself *euskaldunberri* [new speaker], I consider myself *euskaldun zaharra* [native speaker] because I... well, my first words were in Basque. When I think, I think in Basque. And when I write... when I write in Spanish, I first think how to say it in Basque. (ZEA-B, 86 /291) (Ortega et al. 2016: 190, original in Basque)

We can see that for this speaker it is the community as a whole that has made her a Basque speaker (school, friends and playmates, neighbours, especially her elderly next-door neighbours, who were 'like her second grandparents'—everybody except her family). She talks in the local dialect and she considers herself Basque-dominant in her bilingual competence. Not only do traditional Basque speakers in her village say of her that 'she talks just the same as us' and that 'she's just like us', but she herself considers herself a *euskaldun zaharra* (old Basque speaker, the Basque way to refer to a traditional native speaker), no different from others in the village and the valley. She was not raised in Basque by her parents but the community raised her.

Our data have shown other interesting ways in which the community has a socialising impact. The following example illustrates what we consider an emerging social norm by which children will be spoken to in Basque:

(14) In X [referring to their town, highly Basque-speaking] it is frowned upon to speak in Spanish to children, it is in fact rare when it happens, it wouldn't look good. People would say, 'Knowing Basque, what is s/he doing talking to a child in Spanish?' (ZU-C, 149) (Ortega et al. 2016: 138, original in Basque)

But it is not just in highly Basque-speaking areas in the BAC and Navarre that we have seen the community coming together in the Basque upbringing of children: many committed Basque-speaking adults in Spanish-speaking areas take upon themselves to speak to children in Basque, precisely so that they hear the language used in everyday life outside school. This is especially the case in the BAC, where overwhelming enrolment in Basque-medium schools (as discussed in the section "Parents: Much More than Language Transmitters") favours expectations that the addressed child will in fact speak the language. We have even found the same practices among adults who may not be completely proficient in Basque or even have limited competence; however limited, the habit is to address the child in Basque, as this male from Irurita (Navarre) reports:

(15) I cannot really explain it, but to children, it comes naturally to me to speak to children in Basque, it doesn't come naturally at all to speak to them in Spanish. (Alberto, FG10: 8) (Kasares 2014: 214, original in Spanish)

We believe that this practice is consolidating as a bottom-up generated social rule that shows the shared responsibility of the community in the socialisation of children.

Lack of space does not allow us to talk about other elements in social and cultural life that also contribute to developing the minority language in children. In Basque, as in other minority languages, leisure activities and cultural products such as theatre, festivals, TV programmes, etc. are an important source of input, often using language quite different to that learned at school or in the family, and which have a positive impact on attitudes and emotional attachment to the language.

Conclusions

In this chapter, qualitative and quantitative data from three independent studies conducted in Navarre and the BAC have been examined in the light of the language socialisation theoretical framework, so far only applied in the Basque case to the situation of Navarre by Paula Kasares (2014). These three studies have been put into dialogue with each other with a number of interesting results. Applying the language socialisation paradigm to the studies on non-Basque speakers and on new speakers of Basque has proven its validity, as new interpretations and insights have emerged. As well as this, these two studies have enriched our understanding of intergenerational transmission of Basque, precisely because the types of subjects researched challenge the traditional way of looking at intergenerational transmission and help make its fundamental limitations visible.

Basque socialisation of children has been shown as inextricably underpinned by the language ideologies and practices of parents. The linguistic upbringing of children in Basque is a conscious and deeply reflective process, usually accompanied by a clear plan that takes into great account the minority status of the language. Basque-speaking parents *socialise* their offspring *in* and *through* Basque, but they clearly establish language use patterns in the home with the aim of socialising their offspring also *to use* Basque. We have seen that the language socialisation paradigm allows—and indeed endeavours—to also integrate families with limited or no competence in Basque. Even if this type of family is the most common in the Basque context, it has not had a place in intergenerational transmission studies and, yet, their role is key to understand the positive social development of Basque. It is not just a matter of scientific rigour but also of social justice to make these families and non-Basque speakers' efforts visible. Just looking at the percentages of new speakers of Basque gives an idea of the scale of non-Basque speakers' involvement in supporting a language they do not speak.

Indeed, the traditional model based on top-down and unidirectional transfer of the language from adults to children fails to explain the process of intergenerational continuity of Basque. Our data clearly show that children are not passive recipients of the language, they are indeed effective agents in a number of interesting ways: by being the ones who bring the minority language to homes where it had no presence; by assuming the role of *teachers* or experts; by acting as gate-keepers; by being the motivation for parents to decide to learn the language and/or get involved in activities and communities of practice to support Basque; and even by socialising other children themselves. All this, again, was invisible in traditional transmission studies, and yet the positive evolution of Basque in the last decades cannot be understood without it.

Basque and its place in society have experienced many changes in the last 40 years. Language socialisation takes these into account, as a socio-historically situated framework, closely linked to concrete situations where languages have specific values. Thus, if macro-sociolinguistic conditions change, subjects may be expected to change their strategies and practices regarding the language socialisation of their children. In fact, we have seen examples of emerging social norms, such as speaking in Basque to any child, or cases of linguistic *muda* that are explained in the light of the increasingly positive attitudes in favour of Basque.

Language socialisation is not limited to (early) childhood, but spans a whole lifetime. The Basque case has proven this true and shown the complex processes that accompany the experience of being a speaker of a minority language, itself immersed in a process of language revitalisation and normalisation. In this regard, the study of the life trajectories of new speakers and *muda* processes has provided interesting insights.

Finally, we hope to have shown how important it is to adopt a holistic approach. Language socialisation does not only happen through transmission in the family and at school, but all domains of social life potentially contribute to the upbringing of children in the minority language, including leisure and sports activities, and cultural products and events. The holistic nature of language socialisation acknowledges that the whole community is involved in the process.

We believe that the language socialisation paradigm can help understand how intergenerational continuity of minority languages really happens, as it makes visible agents that have a true impact but which are often invisible. Acknowledging this diversity of agencies can also help develop community-based strategies, as well as language planning action.

References

Amorrortu, E., A. Ortega, I. Idiazabal, and A. Barreña. 2009. *Actitudes y prejuicios de los castellanohablantes hacia el euskera*. Vitoria-Gasteiz: Servicio Central de Publicaciones del Gobierno Vasco.

Barron-Hauwaert, S. 2004. *Language Strategies for Bilingual Families: The One-Parent-One-Language Approach*. Clevedon: Multilingual Matters.

Chrisp, S. 2005. Māori Intergenerational Language Transmission. *International Journal of the Sociology of Language* 172: 149–181.

Ciriza, M.P. 2019. Bringing Parents Together: An Innovative Approach for Parental Involvement in an Immersion School in the Basque Autonomous Community. *Journal of Multilingual and Multicultural Development* 40: 50–63.

Duranti, A., E. Ochs, and B.B. Schieffelin, eds. 2012. *The Handbook of Language Socialization*. Malden, MA: Wiley-Blackwell.

Fellin, L. 2002. Language Ideologies, Language Socialization and Language Revival in an Italian Alpine Community. *Texas Linguistic Forum* 45: 46–57.

Fishman, J.A. 1991. *Reversing Language Shift: Theoretical and Empirical Foundations of Assistance to Threatened Languages*. Clevedon: Multilingual Matters.

Friedman, D.A. 2012. Language Socialization and Language Revitalization. In *The Handbook of Language Socialization*, ed. A. Duranti, E. Ochs, and B.B. Schieffelin, 631–647. Malden, MA: Wiley-Blackwell.

Garrett, P.B., and P. Baquedano-López. 2002. Language Socialization: Reproduction and Continuity, Transformation and Change. *Annual Review of Anthropology* 3: 339–361.

Gobierno de Navarra. 2011. Mapa sociolingüístico de Navarra. Euskarabidea –Gobierno de Navarra. https://www.euskarabidea.es/fitxategiak/irudiak/fckeditor/mapa-sociolinguistico-2011_informe-2.pdf. Accessed 25 January 2022.

Gobierno de Navarra. 2019. *El uso del euskera en el alumnado de Navarra, 2018–2019. Investigación Izaskun Arrue*. Unpublished report. Pamplona: Euskarabidea–Instituto Navarro del Euskera.

Gobierno Vasco. 2005. *III Mapa sociolingüístico 2001*. Vitoria-Gasteiz: Servicio Central de Publicaciones del Gobierno Vasco. https://www.euskara.euskadi.eus/contenidos/informacion/argitalpenak/es_6092/adjuntos/iii_mapa_sozi olinguistico.pdf. Accessed 25 January 2022.

Gobierno Vasco. 2019. *Sixth Sociolinguistic Survey 2016*. Vitoria-Gasteiz: Servicio Central de Publicaciones del Gobierno Vasco. https://www.euskadi.eus/contenidos/noticia/eas_mas_noticias/en_def/adjuntos/inkesta_EN.pdf. Accessed 25 January 2022.

Gobierno Vasco. 2021. Matrícula 2020–21. Alumnado por nivel, modelo y red. https://www.euskadi.eus/contenidos/informacion/matricula_graficos_evolutivos/es_def/adjuntos/EAE_eredua_OBLIG.pdf. Accessed 25 January 2022.

He, A.W. 2012. Heritage Language Socialization. In *The Handbook of Language Socialization*, ed. A. Duranti, E. Ochs, and B.B. Schieffelin, 587–609. Malden, MA: Wiley-Blackwell.

Hernández, J.M. 2007. *Euskara, comunidad e identidad. Elementos de transmisión, elementos de transgresión*. Madrid: Ministerio de Cultura.

Hernández, J.M. 2015. Familia hizkuntz politika: Transmisioa ulertzeko eredu berri baten bila. *BAT Soziolinguistika Aldizkari* 94: 47–62.

Kasares, P. 2014. *Euskaldun hazi Nafarroan. Euskararen belaunez belauneko jarraipena eta hizkuntza sozializazioa familia euskaldunetan*. Bilbao: Euskaltzaindia.

Kasares, P. 2017. La transmisión intergeneracional desde la socialización lingüística: El caso vasco. *Treballs De Sociolingüística Catalana* 27: 133–147.

Kasares, P. 2020. Familias vascohablantes: propuesta de definición desde la socialización lingüística. In *Fontes Linguae Vasconum 50 urte. Ekarpen berriak euskararen ikerketari / Nuevas aportaciones al estudio de la lengua vasca*, ed. E. Santazilia, D. Krajewska, E. Zuloaga, and B. Ariztimuño, 351–362. Pamplona/Iruña: Gobierno de Navarra.

Luykx, A. 2003. Weaving Languages Together: Family Language Policy and Gender Socialization in Bilingual Aymara Households. In *Language Socialization in Bilingual and Multilingual Societies*, ed. R. Bayley and S.R. Schecter, 25–43. Clevedon: Multilingual Matters.

Nandi, A. 2017. Language Policies on the Ground: Parental Language Management in Urban Galician Homes. Unpublished Doctoral Thesis, Heriot-Watt University.

Nandi, A. 2018. Parents as Stakeholders: Language Management in Urban Galician Homes. *Multilingua* 37 (2): 201–223.

Ochs, E., and B.B. Schieffelin 1992 [1984]. Language Acquisition and Socialization: Three Developmental Stories and Their Implications. In *Culture Theory: Essays on Mind, Self and Emotion*, ed. R.A. Shweder and R.A. LeVine, 276–320. Cambridge: Cambridge University Press.

Ochs, E., and B.B. Schieffelin. 2008. Language Socialization: An Historical Overview. In *Encyclopedia of Language and Education*, ed. P.A. Duff ad N.H. Hornberger, 2nd ed., vol. 8, 2580–2594. Boston, MA: Springer Science+Business Media.

Ortega, A., E. Amorrortu, J. Goirigolzarri, and J. Urla. 2016. *Los nuevos hablantes de euskera: Experiencias, actitudes e identidades*. Bilbao: Universidad de Deusto.

Ortega, A., J. Urla, E. Amorrortu, J. Goirigolzarri, and B. Uranga. 2015. Basque Linguistic Identity Among New Speakers of Basque. *International Journal of the Sociology of Language* 231: 85–105.

Pujolar, J., and I. Gonzàlez. 2013. Linguistic 'Mudes' and the De-ethnicization of Language Choice in Catalonia. *International Journal of Bilingual Education and Bilingualism* 16 (2): 138–152.

Romaine, S. 1995. *Bilingualism*, 2nd ed. Oxford: Blackwell.

Sánchez Carrión, J.M. 1987. *Un futuro para nuestro pasado*. Donostia-San Sebastián: Elkar.

Schieffelin, B.B., and E. Ochs. 1986. Language Socialization. *Annual Review of Anthropology* 15: 163–191.

Skutnabb-Kangas, T., and R. Phillipson. 1989. 'Mother Tongue': The Theoretical and Sociopolitical Construction of a Concept. In *Status and Function of Languages and Language Varieties*, ed. U. Ammon, 450–477. Berlin: Mouton de Gruyter.

Smith-Christmas, C. 2016. *Family Language Policy: Maintaining an Endangered Language in the Home*. Basingstoke: Palgrave Macmillan.

Zalbide, M. 1998. Normalización lingüística y escolaridad: Un informe desde la sala de máquinas. *Revista Internacional De Estudios Vascos* 432: 355–424.

Zinkunegi, J.F. 1995. Euskararen transmisioa Euskal Autonomi Elkartean [Transmission of Basque in the BAC]. *BAT Soziolinguistika Aldizkaria* 15: 75–88.

Transmission of Breton Among Immersion-School Students: The Impact of Home Language

Holly Kennard

Introduction

Breton, a Celtic language spoken in Brittany, has undergone decades of obsolescence, with social and political pressure gathering speed in the nineteenth century and lasting beyond the Second World War. Since then, efforts to revitalise the language have gradually been increasing, in an attempt to halt the decline of the language, and, crucially, to ensure that it is spoken by younger people. These efforts have focused both on raising the profile of Breton, for example, through visible bilingual signage and on Breton-medium schooling. The exact number of Breton speakers has been difficult to estimate, and until recently, the most accurate estimates came from Broudic's (2009) survey, which gave a figure of 206,000 Breton speakers, of whom 46% were aged over 75, and only 4%

H. Kennard (✉)
University of Oxford, Oxford, UK
e-mail: holly.kennard@ling-phil.ox.ac.uk

M. Hornsby and W. McLeod (eds.), *Transmitting Minority Languages*, Palgrave Studies in Minority Languages and Communities,
https://doi.org/10.1007/978-3-030-87910-5_10

were aged 16–19; however, this was an increase from just 3% in 1997. In 2018, a new, more wide-ranging survey was undertaken (Moal 2018) and preliminary results indicate that the number of speakers remains stable at around 207,000 fluent speakers (though this could also indicate that the 2007 survey underestimated the number of speakers). The mean age of speakers in this survey was 70, and only 5% of speakers were aged under 40.

This increasingly elderly speaker population reflects the loss of the transmission of Breton within the family. Parent-to-child transmission of Breton effectively ceased following the Second World War; this can be seen clearly in Broudic's (1999) discussion of St Méen (northern Finistère), where in 1946, all schoolchildren spoke Breton, but by 1952, only 10% did. This exemplifies Dorian's (1981) 'demographic tip', whereby 'a language which has been demographically highly stable for several centuries may experience a sudden tip' (Dorian 1981: 51). While this may seem sudden, it results from a gradual build-up of negative feeling towards the language, which leads parents not to transmit it to their children. This negative feeling stemmed from the increasing stigmatisation of Breton as 'backward' and undesirable, but was compounded by the post-war political atmosphere in France: Breton separatist groups such as *Breiz Atao* aligned themselves with the Nazi regime, and actively opposed local Resistance movements (McDonald 1989).

Today, there is a small but growing community of younger 'new speakers' of Breton, and it has been observed that there are differences between the 'traditional' Breton of older speakers and that of new speakers. This is largely because, as a result of the gap in intergenerational transmission, the Breton modelled to these new speakers is generally a standardised variety, which abstracts away from the regional variation of traditional varieties; these speakers are also more susceptible to interference from French. It has been claimed that new speakers' Breton differs from traditional Breton in a number of ways: it is said to have a 'Celticised' lexis, and to avoid French loanwords (Jones 1995); it does not maintain phonological processes such as stress and liaison (Madeg 2010); it lacks certain key morphophonological features such as mutation, parts of the verbal paradigm and inflected prepositions (Dressler 1972; Hewitt 1977; McDonald 1989); and it has a preference for SVO word order

(McDonald 1989). While it is clear that many new speakers do 'sound different' from older speakers, more recent research into the Breton of new speakers is starting to challenge some of these claims (see, e.g., Le Ruyet 2011; Davies-Deacon 2017; Kennard and Lahiri 2017; Kennard 2018b), and to provide a more nuanced and detailed picture of the Breton spoken by younger speakers.

Breton-Medium Education

A central part of efforts to revitalise Breton, Breton-medium education began in 1977 with the establishment of *Diwan* (Bocquenet 1985). Although the *Loi Deixonne* had permitted the teaching of minority languages in France since 1951, the reach of this was limited, and the *Diwan* schools (*Diwan* meaning 'seed') were set up in response to a perceived lack of Breton provision in the schooling system (Kuter 1999). What began as a single school for children aged 2–6 now covers the whole span of education up to age 18; however, while there are many *Diwan* primary schools (*skolioù*; 48 in total, across Brittany), there are only six *skolajoù*, for pupils aged 11–15, and one *lise*, for pupils aged 15–18, which has implications for children continuing Breton beyond age 11. Bilingual Breton-French streams within the state and Catholic education systems followed the establishment of *Diwan*; however, while under the *Diwan* system, the focus is on immersion in Breton, and French is introduced gradually, in a state primary stream pupils receive equal amounts of Breton and French and learn to read and write in French before Breton. This bilingual stream continues at the secondary level, but pupils receive fewer hours of Breton in comparison to French.

Breton-medium schools play a crucial role in the acquisition of Breton by younger speakers. The 2018 survey (Moal 2018) suggests that 90% of Breton speakers aged 15–24 acquired Breton through formal education. The number of pupils in Breton-medium education is small, but growing. In September 2019, 18,890 pupils attended Breton-medium education across Brittany and in the Loire-Atlantique[1] *département* (Ofis Publik ar Brezhoneg 2020), and this is growing year-on-year.[2] This means that around 3% of pupils in Brittany attend Breton-medium schooling (Académie de Rennes 2019).

Breton-medium schools face a number of challenges, many of which are not unique to Breton, but common to a number of language revitalisation contexts. The first is the question of 'which Breton' should be taught in schools (Poisard et al. 2014). There exists a great deal of regional variation in Breton, and many older speakers find the accepted standard inaccessible, because they were educated in French and only use Breton in a highly local context.[3] The differences between local varieties are often commented on by older speakers, both as a source of local pride, but also to claim the impossibility of teaching Breton to younger generations (Le Dû and Le Berre 1996). Largely, schools use the standard variety, which is more practical from the perspective of publishing teaching materials, but may widen the gap between older and younger speakers, with some claiming that these two groups are unable to understand one another (Le Dû 1999).

Additionally, teachers might bring regional features from their native area to schools elsewhere. The *Lise Diwan* in Carhaix brings together pupils from across Brittany, who may also have encountered a range of regional Breton features. This is especially true of pupils from the *Gwened* region in the southeast, which has a notably different dialect of Breton (e.g. in relation to stress and palatalisation). Some younger speakers now come from areas in Upper Brittany, such as Rennes and Nantes, which are not traditionally Breton-speaking: naturally they do not have any exposure to a local variety of Breton, and so tend to use the standard variety. These sorts of issues have led to questions about what constitutes 'authentic' Breton (Hornsby 2014).

A separate issue is that of language use outside the classroom. Pupils may be confident using Breton in an educational setting, but in peer-group interactions in a social context, this may be more difficult, with French as the default. This in turn leads to the issue of continued Breton usage beyond the time spent in Breton-medium education. First, as mentioned above, there are far fewer secondary-level *Diwan* schools than primary schools, and the provision for Breton in the state *Div Yezh* stream decreases at the secondary level. This is partly because fewer pupils choose to continue with Breton beyond age 11, and Broudic (2010) discusses reasons for this: the choice may be made by the pupil, not the parent; secondary education is seen as 'more important' than primary education, and so the majority language, French, is seen as more suitable; and finally, the necessity for many pupils to travel a long way and/or board may make Breton secondary education less attractive. Pupils who cease to attend Breton-medium education aged 11, or over the course of their teenage years, may find that they cease to use the language altogether after this point.

This has an impact on the use of Breton after the end of formal schooling, particularly in the light of the fact that students may struggle to use Breton outside a classroom setting. Baudu (2015) interviewed a number of former *Lise Diwan* pupils who had children of their own and found a mixed picture of language use, often linked to the unfamiliarity of informal Breton. One participant said 'I feel fake when I speak Breton to [my children], I feel like I'm acting, playing a role a bit' (Baudu 2015: 64). Speakers may not have the linguistic resources to use Breton in the domain of daily family life, which in turn acts as a barrier to the transmission of Breton within the home.

Language transmission within the home has been shown to be important in younger speakers' language use in other minority language contexts. Research into gender and mutation in Welsh, for example, found that children from Welsh-speaking homes were more proficient than children from English-speaking homes (Gathercole and Thomas 2005; Thomas and Gathercole 2007; Thomas and Mayr 2010; Thomas et al. 2014). However, this does not seem to be true of all features, or in all minority-language contexts, since there may be other factors at work: Mayr et al.'s (2017) study of monophthongs found that there was little difference between adolescents from Welsh-speaking and English-speaking homes, while Nance (2015) investigated vowels and laterals in adolescent Gaelic speakers and found few differences between speakers from English and Gaelic backgrounds.

Taking all of this into account, this chapter examines the impact that a young Breton speaker's linguistic background might have on their use of certain morphophonological features. Given the claims regarding new speakers' use of morphophonology, we might expect to find a range of variation, with some speakers closer to standard usage than others.

The rest of the chapter is structured as follows: Section "Fieldwork" discusses the linguistic backgrounds of the fieldwork participants; details of the morphophonological features and findings from the fieldwork are presented in Section "Findings", and the implications of these are discussed further in Section "Discussion".

Fieldwork

Lise Diwan Students and Linguistic Background

Over the course of several fieldwork visits in 2017–2018, 103 pupils at the *Lise Diwan* in Carhaix participated in research investigating a variety of features of Breton morphophonology. Of these, 55 reported speaking Breton at home (i.e. 53.4%). This is quite a large proportion and contrasts with Kennard's (2018b) study, involving schoolchildren aged 8–14, none of whom spoke Breton at home with their parents, and only one of whom had a family member who spoke Breton. It is possible that the higher proportion of *Lise* pupils speaking Breton is because these speakers are older, aged 15–18. The level of commitment to Breton is a factor in whether or not pupils continue in Breton-medium schooling beyond the primary level (Broudic 2010); thus, it is possible that these pupils come from families who are more invested in Breton and are more likely to have Breton at home.

Asking pupils whether they speak Breton at home provides quite limited information about the amount of Breton input they receive outside school and does not distinguish between a home where parents take an interest in children's homework, but the language of communication is French, and a home where all interaction is in Breton. Questions about home language usage therefore need to be somewhat more nuanced, and to consider the kind of Breton spoken by relatives and how they came to speak Breton. A subgroup of 33 pupils (henceforth, *Liseidi* 'lycée pupils') who participated in the above research were asked further questions about language use at home. They were aged between 14 and 18 at the time of the fieldwork (mean age =

16.0) and come from homes all over Brittany, including the traditionally French-speaking areas of Upper Brittany.

Participants were asked to complete a short questionnaire (in French) containing four questions about their linguistic background: (i) Do you speak Breton as your native language? (ii) Do you speak another language fluently? (iii) Do you speak Breton at home? (iv) If yes, with whom? The second question was asked in case any participants had another first language at home, but in fact none did, and so this will not be considered further. More interesting are the responses to the other questions. Of 33 participants, 14 considered themselves to have Breton as a native language, while 19 did not. Speaker identity is a key issue in the field of minority language revitalisation, so this question was asked to gauge how participants positioned themselves within the Breton-speaking community. On its own, the response does not provide very much information, but it is more interesting taken in conjunction with the responses to question (iii). Here, participants were given a forced choice between 'Yes, often', 'Yes, sometimes' and 'No'. A summary is given in Table 1.

Unsurprisingly, those who self-report as native Breton speakers also report that they speak Breton at home, at least sometimes, with only one exception. Equally, those who report that they speak Breton at home 'often' also regard Breton as a *langue maternelle*, with just one exception.

The final question, which asked participants with whom, in their household, they spoke Breton, drew a variety of responses, summarised in Table 2. More detailed information about each participant is given in Table 3. Participants were free to give any response they chose, and many speak Breton with more than one family member.

Of particular interest for this chapter are those speakers who use Breton with a family member of a different generation, rather than only

Table 1 Participants' responses to fieldwork questions

		Do you speak Breton at home?			
		Often	Sometimes	No	*Total*
Do you speak Breton as your native language?	Yes	6	7	1	*14*
	No	1	8	10	*19*
	Total	*7*	*15*	*11*	*33*

Table 2 Breton-speaking family members of *Liseidi*

Family member	Number of responses
Parent (mother, father or both)	12
Sibling(s)	14
Grandparent(s)	4
Whole family	2

Table 3 Details of Breton-speaking familiy members of *Liseidi*, and how often Breton is spoken

Participant	Speaks Breton at home with ...	How often?
AS	Sisters; grandparents	Sometimes
EP	Whole family	Often
GK	Brothers and sisters	Sometimes
GS	Sisters; father	Sometimes
GZ	Brother	Sometimes
HA	Whole family	Often
HS	Brother	Sometimes
JU	Sister	Sometimes
ML	Sisters	Sometimes
MM	Parents; sisters	Sometimes
MW	Mother	Often
OK	Parents; brothers	Often
PP	Mother	Often
QP	Parents; brother; sister	Sometimes
QV	Brothers; father	Sometimes
RY	Grandparents	Sometimes
SO	Parents, sisters	Sometimes
TJ	Sister	Sometimes
UU	Parents; sister; grandmother	Sometimes
UX	Mother; grandmother	Often
XL	Father	Sometimes
XN	Father; sister	Often

siblings, since this may shed light on possible intergenerational transmission within the home. It is interesting to note additionally, as shown in Table 3, that those speakers who use Breton 'often' at home all use Breton with at least one parent; those who only use Breton with siblings report speaking the language at home 'sometimes', which is hardly surprising if their parents do not speak Breton and the language of the home is French.

Further Interviews on Linguistic Background

As well as completing the written questionnaire regarding home language usage, a smaller group of 14 participants, all of whom had responded that they used language at home with a parent or grandparent, were asked additional questions as part of a linguistic interview. The goal was to discover more about the linguistic background of other Breton-speaking family members: how they had acquired or learnt Breton, and how much they used it with the participant in question. Examining the paths that parents had taken to becoming Breton speakers revealed both a range of experiences and some common trends. In all but one of the families, the parent or parents had not grown up speaking Breton, but had usually learned the language in adulthood. For several, this was alongside their child as he or she attended a *Diwan* primary school, as the excerpt in (1) demonstrates:

(1) Speaker XL
Int: You speak Breton at home sometimes, is that right?
XL: Yes, mainly with my dad.
Int: Did he learn Breton as well?
XL: Yes.
Int: Also at Diwan?
XL: No, erm, while erm … when I was at primary school he learnt as well alongside me.

It is particularly interesting to note, then, that none of the parents had attended *Diwan* as pupils themselves, which echoes Baudu's findings discussed above. Rather, the majority had learned Breton in adulthood, usually primarily through private study, but also through evening classes, Breton-language courses such as those provided by *Stumdi*,[4] and through intensive training. Four of the participants had parents who were themselves teachers in *Diwan* schools, three at the primary level and one at secondary level (*collège*). All four had learnt Breton in adulthood, and XN's discussion is typical of this (see (2)):

(2) Speaker XN
Int: So, you speak Breton at home, is that right?
XN: Yes, yes, also with my sister.
Int: Oh right, so your father, did he learn Breton?
XN: Yes, he learned Breton.
Int: At the Diwan schools as well, or –?
XN: No, not in the Diwan schools, he learned it when he was twenty, I think, on his own, and then he became a Breton primary school teacher.

Not all parents had acquired Breton exclusively in adulthood. Two parents had also acquired some passive knowledge of Breton in childhood from their own Breton-speaking parents (the pupils' grandparents). However, even between these two cases, there are differences in the outcomes from this exposure to Breton at an early age. For OK's mother, this was then supplemented by further studies in Breton, bringing her to full fluency, while for QV's father, this left him with a very good passive understanding of Breton, but difficulties communicating complex ideas.

(3) Speaker OK
Well erm, my mother actually heard [Breton] when she was young. Her parents spoke to her in French but erm they spoke Breton between themselves so she ha- … and with her grandmother as well, so she understood everything. And in fact when she arrived at the Lycée there was a Breton option, and she said to herself 'oh well, why not?' and she learnt it, and so she continued.

(4) Speaker QV
QV: He [my father] understands Breton very well. And as for speaking, he knows everyday words, but when it gets more … let's say … complicated, erm … He doesn't manage. It's a bit too technical.

Int: So, did he learn Breton?
QV: Yes, because my grandparents didn't use Breton, and in fact, erm, at that time, it was shameful to speak Breton; you had to learn French. So they only speak Breton amongst themselves, they learned Breton. So, they spoke in French … erm to their children, that is my father, and his sisters, but erm, but after a while he learned to understand.

In addition to this passive knowledge, one speaker (UX) has a parent who is a native Breton speaker; her linguistic background will be discussed below in Section "Case Studies: Participants".

One final interesting point to raise is the motivation behind parents' choice to learn Breton. For those who learned Breton alongside their children, this is fairly clear, but two participants had additional information to add about their parents' reasons for learning Breton. EP explained that while her father had started to learn Breton as an optional subject at secondary school, and then continued these studies later, her mother had chosen to learn Breton after meeting her father, and he had helped with her studies.

(5) Speaker EP
My dad learnt Breton first, he started it at secondary school with a Breton option, and he continued it afterwards; and my mum, when she met my dad she didn't know how to speak Breton but learned partly with my dad. However, my brothers and I have spoken Breton since we were very small, yeah.

OK, whose mother had acquired a passive knowledge of Breton in childhood (see (3) above), explained that her father had learnt Breton in adulthood, having grown up in a non-Breton-speaking area, and was inspired by his discovery of the *Diwan* schooling system:

(6) Speaker OK
And my father, he's from the Nantes area, and erm, he came erm, well, to Finistère when he was young, to be a children's activity leader. And

> that was when he discovered the Diwan school in [Town]. And he went there [...] and he decided to learn Breton.

It is clear that the participants in this study come from a wide range of linguistic backgrounds. The next section will focus on a subset of participants with contrasting backgrounds in an attempt to identify patterns in their spoken Breton that might be linked to their use of the language at home, and the type of speakers they interact with in the home environment.

Case Studies: Participants

Seven teenaged speakers of Breton from different linguistic backgrounds have been chosen as case studies: EP, JU, MM, QP, QV, UX and XH. A summary of their responses to the questions asked during the fieldwork is given in Table 4, and these are then discussed in more detail below.

Table 4 Case study participants: linguistic backgrounds

Participant (M/F, age)	Breton at home?	How often?	With whom?	Interlocutors' paths to Breton
EP (F, 16)	Yes	Often	Whole family	Father *collège* Mother with father
ML (M, 17)	Yes	Sometimes	Siblings	*Diwan*
MM (F, 15)	Yes	Sometimes	Parents; siblings	Both parents Stumdi
QP (F, 17)	Yes	Sometimes	Mother; siblings	Mother intensive course
QV (M, 16)	Yes	Sometimes	Father; siblings	Father passive knowledge
UX (F, 16)	Yes	Often	Mother; grandmother	Mother native speaker Grandmother passive knowledge + later study
XH (F, 17)	No	NA	NA	NA

These seven participants have been chosen to reflect the wide range of linguistic backgrounds that the *liseidi* have, including the different paths to speakerhood that their interlocutors at home have taken, and the fact that more participants responded that they spoke Breton at home 'sometimes' than 'never' or 'often'. More female than male speakers took part in the study, hence there are 5 female and 2 male participants among the case studies.

XH (F, 17) does not speak Breton at home, and therefore comes from a completely French-speaking background. She does not identify as *bretonnant*. Four of the speakers, ML, MM, QP and QV, report speaking Breton at home 'sometimes'. ML only speaks Breton with his sisters, all of whom are also *Diwan* pupils; neither of his parents speaks Breton. The other three also speak Breton with at least one parent. MM's parents learnt Breton in adulthood through the Breton training organisation *Stumdi*. QP's mother comes from a French-speaking background, but having studied Breton took an intensive language course before training to become a Breton-immersion teacher at primary level. Interestingly, QP does not identify as *bretonnant*, while the other three speakers who use the language at home do.

(7) Speaker QP
QP: My mum, she's a Breton primary school teacher
Int: Oh right! So did she learn it?
QP: Erm no … erm …
Int: When she was small?
QP: Well, quickly, you know … but in any case she did Breton studies
Int: Okay. So she wasn't at Diwan?
QP: No, she was at a French lycée

QV has a particularly interesting linguistic background. As discussed above, his father grew up with a passive knowledge of Breton, but finds speaking it more difficult (see excerpt in (4)). Although QV uses Breton 'sometimes' at home, mainly with his father and siblings, he also spoke about using Breton in other non-school contexts, as the excerpt in (8) shows.

(8) Speaker QV
Int: It's great that you have family who speak Breton
QV: I don't just speak Breton with my family
Int: Yeah?
QV: I do theatre in Breton
Int: Oh right?
QV: That helps as well
Int: Yes, yes
QV: Then, there's the 'lise' as well
Int: Of course
QV: Then apart from that … my brothers speak Breton as well, they were at Diwan […] My big brother, my oldest brother, left Diwan in year 4 [i.e. aged 15], then the other before year 3 [i.e. aged 13], and so they don't speak Breton as much

Finally, EP and UX often speak Breton at home with their families. EP reported that she spoke Breton with the whole family, and that her parents had learned Breton in adulthood (see excerpt in (5) above). UX has an interesting and unusual linguistic background, as her mother identifies as a native speaker of Breton, while her maternal grandmother grew up with a passive knowledge that she later built on with further study in adulthood. UX was the only participant who described her linguistic background in this way, but this restoration of intergenerational transmission is ultimately the aim of revitalisation efforts such as Diwan.

(9) Speaker UX
Int: And you speak Breton at home as well?
UX: Yes
Int: With your mother?

UX: Yes
Int: So, did she learn Breton?
UX: Yes, she ... it's her own native language too
Int: Oh yes? Ah well that's great! That's quite unusual.
UX: Yes
Int: So, your grandmother as well –
UX: Yes, she learnt it, however
Int: Yes, yes, so did she not speak it from childhood, is that it, or ...?
UX: My grandmother? Er well, her family spoke Breton but as it wasn't very correct, it was forbidden and all that, she had to learn, properly, when she was an adult.

Since these participants come from different linguistic backgrounds, this may have influenced not only their attitudes towards the language, but also the kind of Breton they speak. Of course, the linguistic environment of the *Lise Diwan* itself also plays a role: this is where most pupils speak the greater part of their Breton, and as it is a boarding school it is a more immersive environment than a day school. It is also important to note the relevance of peer-group language for adolescent speakers (although of course, the level of home language usage is likely to play a role as well; this is discussed further in Section "Discussion"). Nance (2020) contrasts studies where home language seems to play a role in minority language acquisition (e.g. Gathercole and Thomas 2009), and others where there appears to be little difference between younger speakers on the basis of home background (e.g. Nance 2015; Morris 2017). She hypothesises that while there may be initial differences between pupils based on home background, these are later levelled out as those who are acquiring the language purely through immersion schooling receive enough input in the minority language to catch up with their peers. The peer group thus becomes more important than the parents' language.

Findings

Breton Morphophonology

The discussion can now turn to an examination of certain Breton morphophonological features as used by these seven speakers; namely, grammatical gender and mutation. These are both areas characteristic of Celtic languages which differ from French, which might make them more difficult for younger speakers to acquire. Breton has two grammatical genders, masculine and feminine, and these are signalled primarily by agreement with the numerals two, three and four, and by patterns of mutation. Mutation is the replacement of the initial consonant phoneme of a word by a different consonant phoneme under certain morphosyntactic conditions (Ball and Müller 1992). Examples from Breton are given in (10).

(10) Initial consonant mutation in Breton
a. *ti* 'house'
b. *ma zi* 'my house'
c. *e di* 'his house'

There are four types of mutation in Breton, but only two, lenition and spirantisation, will be discussed in this chapter. They affect only a subset of consonant phonemes, and the phonological changes they involve are illustrated in Tables 5 and 6.

Table 5 Breton lenition

Unmutated	p	t	k	b	d	g	gw	m
Mutated	b	d	g	v	z	h, x[5]	w	v

Table 6 Breton spirantisation

Unmutated	p	t	k
Mutated	f	z	h, x[5]

Mutations can be triggered by a preceding word, as in (10), such as a particle, possessive or preposition, but can also be affected by morphosyntactic properties of lexemes such as gender and number. Key to the discussion in this chapter is the fact that feminine singular nouns undergo lenition following the definite and indefinite articles, but masculine singular nouns do not. However, masculine singular nouns beginning /k-/ undergo spirantisation in the same context.

Breton is said to have an opaque system of grammatical gender, as has been described for Welsh (Thomas and Gathercole 2007), meaning that the cues to gender are contradictory and not readily available. This can be seen in Breton in three main ways:

i. Not all consonants undergo mutation; e.g. s-initial nouns do not change regardless of gender.
ii. There is no one-to-one relationship between a particular mutation and a particular gender; e.g. lenition is found in feminine singular nouns following the article, but also in masculine plural nouns referring to humans. Lenition thus marks both masculine and feminine, and singular and plural.
iii. There are a number of exceptions to the regular mutation rules; e.g. d-initial feminine nouns never lenite following the article.

A summary of mutation in singular nouns following the articles is given in Table 7.

In addition to mutation of the nouns themselves, Breton also signals grammatical gender through lenition of attributive adjectives, which follow the noun. Adjectives undergo lenition when they follow a feminine singular noun, but not a masculine singular noun. However, this is also subject to phonological constraints: adjectives beginning with voiceless stops only lenite when the preceding noun ends in a sonorant. Other lenitable adjectives are not subject to this constraint. This is summarised in Table 8.

Finally, gender is also signalled by agreement with the numerals two, three and four, which in Breton precede singular nouns. These numerals also trigger their own mutations on the nouns that follow them, but

Table 7 Mutation of singular nouns following the articles

	Masculine	Masculine: /k-/	Feminine	Feminine: /d-/
Unmutated	pesk 'fish'	kazh 'cat'	kador 'chair'	dremm 'face'
Mutated	ur pesk 'a fish'	ur c'hazh 'a cat'	ur gador 'a chair'	un dremm 'a face'
Mutation type	None	Spirantisation	Lenition	None

Table 8 Mutation of adjectives

	Masculine	Feminine, final sonorant	Feminine, final obstruent
	pesk 'fish'	kador 'chair'	bag 'boat'
bras 'big'	ur pesk bras	ur gador vras	ur vag vras
kozh 'old'	ur pesk kozh	ur gador gozh	ur vag kozh

Table 9 Forms of the numerals

	Masculine *kazh* 'cat'	Feminine *bag* 'boat'
'two'	daou gazh	div vag
'three'	tri c'hazh	teir bag
'four'	pevar c'hazh	peder bag

this is completely regular, and not affected by the gender of the noun in question. A summary is given in Table 9.

Three features have been chosen as representative of this area of morphophonology, and will be considered for the seven case studies in this chapter:

1. Mutation in nouns following the (indefinite) article
2. Form of the numeral 'two'
3. Mutation in attributive adjectives following the noun

Fieldwork Elicitation

To obtain the data under discussion in this chapter, two main elicitation tasks were used. Participants were asked to name items in Breton, which were presented using PowerPoint on a laptop screen. In the first, the items were presented in groups of four: first one item, then two, then three, then many. Participants were asked to name the items in Breton by saying 'an X', 'two Xs', 'three Xs', 'Xs' in turn. Thirty-four[6] nouns were used, of which 14 were masculine (8 mutable, 6 not) and 20 were feminine (12 mutable, 8 not). In the second exercise, participants were shown pairs of images, one with a small item, and one with a larger version of the same item. They were asked to name the items by saying 'a big X; a small X'. The same list of nouns was used as in the first elicitation task, with one exception (*sant* 'saint' was not included, because it was felt 'a big saint; a small saint' was semantically odd).

The fieldwork in question surveyed not only the *liseidi*, but also adult speakers; both those who had grown up speaking Breton, and those who might be better identified as 'new speakers'. Their data will not be discussed in this chapter, other than as an occasional base of comparison.

Use of Morphophonology

It seems reasonably intuitive to assume that receiving Breton input at home would improve teenaged speakers' proficiency in Breton. However, it is also sensible to assume that the amount of Breton spoken at home will also play a role. Looking at the case studies, then, we might expect to see a difference between those who speak Breton often at home (EP and UX), in comparison to XH, who does not speak Breton at home, and that those who speak Breton at home sometimes (ML, MM, QP and QV) would be somewhere in between. We might also see finer-grained differences between these last four, depending on their family members' use of Breton. The questions being investigated can therefore be summarised as follows:

1. To what extent does the language of the home affect teenaged speakers' use of key features of Breton morphophonology (gender and mutation)?
2. How relevant is the amount of Breton spoken at home?
3. How relevant are family members' own linguistic backgrounds in the use of the speaker's Breton?

Rather than categorising speakers' usage as 'correct' or 'incorrect', the findings are expressed in terms of 'expected usage': that is, what would be expected in adult speakers and/or Standard Breton. In fact, the adult speakers who took part in the same linguistic fieldwork (both adult new speakers and older speakers who grew up in a Breton-speaking environment) do not always conform to Standard Breton usage, or indeed more regionally based descriptions of the language. It would therefore be odd to assume that the *liseidi* would do so consistently. As a group, the *liseidi* tend to lag behind adult speakers' usage (see Table 11 for details of average usage), but if we examine the data across all three morphophonological features first of all, it seems as though the expectations above are borne out. Table 10 is an expanded version of Table 4, giving an indication of the extent to which the speakers under discussion conform to the expected morphophonology for adult native speakers.

It is clear that EP and UX, who often use Breton at home, are consistently the closest to expected usage and adult norms. They use the expected mutated form following the article in all (UX) or almost all (EP) contexts, use the expected form of the numeral most of the time and lenite adjectives following feminine nouns more than any of the other speakers. The average usage for all of the *liseidi* is given in Table 11, along with the average usage for adults who completed the same fieldwork tasks as a means of comparison. EP and UX are above the average for the *liseidi* for all three features and conform to adult usage for all but the adjectival mutation. It is interesting to note that although the parents of EP and UX followed different paths to becoming speakers of Breton, there is little to choose between them in terms of morphophonology.

The speakers who use Breton at home sometimes, with a variety of different interlocutors of differing backgrounds, unsurprisingly show a degree of interspeaker variation. ML and QV are most similar to one another, being somewhat below the *liseidi* average for all three morphophonological features. This is particularly striking for the mutation of adjectives following feminine nouns, which QV does not do at all, and ML does in only one instance. They thus produce utterances such as (11).

(11) Adjectives: QV and ML
a. *ur vag **b**ras* 'a big boat' [expected: *vras*]
b. *ur volenn **b**ihan* 'a small bowl' [expected *vihan*]

Table 10 Use of morphophonological features by case study participants. (a) Mutation of nouns (masculine and feminine) following the indefinite article: percentage as expected; (b) Form of numeral 'two' before masculine and feminine nouns: percentage as expected; (c) Mutation of adjectives *bras* 'big' and *bihan* 'small' following feminine nouns: percentage lenited. See Tables 7–9 for details

Participant (M/F, age)	Breton at home?	How often?	With whom?	Interlocutors' paths to Breton?	% expected mutation following article[(a)]	% form of numeral[(b)]	% mutation of adjective[(c)]
EP (F, 16)	Yes	Often	Whole family	Father *collège* Mother with father	97.3	83.3	55
ML (M, 17)	Yes	Sometimes	Siblings	*Diwan*	75	43.	5
MM (F, 15)	Yes	Sometimes	Parents; siblings	Both parents Stumdi	76.5	82.1	40.6
QP (F, 17)	Yes	Sometimes	Mother; siblings	Mother intensive course (teacher)	90.5	41.2	12.1
QV (M, 16)	Yes	Sometimes	Father; siblings	Father passive knowledge	75	48	0
UX (F, 16)	Yes	Often	Mother; grand-mother	Mother native speaker Grandmother passive knowledge + later study	100	82.9	57.9
XH (F, 17)	No	NA	NA	NA	94.7	65.6	22.6

Table 11 Average usage of key morphophonological features

Speaker group	% expected mutation following article	% form of numeral	% mutation of adjective
Liseidi	85.6	64.1	33.3
Adults	95.7	86.0	69.4

In contrast, MM and QP are much more variable, being comparable to ML and QV in some features, but much closer to adult norms in others. QP uses the expected mutation following the article in over 90% of instances, but her usage of the numeral 'two' and her lenition of adjectives are both below average for the *liseidi*. MM, on the other hand, does not use the expected mutation following the article in as many contexts, yet her use of the numeral and adjectival mutation is much closer to adult usage, as the examples in (12) and (13) illustrate. These findings point to a much patchier understanding of Breton morphophonology among these students than among those who speak Breton more frequently at home, and the implications will be discussed further below.

(12) Mutation following the article
a. Expected mutation: lenition (QP)
ur volenn 'a bowl'
b. Unexpected mutation: no mutation (MM)
ur bolenn 'a bowl'

(13) Form of the numeral 'two'
a. Expected numeral
div blac'h 'two girls' (MM)
b. Unexpected numeral
daou blac'h 'two girls' (QP)

Finally, we might expect XH to diverge the most from expected adult usage, given that she does not speak Breton at all at home, but in fact this is not the case. Despite having no Breton input outside the school environment, she uses the expected morphophonological features to a greater extent than ML and QV, and at times is approaching adult norms. This is a surprising finding and points towards a great deal of variation amongst speakers, and the relevance of individual factors such as speakers' aptitude for learning languages.

Discussion

With this overview in place, the discussion can now turn to the implications of these findings for understanding the role played by the use of Breton in the home environment in teenaged speakers' proficiency. Naturally, there are limitations with this study. It relies on self-reporting; what speakers mean when they say they speak Breton at home 'sometimes' or 'often' is not quantified, and there is likely to be variation between speakers that is not captured here. Although we have some indication of the 'type' of Breton that parents and other relatives speak, their Breton has not been analysed for this study. It might have been possible to see family based trends if this had been the case (e.g. lack of lenition of adjectives following feminine nouns, or normative use of the numeral 'two'). This type of in-depth study, which examines both teenaged speakers' Breton and the Breton of their caregivers and other Breton-speaking relatives, would shed a lot more light on exactly how important input from the home is in influencing how they speak the language.

That aside, it seems clear that using Breton often at home, with a variety of family members, leads to a more adult-like production of Breton morphophonology. Lenition of adjectives following feminine nouns is much lower than descriptions of Standard Breton would lead us to expect, but this appears to be very variable even among adult speakers. It is not surprising to find a relatively low rate of usage among the *liseidi* when the input they receive is so variable. However, what is particularly interesting about EP and UX is that despite the fact that their Breton-speaking parents have acquired the language in quite different ways, they do not differ greatly from one another in the features under discussion here, suggesting that uninterrupted intergenerational transmission may be less influential than simply using Breton as the default language of the home.

What these findings also seem to suggest is that the intergenerational use of Breton may be more influential in supporting the acquisition of certain morphophonological features than peer-group usage. This can be seen for speakers ML and QV, who both use Breton at home 'sometimes', but are less proficient in these morphophonological features than the other speakers. ML uses Breton at home sometimes, but only with his siblings, who also attend the *Diwan* schooling system. They do not speak Breton with their parents. While it is heartening to hear of *Diwan* pupils using Breton outside the classroom, given that this is one of the biggest challenges facing the immersion-school system, it seems that it may have a relatively small impact on speakers' use of Breton morphophonology (though it may, of course, improve other aspects of their Breton not studied here, such as lexis and fluency). Using Breton with siblings at home therefore seems to be an extension of the peer-group environment at the *Lise Diwan* itself.

As discussed above, QV has a particularly interesting linguistic background. Although he sometimes speaks Breton at home with his father and brothers, he seems to view his additional Breton-language activities as more relevant to his use of Breton than his home environment. He is clearly a keen language user, who is incorporating Breton into every part of his life, but this does not translate into a more adult-like morphophonology. Again, this seems to indicate that intergenerational, family wide use of the language may be more influential.

As this is only a set of case studies, any conclusions drawn regarding the role of Breton in the family are necessarily limited. Nowhere is this clearer than with speaker XH. Despite never speaking Breton at home, her use of the expected morphophonology is largely average for the *liseidi*, and ahead of ML and QV. This suggests that while using Breton at home often with parents is beneficial for immersion-school pupils, not having this input does not necessarily mean that teenaged speakers will lag behind their peers. The variation that MM and QP exhibit, displaying adult-like proficiency in some areas but not others, also supports this, and points to a somewhat patchy acquisition of Breton morphophonology among some speakers. However, it is interesting that even weak trends can be observed here, given that other studies of adolescent speakers of minority languages have found the impact of home background to be minimal (Mayr et al. 2017; Nance 2020). Given findings by Thomas and Gathercole (2007), inter alia, it is possible that the effect of linguistic background on the morphology and morphophonology is more persistent than in the phonology, but this is merely conjecture, and a wider-ranging study would be required to investigate this.

Notes

1. Although the *département* Loire-Atlantique was part of the historic region of Brittany, it is not today part of the Brittany administrative *région*. Despite the fact that Nantes was for a time the seat of the dukes of Brittany, the city itself has never been Breton-speaking; however, Breton was spoken in rural parts of Loire-Atlantique as late as the twentieth century (Mathelier 2017). In September 2018, there were 798 pupils in Breton-medium education in this region (Ofis Publik ar Brezhoneg 2020).
2. Figures from previous years: 2018–18,337; 2016–17,024; 2015–15,696. The *Ofis Publik ar Brezhoneg* webpage is updated every year, and previous years' figures do not remain available; however, these figures can be found in Kennard (2017, 2018a, 2018b).
3. This echoes Dorian's (1981) findings for East Sutherland Gaelic, where speakers were unable to follow Gaelic-language radio broadcasts because the variety used, the standard, was so unfamiliar.
4. *Stumdi* is a Breton teaching organisation that offers a range of different courses in the Breton language.
5. The grapheme <c'h> , which is used for both lenited /g/ and spirantised /k/ (as well as existing as a non-mutated form) is variously pronounced /h/ and /x/ by different speakers and in different contexts.
6. A further two nouns were in fact included in the elicitation task, but as they are listed as having either gender, they will not be considered further.

References

Académie de Rennes. 2019. L'académie en chiffres à la rentrée 2019. http://www.ac-rennes.fr/cid102458/l-academie-chiffres.html. Accessed 15 April 2020.

Ball, M.J., and N. Müller. 1992. *Mutation in Welsh*. London: Routledge.

Baudu, T. 2015. 'From Pupil to Parent': Understanding Former Diwan Pupils' Attitudes, Challenges and Opportunities in Revitalizing the Breton Language Transmission Within the Family. Unpublished MA Thesis, Bangor University.

Bocquenet, L. 1985. Pourquoi DIWAN? *Multilingua* 4 (4): 211–215.

Broudic, F. 1999. Les jeunes et la langue bretonne au XXe siècle: Une évolution en deux temps et demi. *Klask* 5: 179–192.

Broudic, F. 2009. *Parler breton au XXIe siècle: Le nouveau sondage de TMO-Régions*. Brest: Emgleo Breiz.

Broudic, F. 2010. *L'enseignement du et en breton: Rapport à Monsieur le Recteur de l'Académie de Rennes*. Brest: Emgleo Breiz.

Davies-Deacon, M. 2017. The Online Presence of Standard and Non-standard Breton. Paper presented at the Annual Conference of the Society for French Studies, University of Durham, 3–5 July.

Dorian, N.C. 1981. *Language Death: The Life Cycle of a Scottish Gaelic Dialect*. Philadelphia, PA: University of Pennsylvania Press.

Dressler, W.U. 1972. On the Phonology of Language Death. *Proceedings of the Chicago Linguistics Society* 8: 448–457.

Gathercole, V.C.M., and E.M.N. Thomas. 2005. Minority Language Survival: Input Factors Influencing the Acquisition of Welsh. In *ISB4 Proceedings of the 4th International Symposium on Bilingualism*, ed. J. Cohen, K.T. McAlister, K. Rolstad, and Jeff MacSwan, 852–874. Somerville, MA: Cascadilla Press.

Gathercole, V.C.M., and E.M.N. Thomas 2009. Bilingual First-language Development: Dominant Language Takeover, Threatened Minority Language Take-up. *Bilingualism: Language and Cognition* 12 (2): 213–237.

Hewitt, S. 1977. The Degree of Acceptability of Modern Literary Breton to Native Breton Speakers. Unpublished Diploma of Linguistics Thesis, University of Cambridge.

Hornsby, M. 2014. 'Une prononciation déficiente, francisée': The Debate Over an "Authentic" Accent in Revitalized Breton. *Zeszyty Łużyckie* 48: 149–171.

Jones, M.C. 1995. At What Price Language Maintenance? Standardization in Modern Breton. *French Studies* 49 (4): 424–438.

Kennard, H.J. 2017. Lexical Stress in New Speakers' Breton: Production and Perception. Paper presented at the 11th International Symposium on Bilingualism, Limerick, Ireland, 11–15 June.

Kennard, H.J. 2018a. 'New' and 'Old' Speakers of Breton in the 21st Century: Insights from Morphophonology. Paper presented at Celtic Sociolinguistics Symposium III, Galway, Ireland, 16–17 November.

Kennard, H.J. 2018b. Verbal Mutation Among Young Speakers of Breton: Acquisition and Maintenance. In *New Speakers of Minority Languages: Linguistic Ideologies and Practice*, ed. M. Hornsby, M. Moriarty, C. Smith-Christmas, and N.Ó. Murchadha, 231–252. Basingstoke: Palgrave Macmillan.

Kennard, H.J., and A. Lahiri. 2017. Mutation in Breton Verbs: Pertinacity Across Generations. *Journal of Linguistics* 53 (1): 113–145.

Kuter, L. 1999. The Diwan Phenomenon: A Catalyst for Change in the Schools of Brittany. In *Les langues régionales de France: un état des lieux à la veille du XXIe siècle. Actes d'un colloque organisé à «The University of Pennsylvania, Philadelphia, USA»*, ed. P. Blanchet, R. Breton, and H. Schiffman, 177–183. Louvain-la-Neuve: Peeters.

Le Dû, J. 1999. La langue bretonne aujourd'hui. In *Les langues régionales de France: un état des lieux à la veille du XXIème siècle. Actes d'un colloque organisé à «The University of Pennsylvania, Philadelphia, USA»*, ed. P. Blanchet, R. Breton, and H. Schiffman, 25–31. Louvain-la-Neuve: Peeters.

Le Dû, J., and Y. Le Berre. 1996. Parité et disparité: Sphère publique et sphère privée de la parole. *La Bretagne Linguistique* 10: 7–25.

Le Ruyet, J.-C. 2011. Effet Buben, liaison et modèles orthographiques bretons. *La Bretagne Linguistique* 16: 97–109.

Madeg, M. 2010. *Traité de prononciation du breton du Nord Ouest*. Brest: Emgleo Breizh.

Mathelier, Y. 2017. *Le breton parlé dans le pays guérandais*. Fouesnant: Yoran Embanner.

Mayr, R., J. Morris, I. Mennen, and D. Williams. 2017. Disentangling the Effects of Long-term Language Contact and Individual Bilingualism: The Case of Monophthongs in Welsh and English. *International Journal of Bilingualism* 21 (3): 245–267.

McDonald, M. 1989. *'We Are Not French!' Language, Culture and Identity in Brittany*. London: Routledge.

Moal, S. 2018. The 2018 Sociolinguistic Survey in Brittany: Some Facts and Development Paths. Paper Presented at Celtic Sociolinguistic Symposium III, Galway, Ireland, 16–17 November.

Morris, J. 2017. Sociophonetic Variation in a Long-term Language Contact Situation: /l/-darkening in Welsh-English Bilingual Speech. *Journal of Sociolinguistics* 21 (2): 183–207.

Nance, C. 2015. 'New' Scottish Gaelic Speakers in Glasgow: A Phonetic Study of Language Revitalisation. *Language in Society* 44 (4): 553–579.

Nance, C. 2020. Bilingual Language Exposure and the Peer Group: Acquiring Phonetics and Phonology in Gaelic Medium Education. *International Journal of Bilingualism* 24 (2): 360–375.

Ofis Publik ar Brezhoneg. 2020. Chiffres clés. http://www.fr.brezhoneg.bzh/5-chiffres-cles.htm. Accessed 15 April 2020.

Poisard, C., M. Kervran, E. Le Pipec, S. Alliot, G. Gueudet, H. Hili, N. Jeudy-Karakoç, and G. Larvol. 2014. Enseignement et apprentissage des mathématiques à l'école primaire dans un contexte bilingue breton-français. *Spirale: Revue de recherches en éducation* 54: 129–150.

Thomas, E.M., and V.C.M. Gathercole. 2007. Children's Productive Command of Grammatical Gender and Mutation in Welsh: An Alternative to Rule-based Learning. *First Language* 27 (3): 251–278.

Thomas, E.M., and R. Mayr. 2010. Children's Acquisition of Welsh in a Bilingual Setting: A Psycholinguistic Perspective. In *Welsh in the Twenty-First Century*, ed. D. Morris, 99–117. Cardiff: University of Wales Press.

Thomas, E.M., N. Williams, L.A. Jones, S. Davies, and H. Binks. 2014. Acquiring Complex Structures Under Minority Language Conditions: Bilingual Acquisition of Plural Morphology in Welsh. *Bilingualism: Language and Cognition* 17 (3): 478–494.

Transmission in Diasporic Contexts

Comparing Family Language Policy in Cyprus, Estonia and Sweden: Efforts and Choices Among Russian-Speaking Families

Sviatlana Karpava, Natalia Ringblom, and Anastassia Zabrodskaja

Introduction

The sustainability of a heritage language's (HL) acquisition, use and maintenance can be affected by such factors as socio-economic status (SES), education and demography and language attitudes within a family and in society (Wardhaugh 2010). In addition, linguistic and cultural

All three authors of this chapter contributed equally and should be considered co-first authors.

S. Karpava
University of Cyprus, Nicosia, Cyprus

N. Ringblom
Stockholm University, Dalarna University, Stockholm, Sweden

A. Zabrodskaja (✉)
Tallinn University, Tallinn, Estonia

M. Hornsby and W. McLeod (eds.), *Transmitting Minority Languages*, Palgrave Studies in Minority Languages and Communities,
https://doi.org/10.1007/978-3-030-87910-5_11

identity, affective and social networking should be taken into consideration (De Houwer 2009). A minority or immigrant language, which corresponds to a HL for the purposes of this study, does not usually have much institutional support, so family may play the primary role in HL socialisation (Melo-Pfeifer 2015). As Albirini (2014) argues, the most important predictor of HL proficiency is language use by children and parents, especially by mothers, taking into consideration quality, quantity, frequency, range and contexts (see Paradis 2004; Schmid 2002, 2007).

We analysed family language policy (FLP) in multilingual families who used Russian as the HL with a particular focus on parental *beliefs* and *everyday practical activities*, constructing safe spaces of language transmission and managing FLP. Our study was based on data from ethnographic sociolinguistic interviews with Cypriot families living in its rural and urban areas, Estonian families from the capital Tallinn and the north-eastern, predominantly Russian-speaking rural region, and Russian-speaking families spread out over most of Sweden. The data collection included questionnaires with parents to find out their general background, SES (socioeconomic status), language proficiency and reported language use and attitudes.

Our chapter articulates the implications of dynamic FLP processes and explores their complexity, showing how FLP can support, reinforce and integrate Russian as a minority language in the diversifying societies of Cyprus, Estonia and Sweden. Based on this aim, our chapter is divided into six sections. These sections address approaches to FLP research, the nature of the HL, the methodological framework of the current research, the set of choices and efforts indicated among study participants in relation to Russian-language transmission and a conclusion.

Research on FLP: An Overview of Recent Developments

The linguistic environment of a child is built by his/her family, which is considered to be a driving force in minority language maintenance and transmission (Schwartz 2010), and a proactive FLP can help to prevent language attrition and/or language assimilation in the next generation (Fishman 1991; Spolsky 2007). The FLP depends on the family structure, the number of members each family has, the role of siblings, grandparents and relatives and social networks (Wong Fillmore 1991; Harris 1995). For example, according to Kyratzis (2004) and Zhu Hua and Li Wei (2005), older siblings are more inclined to use the MajL (majority language) with their parents and younger brothers and sisters (La Piedra and Romo 2003; Gregory 2004), thus, restricting the possibility of HL use, maintenance and transmission.

On the one hand, families with one child or fewer children have more time and opportunities for interaction. On the other hand, in a single-child family, there is no interaction with other siblings, which can lead to language shift. Some parents may insist on the use of the HL, even if their children refuse; they can correct their mistakes and do not allow them to code-switch and implement translanguaging, which can lead to conflicts, burdens and frustration in a family. Family cohesion is strengthened by consensual language use, emotional ties and cultural pride, while a lack of cohesion and a conflictual relationship among immigrant family generations can lead to emotional distance, language shift or even language loss (Tannenbaum 2005; Spolsky 2004, 2007). Schwartz (2010) asserts that family cohesiveness and emotional relations are crucial for the FLP, which is in line with the research conducted by Wong Fillmore (2000) and Okita (2002).

Parental beliefs and attitudes shape the FLP (Barkhuizen 2006). The language ideologies held by the parents might not coincide with their actual language practice and strategies, explicit and implicit FLP or conscious and subconscious choices (De Houwer 1999; King 2000; Schwartz 2008). Parents can even make spontaneous decisions and have an unplanned FLP by accepting or adapting to the generally prevailing social norms and language ideologies in the country (Spolsky and Shohamy 1999; Schwartz 2008, 2010). Inconsistency in theory and practice leads to a discrepancy between parents' commitment to HL maintenance and its actual realisation and the effectiveness of efforts (Schwartz 2008, 2010).

Tannenbaum (2003) reports that immigrant children and adults can have different language use preferences and choices: they found that parents were more sensitive to the context/domain of communication (use of HL in intimate interactions and the MajL in the public domain) than their children.

Thus, members of the same family can demonstrate diverse views on bilingualism/multilingualism (Zhu and Li 2016). Family composition, personal experiences and parents' attitudes are crucial factors that affect the FLP (Protassova 2018); the same is true of external factors, home environment, exposure to the HL, HL schools and bilingual education. The family type, the number and order of children, continuity of family structure (if there has been a separation or divorce), educational level, SES, age of onset of the MajL (AoO), length of residence (LoR) in a host country, acculturation, integration, linguistic and cultural identity, parents' attitudes and beliefs: these all contribute to the FLP to different extents (Schwartz 2010).

Grin (2003) and Lo Bianco and Peyton (2013) maintain that there are three factors associated with language maintenance and language revitalisation: capacity, opportunity and desire. Socio-political and economic factors affect the FLP (Curdt-Christiansen 2009). According to Spolsky (2012), the FLP is associated with the family and wider community, as well as societal and educational levels. Schwarz and Verschik (2013) argue that the FLP is multidimensional and is comprised of the agency of parents, children and teachers, as well as how the family is affected by ideology, micro- and macro-factors, which is in line with the findings of Smith-Christmas (2015).

The FLP depends on ideology, management and practice and intra- and inter-family factors (Spolsky 2004; King et al. 2008; Schwartz 2010). Intra-family factors include parents' decisions about whether or not to support the minority language and the FLP; inter-family factors encompass subjective and objective aspects of ethnolinguistic vitality (Allard and Landry 1992), community or society language policy, acculturation, power relations, socio-economic and political factors, SES and linguistic and cultural awareness (Lambert and Taylor 1996; Schwartz 2010). Parental education and SES are other factors to be taken into consideration: parents with higher levels of education and SES seem to have greater success in maintaining the minority language (Kloss 1966; Williams 1987; Lambert and Taylor 1996; King and Fogle 2006).

Parents and/or children may see advantages in bilingualism/multilingualism in terms of better opportunities for education and well-being in future, as well as the family's linguistic, cultural and cognitive development (Bialystok and Werker 2017). Children might refuse to speak the HL due to pressure from their peers, time and school curriculum restrictions, lack of schooling, inadequate input and/or low learning motivation. Their refusal or acceptance can change during the course of their lives, reflecting changes in the wider society. Children need encouragement and motivation from their parents and relatives (Protassova 2018). Without sustained effort from parents, children can become passive and unbalanced bilinguals.

Not every family is successful in terms of HL transmission due to their desire to integrate into the MajL society. Each family builds its own integration strategy with regard to the mainstream society, including acculturation towards the host culture: the longer their LoR, the more they want to adopt the host culture identity and to improve their social status (Ben-Rafael et al. 1997; Donitsa-Schmidt 1999; Pease-Alvarez 2003). Language practice and management (including parental language choices, preferences and decisions regarding intergenerational home communication, control of language use (Caldas and Caron-Caldas 2000, 2002; Schwartz 2010), linguistic repertoire, code-switching/-mixing and translanguaging) affect HL retention or rejection (Fishman 1991).

To summarise, in order to maintain the HL, a lot of parental effort is needed, as well as intellectual and emotional investment (Schwartz 2010), 'invisible' work and responsibility for FLP planning and management, coordinating, scheduling and organising (Pease-Alvarez 2003; Schwartz 2010).

The Nature of the HL

The HL cannot be learned without purposeful effort and practical input from minority/immigrant family members in the host country (Park 2013; Melo-Pfeifer 2015; Fairclough and Belpoliti 2016). The HL can also be described as 'community, ancestral, ethnic, immigrant, minority, home or non-official' (Fairclough and Belpoliti 2016: 186; Makarova et al. 2019) and is a weak language in comparison to the dominant language of the host country, in the particular national territory. In this study, the HL is important, since it is more relevant in a situation of simultaneous bilingualism in which the observed parents tried to raise their children.

HL maintenance also depends on language attitudes towards minority and majority languages (Pearson 2007; Santello 2015). Positive and proactive attitudes can create a 'supportive home environment' (Park 2013: 39) that can facilitate HL development, use at home and use in a wider social circle (Guardado 2002; Park and Sarkar 2007; Chumak-Horbatsch 2008).

These attitudes are formed by the wider society and can lead to assimilation or isolationist tendencies and language practices at home (Borland 2006; Canagarajah 2008; Curdt-Christiansen 2009). Without sufficient school or institutional support, only strong will and powerful effort by the parents, as well as an explicit and implicit FLP, can prevent minority language shift and loss (Pérez-Leroux et al. 2011; Schwartz and Moin 2012; Kulyk 2015; Melo-Pfeifer 2015; Makarova et al. 2019). Whether a child is willing to use the minority language or not can depend on his/her family, but also on the wider social network, peers, siblings, relatives, friends and teachers (Wardhaugh 2010; Ghimenton 2015). Socio-cultural contexts and parental attitudes should also be taken into consideration (Song 2016).

Antonova-Ünlü and Li Wei (2016) found that there is an emotional connection between a child and his/her mother's spoken language in mixed-marriage families. Very often, children can use only the MajL and insist on using it even if their parents address them in the minority language (Kopeliovich 2010). HL maintenance can have a positive effect on cognitive development, academic achievement and social well-being, while loss of the HL can have a negative impact on the social and psychological development (e.g. self-image and cultural identity) of a child (Kouritzin 1999; Cummins 2001; Park 2013).

Previous research on Russian-speaking parents and FLP showed that they have positive attitudes towards Russian-language development among their children (Friesner 2007; Nesteruk 2010; Altman et al. 2014) and towards Russian culture (Friesner 2007). It is estimated that the Russian-speaking diaspora outside Russia exceeds 30 million people, and the view of Russian as a commodity, a language that has high status and utility for communicative efficiency, career progress and well-being, can foster parents' efforts in HL use, maintenance and transmission, as the knowledge of the language can help children in their future life opportunities and competitiveness (Protassova 2018). This makes the FLP worth investigating across countries with different Russian migrant groups. While nowadays Russian is becoming more and more prestigious in Cyprus, Russian immigrants have never been a large minority, but they do represent a high prestige group in Sweden. In Estonia, Russian-language use is stigmatised because of Estonia's past as a Soviet Republic. These sociolinguistic similarities and differences have been discussed elsewhere (Karpava et al. 2018: 108–109; 2019: 624–626).

In Cyprus, there are around 11,000 Russian-speaking people permanently residing on the island: members of immigrant (both spouses Russian) and mixed-marriage families (Greek Cypriot husbands and Russian wives). Their dominant language constellation comprises Russian, Greek and English, to various degrees (Karpava 2020). In Sweden, there are 29,000 Russian-speaking people and their number is increasing. They are the members of immigrant and mixed-marriage families (mostly Swedish husbands and Russian wives). Russian people live all over the country and are not concentrated in specific districts/cities, even though the majority of them live in large cities like Stockholm, Malmö and Gothenburg. The community of Russians in Estonia is estimated at 320,000, which is 24% of the total population (1.3 million). The sizable Russian-speaking population of Estonia lives very compactly: only 20% are scattered in Estonian-speaking areas. Almost half of the Russian-speaking population lives in Tallinn and a third in Ida-Viru County. Russian-speaking people live in a bilingual society in which Estonian is the dominant and prestigious language: to get Estonian citizenship, among other requirements, one must pass an Estonian language proficiency examination and an examination of knowledge of the Constitution of the Republic of Estonia and the Citizenship Act. This influences parental decisions about educational trajectories, especially if one takes into account that the Estonian language proficiency examination is not required if a person has received basic, secondary or higher education in Estonian. Estonia's Russian speakers do not constitute a single unitary category with a uniform value system and attitudes but show different tendencies with regard to culture and language maintenance or assimilation.

Methodological Background

This study is a part of a larger ethnographic research project on the FLP among Russian-MajL-speaking families in Cyprus, Estonia and Sweden (Karpava et al. 2018, 2019). For this chapter, we have implemented the framework of a conversation-analytic ethnographic approach for data analysis and data interpretation. We were also inspired by Altman et al. (2014) and Dixon et al. (2012), who implemented interviews with both parents and children with the focus on language use and choice, children's self-rated proficiency and linguistic performance and revealed different types of FLP: strict pro-Russian, mild pro-Russian and pro-bilingual.

Both the questionnaire and the interviews consisted of demographic and specific questions dealing with country of origin, LoR in the host country, AoO, number and age/gender of children, FLP at home, and MajL and HL knowledge and use within and outside the family. Additionally, we conducted in-depth, semi-structured interviews with parents. Together with the field notes from family observations and other ethnographic tools, we made observations which provided us with insight into families' *authentic* environments and spontaneous linguistic practices in order to get information about the inner world of minority groups in Estonia and immigrants in Cyprus and Sweden regarding their FLP management, parental beliefs and attitudes, choices and efforts regarding HL use, maintenance and transmission, their success and challenges, ideologies and practices. We see our approach as complementary to the mixed-methods approach, where triangulation and a combination of quantitative and qualitative approaches, data collection and data analysis are adopted in order to avoid bias and the halo effect, increasing the validity and reliability of the study (Brannen 1992; Johnson 1992; Mackey and Gass 2005).

In this chapter, we decided to purposely select 20 families from each country in order to make the present study more rigorous methodologically and to look for similarities and differences in how parents preserve the HL by making their children active Russian-MajL bilinguals and how their efforts influence the children's bilingual upbringing. In Cyprus, we chose ten mixed-marriage families (Greek Cypriot husband and Russian-speaking wife) and ten immigrant families (both spouses are Russian). They came to Cyprus due to family, economic, business, political or educational reasons and have been in the host country from 6 to 15 years. Their ages ranged from 32 to 55. There were 1–3 children in the families, ranging from 4 to 15 years old. A good command of the Greek language was confirmed mainly by the representatives of the first group, whereas only 50% of the Russian immigrants knew the MajL. This could be explained by their use of the English language (nearly 70% of the participants), employment in the Russian or international business sphere and orientation to temporary residence in Cyprus.

In Sweden, 12 mixed-marriage families, 6 immigrant families and 2 single mothers with children were studied. In mixed-marriage families, the family was the main reason for immigration, while in the immigrant families, the reasons varied—from the political to the economic. The age of the participants ranged from 28 to 51. In the families, there were 1–3 children aged from 2 to 17. Most participants (but not all) had a good command of the Swedish language, had a job and identified with both cultures.

As for the Estonian data, the situation with families was rather complicated: it became quite a challenge to describe who were Russian speakers and Russian-Estonian bilingual speakers based on the families' linguistic and cultural backgrounds that we had collected. Individuals had their own means of self-identification and often felt that they were more 'Russian-speaking Estonians' than 'Estonian Russians'. Living in Estonia, these parents did not experience any language barriers when there was a need to be socially involved and politically informed. In the Estonian sample, the 20 families (in the age range of mainly 26–40 years) had children between the ages of 3 and 18 years who attended kindergartens and/or schools with Estonian as the language of instruction. Families maintain close (family, cultural and economic) ties with Russia, and this impacts on their ethnic, cultural and linguistic identities.

Thus, what all the Russian-speaking families had in common was that Russian was at least one of the HLs of the parents. The main criterion for our purposive sampling was that the chosen families had children who attended kindergartens, pre-schools and/or schools with the MajL as the language of instruction (this was especially crucial in Estonia, where Russian-medium schools are available up to the end of stage III (grade 9) of the basic level, age level 15 years). Based on questionnaires received from the parents, we were able to draw some conclusions about the linguistic repertoires of our families. We were also interested in parents' answers regarding the quality and quantity of Russian input that existed inside and outside the families in these countries, and in finding out whether there were any connections regarding the parents' attitudes and the use, maintenance and transmission of the HL (in our case immigrant and minority) contexts.

Results

This section focuses on the parental attitudes and beliefs regarding Russian as the HL transmission with which the study participants constructed linguistic ideologies, consistent with their views on language per se and creating their daily practices, and taking real-life actions and facing numerous challenges during their everyday lives. We choose to identify these crucial components for FLP and HL transmission and maintenance. Each subtopic has multiple rather than linear dimensions. We understand that the presentation of these characteristics might be difficult in the selections but we tried to remain heuristic and as objective as possible when narrowing the complexity of the variation among FLPs used by our informants in the three countries.

Determining the Reasons Behind the Ideologies Influencing Daily Practice

Generally speaking, parents seemed to have positive attitudes towards bilingual and trilingual upbringing, including literacy. This desire was often motivated by the belief that multilingualism was beneficial for the child. Russian was perceived as a commodity: there was a belief that Russian as a successfully acquired HL might be needed in the child's future career, as shown in Extract (1) from the Swedish data:

> (1) Children should know their native language . . . and it's clear that no one other [than the parents] will give them this. Plus, there is a natural understanding that knowledge of Russian is a huge advantage in their future careers. There are numerous multilingual advantages that have been scientifically proven. In particular, it is important for the early development of children and for their ability to perceive different points of view / world-views.

If Russian-speaking immigrants in Cyprus, especially in monolingual families with both spouses being immigrants from Russia or Russian-speaking countries, do not know Greek and/or are not willing to learn it and to integrate into the mainstream society, this can facilitate HL use, maintenance and transmission, as is demonstrated by Extract (2) and Extract (3).

> (2) I am not learning Greek as I am not going to stay in Cyprus.
> (3) There is no integration with Cypriot society and the reason lies in the lack of my language skills.

Here we see the major differences between Russian-speaking parents living in Cyprus, Estonia and Sweden. In Sweden, where the parents intend to stay for the rest of their lives (often because of their economic well-being), they wish to integrate into Swedish society and often study Swedish with the children. These parent/s might even *switch* to the MajL themselves, as shown in Extract (4):

(4) I have been living in Sweden far too long. [I do not speak Russian] because I do not live now, and I am not going to live in a Russian-speaking environment.

Our observations have shown that it is important to note the following when analysing language ideologies and everyday actions: the parents' level of education, success and failures in their current career and future life opportunities, their own MajL competence and the status of being majority or minority community members. This all directly affects the FLP and the success of the development of the HL by the children. Extract (4) expressed the kind of view that comes from highly educated parents who have enjoyed career success in Sweden.

This interactive position is echoed in a self-reflective idea expressed by an Estonian informant in Extract (5):

(5) In our everyday life we use Estonian more and more and he [their child] uses it in his studies. We have already become somewhat Estonianised and feel like we cannot define our family language or culture as either Russian or Estonian; we are in the middle.

Nevertheless, some Russian-speaking mothers living in Sweden say that they simply cannot speak any other languages to their children: this may be due either to a more general situation, as in Extract (6), or a more practical factor, as in Extract (7):

(6) I cannot talk with the child in other languages.
(7) My husband works for an international company and does not speak Swedish at all.

The distinction between LoR in a host country also arises when comparing Extract (2) and Extract (7), connected with Cyprus and Sweden, respectively. As for Estonia, future plans are notably influential with respect to HL transmission: it is usually highly supported when parents are going to send their children to the Russian Federation for higher education and is not considered to be a useful language if higher education in other languages is preferable. This also applies in cases of even young children as their parents try to plan far ahead.

In Estonia, we often encountered opinions such as that in Extract (8), where parents refer to former Soviet times when Estonian was not needed and not used often in society, but due to the sociolinguistic changes after the restoration of independence in 1991, the status of Estonian rose and it became a useful tool:

> (8) I believe that in our time the more languages a child knows the better. Therefore, Russian parents should try to teach the child Estonian. And, if possible, they should support language courses in a third language.

The ideological position 'The more languages a child knows, the better' was identified in all three countries. This might seem encouraging for the maintenance of Russian as the HL but, as we will see in the section "Real-Life Actions and the Role of Challenges", situational constraints may come into conflict with this intention. It should also be noted that, in Cyprus, some of the immigrants continue to be monolingual Russian speakers without putting in much effort to expand their linguistic repertoire as the sociolinguistic situation allows them to do this, which is not the case in Sweden, where the majority of families have a good command of Swedish. As for Estonia, all of the participating families have sufficient proficiency in Estonian because they are originally from Estonia, have graduated from the Estonian higher educational system, work in Estonian environments and communicate in Estonian both at work and in their daily social lives.

The status of a language, and especially its apparent instrumental value, is an important goal-oriented factor. For example, the widespread use of English in Cyprus can also prevent immigrants from learning Greek as they can easily operate in the society knowing only English because 'everyone [in the local population] speaks English' or supports its use in external communication, as is stated in Extract (9), where the interviewee continues her thought:

> (9) Everywhere they [local people] try to help you if you do not know Greek.

The situation is somewhat different in Sweden, where Swedish language use is required to be fully accepted in out-group communication. The same tendencies are also noticed in Estonia, where language issues cause linguistic tensions and lead to interethnic discord. Our overall impression is that what actually happens with language use inside the family and parents' language ideologies in particular largely determines the degree to which heritage culture is transmitted. That said, there are a number of reasons why such a position towards Russian as HL transmission is chosen. The main reason though, in all three countries, is connected with MajL spouses' understandings of what language is really *needed* or what is *right* in language learning processes. The approach is often monolingually biased. This in turn leads to their position against the use of Russian by Russian-speaking partners and the banning of Russian indoor (private) and outdoor (public) communication.

The attitude towards HL transmission in the case of Russian that can be extended to both the Swedish and Estonian contexts is the parents' ideology of 'linguistic purism' and the promotion of the idea of speaking a 'pure language', which is exemplified in Extract (10) and Extract (11):

> (10) Speaking with errors and an accent is awful.
> (11) She [a daughter] has to speak in Russian fluently (pauses) and appropriately.

Such linguistic purism makes Russian-speaking parents and their MajL spouses from Sweden and Estonia favour a one parent-one language (OPOL) approach at home. In practice, the OPOL approach is far from straightforward and might lead to translanguaging (see Karpava et al. 2019). In Cyprus, mixed families seem to be more flexible and allow code-switching or translanguaging, as they have fewer linguistic concerns, as seen in Extracts (12) and (13):

> (12) I need to admit that we code-switch or code-mix a lot, this is the reality. I say something to my husband in Greek, but then I will use Russian with my kids, even though they know Greek … my husband does not know Russian, so we need to translate for him into Greek.

> (13) There is a mixture ... Greek, Russian, sometimes English ... sometimes I even cannot control which language I speak, especially when I am tired or anxious ... or in a hurry. I don't know whether it is right or wrong, but this is what we have in our family.

Here, we should acknowledge that general language policy and public promotion of one single official language in a country facilitate its replication on the family level when parents report trends, patterns and tendencies that are often in complete alignment with the official ideologies . What makes Sweden and Estonia similar is the replacement of Russian holidays with majority (Swedish or Estonian) ones in some families (especially after having spent several years in the country—as far as Sweden is concerned) which is demonstrated in Extract (14) and Extract (15):

> (14) You know, I do not celebrate the Russian Easter. Last week we celebrated the Swedish holiday and that was enough for us.
> (15) We live in Estonia and the Estonian culture and traditions are closer to us. In our family, we celebrate only Estonian holidays. We do not celebrate Christmas on 7 January but only on 24 December.

Clearly, parents' attitudes depend very much on the perceived need to follow the mainstream society or to be in line with a MajL parent's cultural preferences.

There is also evidence from the three data groups that communication patterns outside the home and especially in professional contexts have important effects on Russian-speaking parents' decisions and attitudes towards transmission of Russian as the HL. If in their working MajL environment Russian-speaking parents are not allowed to use Russian openly and might be encouraged to use only the MajL, then this downgrade of Russian in a professional context leads to the situation where Russian speakers find themselves using Russian only with their friends, relatives and children at home. This latter scenario becomes possible, if their MajL spouses have positive attitudes towards bilingualism and code-switching as a family shared linguistic repertoire. Obviously, this social treatment of Russian can have detrimental effects on the development of HL fluency and literacy among the children.

Real-Life Actions and the Role of Challenges

For parents, it is important to provide various opportunities for actual and purposeful use of Russian with and by the children. One phenomenon that was identified is that families with high SES and higher educational backgrounds understood the necessity of simultaneous bilingualism (or functional multilingualism). Thus, they tried to develop Russian literacy, reading and writing skills among their children. They eagerly bought Russian-language books and magazines, watched Russian TV channels, listened to Russian radio and sent their children to Russian heritage (Saturday/Sunday) schools, especially in Cyprus, in its urban areas in particular, where both public and private teaching centres offer Russian lessons. In the Swedish school system, there is the legal right for mother tongue (Russian in our case) instruction for the children who speak other languages, which includes the teaching of a language as a subject in the school curriculum. In Sweden and Estonia, some parents also choose extra-curricular activities for their children in Russian. In Estonia, there exist Russian-language Sunday/evening schools and private courses for Russian-speaking children studying in Estonian.

The parents emphasised the importance of cultural links with Russia and Russian-speaking countries. Extracts (16), (17) and (18) deal with the attitudes within such families in Cyprus, Estonia and Sweden, respectively:

> (16) We do not have a lot of Russian books at home, and those are mainly textbooks; we bring them from St. Petersburg in summer. Our Russian language teacher tells us beforehand which textbooks we will need. It is also possible to buy them here in Cyprus in a shop, but you need to order them.
> (17) I would say that the dearest to our hearts are the Russian TV channels.
> (18) I always bring books back from Russia with me. When we are there, the first thing we do is go to a bookstore.

A common pattern in everyday actions regarding HL preservation in Cyprus and Sweden was Russian-speaking parents' solidarity and bonding with other immigrants from Russia or Russian-speaking countries: for example, they help each other get Russian books and educational materials for their children and exchange them via close-knit social networks. In Estonia, there is no need for such group actions because of the close proximity to Russia, and there are lots of bookstores where it is possible to get all kinds of Russian-language books fairly cheaply.

For HL teaching, extra-curricular activities are important throughout childhood, but especially in the early years of natural language development in order to create a habit of speaking Russian in all situations. The lack of communication opportunities in the HL might result in a child's poor ability to use the HL for different communicative needs. But even if both parents share the basic assumption that the HL must be transmitted, this might vary within the lifespan of children, and the process of Russian use becomes influenced by several fundamental factors.

Our data demonstrate that in Cyprus as children get older, they do not have enough time for extra-curricular Russian classes as they attend Greek-speaking or English-speaking schools, they need to cover a lot of material and cannot handle the extra cognitive load. This is seen in Extract (19):

> (19) Unfortunately, we do not attend a Russian school any more; we have learned how to read and write, but now we do not have enough time as my son is in lyceum and he needs to prepare for his Greek exams.

From the Swedish data, we learned that although Sweden provides students with a legal right to mother tongue instruction, additional efforts must be made by Russian-speaking parents, especially since help for Swedish-Russian bilingual families is mostly available only in the larger cities. Thus, families in remote and small communities do not have access to Russian-language support services and have to rely on their own resources, according to some of the parents in our study.

Still, the availability of extra-curricular activities in Russian does not immediately lead to long-term plan implementation. Real-life actions are influenced by parents' ideologies or linguistic factors. Rationalisation and extra-linguistic aspects are more important when arranging child's learning activities outside the classroom, as we see in Extract (20), from the Estonian data:

> (20) We began with a Russian-language music club but then our teacher left and an Estonian speaker started to teach the piano to our daughter. They switched to Estonian naturally… No, we did not want to change that hobby group because it is near our home and she does not have to go far.

It is also important to be aware of the role of multilingualism in families. Russian-speaking spouses in mixed-marriage families in Sweden and Cyprus have to learn and know the MajL in order to communicate with their partners and children; in Estonia, all of the Russian speakers have at least some knowledge of Estonian because they were born in Estonia. Our research has shown that as children receive Russian and MajL input from both parents, this leads to code-switching and translanguaging (Karpava et al. 2019). In such families, parents, especially Russian-speaking mothers in Cyprus and Sweden, should put more effort into supporting Russian as the HL. Good examples are provided by Extract (21) and Extract (22), respectively:

> (21) Before I spoke very little with her, as I spent very little time at home; now I have changed jobs and I am at home in the afternoon. Besides, we have sent her [their daughter] to a Russian kindergarten and her progress is obvious, as she has a very good teacher.
> (22) No, by itself, of course, nothing will work out. There is a need for focused efforts. I have to speak and speak, and just ignore her [the child] if she answers me in Swedish.

This has obvious limitations because for the communication process, time is needed and if mothers have full-time jobs, then the frequency of Russian usage cannot be guaranteed over time. Sometimes grandparents or relatives can take a leading role in literacy development and HL maintenance and transmission; see Extract (23) exemplifying a Russian speaker's experiences living in Cyprus:

(23) I teach my younger child; she likes to circle letters and she learns how to read syllable by syllable. It is difficult and there is not enough time, but her grandmother helps when she visits us.

As we see from the above example, a Russian-speaking mother is describing what her child *likes* and *does*, not forgetting to mention *difficulties* and how these are overcome in their family with the help of a grandmother. But often parents' actions as home teachers and their desire to transmit the HL are constrained by idealised thinking, e.g. 'A child *must* know the mother tongue of the parents'. This strategy is claimed by Russian-speaking parents in Sweden and Estonia, where the prescriptive 'must learn' approach seems to be adopted through the lens of official language policy, in which linguistic purism and clear single official language institutional support are combined: if officials impose a one-nation–one-language ideology from above, then families construct their own paradigms from below, where an HL starts receiving non-official internal support and value. These issues in HL transmission could serve as an important focus for future participant observation ethnographic studies.

Conclusion

Within the field of FLP research, the transmission of Russian as a subject of particular interest provides a rich source of empirical evidence that highlights minority parents' attitudes towards the HL, their efforts and choices. The wish of Russian-speaking parents to transmit Russian as the HL is mostly motivated by their desire to transmit their mother tongue to their children and thus keep it active within the family. Many parents mention that it is their natural (i.e. emotional) choice and some also mention the practical value of knowing Russian (and benefiting from simultaneous bilingualism).

The key components that affect HL literacy development include links with relatives in Russia and trips (home) to Russian-speaking countries, or HL social habits, such as joint TV watching, listening to music and using internet resources, as well as intentional communication with siblings and/or peers; this also involves extra-curricular activities. Similar in their intentions are Russian-speaking parents living in Cyprus and Sweden, who understand the importance of Russian literacy development, but might not have enough time to teach their children.

A number of factors can intervene between intended and actual FLP that determine families' daily choices. The most important one is a transition in parents' linguistic and cultural behaviour in response to their new identity, especially in Estonia and Sweden. In general, these parents tend to be more concerned with their children's mastery of the dominant MajL, and thus they are not consistent in using only Russian with their children at home and especially outside it. We need to bring the issue of social integration and inclusion into the discussion of HL transmission and use, which has to do in part with the perceived cultural value of Russian. In the case of Estonia, sometimes particularly negative and even downright hostile attitudes towards Russian (on the part of MajL speakers) are noted. This forms a distinguishing factor in differences between the three countries: while the situation in Cyprus is different, as the Greek Cypriots are generally very positive towards Russian, Sweden falls somewhere in between.

Another topic discussed was the input that a child received in the HL and which was not sufficient to develop a high command of Russian. It should be taken into consideration that many of the Russian-speaking mothers in Cyprus are housewives who have part-time jobs, while Russian-speaking mothers in Sweden tend to work full-time and send their children to Swedish-medium pre-schools. This affects the results of HL transmission since the children in Cyprus receive greater Russian input than their counterparts in Sweden, due to having more conversational time with their mothers.

To conclude, even though in order to transmit Russian to their children parents act as Russian-language teachers, buy Russian books and organise Russian-language extra-curricular activities, this might not be sufficient without the conscious and consistent use of the HL by the Russian-speaking parents: speaking spontaneous Russian in everyday situations at home as well as in public spaces.

Acknowledgements This paper was supported by basic funding for research areas of national significance at the Institute of Estonian and General Linguistics of the University of Tartu. The theoretical results are part of the project IUT20-3 'Sustainability of Estonian in the era of globalisation' (EKKAM). Natalia Ringblom would like to acknowledge the support of the Åke Wiberg Foundation in conducting this research. Data collection and analysis in Cyprus were supported by the internal start-up funding programme of the University of Cyprus: *Heritage Language Maintenance, Variation and Change* (2020–2022).

References

Albirini, A. 2014. Toward Understanding the Variability in the Language Proficiencies of Arabic Heritage Speakers. *International Journal of Bilingualism* 18: 730–765.

Allard, R., and R. Landry. 1992. Ethnolinguistic Vitality Beliefs and Language Maintenance and Loss. In *Maintenance and Loss of Minority Languages*, ed. W. Fase, K. Jaspaert, and S. Kronn, 173–195. Amsterdam: John Benjamins.

Altman, C., Z. Feldman-Burstein, D. Yitzhaki, S. Armon-Lotem, and J. Walters. 2014. Family Language Policies, Reported Language Use and Proficiency in Russian-Hebrew Bilingual Children in Israel. *Journal of Multilingual and Multicultural Development* 35: 216–234.

Antonova-Ünlü, E., and W. Li. 2016. Aspect Acquisition in Russian as the Weaker Language: Evidence from a Turkish-Russian Child. *International Journal of Bilingualism* 20: 210–228.

Barkhuizen, G. 2006. Immigrant Parents' Perceptions of Their Children's Language Practices: Afrikaans Speakers Living in New Zealand. *Language Awareness* 15: 63–77.

Bialystok, E., and J.F. Werker. 2017. The Systematic Effects of Bilingualism on Children's Development. *Developmental Science* 20: 125–135.

Borland, H. 2006. Intergenerational Language Transmission in an Established Australian Migrant Community: What Makes the Difference? *International Journal of the Sociology of Language* 180: 23–41.

Caldas, S., and S. Caron-Caldas. 2000. The Influence of Family, School, and Community on Bilingual Preference: Results from a Louisiana/Québec Case Study. *Applied Psycholinguistics* 21(3): 365–381.
Caldas, S., and S. Caron-Caldas. 2002. A Sociolinguistic Analysis of the Language Preferences of Adolescent Bilinguals: Shifting Allegiances and Developing Identities. *Applied Linguistics* 23: 490–514.
Canagarajah, A.S. 2008. Language Shift and the Family: Questions from the Sri Lankan Tamil Diaspora. *Journal of Sociolinguistics* 12: 143–176.
Chumak-Horbatsch, R. 2008. Early Bilingualism: Children of Immigrants in an English-Language Childcare Center. *Psychology of Language and Communication* 12: 3–28.
Cummins, J. 2001. Heritage Language Teaching in Canadian Schools. In *An Introductory Reader to the Writings of Jim Cummins*, ed. C. Baker and N. Hornberger, 252–257. Clevedon: Multilingual Matters.
Curdt-Christiansen, X.L. 2009. Invisible and Visible Language Planning: Ideological Factors in the Family Language Policy of Chinese Immigrant Families in Quebec. *Language Policy* 8: 351–375.
De Houwer, A. 1999. Environmental Factors in Early Bilingual Development: The Role of Parental Beliefs and Attitudes. In *Bilingualism and Migration*, ed. G. Extra and L. Verhoeven, 75–96. Berlin and New York: Mouton de Gruyter.
De Houwer, A. 2009. *Bilingual First Language Acquisition*. Bristol: Multilingual Matters.
Dixon, Q., S. Wu, and A. Daraghmeh. 2012. Profiles in Bilingualism: Factors Influencing Kindergartners' Language Proficiency. *Early Childhood Education Journal* 40: 25–34.
Fairclough, M., and F. Belpoliti. 2016. Emerging Literacy in Spanish Among Hispanic Heritage University studEnts in the USA: A Pilot Study. *International Journal of Bilingual Education and Bilingualism* 19: 185–201.
Fishman, J.A. 1991. *Reversing Language Shift: Theoretical and Empirical Foundations of Assistance to Threatened Languages*. Clevedon: Multilingual Matters.
Ghimenton, A. 2015. Reading Between the Code Choices: Discrepancies Between Expressions of Language Attitudes and Usage in a Contact Situation. *International Journal of Bilingualism* 19: 115–136.
Gregory, E. 2004. 'Invisible' Teachers of Literacy: Collusion Between Siblings and Teachers in Creating Classroom Cultures. *Literacy* 38: 97–105.
Grin, F. 2003. *Language Policy Evaluation and the European Charter for Regional or Minority Languages*. London: Palgrave Macmillan.

Guardado, M. 2002. Loss and Maintenance of First Language Skills: Case Studies of Hispanic Families in Vancouver. *The Canadian Modern Language Review* 58: 341–363.

Harris, J.R. 1995. Where Is the Child's Environment? A Group Socialization Theory of Development. *Psychological Review* 103: 458–489.

Johnson, R.C. 1992. Offspring of Cross-Race and Cross-Ethnic Marriages in Hawaii. In *Racially Mixed People in America*, ed. M.R. Root, 239–249. Thousand Oaks, CA: Sage.

Karpava, S., N. Ringblom, and A. Zabrodskaja. 2018. Language Ecology in Cyprus, Sweden and Estonia: Bilingual Russian-Speaking Families in Multicultural Settings. *Journal of the European Second Language Association* 2 (1): 107–117.

Karpava, S., N. Ringblom, and A. Zabrodskaja. 2019. Translanguaging in the Family Context: Evidence from Cyprus, Sweden and Estonia. *Russian Journal of Linguistics* 23 (3): 619–641.

King, K.A. 2000. Language Ideologies and Heritage Language Education. *International Journal of Bilingual Education and Bilingualism* 3: 167–184.

King, K., and L. Fogle. 2006. Bilingual Parenting as Good Parenting: Parents' Perspectives on Family Language Policy for Additive Bilingualism. *International Journal of Bilingual Education and Bilingualism* 9: 695–712.

King, K.A., L. Fogle, and A. Logan-Terry. 2008. Family Language Policy. *Language and Linguistics Compass* 2: 907–922.

Kloss, H. 1966. German-American Language Maintenance Efforts. In *Language Loyalty in the United States: The Maintenance and Perpetuation of Non-English Mother Tongues by American Ethnic and Religious Groups*, ed. J.A. Fishman, 206–252. The Hague: Mouton.

Kopeliovich, S. 2010. Family Language Policy: A Case Study of Russian-Hebrew Bilingual Family: Toward a Theoretical Framework. *Diaspora, Indigenous, and Minority Education* 4: 162–178.

Kouritzin, S.G. 1999. *Facets of First Language Loss*. Mahwah, NJ: Lawrence Erlbaum.

Kulyk, V. 2015. The Age Factor in Language Practices and Attitudes: Continuity and Change in Ukraine's Bilingualism. *Nationalities Papers* 43: 283–301.

Kyratzis, A. 2004. Talk and Interaction Among Children and the Co-construction of Peer Groups and Peer Culture. *Annual Review of Anthropology* 33: 625–649.

La Piedra, M., and H. Romo. 2003. Collaborative Literacy in a Mexican Immigrant Household: The Role of Sibling Mediators in the Socialization of

Pre-school Learners. In *Language Socialization in Bilingual and Multilingual Societies*, ed. R. Bayley and S. Schecter, 44–61. Clevedon: Multilingual Matters.

Lambert, W.E., and D.M. Taylor. 1996. Language in the Lives of Ethnic Minorities: Cuban American Families in Miami. *Applied Linguistics* 17: 477–500.

Mackey, A., and S.M. Gass. 2005. *Second Language Research: Methodology and Design*. Mahwah, NJ: Lawrence Erlbaum Associates.

Makarova, V., N. Terekhova, and A. Mousavi. 2019. Children's Language Exposure and Parental Language Attitudes in Russian-as-a-Heritage-Language Acquisition by Bilingual and Multilingual Children in Canada. *International Journal of Bilingualism* 23: 457–485.

Melo-Pfeifer, S. 2015. The Role of the Family in Heritage Language Use and Learning: Impact on Heritage Language Policies. *International Journal of Bilingual Education and Bilingualism* 18: 26–44.

Nesteruk, O. 2010. Heritage Language Maintenance and Loss Among the Children of Eastern European Immigrants in the USA. *Journal of Multilingual and Multicultural Development* 30: 271–286.

Okita, T. 2002. *Invisible Work: Bilingualism, Language Choice and Childrearing in Intermarried Families*. Amsterdam: John Benjamins.

Paradis, M. 2004. *A Neurolinguistic Theory of Bilingualism*. Amsterdam: John Benjamins.

Park, S.M., and M. Sarkar. 2007. Parents' Attitudes Towards Heritage Language Maintenance for Their Children and Their Efforts to Help Their Children Maintain the Heritage Language: A Case Study of Korean-Canadian Immigrants. *Language, Culture and Curriculum* 20: 223–235.

Pearson, B.Z. 2007. Social Factors in Childhood Bilingualism in the United States. *Applied Psycholinguistics* 28: 399–410.

Pease-Alvarez, L. 2003. Transforming Perspectives on Bilingual Language Socialization. In *Language Socialization in Bilingual and Multilingual Societies*, ed. R. Bayley and S. Schecter, 9–24. Clevedon: Multilingual Matters.

Pérez-Leroux, A.T., A. Cuza, and D. Thomas. 2011. From Parental Attitudes to Input Conditions: Spanish-English Bilingual Development in Toronto. In *Bilingual Youth: Spanish in English-Speaking Societie*, ed. K. Potowski and J. Rothman, 149–176. Amsterdam: John Benjamins.

Protassova, E. 2018. Multilingual Education and Family Language Policy. *International Journal of Multilingual Education* 11: 102–111.

Santello, M. 2015. Bilingual Idiosyncratic Dimensions of Language Attitudes. *International Journal of Bilingual Education and Bilingualism* 18: 1–25.

Schmid, M. 2002. *First Language Attrition, Use and Maintenance: The Case of German Jews in Anglophone Countries*. Amsterdam: John Benjamins.
Schmid, M. 2007. The Role of L1 Use for L1 Attrition. In *Language Attrition: Theoretical Perspectives*, ed. B. Köpke, M. Schmid, M. Keijzer, and S. Dostert, 135–154. Amsterdam: John Benjamins.
Schwartz, M. 2008. Exploring the Relationship Between Family Language Policy and Heritage Language Knowledge Among Second Generation Russian-Jewish Immigrants in Israel. *Journal of Multilingual and Multicultural Development* 29: 400–418.
Schwartz, M. 2010. Family Language Policy: Core Issues of an Emerging Field. *Applied Linguistics Review* 1: 171–192.
Schwartz, M., and V. Moin. 2012. Parents' Assessment of Their Preschool Children's Bilingual Development in the Context of Language Policy. *Journal of Multilingual and Multicultural Development* 33: 35–55.
Schwarz, M., and A. Verschik. 2013. Achieving Success in Family Language Policy: Parents, Children and Educators in Interaction. In *Successful Family Language Policy: Parents, Children and Educators in Interaction*, ed. M. Schwartz and A. Verschik, 1–20. Dordrecht: Springer.
Song, K. 2016. Okay, I Will Say in Korean and Then in American': Translanguaging Practices in Bilingual Homes. *Journal of Early Childhood Literacy* 16: 84–106.
Spolsky, B. 2004. *Language Policy*. Cambridge: Cambridge University Press.
Spolsky, B. 2007. Family Language Management: Some Preliminaries. In *Studies in Language and Language Education: Essays in Honour of Elite Olshtain*, ed. A. Stavans and I. Kupferberg, 429–449. Jerusalem: The Hebrew University Magnes Press.
Spolsky, B. 2012. Family Language Policy—The Critical Domain. *Journal of Multilingual and Multicultural Development* 33: 3–11.
Spolsky, B., and E. Shohamy. 1999. *The Languages of Israel: Policy, Ideology and Practice*. Clevedon: Multilingual Matters.
Tannenbaum, M. 2003. The Multifaceted Aspects of Language Maintenance: A New Measure for Its Assessment in Immigrant Families. *International Journal of Bilingual Education and Bilingualism* 6: 374–388.
Tannenbaum, M. 2005. Viewing Family Relations Through a Linguistic Lens: Symbolic Aspects of Language Maintenance in Immigrant Families. *Journal of Family Communication* 5: 229–252.
Wardhaugh, R. 2010. *Introduction to Sociolinguistics*. Oxford: Wiley-Blackwell.
Williams, G. 1987. Bilingualism, Class Dialect and Social Reproduction. *International Journal of the Sociology of Language* 66: 85–98.

Wong Fillmore, L. 1991. When Learning a Second Language Means Losing the First. *Early Childhood Research Quarterly* 6: 323–346.

Wong Fillmore, L. 2000. Loss of Family Languages: Should Educators Be Concerned? *Theory into Practice* 39: 203–210.

Zhu, H., and W. Li. 2005. Bi- and Multi-lingual Acquisition. In *Clinical Sociolinguistics*, ed. M. Ball, 165–179. Oxford: Blackwell.

Zhu, H., and W. Li. 2016. Transnational Experience, Aspiration and Family Language Policy. *Journal of Multilingual and Multicultural Development* 37: 655–666.

Ben-Rafael, E., E. Olshtain, and I. Geijst. 1997. Identity and Language: The Social Insertion of Soviet Jews in Israel. In *Russian Jews on Three Continents: Migration and Resettlement*, ed. N. Levin-Epstein, Y. Ro'i, and P. Ritterband, 364–388. London: Routledge.

Brannen, Julia, ed. 1992. *Mixing Methods: Qualitative and Quantitative Research*. Aldershot: Avebury.

Donitsa-Schmidt, S. 1999. Language Maintenance or Shift—Determinants of Language Choice Among Soviet Immigrants in Israel. Unpublished doctoral thesis, University of Toronto.

Friesner, M. 2007. Language Policy and Multiple Transnational Identity: The Case of Russian Immigrants in Montreal. *Working Papers in Educational Linguistics* 22: 25–44.

Karpava, S. 2020. Dominant Language Constellations of Russian Speakers in Cyprus. In *Dominant Language Constellations, Educational Linguistics*, ed. J. Lo Bianco and L. Aronin, 187–209. Cham: Springer Nature.

Lo Bianco, J. and J.K. Peyton. 2013. Vitality of Heritage Languages in the United States. *Heritage Language Journal* 10: i–viii.

Park, S. M. 2013. Immigrant Students' Heritage Language and Cultural Identity Maintenance in Multilingual and Multicultural Societies. *Concordia Working Papers in Applied Linguistics* 4: 30–53.

Smith-Christmas, C. 2015. *Family Language Policy: Maintaining an Endangered Language in the Home*. Basingstoke: Palgrave.

Effective Family Language Policies and Intergenerational Transmission of Minority Languages: Parental Language Governance in Indigenous and Diasporic Contexts

Anik Nandi, Ibon Manterola, Facundo Reyna-Muniain, and Paula Kasares

Introduction

Under the effects of globalisation, the pressure of dominant languages on minority languages is relentless, partly because many users of smaller languages can see more opportunities if they shift to a dominant one.

A. Nandi (✉)
Faculty of Humanities, Liberal Arts & Social Sciences, Alliance University, Bengaluru, India
e-mail: a.nandi@hum.leidenuniv.nl

I. Manterola
Universidad del País Vasco/Euskal Herriko Unibertsitatea (UPV/EHU), Vitoria-Gasteiz, Spain
e-mail: ibon.manterola@ehu.eus

F. Reyna-Muniain
Christian Albrechts Univesität zu Kiel, Leibnizstraße, Germany
e-mail: reynaf@romanistik.uni-kiel.de

M. Hornsby and W. McLeod (eds.), *Transmitting Minority Languages*, Palgrave Studies in Minority Languages and Communities,
https://doi.org/10.1007/978-3-030-87910-5_12

Despite these pressures, however, minority language speakers, whether in indigenous or diasporic contexts, maintain or reclaim to varying degrees their languages as active agents through everyday interactions and through the transmission of the language within the home (Li 2018). Using the lens of language policy, broadly understood as any conscious decision or choice made about language(s) by social actors such as the state, community or individual,[1] this chapter will present a systematic account of the family dynamics of intergenerational transmission of minority languages in three Spanish-dominated bi/multilingual settings: Galicia and Navarre (Spain) and Buenos Aires (Argentina). Case examples from Galicia and Navarre will centre on indigenous minority language-speaking parents (of Galician and Basque in their respective regions). Going beyond the territorial boundaries of Spain or Europe, in Buenos Aires, we will investigate the language practices of third-generation migrant parents of Galician origin who use their heritage language to construct their individual, local and also transnational identities. The focus will be on new speaker parents who have made a conscious decision to bring up their children in either Galician or Basque, languages which they themselves did not acquire at home. We use the term 'new speakers' to refer to individuals who did not learn a minority language through family transmission at home or through exposure to its use within the local community, but instead acquired it through the education system or as adult learner (in the case of the Basque and Galician speakers studied).

The contemporary rise of the 'new speaker' profiles in our contexts of research and other European minority language situations (e.g. Catalan, Breton, Welsh and Gaelic) has in various ways come to epitomise what O'Rourke et al. (2015: 1) underscored as the 'challenging opportunity'. Studies conducted on new speaker profiles in diverse European minority language revitalisation settings for nearly a decade demonstrate that new

P. Kasares
Departamento de Ciencias Humanas y de la Educación, Universidad Pública de Navarra (UPNA), Pamplona, Spain
e-mail: paula.kasares@unavarra.es

speakers are capable of increasing the demographic strength and social status of these languages.[2] Although family transmission has for long been considered a crucial domain of linguistic vitality, new speakers bring complexity to this paradigm. In particular, new speakers prompt questions about their role as parents and as potential agents of sociolinguistic change in language revitalisation processes (O'Rourke and Nandi 2019). Drawing from in-depth fieldwork interviews, this chapter concentrates on the interaction between macro-level language policy and parental agency in relation to Galician and Basque-speaking new speaker parents who live in urban settings. We investigate how individuals as well as collective linguistic practices of these parents act as language 'governmentality' measures (Foucault 1991), influencing their children's acquisition and learning of minority languages. The endeavour is also to reveal the key challenges they encounter whilst implementing these policies.

The target research samples of this study are parents from urban/semi-urban backgrounds aged between 30 and 55, from various occupations representing to a large extent the educated middle class in their respective societies. Notably, in the bilingual settings of Galicia and Navarre, the upper age range of the sample ensures the inclusion of parents who experienced the education system's transition from Franco's regime to the current system of autonomous communities. It is also worth mentioning here that this chapter has derived from a larger body of three doctoral studies. The data in Galicia were drawn from in-depth semi-structured interviews and two focus group discussions conducted between 2013 and 2015 with eighteen families from five urban/semi-urban areas of Galicia (Nandi 2017b). Data from Navarre were collected between 2011 and 2012 through ethnographic observation in school contexts, in-depth interviews with schoolteachers and linguistic biographies based on ten interviews with parents (Kasares 2014). In Buenos Aires, the data were taken from a corpus of sixty semi-structured interviews and 400 questionnaires carried out between 2013 and 2018 with third-generation Galician migrants (Reyna-Muniain 2021). This chapter uses interview data from two families from each context. All the families who participated in the contexts of our research were made up of at least one new speaker parent. Amongst the four parents interviewed in Galicia, three are new speakers and one father is a traditional speaker. Whereas three participants are new speakers in Navarra, one mother is predominantly a Castilian speaker with a limited competence in Basque (i.e. she understands the language but cannot speak it). Finally, in the context of Buenos Aires, the two parents interviewed are new speakers of Galician whose respective partners speak Argentine Spanish.

This chapter commences with a discussion on the role of parental agency in developing bottom-up family language policies from a critical perspective. This is followed by a brief outline of the sociolinguistic situation of each context, including its formal language policies and their immediate impact on the urban milieu. Finally, it culminates with a thematic analysis of the collected data.

Parents as Policymakers: Researching Family Language Policy from a Critical Perspective

The state plays a pivotal role in top-down language governance by formulating policies and then implementing them in the public domain through different *ideological state apparatuses* (Althusser 1971), such as the school, religious institutions and mass media. Even though these apparatuses are not necessarily under the state's control, policymakers often use them to introduce top-down ideologies. Family, which is considered a micro social unit, is not beyond larger social structure. Therefore, when there is a perennial transference of majoritarian influences, state policy and media messages from the public sphere into the home space, the school and home spaces can become intertwined. Although each family has its own norms for language use, adult family members who act as policy stakeholders at home are not completely detached from top-down ideologies (Nandi and Devasundaram 2017). Even though research on multilingual families is now a well established domain of enquiry, Family Language Policy (henceforth FLP) really emerged as an independent field only in the last decade. It quickly became an important domain in minority language research, taking into account the 'overt decisions parents make about language use and language learning as well as implicit processes that legitimise certain language practices over others at home' (Fogle 2013: 83).

Language policies, whether governmental, in the community or inside the family, include three interrelated, albeit independent, factors (Spolsky 2004): language ideologies (what people believe about language), management or planning (endeavours people make for language maintenance) and practices (what they really do). Language ideologies include beliefs, attitudes and norms that determine the value of a language and how it should be used in everyday contexts. They play a pivotal role in any act of prioritisation concerning the use or non-use of certain language(s) or linguistic vernacular(s) at home. In the family context, parents as primary caregivers often transmit their ideologies through their language practices (i.e. language selection in interaction) and hence socialise their children into this ideology (Curdt-Christiansen and Lanza 2018). Such practices amongst adult family members determine to a large extent the expected linguistic behaviours that establish the de facto language use in various domains and for different purposes. De facto everyday language use inside the home domain is essentially different from language ideologies and beliefs since it demonstrates what caregivers really do, instead of what they believe should be done to maintain a language.

Language 'management' or planning decisions, on the other hand, can be understood as conscious and overt actions made by actors who maintain or intend to exert control over the subjects in a specific context to modify their language behaviour (Spolsky 2009: 1–4). Since parents are often the *in-situ* language planners at home, language management inside the family includes the choices and efforts that parents make to preserve a language. However, the distinction between language management and practices inside the home, as Curdt-Christiansen (2014: 38) notes, is difficult to make since parents often control and/or intervene in their children's discourse behaviour in everyday interaction. Such monitoring techniques evoke discourses of language 'governmentality' and 'biopower' (see Foucault 2007; cf. Nandi 2017b). Language governmentality is an extension of Foucault's (1978) notion of 'governmentality'. Since the early 1990s, Foucauldian notions have been widely used by critical language policy researchers to assess policy implementation at different levels and the role of human agents within it (see Tollefson 1991; Johnson 2013).

Governmentality, in its primary sense, can be understood as the art of governance (Foucault 2007). In the Foucauldian use of the term, it is an 'analytical toolbox' (Rose et al. 2006: 18) that evaluates the societal power dynamics in terms of 'the conduct of conducts' (ibid.), referring to a form of activity intending to shape, direct, influence or in some cases, regulate the conduct of a person or a population. Although Foucault does not offer a concrete, categorical definition of governmentality, he explains 'governmentality' as:

> The ensemble formed by institutions, procedures, analyses and reflections, calculations, and tactics that allow the exercise of this very specific, albeit complex, power that has the population as its target, political economy as its major form of knowledge, and apparatuses of security as its essential technical instrument. (1991: 102)

As such, it can be understood as a complex form of power, which is by no means restricted to the compasses of the state or within its policies. Instead, it is ubiquitous whenever people or particular groups intend to 'shape their own conduct or the conduct of others (e.g. within families, workplaces, schools etc.)' (Walters 2012: 11). Foucault interprets power with reference to 'strategies' that are produced through the nexus of the power relations, in part through a diverse range of discursive practices originating from different institutions, social relationships and forms of interaction which decide certain ways of speaking, being and acting 'normal'. In this vein, language governmentality can be described as how decisions regarding language(s) are made across a diverse range of establishments, including the family, the education system and mass media, through a diverse range of mechanisms, such as books, regulations and interventions to normalise certain language practices, ideological belief systems and actions of individuals. As such, parental language management decisions and practices can also be analysed as one form of language governmentality.

Parents being the hegemons in the FLP environment also relate to the discourses of 'biopolitics' or 'biopower'. In a Foucauldian sense, governmentality absorbs biopower. He defines it as 'the set of mechanisms through which the basic biological features of the human species became the object of a political strategy, of a general strategy of power' (Foucault 2007: 1). As such, biopolitics can be explained as a technology of power that fosters on the basis of disciplinary power. Whereas discipline is about governing individual bodies, biopolitics is about controlling entire populations. Inside the family domain, biopower is often reproduced through parental agency and various control mechanisms used by them as progenitors. Thus, parents, as principal caregivers, often adopt the role of custodians over their children's everyday language conduct, 'perceiving this "ownership" as a putative parental right' (Nandi 2018: 208; cf. Blommaert 2019). The next section offers a brief outline of the sociolinguistic situation of each context, including its top-down language policies and their immediate impact on the urban settings.

Locating the Research Sites

Although it appears that settings like Navarre, Galicia and Buenos Aires could not be more different regarding linguistic diversity,[3] language policies in these contexts are ideologically connected as they were developed primarily to resolve 'conflicts' between dominant and minority language(s). Although the use of Castilian was made obligatory as the only language for administration, education and media during Franco's dictatorship (1939–1975), the post-Franco regime witnessed Spain's transition to democracy, leading to a new legal framework for its regional languages. This new constitutional regime conferred diverse degrees of co-officiality to Galician and Basque alongside Castilian within what became the Autonomous Communities of Galicia and Navarre respectively. Although the top-down policy rhetoric in Galicia and Navarre contests the 'one language–one nation' ideology by offering constitutional recognition to their minority languages, in practice, governmental policymakers in these settings have marginalised minority languages and attempted to perpetuate systems of socio-lingual inequity through *laissez-faire*[4] implementations (see O'Rourke 2011 for Galicia and Erize 2001 for Navarre). In Argentina, and more specifically in Buenos Aires, the monocultural and monolingual Spanish-dominant policy of the nineteenth century has evolved into a clearly multicultural policy at the beginning of the twenty-first century, where the public institutions promote the social visibility of cultural diversity (Banfi 2018; Reyna-Muniain 2021). Ultimately, with weak 'top-down' support for the language, intergenerational transmission of Galician and Basque in their respective contexts largely depends on 'bottom-up' interventions from parents and grassroots-level community endeavours.

Regarding the current sociolinguistic situation of Basque in Navarre, there has been an increase of around 3.5% amongst Basque speakers in the last twenty-five years (Eusko Jaurlaritza-Gobierno Vasco 2019: 148). In official surveys conducted between 1991 and 2016, the question of whether the public organisations should promote the use of Basque has also received an increasingly positive response (see Eusko Jaurlaritza-Gobierno Vasco 2019). Concerning the day-to-day use of Basque, in 2016 nearly 7% of the conversations that took place in the streets in Navarre were in Basque (Soziolinguistika Klusterra 2017: 6). However, in the city of Pamplona/Iruña (mixed zone), where data for this study were collected, the percentage was 3% (Soziolinguistika Klusterra 2017: 9). In educational settings, a strong parental commitment towards the promotion and maintenance of Basque amongst children was also noted. For instance, during the school year 2018–2019, nearly 27% of the total school population attended Basque-medium schools and around 20% of students were schooled in Castilian-medium programmes where Basque was only taught as a subject (Goikoetxea and Orzaiz 2019). It is also worth pointing out here that a large majority of Basque-speaking parents who put their children in Basque-medium schools in Navarre fit in the aforementioned category of new speakers, who constitute 47% of the total population aged between 35 and 49 (Eusko Jaurlaritza-Gobierno Vasco 2019: 169).

In Galicia, contemporary sociolinguistic data on Galician demonstrate that there is a persistent language shift towards the dominant language—Castilian (Instituto Galego de Estatística 2018). Top-down language policy for Galician revolves around what is referred to as *Normalización Lingüística* (Linguistic Normalization). Over the past three decades, institutional language policy discourses in Galicia focused mainly on the area of education, which supports the progressive incorporation of Galician in the school curricula, with the aim of establishing bilingual programmes in all Galician schools. However, the policy stakeholders of the conservative centralist government which had been in power almost uninterruptedly during the initial years of language policy in Galicia (1982–2004) took very little interest in implementing the policy initiatives on the ground. They were more interested in not upsetting certain Castilian-speaking urban middle-class people in Galician society (Nandi 2017a). In 2010, the conservative government introduced further changes to the educational language policy through a new decree, *O Decreto de Plurilingüismo* (The Decree of Plurilingualism, henceforth DDP). Although this new policy claims to ensure the continuation of Galician in primary and secondary schools alongside Castilian, it allows the medium of instruction to be that of the children's home language. Since Castilian has been, and continues to be, the most widely spoken language in urban/semi-urban areas, a majority of Galician children tend to be brought up speaking Castilian by Castilian-speaking parents. Therefore, with the application of this policy, Castilian automatically becomes the medium of instruction in the urban pre-primary education curriculum, further constraining the conduits of access to Galician amongst pre-school students. It is also important to note that ever since this educational policy was put into practice, language shift in the urban contexts has proportionally gained momentum (Monteagudo et al. 2020). Dissatisfaction with such top-down policies has in many ways unsettled the mood of a pro-Galician urban demographic, including those so-called active new speaker parents (O'Rourke and Nandi 2019: 497–498) who are the primary focus of our case study in Galicia. This profile refers to a group of highly dedicated individuals who are devoted to the cause of revival of Galician from the bottom up. Although this demographic represents a very small slice (around 0.05%) of the total Galician population above 14 years, they invest time and effort in the language and commit seriously to using it (Seminario de Sociolingüística 2017).

Governmental language policy in Argentina towards the end of the nineteenth century was predominantly monocultural and monolingual. Only Spanish-speaking white people were considered to be full citizens, whereas the native indigenous population and immigrants were excluded (Monteagudo and Reyna-Muniain 2019). This mindset was challenged in the early twentieth century due to the emergence of transnational identities as Argentine society witnessed an inward migration from various European countries. Currently, Argentina can be considered a superdiverse domain that has become a melting pot for both autochthonous and diasporic cultures. In this scenario, the Galician community is one of the most relevant minority groups in Argentinian society, given its history and size (Núñez Seixas 2001). For instance, by 1936 there were two and a half million inhabitants in Buenos Aires, of which 10% were Galicians (Villares 2014: 475). The gradual disappearance of native speakers and the extremely weak intergenerational transmission of the language encouraged cultural and linguistic assimilation. During the last few decades, several attempts have been made to reverse the process of language shift. Many Galician descendants show an increasing interest in Galician identity and language. In contrast to their grandparents and great-grandparents, these new generations of descendants have achieved high educational and socio-economic status, including the mastery of one or more foreign languages. They seek to recover the individual as well as collective memory and to reclaim the identity that the 'one nation-one language' policy repressed and stigmatised for decades. These individuals participate in diverse collective, self-regulated and voluntary initiatives and projects that aim at the revitalisation of Galician identity, language and culture (Gugenberger 2018). One such initiative was the creation of the *Instituto Argentino Gallego Santiago Apóstol* (Santiago Apóstol Argentine Galician School, hence IAGSA), established in 1998. IAGSA is the first Galician Heritage Language School covering pre-school, primary and secondary levels. Galician is one of the curricular subjects as well as one of the languages used as a medium of instruction alongside English and Spanish (Reyna-Muniain et al. 2019). We will centre our study on parents who learnt Galician as adults and send their children to this school as a part of their home language policies. The following section reveals how new speaker parents across indigenous and diasporic settings exercise their agency and become policy stakeholders in their respective homes and in the community.

Parental Agency in Developing Effective Family Language Policies

This section demonstrates how new speaker parents act as both visible and invisible language planners and attempt to influence their children's behaviour towards minority languages such as Basque and Galician.

Contesting the Conventionalisation of Spanish Through Family's Language Management

Reported language practices of the parents across the contexts of our research seem to confirm that each parent exercises their own individual agency in the family through a wide range of language management tools to exert control over their children's language behaviour. In addition, all minority language-speaking parents from indigenous settings (i.e. Navarre and Galicia), especially those who could be considered language activists, unanimously confirmed that they had absolutely no reservation in choosing the minority language as their vehicular language at home. For instance, Marta, a new speaker mother from Navarre who works as a university lecturer, clearly states that she and her partner (also a new speaker) already had Basque as their primary language at home. Therefore, when their son was born, there was no change in the family's language practices. Later, whilst seeking childcare support, the couple maintained a strict language requirement and deliberately chose a Basque-speaking nanny:

Marta: We already spoke in Basque. When our first child was born, there was no change (in our language practice). We did not even think of it (the language issue). [...] when I started teaching, and we had to hire a babysitter. She used to come in the mornings, and she was a Basque speaker. Obviously, it had to be that way.

[Recorded individual interview (authors' translation), 24.01.12]

Language policy in its primary sense has been described as being 'all about choices' (Spolsky 2009: 1) and language management within the family refers to conscious and explicit efforts made by parents to achieve their expected linguistic outcomes (see the section "Parents as Policymakers: Researching Family Language Policy from a Critical Perspective"). As such, Marta and her partner's conscious decision to hire a Basque-speaking nanny to ensure a more Basque-centred home 'language ecology' (Haugen 1971) for the child is crucially instantiated by its deployment as language management. Moreover, her firm verbal statements, such as 'Obviously, it had to be that way', underscore the couple's commitment to the intergenerational transmission of Basque. Such practices where the parents attempt to control child's external language input can also be identified as an evidence of biopower exercised through parental agency as Marta considers this 'authority' (cf. Nandi 2018: 213) to hire a language-specific childminder in a Castilian-dominated bilingual context.

In the sociolinguistic context of Galicia, active new speaker parents demonstrate an awareness of the cultural as well as ideological hegemony of Spanish in the society. Although institutional support for Galician since the 1980s encourages its progressive inclusion and active use in the school sector, Spanish tends to prevail as the unmarked linguistic code of socialisation amongst school-goers in urban Galicia (Nandi 2019). It thus follows that the use of Galician outside the classroom is often seen as deviant or out of place, causing alienation and anxiety amongst children coming from Galician-speaking households (Seminario de Sociolingüística, in press). In such circumstances, these parents often emphasise 'prestige planning' (Kaplan and Baldauf 1997) for Galician inside the home. Prestige in this context is directly linked to identity and pride that encourages the children to use the minority language. For instance, Lara, a mother from Santiago de Compostela whose eldest son studies in a public primary school, explains to him that he should not feel alienated or ashamed for speaking Galician:

Lara: Since Bruno started the school, he sometimes tells us that he feels uncomfortable because most of his classmates speak Spanish and they often make fun of him if he speaks in Galician. In

> such circumstances, we talk to him and tell him that Galician is part of our identity, which he shouldn't renounce. He knows that Galician is our home language and we frequently chat with him about the linguistic coexistence in Galicia. In fact, we have been explaining this to him since he was very young, precisely because we wanted to prepare him to confront such situations by understanding them.
>
> [Recorded focus group discussion (authors' translation), 14.12.14]

To a greater extent, Lara's strategy involves accentuating the symbolic capital of Galician at home, by instilling a sense of pride and self-identification in the use of the language. The purpose of the couple's active promotion of Galician at home is for their child to articulate and enact their Galician identity without 'fear' or 'shame' in the Spanish-dominated exterior. Through continuous counselling, Lara and her partner provide the child with the essential psychological strength and linguistic skills to contest the dominant discourse on his own. Their sense of responsibility, linguistic commitment and claimed practices towards Galician further underline how these parents exercise their language governmentality measures inside the family.

In the sociolinguistic context of Buenos Aires, second and third-generation new speaker parents of Galician origin use their heritage language to maintain connection with their past, to establish a bond amongst generations and ultimately, to enrich their children's linguistic repertoire (Reyna-Muniain et al. 2019). For instance, Martín, a father from Buenos Aires who learnt Galician as an adult, now encourages his children to learn the minority language by underlining its typological closeness with Portuguese, a dominant language with more than 215 million speakers worldwide:

Martín: My wife and I, we both consider that knowledge of Galician or any other language is always a win-win situation, one can never lose. [...] We can use our vacation in Brazil as an example. As soon as we reached Brazil, they (children) understood the close

> proximity between Galician and Portuguese and their knowledge of Galician became a practical advantage. Back home Galician was not something useful except its cultural value. But its proximity to the Portuguese-speaking world is real. No doubt about that, it is real.
>
> [Recorded individual interview (authors' translation), 11.10.17]

Martín and his partner's utility-based approach to encourage their children to learn Galician is bolstered by a recurrent discourse amongst the second or third-generation immigrant new speakers which emphasises Galician's close linguistic proximity to Portuguese (Reyna-Muniain 2014).[5] In the Galician sociolinguistic situation, the issue of Portuguese is connected to the ideologies of reintegrationism (see below). A small group of activist parents continue to use this ideology as a counter-hegemonic strategy to contest the symbolic dominance of Castilian by opposing *Real Academica Galega* (RAG)'s orthographic rules. Previous research in this area demonstrates that such an argument was an integral part of Galician cultural movements (1940–1960) in Argentina and it has been reasserted in heritage education, at home and in the community ever since (Rodríguez-Brandeiro 2006). The above extract also refers to the discourses of additive bilingualism. It occurs when a speaker of a dominant language becomes bilingual in a foreign or second language through learning for a better lifestyle, job opportunities or education without affecting the L1 (de Mejía 2002). This sort of bilingualism is often associated with the middle class and educated members of the society, as is the case with this family where the parents retain sufficient economic capacity to take their children to Brazil on vacation to make them understand the practical value of knowing Galician through everyday language use (cf. Curdt-Christiansen 2014). Such planned learning activity organised by parents can be understood as one form of language management.

Extended Family Language Policies and Collective Language Governmentality

Apart from the above micro-level individual efforts, parental language governmentality may also adopt a broader social role through grassroots-level mobilisations in language revitalisation settings, as occurred in Spain's Basque Country regions during the Franco regime. Since the teaching and learning of Basque was prohibited in public schools, a group of like-minded pro-Basque people (e.g. parents, educators and other members of civil society) extended their family language policies to education and created Basque-medium clandestine schools, the so-called *Ikastolak*, to respond to the government's anti-Basque policies (Urla 2012). With the establishment of the autonomous educational system in the early 1980s, Basque-medium education was progressively extended to the public schools. Both *Ikastolak* and public schools not only use Basque as their medium of instruction for school activities, but they are also committed to promote its use within the school space as a language of socialisation (Idiazabal and Dolz 2013; Manterola 2019). For instance, Adur, a father who takes his children to a Pamplona/Iruña-based public Basque-medium school, explains how the school space became a place of socialisation in Basque not only for the children, but also for their parents:

Adur: ... with the parents [who take their children to the school] it goes really well, because it's not only me, other parents also speak in Basque with children. They [children] may speak sometimes in Spanish and we remind them 'eh you (all) speak in Basque!' and they change to Basque. [...] In the playground, we already know who [parent] speaks Basque. So, we meet and start talking in Basque.

[Recorded individual interview (authors' translation), 27.02.12]

The above scenario reveals how individual families' language management takes a more collective form as various activist parents transform the school space into a context of socialisation in Basque for everyone.

A sense of community can also be explored in Adur's attestations such as 'it's not only me, other parents also speak in Basque with children' and 'we meet and start talking in Basque' indicating the day-to-day language practices of these parents. Although their claimed commitment to Basque is sometimes offset by their children's intermittent lapses into Spanish, these parents often assume the role of custodians over their children's language behaviour and remind them to speak exclusively in Basque in the school space. In Spanish-dominated urban areas of Navarre, such practices can also be interpreted as providing an organisational basis for the bottom-up contestation to the linguistic supremacy of Spanish coordinated by individual pro-Basque parents.

In Galicia, the active new speaker parents were openly critical of official language policy in education and underlined the insufficient provision for the minority language in the current trilingual model. Since public schools were becoming a space for de-Galicianisation, a collective of pro-Galician parents formed cooperatives to fund Galician-medium schools following the *Ikastolak* model in the Basque Country. One such school is *Escolas de Ensino Galego Semente* (Semente Galician Education Schools). Established in 2011, it is a language immersion school that started as an exigent response to the state's extant language policy—'The Decree of Plurilingualism'. It was funded by a group of pro-Galician activists who sought to reverse the language shift from Galician during children's early years. Although the school started with only three students in the first year, in 2015–2016, when the fieldwork of this study took place, this nursery school had around forty students. Amongst the five new speaker families interviewed in Santiago de Compostela in Nandi's study, four took their children to this school. Samuel, a father who is also one of the founding members of the School, explains more about this proactive strategy of bottom-up resistance:

Samuel: We have been part of the *Semente* project since the very beginning. This initiative brought together a number of collaborators who activated a social mobilisation to create a school. It keeps more connection with the *Ikastolak* of the Basque Country in the sixties. This non-profit social initiative is a product of grassroots-level language activism.

[Recorded individual interview (authors' translation), 20.06.14]

The above comment underlines how activist parents collectively have started widening the symbolic space for Galician. In a community such as Galicia, where the existence of traditional speakers shrinks perceptibly due to language shift, these pro-Galician parents, by creating alternative bottom-up language policies, can play an important role in the language revitalisation process from the ground. During field research, it was also observed that the classrooms of *Semente* School were filled with children's literacy materials exclusively in Galician, including posters, lyrics of traditional Galician songs, storybooks, audio and video resources. These materials can be borrowed for a short period and interested parents can use them to develop an effective home literacy environment in Galician. In addition, after school, the school space converts into a language learning zone, often holding different extracurricular activities with the children to reinforce their oral and written skills in Galician. Such larger cohesions formed by like-minded parents straddling the school, social and home spheres to challenge the supremacy of Spanish can be interpreted as one form of collective language governmentality.

The diaspora context presents a different conjuncture as compared to that of the home country. The Galician community in Buenos Aires, integrated in the Argentine society, is surrounded by a multicultural environment. In this context, the parents of the community in Buenos Aires value the IAGSA's importance as a tool for preserving the heritage language and culture of the community and they are engaged with the educational project.

Martín: [It requires] economic [effort], and the parents' work, and we live far away. Yes, of course, we live in another part of town. It is a sacrifice for the children and for us. Also, for them because it determines who their friends are. They no longer have friends in the neighbourhood. (They have friends from the Galician community instead) [...] The school feels like it's part of our house, like a continuity of the home.

[Recorded individual interview (authors' translation), 10.10.17]

Thus, the choice of the IAGSA seems to imply a determination of the social network of children and the family in general. As it has already been pointed out, the IAGSA interacts with the ideological and strategic aspects of the FLP of the members of the educational community (see Reyna-Muniain et al. 2019). It is important to note that the parents and the IAGSA share the goal of language management to empower children, as expressed by the school principal:

> because it is part of their origins in many cases but also because it will be useful for them in the future. The largest South American power today economically. And say tomorrow many of them will be working in Brazil. And that knowledge of the Galician language will also be in a subtle way. Then they learn the Galician language as something more that will make them better people. And that gives them a different way of thinking.
> [Recorded individual interview (authors' translation), 19.10.17]

The school also contributes to the awareness of children about the importance of learning the Galician language for self-improvement, as another mother's narrative excerpt shows:

Liliana: 'Have you already taken the Portuguese exam? How was it? – It was so easy! – Why was it easy? You never studied Portuguese and it was never spoken at home. I speak Portuguese and you spoke some when you travelled to Buzios (Brazil). But you never learned any Portuguese – No! But with some Galician! Naturally, I had to study the accentuation rules with those weird accents. But then I went over some of the Galician language and I just went for it! – She got a B!'
[Recorded individual interview (authors' translation), 06.01.14]

As a university student in tourism studies, Liliana's daughter is learning several languages. In this context, Liliana is aware that the learning of a heritage language is not only important in terms of pride, but it also implies an added value of profit (Duchêne and Heller 2012). These dynamics show how Galician in relation to Portuguese is revalued not only within the frame of symbolic capital (Bourdieu 1984), but also, simultaneously, in the matter of immediately transferable capital that makes passing her exam quite effortless.

Conclusion

In this paper, we have set out to study the potential of new speaker parents to generate visible and invisible language policies on the ground, influencing their children's acquisition of either Galician or Basque, languages which they themselves did not acquire through intergenerational transmission. Based on their individual as well as collective linguistic practices from both sides of the Atlantic, we have argued that each of them exercises their own agency in the home. We have also shown that their individual language management and practices, when galvanised into collective mobilisations (involving *Ikastolak*, *Semente and IAGSA*), can influence their immediate society's language behaviour. In minority language-speaking communities where the existence of traditional speakers shrinks perceptibly due to language shift, these new speaker parents, by creating alternative bottom-up language policies, can occupy an important role in the language revitalisation process from the ground. As such, their reported linguistic practices could be interpreted as counter-hegemonic strategies to destabilise the normalisation and legitimisation of the dominant discourse of Castilian Spanish, especially in the context of Navarra and Galicia.

Moreover, in the context of Navarre, it has also been observed that parental strategies such as the ones described in this chapter influence the development of children's agency. As the socialising environment creates spaces for language use and promotes children's positive attitudes towards Basque, children bring home experiences, learning and motivations (cf. Kasares 2014). In this way, they also become active agents of language policy practised at home. Akin to Navarre, in the Galician community of Buenos Aires, children schooled in the IAGSA not only reactivate positive emotions amongst adult members of the family through recollection, but also encourage the use of Galician in the home, which in turn, supports the revival of cultural and linguistic identity (cf. Reyna-Muniain 2018). The weight of the cultural heritage of the minority language seems to be a relevant motivational component for new speakers in the diasporic context of Buenos Aires. In addition, the attempts at the intergenerational continuation of Galician clearly merge into the historical moment of the construction of a plurilingual and multilingual city. Although the maintenance of Galician cultural identity appears to be a major motivational factor in parental language policies, the incorporation of the language in the educational system has intensified the impact of such policies, increasing the value of Galician vis-à-vis linguistic commodification. These findings contribute to a better understanding of the dynamics of a minority community diaspora such as the Galician one, which has been extensively studied with reference to identity and culture, but not so much in relation to the family language policies.

In essence, the above case studies involving pro-minority language parents in their respective contexts further exhibit the inherent flexibility in the deliberation between Castilian and Galician or Basque. The sites for intersection and imbrication of the two linguistic discourses are subject to continuous negotiations, variations and mutations on a daily basis through various actors and stakeholders. These reagents include the media, tacit social modes and language practices, and also children, whose agency may affect the linguistic choices and behaviours of peers as well as of older members of the family. All these actors and stakeholders are linked to governmentality and biopower, which, as our multisite study underscores, can stem not only from the government, but also from parental control over children. These interlinked multivalent factors map out in concentric circles of power, from the micro level of parental jurisdiction to the custodians of political power at the executive policy-making echelons of the government (including regional to federal levels and the layers in between). In essence, these activist parents from autochthonous as well as diasporic contexts must negotiate the conflicts between the realities of social pressure, political imposition and public education demands on the one hand, and the desire for cultural loyalty and linguistic intergenerational transmission on the other.

Acknowledgements This chapter benefits from a Short Term Scientific Mission (STSM) that took place in April 2017 under the auspices of the European COST Action 1306 *New Speakers in a Multilingual Europe: Opportunities and Challenges* (2013–2017).

Notes

1. See Spolsky (2004) and Johnson (2013) for a detailed discussion on various definitions of language policy.
2. See Hornsby (2015), McLeod and O'Rourke (2015), Ortega et al. (2016), Smith-Christmas et al. (2018) for case studies from different European minority language situations.
3. Whereas Galicia and Navarre are predominantly bilingual Autonomous Communities (Castilian-Spanish and Galician and Basque in their respective territories), Buenos Aires is linguistically superdiverse, with Arabic, Mandarin, Japanese, Korean, a range of European and various indigenous languages being spoken alongside Spanish (Porto 2014).
4. Policies with minimal or no implementation on the ground to maintain a sociolinguistic status quo.
5. Similar discourses are also present in Galicia itself, which are often linked to the re-integrationist movement of Galician language standardisation in the early 1980s, whereby a group of language activists opposed the linguistic standard proposed by the *Real Academica Galega* (RAG) and proposed an orthography closer to that of Luso-Brazilian (Portuguese) system (Peres-Gonçálves 2014). Although their proposal was rejected by the Galician Government decades ago, some parents in the *Semente* school (see section "Extended Family Language Policies and Collective Language Governmentality") are supporters of this ideology and continue to use the re-integrationist orthography for some of their literacy materials (see Nandi 2017a).

References

Althusser, L. 1971. *Lenin and Philosophy and Other Essays*. New York: Monthly Review Press.

Banfi, C. 2018. Heritage Languages in Argentina. In *Heritage Language Policies Around the World*, ed. C. Seals and S. Shah, 48–66. London: Routledge, Taylor & Francis Group.

Blommaert, J. 2019. Family Language Planning as Sociolinguistic Biopower. In *Family Language Policy: Dynamics in Language Transmission Under a Migratory Context*, ed. S. Haque and F. Le Lièvre, 1–9. Munich: Lincom Europa.

Bourdieu, P. 1984. *Distinction: A Social Critique of the Judgement of Taste*. Cambridge, MA: Harvard University Press.

Curdt-Christiansen, X.L. 2014. Family Language Policy: Is Learning Chinese at Odds with Learning English? In *Learning Chinese in Diasporic Communities*, ed. X.L. Curdt-Christiansen and A. Hancock, 35–55. Amsterdam: John Benjamins.

Curdt-Christiansen, X.L., and E. Lanza. 2018. Language Management in Multilingual Families: Efforts, Measures and Challenges. *Multilingua* 37 (2): 123–130.

De Mejía, A.-M. 2002. *Power, Prestige and Bilingualism: International Perspectives on Elite Bilingual Education*. Clevedon: Multilingual Matters.

Duchêne, A., and M. Heller. 2012. *Language in Late Capitalism: Pride and Profit*. New York: Routledge.

Erize, X. 2001. El discurso contrario a la 'normalización' de la lengua vasca en Navarra (1997–2002). *Revista Internacional De Estudios Vascos* 46 (2): 661–682.

Eusko Jaurlaritza-Gobierno Vasco. 2019. *Sixth Sociolinguistic Survey*. Vitoria-Gasteiz: Servicio de Publicaciones del Gobierno Vasco.

Fogle, L.W. 2013. Parental Ethnotheories and Family Language Policy in Transnational Adoptive Families. *Language Policy* 12 (1): 83–102.

Foucault, M. 1978. *The History of Sexuality: An Introduction*, vol. I. New York: Random House.

Foucault, M. 1991. Governmentality. In *The Foucault Effect: Studies in Governmentality*, ed. G. Burchell, C. Gordon, and P. Miller, 87–104. Chicago: University of Chicago Press.

Foucault, M. 2007. *Security, Territory, Population: Lectures at the College de France 1977–78*. Basingstoke: Palgrave Macmillan.

Goikoetxea, G., and I. Orzaiz. 2019. Euskarak eutsi, erdarek irabazi. *Berria*, 20 February.
Gugenberger, E. 2018. *Theorie und Empirie der Migrationslinguistik: Mit einer Studie zu den Galiciern und Galicierinnen in Argentinien.* Münster: Lit Verlag.
Haugen, E. 1971. The Ecology of Language. *The Linguistic Reporter Supplement* 25: 19–26.
Hornsby, M. 2015. *Revitalizing Minority Languages New Speakers of Breton, Yiddish and Lemko.* Basingstoke: Palgrave Macmillan.
Idiazabal, I., and J. Dolz. 2013. Introducción: Diversidad lingüística y formación plurilingüe. In *Enseñar lenguas en contextos multilingües,* ed. J. Dolz and I. Idiazabal, 9–28. Bilbao: UPV/EHU.
Instituto Galego de Estatística (IGE). 2018. *Enquisa de Condiciones de Vida das Familias. Coñecemento e Uso do Galego. Ano 2017*. Santiago de Compostela: Instituto Galego de Estatística (IGE). www.ige.eu/web/mostrar_actividade_estatistica.jsp?idioma=gl&codigo=0206004. Accessed 5 January 2021.
Johnson, D. 2013. *Language Policy*. London: Palgrave Macmillan.
Kaplan, R., and R.B. Baldauf Jr. 1997. *Language Planning: From Practice to Theory*. Clevedon: Multilingual Matters.
Kasares, P. 2014. *Euskaldun hazi Nafarroan. Euskararen belaunez belauneko jarraipena eta hizkuntza sozializazioa familia euskaldunetan.* Bilbao: Euskaltzaindia.
Kasares, P. 2017. La transmisión intergeneracional desde la socialización lingüística: El caso vasco. *Treballs De Sociolingüística Catalana* 27: 133–147.
Li, W. 2018. Linguistic (Super)Diversity, Post-multilingualism and Translanguaging Moments. In *The Routledge Handbook of Language and Superdiversity*, ed. A. Creese and A. Blackledge, 16–29. London: Routledge.
Manterola, I. 2019. A Study of Recipes Written by Basque L2 Immersion Students: Any Evidence for Language Revitalization? In *L2 Writing Beyond English*, ed. N. Yigitoglu and M. Reichelt, 117–124. Bristol: Multilingual Matters.
McLeod, W., and B. O'Rourke. 2015. New Speakers of Gaelic: Perceptions of Linguistic Authenticity and Appropriateness. *Applied Linguistics Review* 6: 151–172.
Monteagudo, H., A. Nandi, and X. Loredo. 2020. La transmisión intergeneracional del gallego en Galicia. Estrategias de mantenimiento y convivencia. *HispanismeS* 16: 1–12.
Monteagudo, H., and F. Reyna-Muniain. 2019. Language and Migration: The Sociolinguistic and Glottopolitical Dynamics of the Galician Community

in Buenos Aires from the Nineteenth Century to the Present Day. *Journal of Multilingual and Multicultural Development* 41 (1): 97–107.
Nandi, A. 2017a. Language Policies and Linguistic Culture in Galicia. *LaborHistórico* 3 (2): 28–45.
Nandi, A. 2017b. Language Policies on the Ground: Parental Language Management in Urban Galician Homes. PhD thesis, Heriot-Watt University.
Nandi, A. 2018. Parents as Stakeholders: Language Management in Urban Galician Homes. *Multilingua* 37 (2): 201–223.
Nandi, A. 2019. Política lingüística familiar. O papel dos proxenitores pro-galego na transmisión interxeracional. *Estudos Da Lingüística Galega* 11: 77–101.
Nandi, A., and A. Devasundaram. 2017. Contesting the Conventionalising of Castilian: The Role of Galician Parents as Counter-Elites. In *Bilingualism and Minority Languages in Europe: Current Trends and Developments*, ed. F. Lauchlan and M. del Carmen Parafita Couto, 12–33. Newcastle upon Tyne: Cambridge Scholars Publishing.
Núñez Seixas, X. 2001. *La Galicia austral: la inmigración gallega en la Argentina*. Buenos Aires: Biblos.
O'Rourke, B. 2011. *Galician and Irish in the European Context: Attitudes Towards Weak and Strong Minority Languages*. Basingstoke: Palgrave Macmillan.
O'Rourke, B., and A. Nandi. 2019. New Speaker Parents as Grassroots Policy Makers in Contemporary Galicia: Ideologies, Management and Practices. *Language Policy* 18 (4): 493–511.
O'Rourke, B., J. Pujolar, and F. Ramallo. 2015. New Speakers of Minority Languages: The Challenging Opportunity—Foreword. *International Journal of the Sociology of Language* 231: 1–20.
Ortega, A., E. Amorrortu, J. Goirigolzarri, and J. Urla. 2016. *Los nuevos hablantes hablantes de euskera: Experiencias, actitudes e identidades*. Bilbao: Universidad de Deusto.
Peres-Gonçálves, T. 2014. *Breve história do reintegracionismo*. Santiago de Compostela: Através editora.
Porto, M. 2014. The Role and Status of English in Spanish-Speaking Argentina and Its Education System: Nationalism or Imperialism? *SAGE Open* 4 (1): 1–14.
Reyna-Muniain, F. 2014. Políticas culturais no exilio galego: Centro Gallego de Buenos Aires, 1940–1960. *Grial: revista galega de cultura* 201: 123–127.

Reyna-Muniain, F. 2018. Política lingüística familiar en contexto de diáspora: Lengua e identidad en la comunidad gallega de Buenos Aires. In *Migración y contacto de lenguas en la Romania del siglo XXI / Migration et contact de langues au XXIe siècle*, ed. C. Patzelt, C. Spiegel, and K. Mutz, 295–322. Berlin: Peter Lang.

Reyna-Muniain, F. 2021. Lengua e Identidad, en el caso de la segunda y tercera generación de emigrantes gallegos en Argentina. Unpublished PhD thesis, Universität Bremen.

Reyna-Muniain, F., I. Manterola, and A. Nandi. 2019. Educación plurilingüe con lenguas minoritarias en contextos de diáspora y su impacto en las políticas lingüísticas en familias neo-hablantes: El caso del gallego en Argentina. *Lengua y Migración/language and Migration* 11 (2): 107–134.

Rodríguez Brandeiro, C. 2006. La transmisión de la cultura gallega a los nietos de la diáspora: Experiencias desde Buenos Aires. In *Buenos Aires. Gallega Inmigración, pasado y presente. Buenos Aires*, ed. R. Farías, 343–358. Buenos Aires: Comisión para la Preservación del Patrimonio Histórico Cultural del Ministerio de Cultura de la Ciudad de Buenos Aires.

Rose, N., P. O'Malley, and M. Valverde. 2006. Governmentality. *Annual Review of Law and Social Science* 2: 83–104.

Seminario de Sociolingüística, Real Academia Galega. 2017. *Lingua e sociedade en Galicia: Resumo de resultados 1992–2016*. A Coruña: Real Academia Galega.

Seminario de Sociolingüística, Real Academia Galega. (in press). *Prácticas lingüísticas na infancia na comarca de Santiago de Compostela*. A Coruña: Real Academia Galega.

Smith-Christmas, C., N. Ó Murchadha, M. Hornsby, and M. Moriarty, eds. 2018. *New Speakers of Minority Languages Linguistic Ideologies and Practices*. Basingstoke: Palgrave Macmillan.

Soziolinguistika Klusterra. 2017. Measurement of the Street Use of Languages. Basque Country, 2016. http://www.soziolinguistika.eus/files/erabilera-ing.pdf. Accessed 14 April 2020.

Spolsky, B. 2004. *Language Policy*. Cambridge: Cambridge University Press.

Spolsky, B. 2009. *Language Management*. Cambridge: Cambridge University Press.

Tollefson, J.W. 1991. *Planning Language, Planning Inequality*. London: Longman.

Urla, J. 2012. *Reclaiming Basque: Language, Nation, and Cultural Activism*. Reno, NV: University of Nevada Press.

Villares, R. 2014. *Historia de Galicia*. Vigo: Galaxia.

Walters, W. 2012. *Governmentality: Critical Encounters*. Abingdon: Routledge.

'We Had to Make a Choice': The Contentious Debate Over Language Replacement in Transnational Adoptive Families

Alice Fiorentino

Introduction

Whenever individuals grow up with more than one language as a means of primary socialisation, it is desirable for them to develop a sense of well-being related to these languages and to their practice. De Houwer (2015) defines *harmonious bilingual development* as 'the experience of well-being in a language contact situation involving young children and their families' and well-being as 'a broad category of phenomena that includes people's emotional responses, domain satisfactions, and global judgments of life satisfaction' (p. 170).

A. Fiorentino (✉)
Dipartimento Di Culture E Civiltà, University of Verona, Verona, Italy
e-mail: Alice.Fiorentino@univr.it

M. Hornsby and W. McLeod (eds.), *Transmitting Minority Languages*, Palgrave Studies in Minority Languages and Communities,
https://doi.org/10.1007/978-3-030-87910-5_13

The conception of language as an individual dimension of well-being is usually explored in multilingual families where potential language-related conflicts are more likely to arise. Braun and Cline (2014: 4–5) propose three categories of multilingual families: '(a) monolingual parents who live in a country where a different language dominates, (b) families with at least one bilingual parent and with many possible variations (e.g. the two parents share one common language, but one of them speaks a different first language, which may coincide with the language of the place where they live), and (c) trilingual parents, born and raised mono- or bilingually and who have acquired a third language due to their marriage' (in Soler and Zabrodskaja 2017: 550). According to this classification, adoptive families would theoretically fall into a fourth category, d) parents born and raised mono- or bilingually and who have acquired a second language due to the adoption of their child. However, as happens in immigrant communities, in adoptive families societal factors like the pressure to integrate the child into the majority culture may play an important role in favouring the replacement of the language of origin by the second language (henceforth 'language replacement').[1] As a result, in the literature dedicated to such families and due to their frequent representation as being halfway between monolinguals and multilinguals, the language question is often only tangentially addressed.

In recent decades, the bilingual repertoire of transnational adoptees has received more attention (cf. Volkman 2005), yet few studies have discussed the meaning of 'harmonious bilingual development' in adoptees, especially where school-aged children are concerned and adoptive parents still lack linguistic understanding and advice. Even when parents realise that awareness of the heritage language may increase older adoptees' future well-being (Lee and Quintana 2005; Shin 2013), they may encounter several difficulties on the way to becoming a multicultural and multilingual family. Studies on education programmes for adopted children in the United States (Lee and Quintana 2005; Shin 2013) showed that these programmes often do little to contribute to the integration of the heritage culture as part of the family identity. Indeed, the parents describe the activities proposed as 'fairly superficial' (Lee and Quintana 2005: 91) and the language teaching as inadequate (Shin 2013:

201), with the counter-productive result that the children develop feelings of frustration and refusal towards this experience. Despite the varied support that the country of adoption can offer to the maintenance of the first language, there still remain several challenges related to bilingual development in transnational adoptees. Considering the difficulties for the parents to guarantee adequate support in maintaining the heritage language with the child, the whole family may have the impression of being faced with an 'either-or' situation, where the replacement of the first language in favour of the new one is perceived as regrettable but inevitable (Fiorentino 2017).

This chapter aims to address the relationship between ideology and language practice in an adoptive family, the *Giuliani*,[2] in order to identify the conditions for the harmonious bilingual development of transnational adopted children. Our previous observation of the *Giuliani* family found that, in the short term, a language practice based on receptive multilingualism (i.e. the parents exhibit comprehension of the language of the child while speaking their own language, cf. Ten Thije and Zeevaert 2007) favours the maintenance of the origin language and, especially, a more gradual transition to the second language (Fiorentino 2020). However, in the long term, societal and family reasons risk reorienting the initial multilingual efforts of this family towards a more monolingual identity. This chapter aims to capture the struggle for a family linguistic identity as it emerges in the parents' talk during the first year after adoption. We will discuss how, beyond the feeling of inevitability, the initial replacement of the origin language may play a role in the formation of the newly constituted family.

We will explore our hypotheses by means of three research questions:

1. what is the initial attitude of the family towards the origin language?
2. when does language replacement happen?
3. what problems arise in connection with language maintenance efforts in transnational adoptive families?

Harmonious Bilingual Development and Language Shift in Transnational Adoption

Zeleke et al. (2018) address the subject of emotional well-being of transnational adoptees in terms of belonging, meaning and understanding. The authors point out that when a child is welcomed into his/her new adoptive family, these three feelings are threatened by the same fact that they do not share the biological, cultural and linguistic background of their parents and siblings. As a result, from a very early age they may feel the desire to adapt to what they perceive to be a 'homogeneous backdrop' (Jacobson 2010 in Zeleke et al. 2018: 1428). Indications of this process are to be found in adoptees' behaviour as they struggle, especially during adolescence, to build up their own identity and to harmonise 'life experiences into an internalised evolving story of the self in order to have a "whole" rather than fragmented self-concept' (Yngvesson 2013 in Zeleke et al. 2018: 1429).

The contentious point of harmonious development in transnational adoption is what Benoit et al. define as '*la dynamique des appartenances*' ('the dynamics of belonging', 2015: 418). Based on the evidence of adult adoptees, the authors observe that an adoptee's identity is a dynamic construction which is constantly renewed in relation to their experience and which is unlikely to be attributable to a single culture, whether that be the country of origin or the adoptive country. From this perspective, maintaining the child's simultaneous connection to the country of adoption and to the heritage culture could eventually help him to form a unique identity in adulthood. In this regard, though, we must take into account the age factor and pay special attention to older adoptees. Indeed, allowing the child to maintain a connection with the origin language can be a positive contribution to the search for understanding, especially for those children who were socialised into that language. Given that growing up with a language means acquiring social and symbolic meanings embedded in its culture (Duranti et al. 2012), for an older adoptee losing touch with this heritage could mean losing important referents of their primary experience. Despite these considerations, and although the impact of family practices on heritage culture maintenance has been widely recognised and discussed (Jacobson 2008), only a few studies have included the language in the sense of 'diversity-related issues' (Fogle 2012; Shin 2014; Zeleke et al. 2018).

Even if efforts for language maintenance fulfil the same important purpose of favouring understanding and meaning, the question remains of what parents can do in concrete terms to facilitate language maintenance and what kind of challenge it represents for the family. Research on multilingual families has found that, based on various sources of advice, parents form their own sets of beliefs and 'employ certain language practices which they think will lead to a certain result' (Palviainen and Bergroth 2018: 264; see also King et al. 2008). To our knowledge, both professional and amateur linguistic advice is generally poor for adoptive families, especially in the long term.

Fiorentino (2017) found that Italian adoptive families receive advice from two main sources: other adoptive families and health professionals. The general advice received by families who had already adopted was not to worry too much about the linguistic aspect and to let the children go down their own spontaneous path of language learning. Professionals may often suggest that the parents show appreciation towards the heritage culture and language, especially during the initial period, but also that they look at linguistic replacement as a necessary—and temporary—step:

> **ELS**: *è normale che sia arrivato a questa fase di rifiuto, è un passaggio che deve fare, poi magari più avanti gli passerà. È tutto da manuale, sembra incredibile ma è così!*
> [It is normal that he reached this phase of rejecting [author's note—of the language of origin], it is a step that he must take, maybe later he will overcome it. He behaved by the book, it seems incredible but it is like that.]

The 'book' mentioned by the mother corresponds in fact to what Italian adoption agencies tell the families about the role of language. According to our research (Fiorentino 2017), the current belief on language development, usually coming from the perspective of the parents, is that adopted children need to temporarily put aside their pre-adoption traumatic experience to develop a stable sense of identity and that their first language could produce a 'throw-back' effect which hinders the healing process. This role of the first language constitutes, according to this widespread belief, the motivation which would explain and endorse language replacement in transnational adoption.

To our knowledge, there is no general debate on the long-term repercussions of language replacement and language shift on the well-being of school-age adoptees. Similarly to what has been found on other multilingual families (Fogle and King 2013), in the absence of any clear recommendation concerning long-term language development, adoptive parents will still carry out a 'de facto language policy' (cf. Shohamy 2006), i.e. a set of language practices implicitly shared by the family members.

Presentation of the Case Study: Method and Data

The present longitudinal study followed the evolution of Juan, a nine year old boy, and his adoptive family during the first years of their life together. The interactional data were collected spontaneously by the parents between September 2017 and February 2018 and the interviews with the family have continued on a regular basis until the present. Data from September 2017 to November 2017 (the period the family spent in Chile, the country of origin of the child) have been presented in a previous study by the author (Fiorentino 2020) (Table 1).

As is normal practice in the framework of transnational adoption, the social and language environment of the child changed considerably during the first year. For approximately three months, while the family was in Chile, the child's main interlocutors were the parents and the brother. In terms of the language knowledge of the family members, Elsa (ELS) had attended an elementary course in Spanish two years previously and Jacopo (JCP) had had Spanish as a regular subject at school for the last two years. Once the family arrived in Italy the network of relationships grew significantly, demanding a further new adjustment to

Table 1 Participants' background information

Speaker	Relation to the child	Age at data collection	Profession	L1
ELS	Mother	39	Accounting firm (employee)	Italian
ALS	Father	43	Transport sector (employee)	Italian
JCP	Brother	13	–	Italian
JUAN	Adopted child	9	–	Spanish

pre-existing family dynamics. At that moment, the presence of Spanish decreased significantly as no member of the extended family was able to address Juan in this language. As for school, the child started to attend the fourth grade of primary school in February on a part-time basis, two months after his arrival in Italy, under the careful monitoring of the parents, especially the mother, who followed the whole process, bringing the child to school for few hours a day for several weeks and helping him with homework and with the Italian language.

We collected and transcribed 27 hours of interactions, following broad conversational analysis conventions which provide the reader with the researcher's interpretation. To counterbalance our perspective on language interactions and to present a wider view of the language choices of the participants, we propose the same method found in Venables et al. (2013), which includes a second stage of post-interview where we asked the family members to reflect on the topic of 'first language shift' and to comment on some excerpts of their conversations. Venables et al. (2013) remark that 'this methodology can be described as CA-informed research' and it 'aimed at combining an emic and etic orientation to analyzing interactional data, thus obtaining a richer exploration of the data' (p. 431).

Analysis

As we mentioned, the data are part of a larger study. In section "First Steps of Family Communication and Multilingual Practices", we will briefly describe how the family coped with the challenge posed by the language contact situation in the first place and how they incorporated the language of the child into their interactions.

In the follow-up analysis, we will show how the family's approach to language evolved once they came back to Italy in November 2017 and especially when the child started to attend school. We will show that, despite the child and his parents continuing to use a multilingual mode of communication until the last recording in February 2018, school attendance represented a turning point for the language choice of participants, resulting in a change of the status of Italian and the relative shift from Spanish. Thanks to the integrated approach used, we will be able to provide a snapshot of the language shift in action within Juan's language repertoire and to identify the moment when this shift began.

Finally, we will provide evidence of the difficulties of maintaining an active link with the origin culture through the language, but also of the role that the second language plays as an emotional tool. This twofold contribution on the complexities of building a multilingual identity in transnational adoptive families constitutes the core of our analysis. We will try to bring to the surface those feelings, fears and representations that could hinder the development of an active multilingual identity for the adoptive family.

First Steps of Family Communication and Multilingual Practices

During the first steps of family communication, the family did not particularly focus on which language was better suited for communication. Their interactions show that, in the country of origin of the child, the parents' focus had not yet shifted to language. The first months of socialisation were devoted to family bonding, and to the building-up of the initial relationships, especially between the parents and the child. The main fact of being away from the country of adoption for two entire months allowed the family to be absorbed in the present and to allay any concerns about the arrival in the new home country.

As previously observed in Fiorentino (2020), the initial approach to family communication was non-directive, meaning that both Italian and Spanish were employed without explicit boundaries. The primary motivation to speak Spanish with the child was naturally linked to the necessity to reach out to him:

> **ELS**: *Non avremmo mai imposto l'italiano'. 'Noi siamo in tre e lui è da solo.*
> [We would have never imposed the Italian. There were three of us, he was alone.]

Even though the family's stay in Chile was a precondition laid down by the Chilean authorities for adoption, it is interesting to note that the experience of mobility significantly increased the parents' curiosity towards Spanish, which reinforced their desire to practise this language:

> **ELS**: *avrei mantenuto lo spagnolo per il piacere di parlarlo, ho superato un blocco, l'esperienza di mobilità che mi ha fatto apprezzare la diversità linguistica.*
> [I would have maintained the Spanish language for the pleasure of speaking it, I ended a mental block which made me appreciate linguistic diversity.]

Our study confirms what had previously been found about transnational adoption, that it increases adoptive parents' awareness and appreciation of their child's culture (Nelson and Colaner, 2017). For all these reasons, the initial non-directive approach to communication results in multilingual discourse based on receptive multilingualism and mixed speech (Fig. 1).

In this excerpt, all family members adopt a language practice which is based on the understanding of the language of the interlocutor, namely receptive multilingualism, allowing Juan to maintain Spanish as his language of communication for a long period of time after his adoption (at least six months). Receptive multilingualism is made possible by the mutual intelligibility between the two related languages—Spanish and Italian—and by the linguistic knowledge of Elsa (ELS) and Jacopo (JCP). In our previous research on receptive multilingualism in adoptive families (Fiorentino 2020), we observed that where mutual intelligibility is not possible, as in a context of unrelated languages—Russian and

[Ita]	**ALS**	**hai lavato i denti 'sta mattina?**
[Eng]		*Did you brush your teeth this morning?*
[Sp = Ita]	**JUA**	**Si**
[Eng]		*Yes*
[Sp = Ita]	**ELS**	No
[Sp]	**JUA**	**Mire**
[Eng]		*Look*
[Ita/Sp]	**ELS**	dai no sta' a contare quella de l'orso
[Eng]		*come on don't tell lies*
[Ita/Sp]	**ALS**	dai vai a lavarti **mira que**
[Eng]		*come on go wash up **watch out***
[Esp]	**JUA**	**si Jacopo tampoco se los lavó**
[Eng]		*but Jacopo didn't brush them either*
[Ita]	**ELS**	ma no sta a **mirar** quel che fa Jacopo
[Eng]		*Don't **look** at what Jacopo does*

Fig. 1 Giuliani. Excerpt 16 (24.10.2017): 'Breakfast'

Italian—the child stopped speaking the first language a few weeks after his adoption.

The extract shows that the initial family approach accords equal weight to both languages as the parents very often mix Italian with Spanish and demonstrate comprehension of this language, which is structurally and lexically very close to their mother tongue. It is important to point out that the parents' approach takes into account the child's initial resistance towards Italian, which explains why he hardly ever uses this language, not even on the rare occasions when he is solicited to do so (Fig. 2).

By means of expressions like '*no importa*', the child refuses to go along with the parent's solicitation about the language and he communicates that he is interacting with the whole process at his own pace. This sign of the child's approach confirms what other scholars have found

[Ita]	ALS	parlagli in italiano 'Jacopo per piacere mi dai un po'
[Eng]		*Talk to him in Italian 'Jacopo please give me a bit of [Italian]*
[Sp]	**JUA**	**Ah yo no sé en Italia**
[Eng]		*Ah I don't know in Italy* [sic]
[Ita]	ALS	Sì tu sei bravo a parlare in italiano
[Eng]		*But you're good at speaking Italian*
[Sp]	JUAN	**no importa**
[Eng]		*it doesn't matter*
Iita]	ALS	Ma sei capace
[Eng]		But you're able to
[Sp]	JUA	**no tengo ganas**
[Eng]		*I don't feel like*

Fig. 2 Giuliani. Excerpt 16 (24.10.2017): 'No importa'

about the active role of the youngest child in the development of family language policy (see also Fogle and King 2013; Smith-Christmas 2016) and it is particularly prominent in the case of adopted children who have struggled with identity reminders linked to languages.

Apart from these rare episodes, however, the parents do not initially show anxiety towards the child's refusal to speak Italian nor do they seem willing to teach the language to him. On the contrary, they consider that the child's attitude reflects his need to come to terms with the change of environment and they embrace the experience of mobility with enthusiasm.

Social Practices Outside the Family: The Increasing Status of Italian

For the first months after Juan's arrival in Italy, multilingual communication, and especially receptive multilingualism, was still widely exploited, especially as a response to Juan's reticence to begin to speak Italian (see Fig. 2). After three months, not only is the principle of 'I speak what I speak best and you speak what you speak best' (Zentella 1997: 89) grounded in their daily communication but language diversity is something that even the young child internalised (Fig. 3).

[Sp]	**JUA**	**Me ayuda a poder abrir esto? Sabe abrirla?**
[Eng]		Will you help me to open this? Can you open it?
[Ita]	**ELS**	Vediamo
[Eng]		Let's see
[Sp=Ita]	**JUA**	**(laugh) me jodió**
[Eng]		You mocked me
[Ita]	**ELS**	(laugh) però prima di mettere il cucchiaino che è bagnato hai già messo lo zucchero?
		(laugh) but before you put the wet spoon inside did you add sugar?
[Ita=Sp]	**JUA**	No
[Ita/Sp]	**ELS**	Eh allora prima di bagnare il/la **cuchara** prima di come si dice bagnare?
[Eng]		Eh so before you wet the spoon you how do you say to moisten?
[Ita]	**JUA**	**Eh ... mojar** **Sabes mamà que yo me eché el azúcar ya (laugh)**
[Eng]		To moisten You know mum I've added sugar already
[Ita]	**ELS**	Te l'ho chiesto!
[Eng]		I asked you!

Fig. 3 Giuliani. Excerpt 1 (20.11.2017): 'El azúcar'

In the excerpt, the mother and the child understand each other while speaking their first language and work cooperatively to fill potential language gaps, especially in the Spanish language, since the child still does not yet speak Italian with his parents. Communication runs smoothly in a receptive mode, which allows Juan to understand what the mother says (e.g. [Ita.] *bagnare* > [Eng.] to moisten) and to provide her with the right equivalent in Spanish.

Recordings from the 30th of December, four months after the adoption, show not only that Juan keeps communicating in Spanish with his family but also that the parents (especially the mother) still considered it wrong to force him to speak Italian (Fig. 4).

[Ita]	**ALS**	Eh insomma [...] l'à prova due metri 'papà prendiamo le rotelline?'
[Eng]		Huh well [...] he tried for two metres 'dad let's take the wheels'
[Sp=Ita]	**JUA**	**Es que aquí está la bici mamá aquí está la bici tengo que hacer así no tengo que pedalear tengo que y ahí puedo enseñar a hacer así**
[Eng]		It's like here there is the bicycle mum here there is the bicycle I must do like this I don't have to cycle I must and then I can teach how to do that
[Ita]	**ALS**	Non ho capito niente io
[Eng]		I didn't understand anything
[Ita]	**ELS**	Senti!
[Eng]		Come on!
[Ita]	**ALS**	Non ho capito dal bon quello che mi ha detto
[Eng]		I seriously did not understand what he said
[Ita]	**JCP**	È meglio che papà non capisca si abitua a parlare italiano
[Eng]		It is better that dad does not understand, he got used to speaking Italian
[Ita]	**ELS**	Non si insiste così!
[Eng]		You don't have to insist like that

Fig. 4 Giuliani. Excerpt 22 (30.12.2017): 'The bicycle'

In the excerpt, we see that different opinions towards the acquisition of Italian begin to emerge in the family discourse. The brother (JCP) suggests that they all speak Italian with him and pretend that they don't understand Spanish (cf. 'minimal grasp strategy' in Lanza 1997) while the mother insists on avoiding any forcing ('you don't have to insist like that').

Follow-up interviews gave an insight into their motivations:

> **ELS**: *quando siamo tornati JCP era nel suo territorio per cui non gli ha più parlato in spagnolo [...] ha adottato tutta una serie di comportamenti e atteggiamenti per dimostrare che qui era il suo territorio*
> [when we were back JCP was in his territory and that's why he stopped speaking to him in Spanish [...] he adopted a series of behaviours and attitudes to show that this was his territory.]

Furthermore, she interprets the husband's statement ('I didn't understand anything') as an implicit request to switch to Italian:

> **ELS**: *penso che non avendo mai provato a capire e a parlare in spagnolo stia facendo una forzatura obbligando il bambino a parlare in italiano[...] se si ostinava a non capire obbligava Guiudan a imparare l'italiano velocemente per necessità*
> [I think that, since he [the husband] has never tried to speak or understand Spanish, he is forcing him by obliging him to speak Italian [...] if he failed to understand him it was like he forced him to learn Italian quickly out of necessity.]

As for the father, he considered Italian as the child's means of empowerment into the new community and that is why, according to him, family language practices should start to focus more and more on language development:

> **ALS**: *in Italia il fatto che JUAN dovesse imparare la lingua era per renderlo autonomo ... non per comunicare con me ma con gli altri.*
> [In Italy the reason that JUAN had to learn the language was to make him autonomous ... not to communicate with me but with others.]

Despite the first manifestations of concerns for the emergence of Italian at the end of December, the family maintained the receptive use of Spanish until at least February, the date of our last recording, six months after the adoption.

Based on data observation, we can state that it was not the arrival in Italy that activated the parents' concern about the language, in contrast to what we observed in some of the families in our previous studies, who described stopping the use of the heritage language as soon as they left the heritage country (cf. 'The umbilical cord broke when we arrived here', Fiorentino 2017: 14). In this family, it was the moment when the child engaged his socialisation outside the family, five months after his adoption, that raised real concerns about the language. The mother mentioned their anxiety about Juan's integration into the new school and about the possibility of the child communicating with his peers:

> **ELS**: *ero preoccupata che lo apprendesse per potersi esprimere, comunicare con i compagni; la scuola non era la priorità per me, avevo solo il timore che non venisse capito.*
> [I wanted him to learn to be able to express himself, to communicate with his peers; school was not the priority for me, I was just worried that they would have not been able to understand him.]

Therefore, as the child did not start to speak Italian spontaneously, as they expected, the parents started to wonder if they had to prompt the child to learn the language by means of explicit intervention. In view of this, they started to solicit and encourage the child to introduce the Italian language by means of translation exercises and drill-type questions (Fig. 5).

Child's In-Group Identification and Distancing from Spanish

Between the end of January and the beginning of February, the child started to attend school and simultaneously Italian started to be more present in his oral production. The following conversation was the first time in our corpus where Juan willingly accepted to speak Italian (Fig. 6).

[Ita]	**ALS**	E questa cos'è?
[Eng]		And what is this?
[Ita]	**JUA**	Forchetta
[Eng]		Fork
[Ita]	**ALS**	Bravo! Numero uno
[Eng]		Good! Number one
[Ita]	**ELS**	E questo?
[Eng]		And this one?
[ita]	**JUA**	Coltello
[Eng]		Knife
[Ita]	**ALS**	Bravissimo
[Eng]		Very good!
[Ita]	**ELS**	Hai visto che sei diventato bravo allora lo sai l'italiano?
[Eng]		You see that you are good at speaking Italian?

Fig. 5 Giuliani. Excerpt 22 (30.12.2017): 'Number one'

In this excerpt, there is no trace of resistance towards Italian (cf. Fig. 2), but on the contrary, this is the first recording where the child actually claims this language as his own (even if the language itself contradicts his will: 'yo no hablo spagnolo hablo italiano'), as a further attempt to position himself. As for the family, we begin to observe a clash between two different attitudes: on the one hand, they keep on practising multilingual communication and, on the other, they try to orientate Juan's language choice ('and those who speak Spanish don't eat'), as a sign of impatience for the child to speak Italian.

Three months after the last recording, at the end of May, during a conversation, the mother told the researcher that Juan had apparently expressed his will to stop speaking Spanish:

[Ita]	**JUA**	e io poi mangia tutte le patatine la pizza
[Eng]		And then I eat all the chips and pizza
[Ita]	**ALS**	le patatine
		chips
[Ita/Sp]	**JUA**	e la mamma **tiene que comer puro porotos**
[Eng]		and mum eats only beans
[Ita/Sp]		questo sono **porotos**
[Eng]		These are **beans**
[Ita]	**ALS**	fagioli
[eng]		beans
[Sp/Ita]	**JUA**	**e la que tiene** ventinove no mangia **e la que tiene** quarantatre no mangia
[Eng]		And those who are twenty-nine years old don't eat and those who are forty-three years old don't eat
[Ita]	**ELS**	e chi parla spagnolo non mangia (laugh)
[Eng]		And those who speak Spanish don't eat
[Sp/Ita]	**JUA**	**Yo no hablo** spagnolo **hablo italiano**
[Eng]		I don't speak Spanish I speak Italian [...]
[Ita]	**ELS**	(laugh) adesso hai parlato spagnolo
[Eng]		(laugh) Now you spoke Spanish
[Ita]	**ELS**	**Hablo? Hablo? Hablo** è italiano **hablo?**
[Eng]		Speak? Speak? Speak is Italian for Speak?
[Ita]	**JUA**	Parlo
[Eng]		Speak
[Sp/Ita]	**JUA**	Che cosa stai facendo? **Después se derrite**
[Eng]		What are you doing? Then it melts

Fig. 6 Giuliani. Excerpt 22 (06.02.2018): 'Yo no hablo spagnolo hablo italiano'

ELS: *ufficialmente Juan non vuole più parlare spagnolo e nemmeno che gli si parli in spagnolo (gli sono rimasti attaccati alcuni vocaboli). Lo ha detto molto chiaramente che lui è italiano e che vuole imparare l'italiano.*
[Officially Juan does not want to speak Spanish anymore nor does he want to be addressed in Spanish (he nevertheless still has an attachment to some words). He made it clear that he is Italian and that he wants to learn Italian.]

The parents would[3] then be confronted with Juan's claim of his own linguistic and cultural identity ('he is Italian and he wants to learn Italian'). According to our previous research (Fiorentino 2017), adoptive parents often consider that the in-group identification could be very powerful in leading to the replacement of the first language, especially in the first years after adoption. Because language and social identity are intertwined (Piller 2002 in Palviainen and Bergroth 2018: 264), it is not surprising that the identification with the culture of adoption through language could constitute a natural outcome of transnational adoption. As in other multilingual settings, for this child, identity would be 'primarily defined in terms of belonging to a single (imagined homogenous) group of speakers of a certain language' (Palviainen and Bergroth 2018: 272).

Even if the parents were not really surprised by Juan's positioning as part of the child's emotional re-elaboration, his claim left them with a bittersweet taste, especially because the abandonment of Spanish affects the family's repertoire as a whole:

ELS: *Ho abbandonato lo spagnolo con dispiacere. Dispiacere perché sentivo che lui si stava negando la possibilità di portare avanti la sua entità di cileno integrandola con la possibilità di essere italiano. In quel momento lingua e cultura coincidono. Lui pensa che 'se mi dimentico di essere cileno posso sentirmi italiano'.*
[I abandoned Spanish with regret. Regret because I felt that he was denying himself the possibility of carrying on his Chilean 'self', integrating it with the possibility of being Italian. In that moment language and culture coincide. He thinks that 'if I forget to be Chilean, I can feel Italian'.]

The 'regret' expressed elsewhere in our corpus of interviews (see also the use of 'unfortunately' in Fiorentino 2017: 14) is emblematic of the ambiguity that adoptive parents feel towards the disappearance of the origin language, especially when they had actively used the language with the child like this mother had. As she notes, the disappearance of the language meant temporarily denying the possibility of integrating part of the Chilean 'entity' into the new one, both for the child and the family.

Language Shift in Action: The Difficulty of Holding Two Cultures Together

Apart from the undeniable difficulty of integrating a foreign language into a monolingual family, bilingualism in the adoptive environment implies strong efforts of transformation and processing. We already mentioned that in-group identification can lead the child to a dominant-language replacement which can result in language shift, especially if the child loses any opportunity to practise the language outside the family. As far as the parents are concerned, research on language maintenance has found that they often feel inadequate in maintaining and supporting the heritage language of the child, as much and perhaps even more than the culture (cf. Nelson and Colaner 2017). However, by means of the follow-up interviews that we had with the mother from February 2018 until September 2019 (two years after the adoption), we argue that the difficulty of language maintenance in transnational adoptive families could have further and deeper explanations.

When asked about the presence of the heritage culture in their daily life, two years after the adoption, the mother described a conflicted attitude:

> **ELS**: *A distanza di due anni sono combattuta: da una parte quando mi dice che è italiano sta rinnegando una parte della sua vita, però quando continua a evocare il Cile mi infastidisce perché in quella parte lì noi non ci siamo [...] mi ingelosisce perché è una parte di vita che mi esclude.*
> [Two years later I am conflicted: on one hand when he tells me that he is Italian he is denying a part of his life, but when he continues to

evoke Chile he annoys me because in that part we are not there [...] I am jealous because it is a part of his life that excludes me.]

It seems that in the medium term, the child's origin culture could be perceived both as disturbing the family's search for emotional stability and 'divisive' for their identity alignment. It is not surprising that a similar consideration is found by Fogle (2012) concerning the practice of Russian in a family living in the United States who had adopted six children from Russia. The use of Russian among the youngest and the oldest siblings was described as a 'divisive force' (p. 155) for the family which makes the parents want to implement the use of English as a common family language.

It is interesting to note that in our case, the heritage language and culture provoke strong feelings not only for the child, but also for the parents. The feelings of exclusion of the child from the culture of the parents and of the parents from the culture of the child represent the same strong need for family belonging which is challenged in both cases by the evocation of the past of the child.

Furthermore, we found that, after two years, the association between this past and the country of origin still persists:

ELS: *ci ritornerò? Tornare vorrebbe dire riaprire canali emotivi che sono stati forti.*
[if I were to come back (to Chile)? Coming back would mean re-opening emotional channels which have been strong.]

Even if their experience in Chile went quite smoothly and they could enjoy the two months spent together in that country, the time the family lived there was clearly charged with difficult and conflicting emotions. Coming to terms with these moments needs a very long time and great effort on the part of the child, as well as on the part of the parents. The risk is that the heritage language and culture remain confined to a role of painful reminders of these memories. It is interesting to note that, from this perspective, for the mother the second language (i.e. Italian) assumes a function of distancing:

> **ELS**: *il momento della rielaborazione dell'esperienza arriva contemporaneamente allo stabilirsi della seconda lingua, quindi avviene nella seconda lingua.*
> [the moment of the re-elaboration of the experience comes simultaneously with the establishing of the second language, namely it is achieved in the second language.]

The mother found that the development of the second language was somehow functional in the elaboration of the past. In her eyes, the development of Italian skills by the child—and probably the establishment of this language as the family language—made coming to terms with the past of the past more achievable. In other words, the second language served to review primary experience through narration and reworking, allowing the child and the family to distance themselves from a chain of painful experiences.

Discussion and Conclusions

In this study we found that, consistent with other contexts of multilingualism, language shift in transnational adoption is also explained by the sum of linguistic and attitudinal factors. The language approach of this family represented a good opportunity to investigate the evolution of the relationship between language shift and language ideology. In fact, during the observation, we never observed strong a priori attitudes in favour of language shift (as was the case with other families in our research). On the contrary, the entire family, especially the mother, displayed curiosity towards the language of the child from the beginning, to the extent of incorporating it in their daily practice for a long time after the adoption, by means of receptive multilingualism. Traces of their positive initial attitudes are found in the definition that the mother gave to her family during our interviews as an international family (**ELS**: *noi siamo una famiglia internazionale*).

We observed that the circumstances that triggered language replacement and modified language attitudes were, at first, external to the family and were particularly linked to school attendance and to the child's will to identify with the new culture by means of the new language. Despite the strong predisposition towards multilingualism which emerged during the first months of family life, as soon as concerns about socialisation arose, the family started to feel the compelling need to teach the child Italian as a means of empowerment within society. In the parents' eyes, the eventual selection of Italian as the in-group language by Juan ('he is Italian and he wants to learn Italian') reinforced what is perceived to be the natural linguistic outcome in transnational adoption, namely language replacement. These data confirm the tension Van Mensel observes about multilingual families in 'building a family identity through a shared and hybrid family repertoire and adapting to the environment, implying a narrowing or restricting of the possibilities afforded by this same repertoire' (2018: 245).

However, even if the development of Italian was highly solicited and the replacement of Spanish expected, language shift emerges in the narratives as not deliberate:

> **ELS**: *Siamo arrivati a fare una scelta, ma in modo non consapevole.*
> [We came to make a choice, but unconsciously.]

Follow-up interviews confirmed the ambiguity towards language shift that was found in previous research (Fiorentino 2017) and allowed an insight into the symbolic (and yet tangible) value that the heritage language represents for the family. As well as reminding the parents of the emotional burden linked to the time spent in the origin country, Spanish evoked their feelings of exclusion from the heritage culture of the child and from his past. In contrast, Italian was described as a linguistic tool which allowed identity alignment and elaboration of primary experience.

By showing the evolution of language attitudes towards the origin language in transnational adoption, this study contributes to the understanding of the challenges implied by multilingual identities in this type of scenario. Interactional data show that adopted children struggle from the beginning between two linguistic identities and play an active role in orienting the language policy of the family. Furthermore, the relationship between first and second languages in the elaboration of the experience which emerged in follow-up interviews was very useful in explaining and clarifying the understanding of language shift in transnational adoption. However, drawing from the observation of this family, it can be suggested that if adoptive parents who are in the difficult position of helping the children to handle two 'entities' want to build on a multicultural inclusive identity, strong associations should be carefully handled.

Notes

1. The term 'language replacement' is used by Hyltenstam et al. (2009) to refer to 'the linguistic effects for the individual child who is moved from one monolingual situation into another' (p. 123). We use the term language replacement here to discuss the 'either-or' choice which can be taken by the parents, by the child, or by both at a certain point, usually a few months after the arrival in the country of adoption and which triggers language shift.
2. All participants, including their family names, have been given pseudonyms.
3. We use the conditional here because we are consciously adopting the mother's perspective and we cannot be sure of what the real intention of the child was.

References

Benoit, L., M.R. Moro, and A. Harf. 2015. Adoption internationale: le point de vue des adoptés sur leurs appartenances culturelles. *Neuropsychiatrie de l'Enfance et de l'Adolescence* 63: 413–421.

Braun, A., and T. Cline. 2014. *Language Strategies for Trilingual Families: Parents' Perspectives*. Bristol: Multilingual Matters.

De Houwer, A. 2015. Harmonious Bilingual Development: Young Families' Well-Being in Language Contact Situations. *International Journal of Bilingualism* 19 (2): 169–184.

Duranti, A., E. Ochs, and B. Schieffelin. 2012. *The Handbook of Language Socialization*. Oxford: Blackwell.
Fiorentino, A. 2017. Strategies for Language Maintenance in Transnational Adoption: Which Role for the Parents? *Journal of Home Language Research* 2: 5–22.
Fiorentino, A. 2020. Receptive Multilingualism and Second Language Acquisition: The Language Transition Process of Adopted Children. *International Journal of Bilingualism*. https://doi.org/10.1080/13670050.2020.1749232
Fogle, L.W. 2012. *Second Language Socialization and Learner Agency: Adoptive Family Talk*. Buffalo, NY: Multilingual Matters.
Fogle, L., and K. King. 2013. Child Agency and Language Policy in Transnational Families. *Applied Linguistics* 19: 1–25.
Hyltenstam, K., Bylund, E., Abrahamsson, N., Park, H. S. 2009. Dominant Language Replacement: The Case of International Adoptees. *Bilingualism: Language and Cognition* 12 (2): 121–140.
Jacobson, H. 2008. *Culture Keeping: White Mothers, Transnational Adoption, and the Negotiation of Family Difference*. Nashville, TN: Vanderbilt University Press.
King, K., L. Fogle, and A. Logan-Terry. 2008. Family Language Policy. *Language and Linguistics Compass* 2 (5): 907–922.
Lanza, E. 1997. *Language Mixing in Infant Bilingualism*. Oxford: Oxford University Press.
Lee, D.C., and S.M. Quintana. 2005. Benefits of Cultural Exposure and Development of Korean Perspective-Taking Ability for Transracially Adopted Korean Children. *Cultural Diversity and Ethnic Minority Psychology* 11 (2): 130–143.
Nelson, L.R., and C.W. Colaner. 2017. Becoming a Transracial Family: Communicatively Negotiating Divergent Identities in Families Formed Through Transracial Adoption. *Journal of Family Communication* 18 (1): 51–67.
Palviainen, Å., and M. Bergroth. 2018. Parental Discourses of Language Ideology and Linguistic Identity in Multilingual Finland. *International Journal of Multilingualism* 15 (3): 262–275.
Shin, S.J. 2013. Transforming Culture and Identity: Transnational Adoptive Families and Heritage Language Learning. *Language, Culture and Curriculum* 26 (2): 161–178.
Shin, S.J. 2014. Language Learning as Culture Keeping: Family Language Policies of Transnational Adoptive Parents. *International Multilingual Research Journal* 8 (3): 189–207.

Shohamy, E.G. 2006. *Language Policy*. London: Routledge.
Smith-Christmas, C. 2016. *Family Language Policy: Maintaining an Endangered Language in the Home*. Basingstoke: Palgrave Macmillan.
Soler, J., and A. Zabrodskaja. 2017. New Spaces of New Speaker Profiles: Exploring Language Ideologies in Transnational Multilingual Families. *Language in Society* 46: 547–566.
Ten Thije, J., and L. Zeevaert. 2007. *Receptive Multilingualism: Linguistic Analyses, Language Policies and Didactic Concepts*. Amsterdam and Philadelphia: John Benjamins.
Van Mensel, L. 2018. 'Quiere Koffie?' The Multilingual Familylect of Transcultural Families. *International Journal of Multilingualism* 15 (3): 233–248.
Venables, E., S. Eisenchlas, and A. Schalley. 2013. One-Parent-One-Language (OPOL) Families: Is the Majority Language Speaking Parent Instrumental in the Minority Language Development? *International Journal of Bilingualism* 17 (4): 429–448.
Volkman, A. 2005. *Cultures of Transnational Adoption*. Durham, NC: Duke University Press.
Zeleke, W.A., L.S. Koester, and G. Lock. 2018. Parents' Understanding of Adopted Children's Ways of Being, Belonging, and Becoming. *Journal of Child and Family Studies* 27 (5): 1428–1439.
Zentella, A. C. 2007 [1997]. *Growing Up Bilingual: Puerto Rican Children in New York*. Oxford: Blackwell.

Conclusion

Wilson McLeod

Although language transmission can sometimes be presented as a straightforward and 'natural' process, the studies in this volume demonstrate how complex the matter actually is in sociolinguistic terms. The range of social, economic, cultural, ideological and linguistic factors that can come into play in relation to transmission is exceptionally wide. As such, the contexts in which transmission is attempted, and the constraints on the process in particular situations, can be highly variable, as noted by Kircher (2019). The chapters presented here demonstrate this diversity and underscore the importance of taking a broad view of transmission that can account for varied and fluid circumstances and different kinds of interventions and that can accommodate different aims and outcomes.

W. McLeod (✉)
Celtic and Scottish Studies, University of Edinburgh, Edinburgh, UK
e-mail: w.mcleod@ed.ac.uk

M. Hornsby and W. McLeod (eds.), *Transmitting Minority Languages*, Palgrave Studies in Minority Languages and Communities,
https://doi.org/10.1007/978-3-030-87910-5_14

Framing and Conceptualising Transmission

As noted in the Introduction, the 'prototypical' model of transmission (Leonard 2021: 160 fn. 3) often appears to be based on a baseline norm of the 'traditional' family (ideally extended rather than nuclear) in a 'traditional' community (with tight, deeply established social linkages, and ideally in a territorially bounded rural setting). Such assumptions are particularly firmly rooted in relation to regional or minority languages such as Welsh (Jones 2021) and often incorporate essentialist, frequently conservative perspectives that appear to assume substantial social and cultural stasis. Against this background, important phenomena such as multilingualism, mobility and changing social norms can seem aberrant or problematic (Ó hIfearnáin 2015: 50).

By the same token, as Romaine observes (2006: 467–468), a connection can also be drawn between the valorisation of 'prototypical' modes of transmission and 'native speaker' ideology, that is, the increasingly contested idea that those who acquire a language in early childhood have unique competence and authority (Doerr 2009). It is notable that Fishman valorises not only intergenerational transmission but intergenerational transmission as a 'mother tongue' (1991: 355–358), with the implication that transmission later in life, or home transmission that requires supplementary inputs such as school education, is somehow second best.

In contrast, the chapters in this volume demonstrate that it is important to have a broad conception or formulation of transmission that grants a role to a diversity of inputs—from school, community practice and peer-to-peer interaction—and that is functional in a wide range of sociolinguistic contexts. In many cases, the extent of sociolinguistic disruption is such that insistence on traditional modes of intra-family, home-based transmission as a *sine qua non* is unrealistic and likely to generate frustration (Romaine 2006).

Ó hIfearnáin notes that there are no longer any 'accidental' Irish speakers, that 'children no longer become competent speakers unselfconsciously without the deliberate input of parents, other family and community members and institutional supports, particularly from educators' (p. 120). For traditionalists such as Hindley (1990: xv), the necessity of intentional intervention would signify 'that Irish as a living language' has effectively 'expired' now that 'there are no longer mothers who speak it to their newborn infants, because it comes unconsciously and naturally to their lips, without measured thought of choice or national sentiment'.

In contrast to this somewhat reductionist model of 'natural' transmission, the studies in this volume make clear that, depending on the extent of their minoritisation, successful transmission of minority languages will generally require structured, programmatic interventions of different kinds, and therefore that the issue of transmission should be considered an element in strategic language planning. Transmission, therefore, ties into the full range of theoretical and practical questions concerning strategies and tactics for successful language planning more generally and requires to be conceptualised accordingly. While there is some debate concerning the extent to which family language policy can properly be considered a form of 'policy' at all (Gazzola et al. forthcoming), it is evident that public policy interventions of different kinds will often come into play in relation to transmission.

As Smith-Christmas and Ruiséal explain, a crucial factor in relation to transmission is how success is to be defined. This is most obviously the case because setting an unreasonable standard or target can only bring frustration and disappointment. An important factor, of course, is the degree of sociolinguistic dislocation that a particular language has undergone. Among the languages considered in this volume, Guernésiais is clearly the most extreme in terms of the break in transmission, although the Breton case is also striking. Any attempt to re-establish transmission following a systemic rupture will be a long-term undertaking; indeed, Olsen-Reeder suggests that 'success may not be quantifiable by any secure means until the arrival of the fourth generation' following the rekindling of transmission (p. 184).

One important factor here is the extent to which usage of the language in the home will be supplemented by other kinds of inputs. Two parents—or just one parent—as the sole source of input represents a relatively impoverished linguistic diet. Successful language acquisition (whether in linguistic terms in relation to 'accuracy' or in social terms in relation to confidence and actual productive use) is more likely if there are multiple, diverse inputs (Unsworth 2016)—but this will be impracticable or even impossible in cases of advanced language shift. Ó hIfearnáin demonstrates how particular families can successfully transmit Irish even after it has ceased to be the vernacular of the wider surrounding community, but that this will become increasingly difficult, and perhaps impossible, if wider community usage drops below a certain level and no longer serves as a secondary support for these families. Conversely, when a broad-based, supportive social ethos in support of transmission develops, as described by Kasares, Ortega and Amorrortu, the prospects become much more favourable. Important here is Olsen-Reeder's point that even speakers with limited competence in the language should be encouraged to use what they can in order to help develop or sustain a linguistic environment that is conducive to transmission. As Ó hIfearnáin makes clear, transmission by a core group requires support from the linguistic periphery of less active and confident speakers 'because that wider community is not completely culturally separate from the active linguistic minority and its desire to maintain itself' (p. 132). This situation can often be helped by a wider sense of community goodwill towards the minority language by non-speakers. De Bres (2010: 522) mentions, in a Māori context, that New Zealanders can express their support for the language without necessarily having to speak or use Māori themselves. Her examples include non-Māori speakers supporting others in their learning of the language, supporting immersion education, using Māori words in conversation and making the effort to pronounce Māori words well.

An important but often overlooked element in the wider phenomenon of language transmission is the role of *intra*generational communication and *intra*generational transmission. Perhaps most obviously, the importance of the linguistic influence of children and adolescents on each other has been amply documented in sociolinguistics generally (e.g. Tagliamonte 2016). In the context of minority language revitalisation, this element is most clearly problematised in relation to children and adolescents who do not use the minority language when interacting with each other, but only with adults (and often only in structured environments such as school). Olsen-Reeder shows, however, that use of the minority language by adults when they interact with each other can have a strong modelling influence on children (or, conversely, that their use of the majority language may set a negative example). In a rather different way, Sallabank demonstrates that peer-to-peer interaction among adult learners may still play a crucial role when there is no current prospect of intergenerational transmission or intergenerational use.

A related set of factors concerns the dynamic nature of transmission—the extent to which language acquisition and socialisation develop over an extended period of time and may therefore require different kinds of interventions at different stages. Initial acquisition in very early childhood has long been emphasised, although to some extent this may be based on the ideology of the 'mother tongue', with its assumption that a language acquired after the earliest years of life is somehow less fundamental to a person's identity and selfhood. Yet beginning the process of acquisition in early childhood does not provide some life-long linguistic inoculation, as it were; Nandi et al. demonstrate that the ongoing process of becoming a speaker of a minority language in contact with a hegemonic language will be 'subject to continuous negotiations, variations and mutations on a daily basis through various actors and stakeholders' (p. 324). More generally, language skills and repertoires may well fluctuate considerably over the lifespan, with a risk of attrition through lack of use (Grosjean 2010). Different kinds of support for different kinds of speakers at different life stages—young children, adolescents, parents of young children, grandparents and so on—may therefore be required. All of these may be considered under the rubric of transmission.

In considering the modes and dynamics of language transmission, it is important to consider the changing nature of families and family life: the impact of differentiated structures (divorce, mobility, adoption), changing gender roles (the feminisation of the workforce to the role of gay or transgender parents etc.) or the increase in the use of institutional childcare and early years providers. Despite their importance in social terms, it is not always clear that such changes will have ramifications in terms of transmission. Some evidently do, as, for example, Chantreau and Moal demonstrate in relation to the impact of the introduction into a home of a new partner and children who do not know the target language. In contrast, it is not immediately obvious why the situation of gay or lesbian parents should be particularly distinctive in relation to language transmission. Additional research on different kinds of family structures would shed more light on these issues. One element here may be intersectionality, the simultaneous and cumulative effect of different social factors that may work to make transmission more challenging (e.g. single parenthood, 'new speaker' status, race, sexual orientation and so on).

Other kinds of social change, notably the increasing role of information and communication technology, may also bear on language transmission. Most obviously, the increased use of electronic communication, especially with smartphones, tends to diminish the extent of intra-family communication. Even when family members share the same home, children have the option of communicating with others rather than their parents and siblings, including at important shared experiences like family dinners (Latif et al. 2020). This will tend to reduce the significance of the parental role in language input. Of course, there will be circumstances in which the greater potential for extra-family communication will actually increase the use of the minority language—but in most cases it will very likely tend to promote greater use of the socially dominant language.

The Role of Language Ideology

An important factor in relation to transmission is the role of language ideology—most obviously in terms of the beliefs of parents and caregivers but also the prevailing views in the surrounding community and society. Instead of encouragement and support, parents who work to transmit a language may encounter different degrees of criticism, rejectionism and institutional resistance. The social and ideological context may vary even for the same language, as demonstrated by the differences in relation to Russian in Cyprus, Estonia and Sweden identified by Karpava, Ringblom and Zabrodskaja. In the case of minority languages, ideological rejectionism will typically be expressed in the conventional rhetoric that dismisses efforts to maintain these languages as 'social mobility contraindicated, parochial and anti-modern' (Fishman 2001:

19). In such a negative environment transmission may require 'counter-hegemonic strategies', as Nandi et al. explain (p. 323); for example, already by the 1970s 'it ha[d] become a political act for' parents in the Gaelic heartland of the Hebrides 'to bring up their children as Gaelic speakers, for almost every move they make has to be against the tide' (Mackay 1996: 27). The ideological context for Gaelic in Scotland has improved in some respects in recent decades, with increasing valorisation and institutionalisation in public life (McLeod 2020), even if this is modest in scale compared to the remarkable transformation in the social context for the transmission of Basque described by Kasares, Ortega and Amorrortu. Nevertheless, Ó hIfearnáin reminds us that 'the deeply rooted anxiety of parents over the ability of their children to master a minority language at home while also learning a major world language can continue to be transmitted for generations even after changes in the majority opinion have led to a more encouraging environment for the minority language's speakers' (2013: 118). Notably, there can be a disconnect between publicly expressed supportive attitudes towards the language and actual private linguistic practice, particularly in terms of using (or not using) the language with one's own children, a particularly personal and intimate context.

Given this dynamics of contestation, it is unsurprising that some parents who undertake language transmission may find that some of their own relatives are unsupportive of their efforts. As Chantreau and Moal and Macleod demonstrate, this may involve an uncooperative (or merely passive) partner. In contexts of language shift, which almost always involve the devalorisation of the minority language, it may also mean that relatives who can speak the language and are in a position to provide support for the transmission project actually work to undermine it in different ways. The role of grandparents may be particularly challenging here; as Hickey notes (2021: 154), 'the beliefs of the grandparental generation arising from their experience of the differences in the status of their languages may conflict with the family language policy of parents, even when parents support transmission of the heritage language'. This can be particularly disappointing to parents as it will often be the case in contexts of language shift that grandparents will have a richer linguistic repertoire than their children who are attempting to transmit the language.

Ideological resistance may also take more specific forms relating to the kind of language that is being transmitted or acquired, particularly when this appears to deviate from 'traditional' usage. Such linguistic deviation is likely when 'alternative' modes of transmission are involved or when transmission becomes less systematic within a community. By transmitting the language to their children, new speaker parents, whose language variety will probably differ in some respects from that of 'traditional' speakers, will help form a new generation of 'neo-native' speakers whose language will probably differ once again. Some traditional speakers may straightforwardly reject the linguistic change that flows from these changing social contexts; in relation to Gaelic, for example, Nancy Dorian notes that some speakers 'make it clear that they would rather see Gaelic pass out of existence than see it survive in what they think of as a bastardised or neutralised Gaelic that differs markedly from any of the kinds previously acquired in the home' (Dorian 2019: 115). Such inflexible attitudes are unlikely to create a positive environment for language use and maintenance; in Dorian's view, 'expanded tolerance' and 'a degree of acceptance' of linguistic change will produce better outcomes (Dorian 2019: 119). The challenges arising in relation to Breton, which involved a particularly dramatic break in intergenerational transmission and considerable language change, have been much discussed, sometimes polemically (Hewitt 2017: 232); Kennard's study is a useful corrective in this regard. Initiatives such as Tús Maith in Corca Dhuibhne, with its emphasis on linguistic 'localness' and authenticity, may play a helpful role in limiting linguistic discontinuity, as Smith-Christmas and Ruiséal demonstrate.

A different aspect of language ideology that bears on transmission involves the increasing attention to the potential economic value of language skills. This fits within a wider economic framing of language in the neoliberal era, conceptualised by Duchêne and Heller (2012) in terms of 'pride and profit', but it also represents a challenge to the traditional idea that minority languages had no 'commercial value' (McLeod 2020: 45–46), an understanding that plays an immense role in parents' decisions not to transmit a minority language. For some but by no means all minority languages, contemporary revivalist discourses may invoke perceived economic benefits in support of transmission or acquisition. The claimed economic value may be specific to the target language at hand (e.g. in relation to perceived improved job prospects in Scotland for those with Gaelic skills [Dunmore 2019: 138–139]) or indeed may connect primarily to a related variety, as shown by Nandi et al.'s example of how Galician can be valorised in Argentina by reference to its linguistic proximity to Portuguese and the economic opportunities available in nearby Brazil. More generally, it may relate to what King and Wang call the 'neoliberal "selling" of the cognitive, academic, and economic advantages of bilingualism' (2021: 129), which may be invoked in relation to minority languages as well as more widely spoken and more obviously 'useful' languages. Macleod notes an example of this kind of framing in connection with Gaelic, so that some parents who attempt transmission are 'driven by the sense of language having an instrumental value as well as being a marker of identity and heritage' (p. 62).

Ideology also comes in to play in relation to community attitudes concerning social boundaries and openness to outsiders. The language support initiatives for Irish in the Corca Dhuibhne Gaeltacht described by Smith-Christmas and Ruiséal are firmly local in their orientation, emphasising community identity and solidarity, but at the same time they draw support from the positive national policy environment for Irish. Conversely, the extent to which community language use of Upper Sorbian is tightly bound up with Catholic religious practice and related festivals makes it difficult to broaden the social base of the language, as explained by Dołowy-Rybińska. This apparent success of this exclusionary strategy in the Sorbian context connects to wider debates about the potential limits of cultural liberalism for minority language maintenance (e.g. Brooks 2017).

A very different set of insights is offered by Smith-Christmas and Ruiséal's study, with its emphasis on strengthening the emotional bonds that children feel with the minority language. This is in contradistinction to the more common dynamic in minority language revitalisation through which the language tends to become associated with authority, formal environments and regulated behaviours, especially in connection with school (Smith-Christmas 2017). The principle that the desire to acquire and use a language plays a large role in successful outcomes in terms of maintenance is of course well established (Grin 2003), while a newer body of research emphasises the importance of emotions in building affinity to a language and its speech community (Walsh 2019).

In conclusion, this volume represents an alternative way of looking at the issue of language transmission, particularly from an intergenerational perspective, and in doing so follows recent trends in sociolinguistics. From a perspective best characterized as post-structuralist, current scholarship tends to contest homogeneity, stability and boundedness as a basis for studying language and instead finds mobility, mixing and political dynamics central in understanding communication (Blommaert and Rampton 2011). This approach recognises the 'messiness of actual usage' (Heller 2007: 13), and if language use has (finally) been recognised as 'messy', so have the processes of transmitting it, which are not always uniform and certainly not always unproblematic. In consideration of this, both the notion of language maintenance and the mechanism of intergenerational transmission as the fundamental element of the process of Reversing Language Shift as viewed by Fishman need to be investigated and reformulated in the light of new examples and theoretical shifts, which this volume has attempted to present from a broad perspective.

References

Blommaert, J., and B. Rampton. 2011. Language and Superdiversity. *Diversities* 13 (2): 1–21.

Brooks, S. 2017. *Why Wales Never Was: The Failure of Welsh Nationalism.* Cardiff: University of Wales Press.

De Bres, J. 2010. Promoting a Minority Language to Majority Language Speakers: Television Advertising About the Māori Language Targeting Non-Māori New Zealanders. *Journal of Multilingual and Multicultural Development* 31 (6): 515–529.

Doerr, N.M. 2009. Investigating 'Native Speaker Effects': Toward a New Model of Analysing 'Native Speaker' Ideologies. In *The Native Speaker Concept: Ethnographic Investigations of Native Speaker Effects*, ed. N.M. Doerr, 15–46. Berlin: De Gruyter.

Dorian, N. C. 2019. Speaking Gaelic – cò tha dì-beathte? In *Cànan Is Cultar/Language and Culture: Rannsachadh na Gàidhlig 9*, ed. M. Bateman and R.A.V. Cox, 105–122. Sleat, Isle of Skye: Clò Ostaig.

Duchêne, A., and M. Heller, eds. 2012. *Language in Late Capitalism: Pride and Profit*. London: Routledge.

Dunmore, S. 2019. *Language Revitalisation in Gaelic Scotland: Linguistic Practice and Ideology*. Edinburgh: Edinburgh University Press.

Fishman, J.A. 1991. *Reversing Language Shift: Theoretical and Empirical Foundations of Assistance to Threatened Languages*. Clevedon: Multilingual Matters.

Fishman, J.A., ed. 2001. *Can Threatened Languages Be Saved? Reversing Language Shift, Revisited: A 21st Century Perspective*. Clevedon: Multilingual Matters.

Gazzola, M., et al. Forthcoming. Introduction. In *The Routledge Handbook of Language Policy and Planning*, ed. M. Gazzola et al. Abingdon: Routledge.

Grin, F. 2003. *Language Policy Evaluation and the European Charter for Regional or Minority Languages*. Basingstoke: Palgrave Macmillan.

Grosjean, F. 2010. *Bilingual: Life and Reality*. Cambridge, MA: Harvard University Press.

Heller, M. 2007. Bilingualism as Ideology and Practice. In *Bilingualism: A Social Approach*, ed. M. Heller, 1–22. New York: Palgrave.

Hewitt, S. 2017. Breton Orthographies: An Increasingly Awkward Fit. In *Creating Orthographies for Endangered Languages*, ed. M. Jones and D. Mooney, 190–234. Cambridge: Cambridge University Press.

Hickey, T. 2021. Family Language Policy: Promoting Partnership in the Early Years to Support Minority Language Revitalisation. In *Language Revitalisation and Social Transformation*, ed. H. Lewis and W. McLeod, 141–173. Basingstoke: Palgrave Macmillan.

Hindley, Reg. 1990. *The Death of the Irish Language: A Qualified Obituary*. London: Routledge.

Jones, R. 2021. The Geography of Minority Language Use: From Community to Network. In *Language Revitalisation and Social Transformation*, ed. H. Lewis and W. McLeod, 37–65. Basingstoke: Palgrave Macmillan.

King, K.A., and L. Wang. 2021. Family Language Policy and Language Transmission in Times of Change. In *Language Revitalisation and Social*

Transformation, ed. H. Lewis and W. McLeod, 119–140. Basingstoke: Palgrave Macmillan.

Kircher, Ruth. 2019. Intergenerational Language Transmission in Quebec: Patterns and predictors in the Light of Provincial Language Planning. *International Journal of Bilingual Education and Bilingualism*. https://doi.org/10.1080/13670050.2019.1691499.

Latif, H., A.S. Kandemir, S. Uçkun, E. Karaman, A. Yüksel, and O.A. Onay. 2020. The Presence of Smartphones at Dinnertime: A Parental Perspective. *The Family Journal* 28 (4): 432–440.

Leonard, W.Y. 2021. Local Power Relationships, Community Dynamics, and Stakeholders. In *Revitalizing Endangered Languages: A Practical Guide*, ed. J. Olko and J. Sallabank, 156–163. Cambridge: Cambridge University Press.

Mackay, D. 1996. *We Did It Ourselves—Sinn fhein a rinn e: An Account of the Western Isles Community Education Project Proisect Muinntir nan Eilean 1977–1992*. The Hague: Bernard van Leer Foundation.

McLeod, W. 2020. *Gaelic in Scotland: Policies, Movements, Ideologies*. Edinburgh: Edinburgh University Press.

Ó hIfearnáin, T. 2013. Institutional Breton Language Policy After Language Shift. *International Journal of the Sociology of Language* 223: 117–135.

Ó hIfearnáin, T. 2015. Sociolinguistic Vitality of Manx After Extreme Language Shift: Authenticity Without Traditional Native Speakers. *International Journal of the Sociology of Language* 231: 45–62.

Romaine, S. 2006. Planning for the Survival of Linguistic Diversity. *Language Policy* 5: 441–473.

Smith-Christmas, C. 2017. 'Is It Really for Talking?': The Implications of Associating a Minority Language with the School. *Language, Culture and Curriculum* 30 (1): 32–47.

Tagliamonte, S.A. 2016. *Teen Talk: The Language of Adolescents*. Cambridge: Cambridge University Press.

Unsworth, S. 2016. Quantity and Quality of Language Input in Bilingual Language Development. In *Bilingualism Across the Lifespan: Factors Moderating Language Proficiency*, ed. Elena Nicoladis and Simona Montanari, 103121. Berlin: De Gruyter.

Walsh, J. 2019. The Role of Emotions and Positionality in the Trajectories of 'New Speakers' of Irish. *International Journal of Bilingualism* 23 (1): 221–235.

Index

M. Hornsby and W. McLeod (eds.), *Transmitting Minority Languages*, Palgrave Studies in Minority Languages and Communities,
https://doi.org/10.1007/978-3-030-87910-5

The manufacturer's authorised representative in the EU is Springer Nature Customer Service Centre GmbH, Europaplatz 3, 69115 Heidelberg, Germany. If you have any concerns regarding our products, please contact ProductSafety@springernature.com

Printed and bound by CPI Group (UK) Ltd, Croydon, CR0 4YY
30/09/2026
02225490-0015